Banking in Oklahoma
Before Statehood

Banking in Oklahoma
Before Statehood

Michael J. Hightower

University of Oklahoma Press : Norman

Also by Michael J. Hightower
Inventing Tradition: Cowboy Sports in a Postmodern Age
 (Saarbrücken, Germany, 2008)
Frontier Families: The Records and Johnstons in American History
 (Oklahoma City, 2011)
The Pattersons: A Novel (Charlottesville, Va., 2012)

An earlier version of chapter 3 appeared as "The Riverboat Frontier: Early-Day Commerce in the Arkansas and Red River Valleys" in *Chronicles of Oklahoma* 89, no. 2 (2011): 176–207.

Library of Congress Cataloging-in-Publication Data

Hightower, Michael J.
  Banking in Oklahoma before statehood / Michael J. Hightower.
    pages cm
  Includes bibliographical references and index.
  ISBN 978-0-8061-4388-0 (hardcover : alk. paper)
1. Banks and banking—Oklahoma—History—19th century. 2. Oklahoma—History—19th century. I. Title.
  HG2611.O5H54 2013
  332.109766'09034—dc23
                                                                    2013009231

1 2 3 4 5 6 7 8 9 10

I dedicate this book to my late father,
Frank Johnson Hightower,
for clueing me in to the joy of history.

Contents

Illustrations

Preface

A few seconds past noon of April 22, 1889, two riders drew rein and looked upon a scene that telescoped nine generations of American frontier settlement into one flashing moment.

Angie Debo, *Prairie City*

Four factors coalesced to illuminate the need for a book on bartering and banking on the Oklahoma frontier—or, more precisely, the need for books, as there was no way to shoehorn this remarkable story and its continuation in modern-day banking and commerce into just one. First, archival collections in the Oklahoma History Center and elsewhere around the state are brimming with primary documents on frontier commerce that have never been fully exploited. Because Oklahoma was so late to develop as a state, its foundational documents, from business charters and correspondence to voluminous newspaper clippings, are perfectly preserved and available in easy-to-access archives. It was high time to mine those archives to learn how past generations of businesspeople deployed capital to shape state and local history.

Second, documentary sources are complemented by oral history collections dating back to the 1930s, when researchers laboring under the auspices of the Works Progress Administration fanned across the state to collect stories from Native Americans already present when parts of the Indian Territory were opened to settlement in 1889 and pioneers who came later. Preserved in the Indian-Pioneer Papers, their stories form the nucleus of collections that have expanded with the advent of new technologies. In this book on Oklahoma banking and commerce, I rely on existing oral histories and interviews that I conducted between 2009 and 2013 with bankers and community leaders statewide. Their families' stories have for the most part been transmitted orally and never circulated very far beyond their communities. *Banking in Oklahoma* brings at least a few of those stories to the printed page and folds them into the broader narrative of banking and commerce in Oklahoma.

A third inspiration for these books strikes at the heart of what it means to be an Oklahoman. As residents of the forty-sixth state to join the Union, Oklahomans take pride in living in a young state. I recently purchased a T-shirt at the Will Rogers World Airport in Oklahoma City that brands the state, and presumably its wearer, as "FOREVER WILD, FOREVER FREE." Newcomers who are slow to get the message exit the airport and encounter a statue of a mounted Will Rogers with a rope in hand and a mischievous glint in his eye—as potent an icon of the frontier as one is likely to find at a metropolitan airport. Yet with each passing year, fewer businesses and banks hewn from the frontier remain standing against the juggernaut of corporate business, and fewer people survive to share their stories, or perhaps their ancestors' stories, of economic and community development. Oklahoma is not as young as it used to be, and neither are the people whose families built its businesses and financed its development. Simply put, the window for capturing the lived experience of pioneer banking and commerce is closing. If we allow that window to close, a vital part of Oklahoma history will be lost forever.

Finally, the financial fiasco of 2008 and its ugly aftermath remind us that banking is a pillar on which civilization rests. Perhaps not since the Great Depression has so much attention—and, arguably, so much disinformation—been lavished on bankers. If ignoring the lessons of history dooms us to repeat it, then surely illuminating those lessons will accrue to the benefit of bankers looking for new perspectives on their profession. For the rest of us, history can help us to understand our present circumstances, and might even light the path to informed financial decisions.

Banking in Oklahoma before Statehood rests on a belief that narrative is the purest form of historical analysis. Narratives survive in the form of memoirs, oral histories, correspondence, newspaper and magazine articles, audiotaped interviews, and similar artifacts that historians treasure as primary sources. By blending the methodological tools of history (documentary research) and sociology (sampling, interviewing, and content analysis), a coherent story of bartering and banking on the Oklahoma frontier emerges. It is a story that transcends the minutiae of time, place, and circumstance to show us what has been important to people, why they did what they did, and why we should care.

A corollary of history-as-narrative is social history, sometimes described as history "from the bottom up." Beneath the level of statecraft that dominates "official history" lies a vast substratum of stories that rarely get recorded and are therefore subject to oblivion with the passage of time. On the battlefield, it is said, history is told by the victors. Yet it is also told by those who, by dint of their money, power, fame, or, more likely, a combination of all three, control the levers of communication. *Banking in Oklahoma before Statehood* aims to right that balance by giving voice to people whose stories have been neither properly told nor widely disseminated. Theirs is not a history gleaned from the canons of official history, but rather a history that percolates up, more or less undiluted, from the swirl of everyday life.

Historians, particularly those with a sociological bent (one hopes that includes pretty much all of us), look for ways to situate their work in a theoretical framework—that is, to show that all the sound and fury actually signifies something. In the course of researching and writing *Banking in Oklahoma before Statehood,* I realized that the story of bartering and banking in Oklahoma is nothing less than a microcosm of the tug-of-war between two systems, capitalism and democracy, that has bedeviled Americans ever since Thomas Jefferson and Alexander Hamilton squared off over the issue of centralized banking.

Capitalism is a cultural system that unleashes the individual's capacity to control resources and initiate projects. It is planted so deeply in our collective consciousness that we rarely stop to think about it, let alone ponder the alternatives that have flourished throughout history and woven themselves into various countries' laws and customs.[1] Even though America's geographical frontier closed in the late nineteenth century, the no-holds-barred brand of capitalism that breathed life into the Oklahoma frontier has remained alive and well throughout the state's history. From fur traders who plied the Arkansas and Red Rivers to modern-day entrepreneurs and power brokers, Oklahoma's cast of characters has included businesspeople with a high tolerance for risk and a big appetite for reward, and they have been enabled by financiers who controlled the flow of currency and credit. In a symbiosis that saw its first stirrings at the dawn of civilization, this dynamic duo has facilitated the acquisition, production, and distribution of the resources that make communal life possible.

For better and worse, and always for a rollicking good time, Oklahoma's businesspeople have contributed to a commercial culture that is brash, bold, and usually a bit rough around the edges. Nowhere is the expression "the almighty dollar" (coined by Washington Irving) more apropos than in Oklahoma, where staking a claim has always been more than a metaphor, and whose undulating woodlands and prairies have proven irresistible to countless pilgrims in search of the Promised Land. In an era when commerce still carried the taint of dishonor among Europe's upper crust, Americans embraced as their guiding ethos the qualities that made for successful entrepreneurship. Alexis de Tocqueville, whose *Democracy in America* set the standard for sociological insight in the 1830s, put his own aristocratic predilections aside to recognize a kind of grandeur in Americans' reliance on wealth as the universal measure of a man's merit. "The Americans," he wrote in his chef d'oeuvre, "bring a sort of heroism to the way they conduct commerce."[2] Nearly a century after Tocqueville's travels in America, the dour President Calvin Coolidge chimed in with his own prescient take on a culture that found its purest expression in Oklahoma: "The chief business of the American people is business."[3]

Closer to home, the teetotaling pioneer Henry Overholser was spot-on when he expressed Oklahomans' commitment to free enterprise. Alarmed by the arrival of the Anti-Saloon League's foot soldiers in his adopted hometown, Overholser rose to the defense of the Oklahoma Territory's saloons: "My friends, Oklahoma City, as has already been said, is a businessman's town, and the people are for anything that will help business. Yes, this town has been founded and run by businessmen, and it will continue to be run by businessmen."[4] For an earthier take on Oklahoma's commercial culture, we rely on George Patterson, the father of William G. Patterson whose model of money lending at Penn Square Bank in the early 1980s remains unchallenged in the annals of pecuniary brazenness. Drawing on his Apache ancestry (his Indian name was

"Kemoha") to probe to the heart of things, the elder Patterson described Oklahoma as a new state, "home to the bullshitter and the wildcatter. You've always had the gambling spirit in Oklahoma."[5]

Democracy is more nuanced than capitalism, but one thing is certain: it is more than a process of free and fair elections. It is perhaps best understood as a system that enables citizens to join together in achieving goals that accrue to the common good—to determine the rules of the game whose outcomes express widely shared needs and interests. Ideally, democracy also serves as a catalyst for economic growth.

Somewhat paradoxically given his analysis of American commerce, Tocqueville identified "equality of condition" as the defining characteristic of American culture. "I readily discovered the prodigious influence that this primary fact exercises on the whole course of society," he wrote in his introduction to *Democracy in America*. "It gives a peculiar direction to public opinion and a peculiar tenor to the laws; it imparts new maxims to the governing authorities and peculiar habits to the governed."[6] Following Tocqueville's travels through the country in the 1830s, Americans pushed the frontier westward until it disappeared altogether. Somewhere along the way, equality born of frontier conditions, to the extent that it ever existed in pure form, disappeared as well, and its legacy morphed into a golden age that survives in the West of our imagination. Its virtual obliteration beneath the tide of westward migration left generations of post-frontier Americans to confront socioeconomic structures that, for better and worse, are a (and perhaps *the*) defining feature of civilization. Yet the ideals enshrined in small *d* democracy remained at the bedrock of American culture, serving as the North Star for settlers aiming to strike a balance between capitalist competition and shared values supporting community development and a sense of fair play.[7]

Americans have long supposed capitalism and democracy to be complementary systems. Yet they rarely strike a balance; when they do, it never seems to last very long, and it is always messy. Writ large, the sparring between these pillars of civilization that shaped banking and commerce on the Oklahoma frontier reflects nothing less than disagreements about the meaning and future of the Republic. It is no exaggeration to suggest that experiments in resource allocation, spawned by the tug-of-war between capitalism and democracy and embedded in commercial activities, constitute the overarching theme of American history.

As stewards of the nation's currency and credit, bankers labor beneath a pendulum—some might suggest a sword of Damocles—as it swings between the profit motive inherent in capitalism and America's promise as a land of opportunity for *all*. The plot thickens when we consider that Oklahoma's bumpy road to statehood was paved during the Gilded Age (1865–1900)—a time when corporate power reached Olympian proportions, disparities in wealth widened into chasms, and money decided elections from city councils to Congress. During those heady years, it became more apparent than ever that capitalism cannot operate without inequality insofar as people enter the marketplace with varying levels of talent and resources, and success brings rewards that reinforce the original differences. In short, democracy depends on equality, whereas capitalism depends on inequality. Choosing an apt metaphor for the Gilded Age, we might think of capitalism as an engine; just as unequal temperatures drive heat engines, inequality drives the engine of capitalism.[8]

To extend the metaphor, America has never been short of mechanics bent on fine-tuning the engine. Rutherford B. Hayes, elected president in 1876, in part because he promised to end Reconstruction, added his voice to a chorus of critics who viewed the influence of big money as nothing short of a betrayal of the Revolution. "This is a government of the people, by the people, and for the people no longer," wrote the ex-president two years before Gettysburg's twenty-fifth anniversary and three years before the Oklahoma country was opened to non-Indian settlement. "It is a government by the corporations, of the corporations, and for the corporations."[9] Populist firebrand Mary E. Lease agreed with the ex-president, but was a bit more specific in describing corporate hegemony as "a government of Wall Street, for Wall Street, and by Wall Street."[10] A decade or so into the twenty-first century, economist Joseph Stiglitz suggested that America's once-vibrant democracy is now on life support. What we have, wrote the Nobel Prize winner, is a government "of the top 1 percent, by the top 1 percent, and for the top 1 percent"— not exactly good news for champions of the American Dream.[11] By late 2011, the Occupy Wall Street movement was searing itself into the nation's consciousness as the latest attempt to fix the engine. As of this writing in 2013, it was clear that the inchoate outpouring of frustration was gaining not only traction but even a hint of organization. Perhaps a whiff of grapeshot was just what Wall Street bankers needed to reconsider their rough treatment of the men and women on the street—that is, the other 99 percent.

The repair shop has long since become a magnet for government officials whose insistence on imposing regulations on the banking industry, whether from Oklahoma City or Washington, D.C., came to play a decisive role in the economy. A dozen years into the new millennium, one wonders if we will ever resolve the tension between capitalism and democracy, or if, like actors in a Greek play, we are fated to replay the drama in new and ever more interesting ways for generations to come.

Because the story of bartering and banking on the Oklahoma frontier is best understood as an extension and adaptation of financial systems developed in the nation's infancy, *Banking in Oklahoma before Statehood* begins, in Part I, with two chapters on the early national period of American history, when British control was ending and new systems were rising to meet the needs of American enterprise. Debates, sometimes peaceful but often not, revolved around the issue of centralized banking. Opposing forces coalesced behind two men: Thomas Jefferson, whose vision of an agrarian republic left little room for banks; and Alexander Hamilton, who believed that America's survival depended on the imposition of centralized banking, much as Great Britain relied on the Bank of England to sustain its empire. The stakes in America's early experiments in banking and commerce were nothing less than the manner in which Americans would produce, acquire, and distribute their surplus—a tad more complicated, to be sure, but fundamentally the same conundrums that bedeviled humankind at the dawn of civilization and that have occupied us ever since.

The scene shifts in Part II to the southwestern frontier, where riverboats and wagon trains were the harbingers of commerce on the prairies. Whether winding their way upriver in a steamboat or driving a team of oxen across the prairie, frontier businessmen confronted two major impediments to establishing commercial footholds in the region that eventually coalesced into the Oklahoma and Indian Territories and, later, the state of Oklahoma: a dearth of currency; and ad hoc methods of banking and finance. Storekeepers filled the void by using their commercial activities as a platform to open de facto banks. Typically, they extended credit to farmers and ranchers until their crops came in or livestock was sold. Flush with cash, customers were able to pay off their accounts, thus enabling storekeepers to buy manufactured goods from wholesalers back east and restock their shelves. By serving as conduits for manufactured goods and providing their customers with currency and credit, these so-called merchant-bankers were jacks-of-all-trades who had to know something about retailing, farming, ranching, and warehousing. Their ingenious methods of banking and finance gradually replaced bartering as the time-honored method of acquiring goods and had momentous implications for the region's commercial development.

Part III covers the territorial period of Oklahoma history when the present-day state of Oklahoma was divided in all respects—politically, economically, topographically, and culturally—into two regions: the Oklahoma Territory in the west, and the Indian Territory in the east. The territorial period began, quite literally, with a bang, when gunshots at high noon on April 22, 1889, were the signal for non-Indian settlers to thunder into the "Oklahoma country" and stake their claims. Thirteen months later, the region that they settled was organized into seven counties—Payne, Logan, Kingfisher, Oklahoma, Canadian, and Cleveland, all clustered in present-day central Oklahoma, and Beaver in No Man's Land, later split into the Panhandle counties of Beaver, Texas, and Cimarron. These counties became the nucleus of the Oklahoma Territory, whose boundaries expanded through additional land runs and lotteries. East of the Oklahoma Territory, lands held by the Five "Civilized" Tribes and their smaller neighbors, known collectively as the Indian Territory, were under increasing pressure from non-Indians who were convinced that tribes were squandering God's bounty with inefficient farming practices and their peculiar custom of owning land in common. From the famed Run of '89 until the admission of Oklahoma into the Union as the forty-sixth state in 1907, the Oklahoma and Indian Territories were known as the Twin Territories, united along a common boundary, but separated in ways that continue to fuel a rivalry between east and west. That rivalry has never entirely dissipated. As one who has lived on both sides of the Great Divide, I speak with some authority in suggesting that it never will.

During the territorial period, bankers took up residence at the heart of commercial culture aiming to align their profession with business practices commensurate with the needs of the new century. Episodes in that rough-and-tumble period are ripped from the pages of western lore: the establishment of banks in tents and ramshackle buildings whose valuables, often stashed in canvas bags and nail kegs, were guarded by armed vigilantes; the Panic of 1893, which swept in from the East and toppled banks in the Oklahoma Territory; the rise of prairie populism and its expression in the free silver debate; the territorial legislature's effort to regulate banking by enacting the Oklahoma Territory's first banking codes in 1897, eight years after the Run of '89; bank robberies and insider shenanigans that branded the Twin Territories as havens for outlaws and risky venues for commercial development; the scramble to establish the first bank in town; rivalries between banks with territorial and national charters, contests that exacerbated tensions and sowed the seeds of distrust; speculation in land and natural resources that led some to riches, others to ruin, and many to both; and land fraud in the Indian Territory that stained America's reputation as the land of opportunity. Challenges in the territorial period were exacerbated by a public relations nightmare, courtesy of writers with a flair for exaggeration who filled the eastern press with tales of frontier mayhem.

Against a backdrop of real-life challenges and outright fabrications, Oklahoma's pioneer capitalists managed to create viable businesses. Their efforts were facilitated by the rapid-fire development of communication and transportation infrastructures. As stewards of currency and credit, bankers were never far from the action, and the institutions they built were both cause and effect of Oklahoma's tortuous journey from frontier to statehood.

One of my first interviewees for this project was John Marshall, a former officer with Liberty Bank in Oklahoma City. In response to a question about the relevance of banking and commercial history to Oklahoma's financial professionals, Marshall offered a comment that cut to the chase and, by the way, was music to an author's ears. "The problem," he said, "is that there isn't much to read."[12]

How true. For too long, historians have shied away from business in favor of topics perceived as more alluring. In Oklahoma, this has produced an embarrassment of riches on cowboys, Indians, and swashbuckling trailblazers, but it has left us with relatively little to read about the role bankers and businesspeople have played in economic and community development. To borrow from historian Angie Debo's iconic imagery, pioneers who participated in the Oklahoma land runs were indeed fortunate to witness and participate in flashing moments when generations of frontier settlement were telescoped into maelstroms of raw energy and pure optimism, the likes of which no one had ever seen, and which nobody would see again. Less dramatic, but certainly no less worthy of our attention, has been the role of businesspeople who have woven their stories into the fabric of state and local history. Today, as the pace of global business reaches warp speed and technology wraps us in an ever-tighter embrace, it is more important than ever to be mindful of the historical forces that spawned the world we live in. Perhaps the danger in not learning from the lessons of history is not so much that we are doomed to repeat it, but rather, that we will never know who we really are.

Before we unfurl our "On to Oklahoma!" banners and, after a brief sojourn to the early national period of American history, proceed with the story of bartering and banking on the Oklahoma frontier, I would like to thank the people who have participated in this project: Bob Blackburn, executive director of the Oklahoma Historical Society, for bringing me in as principal researcher for the Oklahoma Bank and Commerce History Project; George Records, for his support and encouragement; the Oklahoma Bankers Association (OBA) and Community Bankers Association of Oklahoma (CBAO) members and staff, whose enthusiasm for the project was evident from day one, and who were more helpful than they know in keeping me on task; bankers and businesspeople who welcomed me into their offices to conduct taped interviews, and who shared historical artifacts that help tell the story of Oklahoma banking and commerce; archivists and librarians at the Oklahoma Historical Society, the University of Oklahoma's Western History Collections, and libraries throughout Oklahoma who enabled my sleuthing; astute Oklahomans who found out what I was up to and alerted me to stories from their parts of the state; University of Virginia librarians for reserving a few feet of shelf space for my native state; and Andrew Shiva, for permission to reproduce territorial banknotes from his collection, and for promoting awareness of America's monetary history through the National Currency Foundation. Special thanks go to Judy Hightower for her feedback on the manuscript as it evolved. Finally, I am indebted to Kelly Parker for her skills as an editor and proofreader and Charles Rankin, Jay Dew, Steven Baker, Sandy See, and their colleagues at the University of Oklahoma Press for bringing this project to completion.

So there is plenty of credit to go around. Mistakes and shortcomings, of course, are all mine.

Oklahoma City and Charlottesville
Fall 2013

PART I

The Early National Period, 1781–1863

CHAPTER ONE

Bank Battles

I believe that banking institutions are more dangerous to our liberties than standing armies. If the American people ever allow private banks to control the issue of their currency, first by inflation and then by deflation, the banks and the corporations that will grow up around them will deprive the people of all property until their children wake up homeless on the continent their fathers conquered.

Thomas Jefferson to Albert Gallatin, Secretary of the Treasury

When dawn broke on October 19, 1781, General Charles Cornwallis and the eight thousand redcoats under his command were in a desperate situation. Behind them was the Chesapeake Bay, whose potential as an avenue of escape had been compromised ever since late August when the Count François-Joseph de Grasse sailed into Yorktown from Santo Domingo with his entire West Indian fleet. His sailors were reinforced by more than three thousand soldiers who served under the Marquis de Saint-Simon. The next month, the admiral Count de Barras used his eight sail of the line to transport the combined forces of Generals Washington and Rochambeau to the Virginia coast. Meanwhile, a detachment of American troops serving under the Marquis de Lafayette was positioned in Virginia, waiting for instructions.

Out of time and short on options, Cornwallis and his soldiers braced for the worst. It came with a vengeance when an allied army of nine thousand Americans under General Washington and seven thousand French under General Rochambeau launched their epic siege of York-town. With French naval forces positioned offshore to prevent the British from escaping, the fighting raged for three weeks until Cornwallis acknowledged the futility of his position. "Our numbers had been diminished by the enemy's fire," wrote a disconsolate General Cornwallis in his account of the Battle of Yorktown, "but particularly by sickness, and the strength and spirits of those in the works were much exhausted by the fatigue of constant watching and unremitting duty. Under all these circumstances I thought it would have been wanton and inhuman to the last degree to sacrifice the lives of this small body of gallant soldiers, who had ever behaved with so much fidelity and courage, by exposing them to an assault which, from the numbers and precautions of the enemy, could not fail to succeed."[1]

At Cornwallis's command, soldiers representing the mightiest empire on earth laid down their arms. In a letter penned on October 20 to Sir Henry Clinton, the general described his defeat by upstart colonists on the banks of Chesapeake Bay. The general's letter began on a simple note that belied its momentous message: "I have the mortification to inform your Excellency that I have been forced to give up the posts of York and Gloucester, and to surrender the troops under my command, by capitulation, on the 19th instant, as prisoners of war to the combined forces of America and France."[2] General Cornwallis closed his correspondence with assurances that His Majesty's soldiers' treatment at the hands of their enemies "has been perfectly good and proper," and that the French in particular were going out of their way to be gracious in victory.[3] Americans had less reason to be kind to King George's soldiers who had turned so savagely against them.

Against all odds, General George Washington had led his ragtag army of citizen-soldiers to victory. The political revolution was over, or would be as soon as the belligerents could draft a formal termination of hostilities. But looming on the horizon was the need for a revolution of an entirely different sort—one that called for brains rather than brawn, and one that had little in the way of precedent that General Washington and his compatriots could call on for guidance. The question was simple: now that the revolutionaries had their country, what, exactly, were they going to do with it?

Of all the issues that spurred the generation of 1776 to action, none was more vexing than finance. For generations, economic life in the colonies had been fairly simple. In the South, planters cleared vast swaths of land to grow sugar, tobacco, rice, and indigo. The middle and northern colonies exploited the forests and seas for their bounty and cleared pastures for their livestock, while New England shipbuilders created what passed for large-scale industry. Frontiersmen at the fringes of civilization relied on their wits and primitive technologies to strip the land of its fauna and to cash in on the fur trade. Small-scale and cottage industries supplied what the land could not, and, for the most part, imports from England took care of the rest.

Economic links between scattered and largely self-sufficient settlements and the mother country were forged in the crucible of an economic theory known as "mercantilism." Accepted as gospel by most people who thought about such things, mercantilism held that gold and silver were the only genuine measures of wealth. Their suitability as media of exchange was due less to their rarity than to their homogeneity. (Even though gold and silver are susceptible to debasement by mixing them with lesser metals, there are easy ways, including water displacement and standardized weights, to distinguish between adulterated blocks of precious metals and blocks of specified purity.)[4] Nations cursed by an absence of these natural resources had no choice but to maintain a favorable balance of trade with other countries and, in the process, accumulate as much precious metal as they could. A corollary of mercantilism was that nations could only grow rich at the expense of others. International trade was thus seen as a zero-sum game, and precious metals were the prizes.

But not everyone was on board with the conventional wisdom. Adam Smith, the Scottish apostle of free enterprise whose *Wealth of Nations,* published in 1776, was the first broadside to puncture mercantilist theory, extolled the virtues of an unfettered marketplace in which wealth came not from trade policies aimed at accumulating gold and silver but rather through the decision making of individuals motivated by enlightened self-interest. For Smith, the supply of and demand for all marketable items, from foodstuffs to the products of industry, found their natural equilibrium through the "invisible hand of the marketplace." Understanding and exploiting that basic principal, and not filling storerooms with gold and silver, was Adam Smith's ticket to prosperity.

Rejection of mercantilism and acceptance of what came to be known as free-market capitalism were far in the future when colonial militias pounded their swords into ploughshares and their leaders pondered their hard-won freedom. Of more immediate concern than abstract economic theory was one of mankind's most enduring conundrums: the lack of a universally accepted medium of exchange, known in the common vernacular as "money." Lacking gold and silver mines and left to their own devices, British colonists resorted to experimentation in their quest to establish a viable economy.

For all their variety, experiments in finance were torn from history's playbook. Since the settlement of Jamestown, bartering had been a mainstay of local economies. When media of exchange were needed to close complicated transactions, various and often ingenious items were drawn into circulation. Taking a cue from Native Americans, colonists in New England used cylindrical beads made from polished shells and fashioned into strings and belts, or wampum, to trade for items of value. So-called commodity money came in the form of such widely available resources as corn, cattle, and furs. In the southern colonies, tobacco and rice were used as money. Records from 1696 indicate that Virginia clergymen were paid an annual salary of 16,000 pounds of tobacco. By the early eighteenth century, legislatures had established tobacco as legal tender for paying taxes and public debts.[5] Up north, students at Harvard College paid their tuition with livestock, meat, and whatever could be gleaned from family closets. One student who later became president of the college settled his bill in 1649 with "an old cow." He gave an account of the construction of the first college building, including an entry that might puzzle university registrars in our own day: "Received a goat 30s. plantation of Watertown rate, which died."[6]

Frustrated colonists might have argued that money in the form of coins was scant improvement over goats and tobacco. Mercantilist policies prevented the creation of a satisfactory circulating medium in the colonies and forbade the export of coinage from Britain. What is more, the drain on specie resulting from the colonies' perennial trade imbalance meant that there was never enough coin to meet demand. The lack of specie, coupled with debtors' desire for credit and low interest rates, fueled colonists' insistence on creating banks. Indeed, royal governors' suppression of inflationary movements was a major cause of the American Revolution.[7] Attempts to attract specie to the colonies were doomed to failure because, as might be expected, people fortunate enough to get their hands on coins hoarded them in their mattresses and buried them under bushes.

As the pace of trade quickened in the eighteenth century, Portuguese and Spanish coins became more common than English coins. The Spanish dollar—the nearest thing to an international medium of exchange—was the most stable and least debased coin in the Western world from the sixteenth to the nineteenth century, and it accounted for half the currency in the North American colonies; the rest consisted of a hodgepodge of British, French, and other national coinage brought in by travelers.[8] Disorder descended into chaos as colonists not only retained the English system of pounds, shillings, and pence but also placed different values on whatever coins happened to be in circulation.[9] The bottom line was that coins in colonial America were not nearly as liquid—that is, readily convertible into other assets—as their holders might have wished.[10]

One solution for the dearth and complexity of coins was for colonists to manufacture their own. Not surprisingly in a land destined to turn entrepreneurship into an art form, a mint was established in Massachusetts, the only colony to do so. Its operations were confined to minting small silver pieces known as pine tree shillings. The mint became such an asset to the Massachusetts economy that the British government did not suppress its production of coins for three decades.[11] Vigorous efforts to compel its managers to turn a portion of their profits over to the authorities met with little success, and the Crown closed the mint when Massachusetts's original charter was revoked in 1684. Attempts to establish mints in Virginia and Maryland never got off the ground.[12]

Reduced to barter and commodity money and hamstrung by a dearth of coinage, colonists had their hands full just trying to maintain a viable economy. The exchange of goods and services was rendered even more troublesome by an absence of banks. This was no accident: British law effectively forbade the establishment of banks in the colonies, which left merchants in charge of basic banking functions. With ingenuity born of necessity, colonial merchants became lenders, exchange agents, shipowners—in short, whatever they needed to be in order to fulfill the financial responsibilities that are now shared by many different corporations under forms of restricted liability.[13] In a pattern that followed the course of westward migration, self-reliant merchants managed their debts with the utmost care. Knowing that debtors' prisons awaited the profligate, one could not be too careful.

When all else failed, *homo oeconomicus* had yet another trick up his sleeve: paper money. Like today's Federal Reserve notes that function as IOUs and reside in our wallets, paper money—sometimes referred to as "bills of credit"—paid no interest. But they were certainly more convenient to carry around than goats and bales of tobacco, and they could be used to buy merchandise and pay taxes. The procedure for getting bills of credit into circulation was fairly straightforward: have a printer engrave various denominations on pieces of paper and induce government officials to sign them; use the notes to buy goods and services or lend them to people; and keep them in circulation by passing a law forcing people to accept them and by promising to redeem them in the future for taxes or loan payments.[14] Of course, when more paper notes were in circulation than were needed for everyday transactions, they lost value—or, in economic jargon, they depreciated.[15] Not surprisingly, folks weaned on frontier scarcity regarded paper money with deep skepticism. Just as alchemists invited derision for claiming they could turn hunks of metal into gold, moneymen with colorful paper dangling from their pockets were often dismissed as fools or perhaps even scoundrels bent on fleecing the public.

The world's first government paper money was printed in medieval China, where both paper and printing were invented long before their appearance in the West. Paper money's debut in North America came in 1690, when Massachusetts was raising money for King William's War, the American theater of the Nine Years' War.[16] Even though notes were often discounted from their face value, they circulated as legal tender and were accepted as payment for taxes and other government obligations. A downside of paper money was that it drove coins out of circulation as people passed notes but hoarded their specie. Quite justifiably, they regarded coinage as a superior store of value.

Eventually, Massachusetts's experiment in paper money was replicated throughout the colonies, but it never replaced specie and commodity money. It did, however, provide people with a kaleidoscopic array of choices in financing the production, acquisition, and distribution of goods. Some currencies were interest-bearing notes. A fair number of them were legal tender, but many were not. There were notes that bore no interest and were accepted as legal tender for future obligations, but not for past debts. Some currencies were legal tender for all purposes. Others were receivable for public payments but not for transactions between individuals. In some instances, funds arising from taxation were pledged for the redemption of notes. Sometimes they were payable on demand; sometimes they were payable in the future. There were currencies issued by committees and currencies issued by designated officials.[17] The smorgasbord varied not only from one colony to the next but also within colonies. In the 1730s, seventeen forms of legal tender were circulating in North Carolina.[18] By 1740, every colony but Virginia was issuing paper money.[19]

Printing paper money went into overdrive during the Revolution. Lacking the power to tax and unable coerce fractious colonies to fund the war effort, the Second Continental Congress printed negotiable bills of credit known as continentals. By 1779, continentals with a face value of some $225 million, a huge sum superimposed upon a preexisting money supply of $12 million, were in circulation.[20] Meanwhile, states and even counties continued to print their own money. Inevitably, the outpouring of paper money spawned an inflationary spiral that sent continentals straight to the privy. Prices doubled in 1776, doubled again the next year, and doubled yet again the next. Between early 1779 and early 1781, prices rose nearly tenfold. Efforts to rein in prices by revaluation were of little use, and the phrase "not worth a continental" entered the American lexicon to describe plunging currency values.[21]

Anyone who thought that freedom from Great Britain would be a panacea for a dysfunctional economy was in for a rude awakening. America launched its experiment in self-government with the Articles of Confederation. Adopted in 1781 to replace the ad hoc administration of the Second Continental Congress, the Articles of Confederation were supposed to unify the former colonies in a loose confederation of states without threatening their autonomy. But without the power to raise an army and levy taxes, the Articles of Confederation were more like the rules that govern today's United Nations than the basis for a sovereign state. Prescient observers recognized the need for a strong hand to guide the ship of state and called for a convention to revise the Articles of Confederation. Opposition came from former colonists who balked at trading an overseas tyrant for a homegrown one. No sooner had the dust settled at Yorktown than the sides squared off in what was to become the central paradox in American governance and its corollary in finance: the protection of democratic rights under the aegis of a central authority.

As if on cue to expose the weaknesses of the Articles of Confederation, a bankrupt farmer and former army captain from western Massachusetts, Daniel Shays, led more than a thousand embittered farmers toward Springfield to exchange their pitchforks for muskets and seize cannon, all as a prelude to forcing the state legislature to drop direct taxation and reduce court fees. The rebels were eventually scattered, and by the early spring of 1787, they no longer posed a threat to the Massachusetts government.[22] Still, the lessons of Shays's Rebellion were not lost on delegates as they gathered for what came to be known as the Constitutional Convention. Anyone could see that a loose confederation of states could never stand up to internal threats, let alone threats from abroad, that were the price of nationhood. To maintain order at home and take its place in the community of nations, America needed a constitution with teeth, and a sound financial structure to support it. Otherwise, there would surely be more Daniel Shayses in America's future.

The Constitutional Convention was still a few years away when Robert Morris, superintendent of finance for the fledgling nation, teamed up with Thomas Willing to launch the Bank of North America—the first real bank, in the modern sense, on the North American continent.[23] It was incorporated by Congress in December 1781 and chartered by the Pennsylvania Assembly early the next year. Capitalized with $400,000, the bank's purpose was to alleviate America's chaotic monetary system and dearth of credit that were the colonies' legacies to the republic.[24] Before politics interceded and temporarily stripped the bank of its corporate status conferred by Congress, the Bank of North America aided in the war effort and postwar recovery.[25] Banking in North America thus began in the crucible of war, when the Continental Congress needed funds to maintain an army that had just sent King George's soldiers packing back to England, and that would surely be needed in the days to come. As über-patriot Thomas Paine noted in his *Dissertations* on the bank's defense, the bank was produced "by the distresses of the times and the enterprising spirit of patriotic individuals."[26]

Morris and Willing looked to European banks, and especially to the Bank of England, as their models. Chartered in 1694, the Bank of

England's ability to arrange government loans and issue bonds that could be traded on the open market was the engine that drove the British Empire to the four corners of the globe. Rather than hoard surplus capital in the form of gold and silver, investors snatched up the Bank of England's bonds and used the income they generated to plow working capital into new enterprises. With its capital mobilized in the service of wealth creation, England was able to compete with more populous nations that were endowed with an abundance of natural resources.[27] The Roman statesman Cicero was clearly onto something when he observed that "the sinews of war are infinite money."

Molding Old World banking practices to the contours of their upstart nation, Morris and Willing set up shop in Philadelphia, which served as America's financial hub long before the ascent of Wall Street. The Bank of North America issued paper money in the form of notes that were redeemable for specie on demand at fixed rates. Transfers of deposits from one person's ownership to another were carried out with checks. Unlike the federal government whose paper money was limited to bills of credit, the Bank of North America offered three kinds of money: notes, coins, and deposits. Much to the delight of its founders, people found the Bank of North America's money to be more flexible than government bills of credit.

Even though the bank succeeded in earning the financial elite's confidence, its principals knew they were in for an uphill climb. Legend has it that Thomas Willing, the bank's first president, instructed employees to carry bags of coin out one door and in the other to create an illusion of vast resources.[28] Lest we judge such deceptive tactics too harshly, we should recall that similar measures were taken during the savings and loan crisis of the 1980s. Readers are invited to draw their own parallels between Willing's tactics and Wall Street shenanigans that triggered the recession of 2008.

In 1784, another bank entered the picture. Chartered as the Bank of New York, this newcomer to American finance was a joint-stock company, and it counted among its founders a former artillery officer who had served with distinction in the War of Independence to become one of General Washington's most trusted officers. First impressions of the young soldier were deceiving. "I noticed a youth, a mere stripling, small, slender, almost delicate in frame," recalled a fellow officer about his first encounter with a twenty-something Alexander Hamilton, "marching beside a piece of artillery with a cocked hat pulled down over his eyes, apparently lost in thought, with his hand resting on the cannon and every now and then patting it as he mused, as if it were a favorite horse or a pet plaything."[29]

Americans would discover soon enough what was going on in Hamilton's fertile mind. At the request of Robert Morris, who had read the former artilleryman's proposals to restructure American banking, Hamilton actually drafted the charter for the Bank of New York in exchange for a seat on its board of directors.[30] Building on the Bank of North America's template, Hamilton and his associates at the Bank of New York were beginning to devise instruments that were more flexible than government bills of credit. They were also establishing institutions aimed at facilitating the growth of both industry and agriculture. As Hamilton noted in 1781, "Most commercial nations have found it necessary to institute banks; and they have proved to be the happiest engines that ever were invented for advancing trade."[31]

It was thus not without precedent that Founding Fathers with a financial bent set their sights on bringing order to America's financial system. The framers of the Constitution met in Philadelphia at a time when Adam Smith's ideas, expressed so convincingly in *The Wealth of Nations,* were coming into vogue. Drawing from a deepening pool of enlightened thinking, Smith relied on logic and empirical evidence to undermine mercantilism and posit the marketplace as the route to prosperity. As a nascent nation, America was not mired in networks of privilege that militated against the adoption of sound financial principles, and there were no monopolies founded on royal favor to be dismantled. More than any nation, America was a tabula rasa—a blank slate on which free-market principles could be etched and incorporated into its founding principles.

On the eve of the Constitutional Convention, Congress followed Jefferson's suggestion to adopt the dollar as America's currency and the decimal system for dividing it into smaller units. "Dollar" came from the German word for valley, *Thal,* and entered the vernacular in the fifteenth century when silver deposits were discovered in Bohemia and minted into coins from the valley. The American dollar became official in 1785 when Congress declared that the "monetary unit of the United States of America be one dollar." Although the cent, five-cent, dime, and fifty-cent coins advocated by Jefferson were adopted, Congress ultimately decided to authorize a quarter-dollar coin rather than a twenty-cent piece.[32] But paper money, particularly on the frontier, remained suspect—or worse. A year before the Constitution was composed, a petition drawn up in Botetourt County in Virginia's Shenandoah Valley denounced paper money as "dishonest in principle and a menace to the morals of the people, because it robbed the industrious of the fruits of their labors."[33]

By the end of a momentous decade that began with the defeat of a mighty empire and ended with a Constitutional Convention aimed at framing laws for the new nation, much had been accomplished in hewing a new financial structure from the chaos of the old: banks were facilitating the flow of currency and credit; mercantilism was yielding to "the invisible hand of the marketplace," otherwise known as free-market capitalism; and a national monetary unit promised to simplify the production, acquisition, and distribution of goods. Virtually without exception, the nation's first bankers were merchants who sought to advance their interests by improving on methods of extending credit. In their new guise as bankers, they turned a dearth of capital to their advantage by devising ever more creative ways to extend credit—that is, to create money, and thereby increase the fledgling nation's store of financial resources.

By 1790, four banks were either open or about to be open for business: the Bank of North America; the Bank of New York; the Massachusetts Bank; and the Bank of Maryland.[34] Eight more banks were set up in 1792, prompting contemporaries to comment on a "bancomania" that was sweeping the land.[35] All were public banks in the sense that they were enfranchised by governmental authorities. Typically in the following years, the state and territorial authorities that granted charters to these and other banks of their ilk were either actual or potential shareholders. Thus were private interests and wealth adapted to public purposes—a symbiosis that rarely achieved a perfect balance, but that aimed to match the privilege of operating under a government charter with the responsibilities inherent in managing other people's money.

But a crucial piece of the financial puzzle was missing. It was left to a thoughtful soldier-turned-banker to provide it.

On September 2, 1789, the United States government created the Treasury Department. Nine days later, the Senate confirmed Alexander Hamilton as the first secretary of the treasury.

By the time of his appointment to the highest financial position in the land, Hamilton was only thirty-five years old. But he had seen enough, both on the battlefield and in his business dealings, to be fed up with inefficiency. At Valley Forge, he watched soldiers mutiny and perish for want of food and clothing. As one of General Washington's most trusted aides-de-camp, he stood by his commander's side and shared his rage over munitions that never arrived and soldiers who were never paid. He surely fumed as the Second Continental Congress issued continentals by the wagon load, only to see their value depreciate until they were scarcely worth the paper they were printed on. During respites from the fighting, Hamilton found a constructive outlet for his frustrations by corresponding with Robert Morris, who would later be a cofounder of the Bank of North America. Hamilton's recommendations for a national bank with partial government ownership, an ability to float foreign loans, and a commitment to providing the national government with short-term loans impressed Morris to such an extent that he later incorporated them into the Bank of North America's charter.[36] Clearly, as the future secretary of the treasury patted his cannon like a favorite horse and gazed thoughtfully into space, his mind was far from empty.

Given his wartime experiences and participation in the Bank of North America and the Bank of New York, it comes as no surprise that Hamilton stepped into his office with a plan to overhaul American finances. By now, his ideas had hardened into a concrete plan of action, and they rested squarely on his conviction that the United States needed a national bank. Inspiration came not only from personal experience but also from his study of European banking systems and his reading of Adam Smith's *Wealth of Nations.* He outlined his plan in his seminal "Report on a National Bank," submitted to the third session of the First Congress in December 1790. The institution that he proposed would be called the Bank of the United States, and it would be placed under *private* rather than *public* direction, with the government owning one-fifth of its shares. Modeled on the Bank of England, the Bank of the United States would function as a depository for government funds, facilitate the transfer of funds between geographic regions, lend money to the federal government and other banks, and regulate the money supply by disciplining state-chartered banks. The institution would also make it easier for citizens to pay their taxes by serving as a lending source. Facilitating the payment of taxes would have the added benefit of stimulating the circulation of money.[37] As Hamilton quipped with uncommon brevity, "by contributing to enlarge the mass of industries and commercial enterprise, banks become nurseries of national wealth."[38]

Opponents of centralized banking were quick to point out the hazards of subordinating states to a new Leviathan. Specifically, foes of centralized banking feared an increase in usury, interference with other kinds of lending, a temptation to overtrade and disturb the natural course of trading, an extension of credit to bankrupts, and the banishment of specie from the country as people responded to a blizzard of paper money by hoarding their coins.[39] Even as he fended off his adversaries with cogent arguments, Hamilton had to overcome the cultural predisposition toward person-to-person loans, the most important type of colonial lending. Well into the early national period, bank opponents complained that person-to-person lending suffered because commercial banks soaked up all excess (that is, loanable) funds by inducing wealthy people to invest in bank stock rather than accommodate their neighbors.[40] On a macroeconomic scale, many failed to grasp the power of a national debt, properly funded and serviced, to bring prosperity to a national economy. John Adams, certainly nobody's fool, was one. "Every dollar of a bank bill that is issued beyond the quantity of gold and silver in the vaults," he said in 1809, "represents nothing and is therefore a cheat upon somebody."[41]

All too often in that acrimonious age, the criticism turned personal. Born to a government functionary on the minor British West Indian island of Nevis and raised on what was then the Danish island of Saint Croix (now part of the U.S. Virgin Islands), Hamilton lacked the pedigree of the other Founding Fathers. As far as John Adams was concerned, Hamilton was nothing more than "the bastard brat of a Scotch pedlar."[42]

Even as insults flew and Congress debated the details of a national banking system, a rising chorus of opposition objected to the bank on constitutional grounds. The ink had scarcely dried on that hallowed document when it was threatened by Hamilton's proposal to create an institution that was not sanctioned by the law of the land. For all the controversy banks have spawned, it is of more than passing curiosity that mention of banking is nowhere to be found in America's founding document.[43] Not to be undone by congressional critics who were quickly hardening into faction, Hamilton hit on an ingenious argument—or, to be more accurate, a Pandora's box whose contents would spill out to bedevil generations to come. Simply put, the secretary declared that the government enjoyed all powers necessary to its functioning and that were not *explicitly forbidden* in the Constitution.

Hamilton's logic was unanswerable. The bill incorporating the bank passed the Senate on January 20, 1791, but not before outbursts of vitriol cast doubt on Congress's claims to civilized behavior. As one senator remarked in his diary, "Some gentlemen would have been ashamed to have their speeches of this day reflected in the newspapers of tomorrow."[44] Debates in the House of Representatives, equally warm and passionate, ended on February 8 and produced a vote of thirty-nine to twenty in favor of chartering the bank. President Washington, keenly aware that acrimony over centralized banking was already casting a pall across his administration, spent some sleepless nights before signing the bill into law on February 25, 1791.[45]

Having won the first skirmish in a bank battle that was far from over, Hamilton could congratulate himself on not one but two victories: he had steered the ship of state toward a financial system commensurate with the needs of the new nation, and he had established the doctrine of "implied powers" that came to dominate legal interpretation of the Constitution. Some fifteen months after his hard-won battle over the Bank of the United States, Hamilton explained what happened: "A mighty stand was made on the affair of the Bank. There was much commitment in that case. I prevailed."[46]

The Bank of the United States was granted a twenty-year charter. Capital stock was set at $10 million—no small sum in a day when the combined capitalization of the nation's three state banks, including the Bank of New York, was only $2 million. Twenty percent of the bank's capitalization was to come from the federal government; the balance was open to public subscription. With 20 percent of the bank's stock, the government was entitled to the same percentage of seats on its board of directors. Notes issued by the bank were limited by a proviso that debts could not exceed deposits by more than $10 million. Finally, periodical statements were to be given to the secretary of the treasury.[47]

On July 4, 1791, bank stock hit the streets and quickly became the most intense initial stock offering in the young nation's history. Investors were downright giddy over the creation of an institution whose currency would circulate nationwide and whose loans would grease the wheels of commerce, agriculture, and manufacturing. Sale of Bank of the United States stock was oversubscribed by 20 percent and sold out within hours in most locations. In early August, the stock price in New York produced a one-month profit in excess of 50 percent. Stockjobbers plying the roads between New York and Philadelphia scrambled to keep up with orders. A few singled out the infamous South Sea Bubble of 1720 as a cautionary tale, but their voices were drowned in a chorus of enthusiasm.[48] Stockholders gathered in October at Philadelphia's city hall to choose a board of directors and elected as their first president Thomas Willing, a principal in the Bank of North America and, arguably, the most prominent commercial banker of his day. The main branch opened at Carpenter's Hall in Philadelphia to receive deposits on December 12, 1791. Loans were extended shortly thereafter.[49]

But not everyone was giddy. Congressional wrangling over the bank bill proved to be only a prelude to a debate that raged unabated into the nineteenth century and, in ways that the Founding Fathers could never have imagined, into subsequent centuries as well. In his Farewell Address, President Washington warned against "the baneful effects of the Spirit of Party, generally," but to no avail.[50] The senior statesman's counsel about the danger of factions fell on deaf ears as the Founding Fathers split into hostile and irreconcilable camps over the issue of centralized banking.

So-called Federalists rallied to the defense of the Bank of the United States, agreeing with Hamilton on the need for an institution to facilitate the flow of credit and currency at home and, at the same time, to establish credibility with foreign governments that were far from sanguine about the United States' prospects for survival. Opponents, more vocal by the day, rallied around Thomas Jefferson and the Republicans whose aversion to centralization of power lies at the heart of America's great experiment in democracy. The bill authorizing the bank had barely been passed when Jefferson and his ideological soul mate, James Madison, excoriated the Federalists as stockjobbers, Tories, and monocrats bent on amassing private fortunes at public expense.[51] All such despicable creatures, observed Madison, were latter-day money changers who had seized control of the temple and made a mockery of the freedoms so recently wrested from King George.

Republican accusations that Hamilton and his henchmen had hijacked the Revolution continued throughout the 1790s and raged unabated after Jefferson's election to the presidency in 1800. "I believe that banking institutions are more dangerous to our liberties than standing armies," asserted Jefferson in a letter to Secretary of the Treasury Albert Gallatin in 1802. "If the American people ever allow private banks to control the issue of their currency, first by inflation and then by deflation, the banks and the corporations that will grow up around them will deprive the people of all property until their children wake up homeless on the continent their fathers conquered."[52] On those occasions when passion yielded to reasoned debate, critics of centralized banking argued that the new behemoth was not entirely necessary and that, perhaps, the nation's finances were not in the shambles portrayed by the Federalists. After all, state indebtedness was decreasing, the nation's credit was improving, and additional revenues from the sale of western lands to individuals and corporations would provide a steady stream of revenue into the nation's coffers for many years to come.[53]

While Federalists and Republicans argued over the merits of centralized banking, the Bank of the United States was taking its place at the center of American finance and working closely with the Treasury Department to ensure the economy's health. Branches were established in the spring of 1792 in New York, Boston, Baltimore, and Charleston. By 1810, branches were up and running in Washington, New Orleans, Savannah, and Norfolk.[54] Twenty-nine commercial banks were doing brisk business in 1800 in towns that included ports capable of accommodating, at the least, the light-draft vessels of the day. Banking was still ancillary to commerce, and commerce was still waterborne and still faced the Atlantic Ocean.[55]

But not for long. Banking made its debut on the far side of the Alleghenies with the founding of what amounted to a bank in Lexington, Kentucky, then the principal town west of the mountains. Given their agrarian roots, Kentuckians were not about to align themselves with moneyed aristocrats back east. So the principals requested incorporation for the Kentucky Insurance Company—an organization whose charter contained nary a word about banks or banking, but that nevertheless authorized lending and issuing notes. The charter was approved on December 16, 1802. Although the Kentucky Insurance Company was supposed to insure riverboats and cargoes, it rapidly developed an open and profitable discount business. Its notes quickly went into general circulation, and its first year's dividend was almost 20 percent—not bad for a pseudo bank on the frontier.[56]

Even though commercial banks were mushrooming and prospering, the Bank of the United States was by far the most powerful bank in the country. Its branches had a monopoly on federal deposits and were the only ones whose banknotes were accepted at par everywhere. And the good news kept on coming: the dollar was the national unit of account; the nation's tax base was rising to a level sufficient to service Revolutionary War debts; a market for debt securities was flourishing; and a private financial-services sector composed of banks, insurance companies, and brokerages was developing.[57] Clearly, the United States was well on its way to monetary standardization. But there was still a long way to go. According to some estimates, 80 percent of American domestic specie in circulation in 1800 consisted of foreign coins.[58]

The entrepreneurial powers unleashed during the early national period launched the United States on its historic growth trajectory, a development that spawned both fear and admiration abroad. As Hamilton noted a year after Bank of the United States's inception, even "the most incorrigible theorist among its opponents would in one month's experience as head of the Department of the Treasury be compelled to acknowledge that [the bank] is an absolutely indispensible engine in the management of the Finances."[59]

The Bank of the United States's charter was set to expire on March 4, 1811. On April 20, 1808, the Senate received the bank's petition for renewal of its charter. The bank's appeal was based on its impressive track record: the government had profited from ownership of its stock; money had been loaned to the government to the tune of $6.2 million; and the bank had come through on its promise "to collect its revenue, and to perform its pecuniary engagements, with ease, economy and security."[60] What is more, Bank of the United States branches had performed valuable services to the public. Willis Alston of North Carolina declared that the Bank of the United States "serves as a controlling power, keeps the state banks in proper bounds, and prevents them from issuing a vast quantity of paper, which would inundate the country."[61] But in the debates over recharter, opponents in Congress were less interested in the bank's accomplishments than they were in its power—an early expression, perhaps, of the "too big to fail" argument.

Some suggested that the Bank of the United States was not quite the monopoly that it was cracked up to be. State-chartered banks were proliferating in its shadow, raking in profits by safeguarding their depositors' money and loaning it to new enterprises at competitive rates of interest for profit. The handful of state-chartered banks that existed in 1790 had mushroomed to nearly thirty by 1800. Their combined capital was an impressive $21.3 million, and there was not a single bank failure until the spring of 1809. In 1811, the roster of state-chartered banks stood at eighty-eight, and they were operating with combined capital of $42.6 million.[62]

Even though well-managed banks were the norm, high profile fiascos fueled suspicions of all banks, commercial ones as well as the Bank of the United States. In the race to attract customers, some bankers ignored the conventional wisdom that banknotes should never exceed capital by a factor of more than three or five. At the far end of a continuum stretching from the prudent to the preposterous, the capital of the Farmers Exchange Bank of Gloucester, Rhode Island, was a modest $45.00 while its banknote issues totaled $800,000—more than 17,000 times its capital![63] The bank, incorporated as recently as February 1804 with authorized capital of $100,000, earned dubious distinction as the young nation's first bank failure in the spring of 1809. Its demise elicited a terse postmortem from Representative Joseph Desha of Kentucky; the bank, he said, "when it was ripped up, had but some odds of forty dollars in its vaults."[64]

Then as now, good news loses traction when disaster strikes, and the failure of the Rhode Island bank definitely caused a stir in the court of public opinion. Bankers' popularity reached its nadir in the West, where opposition to the Bank of the United States was strongest, banking laws were weakest, and sentiment against eastern capital was deeply ingrained in a culture of self-sufficiency and rugged individualism. Westerners and frontiersmen were particularly galled to discover that Europeans owned a significant amount of stock in the Bank of the United States. Simply put, central banking did not seem to be a sine qua non of economic development, and it might even open a portal to foreign domination of the financial system.

The three-year battle to recharter the Bank of the United States ended in a showdown on February 20, 1811, when Vice President George Clinton cast a tie-breaking vote against renewing its charter.[65] In what was surely the most important vice presidential act in the nation's history to that point, Clinton ended a twenty-year experiment in centralized banking and opened the floodgates to state chartering.

Between 1811 and 1816, the number of state-chartered banks ballooned from 88 to 246. With little experience to guide them, state legislatures did not have much advice to offer bank managers, and they failed to develop reporting systems to make sure that bankers behaved themselves. Inexperience did not prevent state legislatures from injecting a dose of politics into the chartering process; what had been deemed corruption in more enlightened eras was business as usual in the early national period. Specie became scarce as Europeans, spooked by a free-for-all that threatened their investments, cashed in their bank stock and withdrew their tender from the American economy. When the War of 1812 brought demands for credit, bankers were happy to comply and issued more credit than they could support. Predictably, state-chartered banks tumbled like dominoes. Nevertheless, banknote circulation skyrocketed from $45 million in 1812 to $100 million in 1817. During the four years between 1814 and 1817, direct losses to the government from poor or worthless banknotes amounted to more than $5 million.[66]

With the advent of peace with Great Britain in 1814, proponents of a return to centralized banking gained the upper hand. A bill to establish a Second Bank of the United States was passed in the House of Representatives on March 14, 1816, by a vote of eighty to seventy-one. After passing the Senate by a vote of twenty-two to twelve, the bill went to President James Madison, and he signed it on April 10. Chartered again for twenty years, the bank was capitalized at $35 million, of which $7 million came from the government. Modeled closely after the First Bank, the Second Bank of the United States was to create a national paper currency, purchase a large chunk of the public debt, and receive deposits of Treasury funds. Its notes and deposits were to be redeemable in specie, and they were given quasi-legal tender status insofar as the federal government would accept them in payment of taxes.[67] The central office was to be in Philadelphia and was slated to open on February 20, 1817, under the leadership of William Jones and twenty-five directors, five of whom were presidential appointees.[68] Perhaps it was seen as a good omen that the Second Bank of the United States opened in January, more than a month ahead of schedule. Not all went according to plan. Under the stewardship of the hard-drinking William Jones, speculation spun out of control and banknote circulation was disappointingly light. Credit was extended and quickly constricted, causing interest rates to spike, farm produce to plummet, and unemployment to soar.

In a foretaste of what the nineteenth century held in store, America found itself in the throes of the Panic of 1819—the same year that the Supreme Court handed down its historic decision in *McCulloch v. Maryland,* determining that the state of Maryland did not have the power to tax the Baltimore branch of the Bank of the United States.[69] Such was the mayhem occasioned by the financial panic that a motion was introduced in Congress to look into setting aside the bank's charter. Instead, the hapless William Jones was replaced by Langdon Cheves (whose name was pronounced "Chivis"), a sound businessman from Charleston, South Carolina, who remained at the helm of the Second Bank of the United States until 1823. Cheves took office the day before Chief Justice John Marshall, repeating verbatim some of Alexander Hamilton's arguments, handed down the Court's decision in *McCulloch v. Maryland* that the power to tax was the power to destroy, thereby saving the Bank of the United States from death by strangulation and embittering bankers with state charters because they had to pay state taxes while the federal bank did not.[70]

Discovering "that there was a great want of financial talent" in Philadelphia, Cheves was fortunate to count on the advice of Nicholas Biddle, a director of the bank whose commitment to public service eventually propelled him to a rendezvous with destiny as the most prominent banker in the land and the personification of centralized banking.[71] Even as Cheves and his directors struggled to undo the damage inflicted by an often inebriated banker and his ill-conceived policies, they knew that the new bank did not have nearly as much clout as its predecessor. The country had grown too much, and too many state-chartered banks had entered the playing field during the five-year hiatus between central banks, for a single institution to control currency and credit to the extent that its proponents had hoped for.

While the Second Bank of the United States struggled to find its legs, banks were still reeling from the effects of the recent panic. By 1825, fully half of the banks founded between 1810 and 1820 had failed. Two of those failures were in the frontier border state of Missouri: the Bank of Saint Louis, in which Senator Thomas Hart Benton was a stockholder, closed in 1819 with heavy losses; and the Bank of Missouri, chartered in 1817 and whose board of directors included the aforementioned senator, closed in 1821. The Missouri banks' failures at roughly the same time as the state was admitted to the Union had the dual effect of casting a shadow across statehood celebrations and convincing Senator Benton that banks were not to be trusted. In subsequent years, Senator Benton opposed federal regulation of the nation's currency and credit, railed against all forms of paper currency, including banknotes, and advocated an exclusively metallic circulation.[72] The senator once quipped, "Are men with pens sticking behind their ears to be allowed to put an end to this republic?"[73] For fifteen years, the Missouri legislature exemplified western distrust of banking institutions by refusing to incorporate another bank. In the absence of paper currency, Missouri businesses relied on Mexican silver specie that was pouring in from the Santa Fe trade.[74]

Yet state chartering elsewhere continued apace, and banknotes littered the financial landscape like the leaves of autumn. Some folks with a flair for entrepreneurship who did not even own a bank printed notes and passed them off for items of value. Publishers discovered a niche by printing banknote detectors that listed, illustrated, and assessed the worthiness of banknote issues, much like bookies publish stats on race horses.[75] Nevertheless, the appearance of banknotes on the frontier was a critical step in allowing people to hold money instead of perishable assets. For all the chaos they created, banknotes hastened economic development by coaxing productive resources from hoards and facilitating trade. The paradigm shift occasioned by the monetization of the economy is reflected in the awe people felt when they got hold of their first banknotes. Farmers who had never seen a banknote handled them gingerly, admiring the fine pictures printed on them, and sharing their wonder with their wives and children. Then they tucked them carefully in the family Bible, where they were kept smooth and nice until the pressures of a monetizing economy lured them into circulation.[76]

By midcentury, thousands of paper-money issues were cluttering the financial landscape. For farmers struggling to wrestle a living from the soil and tradesmen scrambling to build businesses, the monetization of the economy had yet to yield its promise. Seemingly not much had changed since a hodgepodge of coins, certificates, and provincial bills of credit had confounded economic development in the bad old days of King George. Maybe goats and bales of tobacco were not such bad bargains after all.

During the early national period, American banking went through its adolescence as the disciplined and restricted economy of the late eighteenth century evolved into the dynamic, complex, laissez-faire economy of the nineteenth. Much as Newtonian physics had redefined humankind's place in the universe and the French Revolution had dropped the curtain on divine-right kingship, so, too, were contracts, negotiable instruments, equities, and other invisible abstractions steamrolling their way through the economy and revolutionizing the production, acquisition, and distribution of goods. In some cases, the law struggled to keep pace with upstart bankers. In other cases, bankers leaned on the law to sanction their experiments, even as the credit they extended to entrepreneurs was becoming the steam engine of finance. Caught, as all are, in the glare of the present, none were prescient enough to recognize the scope of the revolution they were fomenting—a revolution in finance destined to conquer the world.

The debate over centralized banking that began with the founding of the Bank of North America in the early 1780s and continued in Congress during the early national period reveals a paradox at the heart of American finance. It is a paradox that fueled the dispute between Federalists and Republicans during the first decade of the nation's existence, roared to life in campaigns to charter the First and Second Banks of the United States, and followed the course of Manifest Destiny across the continent. Inevitably, the paradox found its way to the lawless lands west of Fort Smith and immeasurably complicated efforts to establish sound banking principles in Oklahoma.

So, what was the problem?

The problem lay in reconciling the twin pillars of American finance: democracy and capitalism. To the eighteenth-century mind, there was no distinction between economic development and culture. The unlimited potential that flowed from the American Revolution represented the latest stage of regenerative culture that had flowed from ancient Greece and Rome and through Western Europe and onto American shores, where a whole continent awaited the blessings that would inevitably come from inclusion in the new nation. The standard Whig belief in personal freedom and political liberty, enshrined in the Constitution and expressed in Jefferson's vision of an agrarian republic, was inseparable from economic development. Frontiersmen and yeoman farmers fired by a commitment to individual liberty thus stood in the vanguard of American democracy, eager to hew a new Athens from the wilderness. Having wrested their independence from King George, Jefferson's heirs had no real plan for progress, other than avoiding the evils that had led Europe down the path of ruin, and nipping centralization of power in the bud. Simply put, commercial and cultural ascendancy were seen as synonymous because they were regarded as mutual beneficiaries of the same liberating process.[77]

But here was the rub. All that explosive power of individual freedom, coupled with endless resources and a dearth of restrictions in the form of taxes and trade policies, produced a chaotic business climate. Entrepreneurs bent on resource exploitation and wealth creation produced an unprecedented free-for-all whose destructive powers increased with advances in technology and communication. The freedom that America's frontiersmen enjoyed in their conquest of the continent was coupled with the freedom to wreak havoc along the way. To facilitate the flow of currency and credit in ways that might accrue to the common good, and to ease America's entry into the community of nations, capitalism needed some taming. For Hamilton and his heirs, centralized banking under the aegis of elite moneymen was key to keeping the nation's finances from spinning out of control. Unlike Jefferson, Hamilton had a plan for economic development, and it rested squarely on entrusting the flow of currency and credit to a strong central authority.

Democracy and capitalism are uneasy bedfellows at best. Their paradoxical relationship has always been part of the American narrative, and it has led to some fascinating experiments in producing, acquiring, and distributing goods. When Jefferson famously quipped in his first inaugural address, "We are all Federalists, we are all Republicans," what he was really saying is that we are all woven from the twin strands of democracy and capitalism.

By the middle of the nineteenth century, only the staunchest of capitalists could claim to repudiate democracy, and most democrats were either capitalists or prospective capitalists.[78] And everybody depended on capitalism, which in turn depended on some form of banking, to fuel their dreams. Pioneers who pushed westward in the nineteenth century were thus enlisted in the tug-of-war between democracy and capitalism. One way or another, they and their descendants and the native populations they encountered along the way were unwitting foot soldiers in the ongoing battle of the banks.

CHAPTER TWO

Free Banking

Banks are engines calculated to do much good if well managed, much evil if badly administered.

Anonymous

On the morning of July 13, 1804, Vice President Aaron Burr and former secretary of the treasury Alexander Hamilton were rowed across the Hudson River in separate boats. Their destination was a secluded spot near Weehawken, New Jersey, far from the center of attention that was their natural milieu. There, in accordance with the customs of the *code duello,* they paced in opposite directions, turned, and exchanged pistol shots. For reasons that remain unclear to this day, Hamilton's bullet went wildly amiss. Burr's bullet did not. It fractured Hamilton's rib cage, ricocheted off a rib, penetrated his liver and diaphragm, and came to rest in his second lumbar vertebra. His physician, Dr. David Hosack, raced to his side. Hamilton knew he was done for. "This is a mortal wound, Doctor," gasped the fallen financier before lapsing into unconsciousness. He died the next day.[1]

On another summer morning, this one in 1831, Major Thomas Biddle heeded the same call to honor on an island in the Mississippi River near Saint Louis. Owing to his nearsightedness, he stood a mere five feet from his antagonist. When the signal to commence fire was given, he raised his pistol and took aim. So did the other man. Simultaneous blasts echoed across the water. When the smoke cleared, both men lay dead.

Had it not been for Major Biddle's prominence, the event might not have attracted much attention. He was a director of the Saint Louis branch of the Second Bank of the United States, and the gunplay that ended his life was precipitated by an insult to his institution by the other man in the duel.[2] His even more prominent brother, Nicholas, had served as president of the Second Bank of the United States since 1823 and was the most powerful banker of his day. If Nicholas had ever doubted his brother's commitment to central banking, all the evidence he needed to the contrary lay sprawled on an island in the Mississippi River.

Towering egos were certainly to blame for the duels that led to Alexander Hamilton's and Thomas Biddle's deaths. Yet the men also went to their graves as extreme examples of the passions that banking stirred during the early days of the Republic. Ever since Federalists and Republicans had squared off over chartering the First Bank of the United States, Americans had gravitated to one of two hostile camps: those who championed local rule and small-scale banking, and others who emphasized the need for a strong central authority to manage the affairs of a growing nation. The latter had the upper hand as long as the Second Bank of the United States was pulling the levers of currency and credit. But the nation was still in the process of creating itself, and bank battles, literally and figuratively, were far from over.

In an absence of laws requiring banks to issue reports on their financial condition, it is difficult to get an accurate impression of local banking before 1834. Understandably, many people were vexed by what would one day be denounced as a lack of transparency. In an essay on banking and currency written in 1831, Secretary of the Treasury Albert Gallatin referred to "the mystery with which it has been thought necessary" in several of the states "to conceal the operations of the banking institutions."[3] It comes as no surprise that secrecy fostered confusion in the public sphere and mismanagement in the banks. Yet even in an age of lax regulation and rampant subterfuge, two principal defects of banking in the early national period could not be hidden: the endless opportunities to issue banknotes and bankers' tendency to make loans on dubious collateral. Until these systemic problems could be corrected, Americans had scant protection from financial panics that roiled the nineteenth-century economy.

The first of these recurrent storms was the Panic of 1819 that William Jones, president of the Second Bank of the United States, met with such incompetence. Its complex causes were basically twofold: an inability of manufacturing industries to regain their footing after the abnormal growth occasioned by the War of 1812 and subsequent embargo, and speculation steeped in a toxic stew of rapid growth and bad banking. Secretary of the Treasury William H. Crawford, who served in that capacity from 1816 to 1825, and Congress scrambled for remedies. What Secretary Crawford and Congress came to understand was the difficulty of adjusting revenue to expenditures in a new and rapidly expanding nation. They were joined on their learning curve by the general-turned-statesman from Tennessee, Andrew Jackson, whose hatred of America's original inhabitants was matched by his contempt for bankers and their nefarious ways. Nicknamed "Old Hickory" for his intransigence on the battlefield, he lost money during the Panic of 1819, and he never forgot it. The experience left him with a distrust of leverage and a hankering for revenge against the Second Bank of the United States that had handled the nation's money with such ineptitude.

While Old Hickory was recouping his losses and plotting his revenge, the Second Bank of the United States was elevating one of its directors to the top job. At a meeting of stockholders in November 1822, Nicholas Biddle, a Philadelphian and valedictorian of his Princeton class whose brother, Thomas, would later meet his Maker in faraway Saint Louis, went from a dark horse to front-runner. Clearly skilled as a money manager, Biddle's talents went far beyond the minutiae of finance and accounting. Long before he was appointed as president of the Second Bank of the United States, he attended Napoleon Bonaparte's coronation as emperor at Notre Dame Cathedral, applied his classical learning to study tours of Italy and Greece (then under Turkish rule and terra incognita to the Western world), and wrote a history of Lewis and Clark's expedition to the Pacific Northwest, described by one admirer as "a first-rate narrative digest, that revealed to the people the travels of Lewis and Clark; and Americans could begin to imagine the nation of the future, stretching three thousand miles from sea to sea."[4] Biddle's appointment was assured when two heavy hitters lined up behind his candidacy: President James Monroe and Secretary of the Treasury William Crawford.[5]

Barely thirty-seven years old at the time of his appointment and with no apprenticeship to his credit, the peripatetic scholar and adventurer seized command of the Second Bank of the United States, then the largest corporation in America and one of the largest in the world.[6]

At the same time, the federal government owned 20 percent of the bank's capital, and its board included a prescribed number of directors who served at the president's pleasure.[7] Working closely and effectively with the Treasury Department, what became known in financial circles as Biddle's Bank grew to be the financial hub of the Mississippi Valley, where its New Orleans branch ranked first in importance and its Natchez branch was larger than the one in Boston. Ensconced at the edge of the frontier, the bank controlled the flow of currency and credit between the increasingly settled East and the trans-Mississippi West, where farmers and exchange dealers relied heavily on the bank's branches to fund their enterprises.[8]

Under Biddle's management, the bank served as the balance wheel of the banking system. It regulated the money supply, restrained the expansion of bank credit, governed the exchanges, safeguarded investment markets, protected the money market from destabilizing actions of the Treasury Department, and facilitated the Treasury Department's operations. Nicholas Biddle invites comparisons with Alan Greenspan, former chairman of the Federal Reserve, insofar as he exercised the power and prestige of the Second Bank of the United States without doing much more than signaling his intentions to infuse the system with funds. In his annual report for 1828, Secretary of the Treasury Richard Rush expressed the opinion of many that Biddle's Bank was doing yeoman's work in the service of American finance: "In faithful obedience to the provisions of its charter, and aided by its branches, the bank had afforded the necessary facilities for transferring the public moneys from place to place."[9]

Unlike central banks in our own day, the Second Bank of the United States operated essentially as a private institution. Fattened by federal deposits and operating in branches from the Atlantic to the Mississippi, it tended to restrict the growth of state and private (that is, unincorporated) banks. To an ascendant coterie of Wall Street financiers in New York, the bank symbolized the well-heeled aristocrats of Philadelphia whose wealth was on display on Chestnut Street. No matter how effectively the bank managed the nation's credit and money supply, there was no getting around the fact that it was a quasi-public monopoly.

Prosperity came at a price, and for libertarians with a zest for free enterprise and free markets, it was too high. Among those unwilling to foot the bill was Andrew Jackson—frontiersman first, soldier second, and now the sworn enemy of centralized banking. His version of the banker's bottom line was simple: Biddle's Bank had to die.

Andrew Jackson was inaugurated as the seventh president of the United States on March 4, 1829. Born in 1767 in South Carolina, the man known to history as "Old Hickory" bore the scars of a hardscrabble life, not all of which were visible. A proclivity for dueling put enough lead in his body to kill mere mortals. It also put a steely glint in his eye that his opponents ignored at their peril. But there was more to Jackson than the soul of a scrappy frontiersman. He was elected to the House of Representatives in 1796 and to the Senate the following year. Finances forced him to return to Tennessee, where he read enough, no doubt shivering by candlelight, to gain admission to the Tennessee bar. He also secured a position on his adopted state's superior court, where he was known as a fair judge who preferred conviction and intuition to book learning to render his decisions.

It was Jackson's heroic stand at the Battle of New Orleans in 1815 that earned him a memorable nickname and, eventually, a shot at the nation's highest office. He ascended to the presidency in a landslide election in 1828 with many firsts to his credit: he was the first president with no connection to the Virginia dynasty; the first self-made man without an aristocratic bone in his body; the first to gain fame through military service; and the first to enter the White House through mudslinging.

President Jackson's inaugural ball put to rest any doubts that a new sheriff was in town when his supporters, clad in homespun clothing and unschooled in civilized refinements, heralded frontier democracy with festivities that sent guardians of propriety running for cover. "Cut glass and china to the amount of several thousand dollars had been broken in the struggle to get the refreshments," wrote Margaret Bayard Smith, the wife of a senator from Maryland and a chronicler of Washington life who had lived in the capital since 1800, in a letter to Mrs. Kirkpatrick. "Ladies fainted, men were seen with bloody noses and such a scene of confusion took place as is impossible to describe,—those who got in could not get out by the door again, but had to scramble out of windows. . . . The noisy and disorderly rabble in the President's House brought to my mind descriptions I had read, of the mobs in the Tuileries and at Versailles, I expect to hear the carpets and furniture are ruined, the streets were muddy, and these guests all went thither on foot."[10] Supreme

Court justice Joseph Story, a staunch Adams man who was at the White House on Inauguration Day, recorded his own take on the hullabaloo following Jackson's swearing-in ceremony: "After the ceremony was over, the President went to the palace to receive company, and there he was visited by immense crowds of all sorts of people, from the highest and most polished, down to the most vulgar and gross in the nation. I never saw such a mixture. The reign of 'King Mob' seemed triumphant. I was glad to escape from the scene as soon as possible."[11]

As far as President Jackson was concerned, real money was specie; paper money and newfangled commercial paper such as bills of exchange, promissory notes, and bank checks were nothing short of fraud. No sooner had the stains been cleaned from the White House carpets than the president put Biddle's Bank in his crosshairs. He made his hostility toward the bank known in his first message to Congress in December 1829 when he questioned the institution's legitimacy on the grounds of both constitutionality and expediency. He turned up the heat in his second annual message in December 1830 when he said that nothing had occurred to lessen "the dangers which many of our citizens apprehend from that institution as at present organized."[12] His jeremiad carried over into Congressional inquiries into the bank's dealings.[13] But it was not until Missouri senator Thomas Hart Benton introduced a resolution in 1831 against rechartering Biddle's Bank that Old Hickory sprang into action.

The aging frontiersman had once declared that he would prefer to undergo the torture of ten Spanish Inquisitions, or perhaps seek asylum in the wilds of Arabia, than recharter the Bank of the United States.[14] Jackson expressed his anguish to his second-term vice president and successor to the presidency, Martin Van Buren, who was similarly ill-disposed toward the bank, in July 1932: "The Bank, Mr. Van Buren, is trying to kill me, *but I will kill it*."[15] Jackson's rhetoric was matched by his ideological soul mate, Senator Benton, whose support likewise came from bank-hating westerners, and who had been sorely stung by the failure of the Bank of Saint Louis in 1819 and the Bank of Missouri in 1821. "All the flourishing cities of the West," thundered the Missouri firebrand, "are mortgaged to this money power. They may be devoured by it at any moment. They are in the jaws of the monster! A lump of butter in the mouth of a dog! One gulp, one swallow, and all is gone!"[16]

Ill-mannered partiers and oratorical flourishes notwithstanding, the Jacksonian crusade against the Second Bank of the United States was not an assault on capitalism. Rather, it was an assault on capitalists who felt most at home on Chestnut Street, and whose aristocratic pretensions were entirely out of synch with the zeitgeist of an industrializing age. New technologies and seemingly endless resources were opening opportunities to an entirely new breed of capitalists—risk takers and investors and speculators who had little patience with the old, conservative merchant class, and who chafed at artificial barriers to getting rich. Amos Kendall, a member of Andrew Jackson's Kitchen Cabinet and one of the bank's most devoted foes, believed that Americans wanted the federal government simply to protect their persons and property, "leaving them to direct their labor and capital as they please, within the moral law; getting rich or remaining poor as may result from their own management or fortune."[17] Another Kitchen Cabinet member and future Supreme Court chief justice, Roger B. Taney (pronounced "Tawney"), made much the same point in his advocacy of an open banking system. He went on record as saying that "there is perhaps no business which yields a profit so certain and liberal as the business of banking and exchange; and it is proper that it should be open as far as practicable to the most free competition and its advantages shared by all classes of society."[18] The conflict was thus not between the static rich and the static poor, but rather between people who were already rich and a dynamic and even revolutionary class of capitalists who wanted to earn their wealth (or, less palatable but certainly possible, lose it) from the opportunities that an expansive America had to offer.

The presidential veto of the bill to recharter Biddle's Bank came on July 10, 1832, along with a blistering message about the threat posed by the "money monopoly": "Is there no danger to our liberty and independence in a bank that in its nature has so little to bind it to our country? The president of the bank has told us that most of the State banks exist by its forbearance. Should its influence become concentrated, as it may under the operation of such an act as this, in the hands of a self-elected directory, whose interests are identified with those of the foreign stockholders, will there not be cause to tremble for the purity of our elections in peace, and for the independence of our country in war?"[19]

Never known for his modesty, Nicholas Biddle believed that presidents and politicians came and went, but that the bank was eternal. But this president came with a mission, and failure was not an option. The relocation of federal funds from the bank's branches to state-chartered banks—Jackson's so-called pet banks—in the fall of 1833 demonstrated that the president was willing to invite a constitutional battle to achieve his goals.[20] Arguably, it was the removal of public deposits, and not the presidential veto, that destroyed the Second Bank of the United States. Deprived of its essential powers, the bank could no longer exert conservative pressures on a galloping economy.

The relocation of federal funds to state banks left little doubt that Biddle's reign was entering its twilight. "The Executive," wrote a deflated Nicholas Biddle in March 1834, "by removing the public revenues has relieved the Bank from all responsibility for the currency."[21] In desperation, Biddle contracted credit, hoping that a recession would shock President Jackson and his minions to their senses. But it was too little, too late, and utterly hopeless. Whatever skills Biddle had acquired as a financier were eclipsed by his ineptitude in hardball politics.

Jackson's veto of the bill to recharter the Second Bank of the United States might well have been the most important veto ever issued by a president. Jackson not only rejected the bank on constitutional grounds but also rejected it because he sincerely believed that it posed a danger to the nation he was sworn to defend. What is more, he expressed his convictions in language that resonates to this day in the annals of presidential rhetoric. Nicholas Biddle likened Jackson's language to "the fury of a chained panther biting the bars of his cage." It was, said the beleaguered bank president, "a manifesto of anarchy, such as Marat, or Robespierre might have issued to the mobs" during the French Revolution.[22] In effect, Jackson was asserting his right to participate in the legislative process, thereby widening the scope of presidential prerogative and challenging Congress's exclusive right to propose and enact legislation. Clearly, a new day was dawning in American governance. From that day forward, the executive was not simply an equal partner with the legislative and judicial branches of government. As an active participant in legislation, the president represented all the people, and his authority bordered on the imperial.

The beginning of the end of Nicholas Biddle's career as the land's most powerful banker came on April 4, 1834, when the House of Representatives agreed by a vote of 134 to 82 that the bank "ought not to be rechartered." Then, by a vote of 118 to 103, legislators agreed that the deposits "ought not to be restored." By a vote of 117 to 105, the House recommended that state (pet) banks continue to serve as depositories for federal funds. Finally, by an overwhelming vote of 175 to 42, the House authorized the appointment of a committee to examine the bank's responsibility for causing the recent panic.[23]

"I have obtained a glorious triumph," crowed the hero of the Battle of New Orleans. At long last, the House had "put to death that mammoth of corruption and power, the Bank of the United States."[24] With little fanfare, the Second Bank of the United States's charter expired in February 1836, and it became just another bank in Philadelphia.[25]

The demise of the Second Bank of the United States opened the floodgates to a surge of state bank chartering, and America departed from a dual banking system in which one national bank coexisted with hundreds of state-chartered banks and embarked on an era of banking empowered exclusively by the states. In short order, control of the nation's money supply devolved from a single institution with a long-term, national perspective to a myriad of local ones, each focused on its own short-term prosperity. Numbers tell the story of the great unraveling. From 1829 to 1837, state banks mushroomed from 329 with capital of $110 million to 788 with capital of $300 million. Between 1830 and 1837, state banknote circulation more than doubled, and loans and discounts increased from less than $200 million to more than $500 million.[26]

The raison d'être of state banks was to receive deposits and make loans, most of which were made in cash rather than lines of credit. Loans were short-term, usually thirty days; long-term notes of sixty days were the exception. Mortgages were reserved for the most credit-worthy customers. To highlight the importance of agriculture, farmers were among the first borrowers to win long-term credit. Not surprisingly, money-making trumped altruism when it came to establishing banks. Merchants and financiers who organized banking divisions were less interested in public service than exploiting their ad hoc banks as sources for loans. As Bank of North America founder Robert Morris quipped way back in 1785, America grew rich by borrowing.[27] "It has come to be a proverb," wrote a shrewd observer in 1857, "that banks never originate with those who have money to lend, but with those who wish to borrow money."[28]

State banks established after the disappearance of the Second Bank of the United States endured their trial by fire in the Panic of 1837. The catalyst for disaster was President Jackson's requirement that public lands be sold only in exchange for gold and silver. The Bank of England responded to the infamous "specie circular" of July 1836 by demanding gold-backed currency for its transactions. Meanwhile, American markets inflated by speculation went into panic mode as credit dried up and anxious citizens hoarded their cash. In the first sixty days of the panic, New York suffered 250 business failures. Boston counted 168 bankruptcies in the first six months.[29] By early fall, 90 percent of the nation's factories were closed, and federal revenues were down by half.[30] In 1837 alone, 618 banks failed, and unemployment was heading off the charts. Job loss was particularly severe in the South and West, where farmers with financial ties to northern financiers paid a heavy price for the expanding web of capitalist enterprise.[31] The Panic of 1837, spawned by Jackson's hard-money doctrine that was utterly out of step with America's progressive and dynamic economy, fit the stereotype of financial panics insofar as it began when bank debt holders suddenly demanded that banks convert their debt claims into cash. When banks responded by suspending their cash conversions, all bets were off, and the panic was on.[32]

Among the innovations spawned by this and subsequent panics was the creation of clearinghouses, supposedly pioneered by sixteenth-century financiers in Naples.[33] New York City bankers served as latter-day pioneers in creating the first American clearinghouse on October 11, 1853.[34] Boston and Philadelphia banks followed suit later in the 1850s, and banks in other large cities soon fell in line.[35] These institutions alleviated the burden of storing large supplies of currency and coin and the inconveniences inherent in physical transfers between banks by creating central chambers in which each bank assigned a clerk. The clerks exchanged claims against each other and paid the difference in money, much as credits are transferred in the same bank, from one account to another, without using cash or coin.[36] Money and banknotes were thus set free for general circulation and commerce. Clearinghouses not only cleared interbank liabilities; they also responded to bank panics by serving as lenders of last resort, issuing private money, and providing deposit insurance. To facilitate these functions, clearinghouses regulated member banks by auditing their risk-taking activities, setting capital requirements, and penalizing members for violating clearinghouse rules. Because of restrictions against branch banking, clearinghouses and their cooperative benefits were limited to citywide coalitions.[37]

President Andrew Jackson, the maverick of his time, thus ushered in the era of free banking (1836–63). His experiment in decentralized banking got off to a raucous start with the Panic of 1837. As banks folded in the perfect storm of collapsing credit and vanishing currency and massive unemployment, demand skyrocketed for new banks, and anyone willing to abide by a common set of state regulations suddenly had an opportunity to enter the banking business. In essence, free banking relieved state legislatures from the drudgery of granting bank charters and allowed individuals to form corporations for the purpose of providing banking services. All they needed was a certificate of incorporation from a state official, and they were off and running. Southerners and westerners in particular had had enough of the money power back east. They viewed free banking as an antidote to the evils of bank chartering that included wholesale bribery of state legislators by rival banking factions. In southern states and regions recently wrested from the frontier, various forms of statewide (but certainly not national!) branching were developed to serve the needs of credit-starved farmers and businessmen. Clearinghouses were a welcome innovation, but they were scant protection from full-blown panics that continued to roil the nineteenth-century economy. In addition to clearinghouses, savings banks emerged during this period, often as philanthropic endeavors.[38]

Jefferson's low opinion of banks (puzzling, given the fact that bank loans funded his expensive tastes) and Jackson's crusade against the Second Bank of the United States left their legacy in the Equal Rights Party, a radical wing of the Democratic Party, better known as Locofocos, that was active from 1835 through the mid-1840s. Grafting pristine Jeffersonian principles onto a nascent labor movement, the Locofocos supported free trade, greater circulation of specie, and legal protection for labor unions, and they excoriated banks as privileged and aristocratic monopolies. "We demand," declared the anti-bank zealots, "that the state governments will no longer authorize the issuing of bills of credit, commonly called bank notes, in open violation of the Constitution of the United States."[39] Meetings sometimes degenerated into brawls as frustrated laborers attempted to reclaim their country from "the desolating influence of paper money."[40]

Cooler heads settled for laws prohibiting branch banking, widely seen as centralization in a particularly sinister guise. Advocates of branching argued that networks of financial institutions tended to stabilize the system and inured to the benefit of small towns that could not support individual banks, but no matter.[41] Distrust of eastern capital had hardened into an ideology, and rugged individualists, particularly in the South and West, would have none of it. Nowhere were banks less popular than Missouri, where the failure of the Bank of Saint Louis in 1819 and the Bank of Missouri in 1821 left the state bankless for more than a decade. When the state legislature became fed up with unreliable currencies flowing in from neighboring states and established the Missouri State Bank in 1837, it authorized the institution to aid in the circulation of specie but not paper money. As one Missouri newspaper editor wrote, "The people of the State of Missouri are opposed to *all Banks*. So are we. But let us not be misunderstood. . . . We mean that we are opposed to national or local Banks as constituted in this country. The Bank of the State of Missouri is different from all the others. . . . Of course, when we express our opposition to Banks, we refer not to ours, but to the miserable paper manufacturers scattered over the country."[42]

Missourians' preference for specie and skepticism toward paper money was borne out when the new bank, founded in the panic year of 1837, became recognized as one of the soundest financial institutions in the nation. Within a month of its opening in the summer of 1837, it became a bank of deposit for the U.S. government and received deposits from traders returning from Santa Fe.[43] Depositors in Arkansas probably thought their northern neighbors were onto something. Two banks were chartered in 1836, the same year that Arkansas was admitted to the Union as the twenty-fifth state, and both failed during the nationwide depression. With a debt of $3 million and no banks, Arkansas's early years of statehood were marked by hard times.[44]

Banks during the free-banking era were governed by a kaleidoscope of state regulations and operated with communication and transportation systems that were anything but reliable.[45] In keeping with Roger Taney's comment in 1834 that banking "should be open as far as practicable to the most free competition and its advantages shared by all classes of society," obtaining a bank charter during the free-banking era was only slightly more difficult than becoming a bricklayer. Hugh McCulloch, president of the Bank of Indiana who was appointed as the first comptroller of the currency in 1863 before serving two nonconsecutive terms as U.S. secretary of the treasury under Presidents Chester A. Arthur and Abraham Lincoln, knew all too well how easy it was to become a banker. "Anybody," he wrote, "who could command two or three thousand dollars of money could buy on margin the bonds necessary to establish a bank, to be paid for in its notes after its organization had been completed."[46] By permitting an indefinite and unlimited number of banks, advocates of free banking sought to restore to the individual the ancient, common-law right to become a banker with nary a thought about managerial competence.[47] Open to all comers, free banking steered between the Locofoco insistence that banks be abolished and the entrepreneurial demand for more of them. Writing in 1834, an anonymous author who might as well be writing today commented on his countrymen's love-hate relationship with their banks: "Banks are engines calculated to do much good if well managed, much evil if badly administered."[48]

As agriculture ceded ground, literally and figuratively, to industry, there was one player in the banking game who felt left out in the cold: the lowly bank depositor. In the halcyon days that fired Jefferson's imagination, trust had acted as the social glue that bound communities in networks of mutual support. Yet the trust that had governed relations between bankers and their customers was ill-equipped to guarantee the safety of deposits. The pace of economic activity was quickening, and conservative practices fostered in tight-knit communities were out of place in an emerging business paradigm that favored risk and innovation.

Legislators in New York had seen the handwriting on the wall before President Jackson paved the way to free banking, and they came to the rescue with a safety fund system to insure the liabilities of New York banks. Conceived during Martin Van Buren's brief stint as governor in 1828 and launched in early 1829, the law required banks to pay annually to the state treasurer a sum equal to one-half of 1 percent of their capital stock until payments amounted to 3 percent. The fund was to be used for redemption of notes of any failed bank.[49] Yet deposit banking was so underdeveloped that the law's framers overlooked the link between debts and deposits. The safety fund system remained in effect from 1829 until 1842, and its virtual collapse in the wake of the Panic of 1837 did not bode well for the prospects of bank guaranty legislation.[50] Clearly, new ways would have to be found to protect bank depositors from the perils of banking in the nascent age of industry.[51]

As state-chartered banks were proliferating like mushrooms and New York's bold experiment in deposit guaranty was going down in flames, few underestimated the challenge of safeguarding democracy in a capitalist land. Centralized banking had certainly failed as a panacea. For all the good they did in terms of monetary policy and as lenders of last resort, the First and Second Banks of the United States had never fostered a level playing field. For twenty years, Biddle's Bank reigned as the largest and most powerful institution in the land. Its president, arrogant and aristocratic to the core, remained a symbol of all the frontier militated against. There is plenty of room to criticize Old Hickory's policies,

GENERAL JACKSON SLAYING THE MANY HEADED MONSTER.

"General Jackson Slaying the Many Headed Monster." This cartoon satirizes President Andrew Jackson's campaign against the Second Bank of the United States and its supporters among state banks. Aiding in the struggle are Vice President Martin Van Buren and Major Jack Downing, a staunch Jackson supporter. Courtesy Library of Congress.

but two things are certain: they were consistent; and they had the support of small *d* democrats eager for assurance that they, and not eastern moneymen, were in control. If the bank was not quite the hydra-headed monster depicted by its enemies, it was certainly a menace in the minds of people who wanted to be left alone.[52] It would be left to future generations of frontiersmen to show that Jackson's flame burned brightly in the Indian country west of Fort Smith.

Banks in the free-banking era not only proliferated at a rapid pace but also began to shape their policies to the contours of a commercial culture that was becoming ever more varied and dynamic. The earliest banks were financed by and for the benefit of merchants, and it was merchants who had received the lion's share of bank credit—understandable, given their domination of commerce at the time of the Revolution and for several decades thereafter. But by midcentury, manufacturing was coming on strong; in many regions it was beginning to overshadow mercantile activities.

Not surprisingly in a nation destined to raise moneymaking to an art form, brash young bankers with a nose for profit nudged their stodgy elders to the side and scoured the land for lending opportunities. The democratization of bank lending was evident in the naming of banks. Whereas early banks adopted no-nonsense names like the Massachusetts Bank or the Bank of Virginia to reflect their connection with and support from the state, new banks arose in response to business arrivistes whose demands for financial services signaled the dawning of a new day. One consequence was the chartering of banks under names such as the Citizens Bank and the Freemans Bank—names meant to reflect their accessibility as well as the democratic and egalitarian spirit that suffused Jacksonian America. Some banks went a step further by adopting names such as the Commercial and Farmers Bank, the Merchants and Planters Bank, and the Traders Bank, all signifying a seismic shift in bank lending away from eastern merchants and toward traders, artisans, and farmers whose pioneering proclivities included finance.[53]

During the three decades preceding the Civil War, Americans lit out for the frontier in droves, and methods of communication and transportation struggled to keep up. In the East, the Erie Canal facilitated trade and travel between the Great Lakes and the growing cities along the

Atlantic coast. Down south, the Cumberland Road opened fertile fields to migrants bound for Kentucky and Tennessee and beyond. Steamboats, pioneered in North America by Robert Fulton when he piloted the *North River Boat* (known after his death as the *Clermont*) past exuberant crowds along the Hudson River on August 1, 1807, expanded trade networks beyond the reach of overland travel.

No sooner had steamboats become a pillar of commerce than railroads fanned out in all directions to take people and products to their destinations with dizzying speed. Expansion was fueled by events that seemed to confirm America's continental dreams: a successful campaign against Mexico that brought the great Southwest within U.S. borders; the discovery of gold in California; and immigration that put legions of laborers to work on roads and bridges and digging for precious metals. Treasury Secretary Robert J. Walker reflected widespread optimism when he wrote repeatedly in his annual reports that America had entered upon "a new commercial era."[54]

Immigration and territorial expansion sent land sales skyrocketing, and wherever land-hungry settlers went, bankers were sure to follow. But in many western states and territories, agrarian distrust of bankers had long since hardened into an article of faith, and it was manifested in prohibitions against banking—period. Secretary of the Treasury Thomas Corwin reported in 1852 that there were "no incorporated banks in regular and active operation" in Arkansas, California, Florida, Illinois, Iowa, Texas, and Wisconsin—seven of the thirty-one states then in existence—or in the two organized territories, Minnesota and Oregon, or in the District of Columbia.[55] Banking was prohibited in Texas from 1845 to 1904 (although a carpetbag constitution permitted it from 1869 to 1876). Further prohibitions were found in Iowa from 1846 to 1857, Arkansas from 1846 to 1864, California from 1849 to 1879, and Oregon from 1857 until about 1880.[56] In Indiana and Missouri, banking was a state monopoly.[57]

In most jurisdictions, banking was prohibited by state constitutions; in others, it was kept out by alert opposition. In the eyes of their enemies, banks were unpopular not only because of their identification with moneyed monopolies, but simply because they were corporations—impersonal, privileged, artificial, and soulless. They were the "*principal cause of social evil in the United States*," wrote Jackson insider and anti-bank zealot William Gouge. In a democracy of plain and honest folk, the only proper money—and, not incidentally, the only money sanctioned by the Constitution—was silver and gold. And like the rain and the warm glow of the sun, precious metal was provided by a benevolent Providence. In spewing their banknotes to an unsuspecting public, elite moneymen were guilty of nothing less than cultivating speculation and exciting the passions, thereby subverting the divine order. "The banks, by expanding their issues, give aliment to the wild spirit of speculation when it begins," wrote the über-conservative Gouge; "and by their contractions they aggravate the evils of the natural reactions."[58] Agrarian conservatism, manifested in Jefferson's vision of a bankless Eden and hardened into ideology by such diverse groups as anti-bank farmers and urban Locofocos, thus reached its zenith at midcentury in a West without banks.

In more settled states where they were permitted, banks were often established for the express purpose of facilitating land purchases. The frenzied activity between 1829 and 1861, interrupted by the Panic of 1837, is reflected in the number of banks established as well as their key indicators: capital; circulation; and loans (see table 1).

In the absence of central banking, state legislatures scrambled to regulate their banks, and the results varied as speculators outdid one

U.S. Banks Established, 1837–1861

		(dollar amounts in millions)		
YEAR	NUMBER OF BANKS	CAPITAL	CIRCULATION	LOANS
1829	329	$110.2	$48.2	$137.0
1835	704	231.2	103.7	365.2
1837	788	290.8	149.2	525.1
1840	901	358.4	107.0	462.9
1843	691	228.9	58.6	254.5
1845	707	206.0	89.6	288.6
1850	824	217.3	131.4	364.2
1855	1,307	332.2	187.0	576.1
1858	1,422	394.6	155.2	583.2
1861	1,601	429.6	202.0	696.8

Source: Davis Rich Dewey, *Financial History of the United States* (New York: Longmans, Green, 1931), 225, 260.

another in their imaginative approaches to channeling credit to commercial enterprises.[59] Coupled with wild-eyed speculation was the lack of uniformity in securing notes. It was all in a day's work for a country merchant to receive and pay out an endless variety of notes, some good, some doubtful, and some devalued beyond the point of no return. The confusion went off the charts as steamboats and then railroads expanded business activity and provided ever more opportunities to circulate paper money. It is impossible to know how many settlers managed to secure a homestead or carve out what was supposed to be a squatter's paradise, only to find that the currency they were counting on to build their dreams was not worth the paper it was printed on.

Empowered with the freedom to print their own currency, state banks by 1860 were circulating an estimated 7,000 different banknotes, including 1,600 or so from defunct state banks. And those were the legitimate notes! An estimated 5,000 counterfeit issues were passing through citizens' hands—worn, tattered, and often perforated many times over with a teller's staple to signify the genuine article.[60] Meanwhile, currency values were up for grabs as gold discovered in the California hills poured into the nation's coffers. Ideally, free banking represented an effort to allow banking resources to expand rapidly to meet the nation's capital needs and, at the same time, safeguard the money thereby created. But in most cases, it exacerbated the disorder and instability of banking. Nowhere was this more evident than in states and territories recently hewn from the frontier, where banks were conspicuous by their absence, and where lax supervision in areas that permitted them spawned "small, swindling concerns" and banknotes whose worth was anyone's guess.[61]

In terms of frontier sociology, the free-banking era was emblematic of a nation whose methods of producing, acquiring, and distributing resources were buffeted by decades of trial and error. The banking system mirrored society as a whole—diverse, disorderly, enterprising, progressive, and rarely encumbered by scrupulous attention to detail.[62] An observer in the 1860s who was clearly fed up with the whole business left a poignant account of currency in the West: "There the frequently worthless issues of the State of Maine and of other New England states, the shinplasters of Michigan, the wildcats of Georgia, of Canada, and Pennsylvania, the red dogs of Indiana and Nebraska, the miserably engraved notes of North Carolina, Kentucky, Missouri, and Virginia, and the not-to-be-forgotten stumptails of Illinois and Wisconsin are mixed indiscriminately with the par currency of New York and Boston, until no one can wonder that the West has become disgusted with all bank issues."[63]

In 1857, there were between 1,500 and 1,600 banks in the United States, and they operated on a continuum from outright thievery and incompetence to conformity with sound banking principles.[64] In some places, banks were highly esteemed and valued; in others, they were disliked, but tolerated; in still others, they were forbidden. Banks varied widely in terms of their structures: unincorporated individuals and partnerships whose longevity in business (and, perhaps, simply their longevity) depended on cultivating trust in their communities; chartered banks whose operations were governed by state or territorial laws; and merchandising establishments that operated as de facto banks. Banks were most visible to the public in the circulation of their banknotes. In terms of lending, the credit they extended was almost exclusively for domestic purposes, and it was geared toward short-term funding. For long-term capital, American businessmen turned to the Old World, where it had accumulated, and to the London money market and British industry, where it was available for speculative ventures. William Gouge voiced the opinion of like-minded libertarians when he said that banks should confine their operations to "deposits and circulation, to business paper having but a short time to run, making it an inflexible rule never to renew the same."[65] Seemingly not much had changed since 1782 in banks' central and essential function: lending short-term money in the form of deposit credit.

For proponents of centralized banking, the Civil War was the last straw. Financing was central to Congress's war effort, and financing much of anything was impossible with an empty Treasury. Turning to the private sector was not much of an option—bank failures and depreciating currencies are hardly the makings of victory on the battlefield. Of the 2,500 state banks created through 1860, more than 1,000 were closed within ten years of formation. By 1862, Congress counted more than $100 million lost through bank failures, mainly in the West. Toss in counterfeiting and outright fraud, and you have all the evidence you need of two stubborn facts: the economy was poised for takeoff, but was shackled by an inefficient banking system; and the U.S. Treasury was emasculated in its efforts to fund the war.[66]

It fell to Treasury Secretary Salmon Portland Chase to brave the political fire storm and propose a third national bank. The ghosts of Jefferson and Jackson were surely howling in protest when, on December 9, 1861, Chase delivered his "Report on the State of the Finances" and outlined what would become, two years hence, the National Banking (or National Currency) Act: "The plan contemplates the preparation and delivery to institutions and associations of notes prepared for circulation under national direction and to be secured by the pledge of the United States bonds."[67] If Secretary Chase was going to finance the war with paper, he was certainly going to control its supply. Beyond immediate objectives, the secretary was fed up with the anomaly of a sovereign authority waging a war to preserve its sovereignty without the most ancient and elementary attribute of government—control of the monetary system.

The National Banking Act, signed into law on February 25, 1863 (in the twenty-second month of the war), by President Lincoln, was the most sweeping revision of the banking system in three decades, and it marked the birth of the national banking era (1863–1913).[68] According to the *New York Tribune,* "There can be no stronger argument in its favor than that it tends to strengthen the Union by closely interwoven ties of common interest in the permanence and credit of the National Government."[69] The law created a bureau in the Treasury Department responsible for executing congressional mandates relating to the issue and regulation of a national currency secured by United States bonds.[70] The national currency created by the law was to take the form of national banknotes, uniform in design and engraved under the direction of the Treasury Department, and be put into circulation by individual banks. Banks could obtain a supply of notes from the federal government only by pledging Treasury bonds as security, and note issues could not exceed 90 percent of the face value of the bonds so pledged. Each bank would then issue the notes, imprinted with its name, and was charged with the duty to redeem them on demand into lawful money—that is, greenbacks. In the event that a bank was unable to redeem its notes, the bonds pledged as security would be sold (or redeemed) by the government, and the proceeds would be used to pay the noteholders.[71]

The head of the bureau, appointed for a period of five years by the president with the advice and consent of the Senate and paid $5,000 annually, was to be known as the comptroller of the currency.[72] His primary responsibilities were to deliver annual reports on the condition of banks to Congress and to make recommendations for improving the banking system.[73] Secretary Chase was fortunate to secure the services of Hugh McCulloch as his first comptroller of the currency. In contrast to most ideologues that gravitate to the nation's capital, the former banker from Indiana showed a flair for flexibility—he came to Washington in 1862 to lobby against the banking bill and wound up staying on to direct its operations.[74]

Anyone who expected an immediate scramble for national charters was sorely disappointed. By November 1863, only 134 national banks had been formed, and five-sixths of them were new institutions rather than conversions from state charters. The sluggish pace of national bank formation prompted Chase and McCulloch to work toward revisions in the law. Their efforts were rewarded in June 1864 with a thoroughly reconstructed law that prohibited real estate loans, raised the minimum capital for city banks, and increased the proportion of capital that had to be paid in before a bank could open for business. At the same time, the legal cash reserve requirement was reduced. The thrust of the revised law was to clamp down on so-called wildcat banks—that is, banks that put banknotes into circulation far from home, and perhaps chose head-quarters "out among the wildcats" where they were hard to find, so that they would never have to actually redeem their notes.[75] True wildcat banks were creatures of the frontier whose wily operators were a major obstacle to the imposition of sound banking principles in the trans-Mississippi West.

The revisions of 1864 hastened the rate of conversions to national charters, but not enough to satisfy advocates of national banking. By late 1864, nearly six hundred national banks had been formed, but fewer than two hundred were conversions. Most national banks were small, and the ones located in major cities remained aloof. As the Civil War wound toward its bloody end, the Lincoln administration and Congress resolved to bring monetary reform to its logical conclusion. "The national banks were intended to supersede the state banks," thundered a frustrated Senator John Sherman of Ohio. "Both cannot exist together."[76]

In March 1865, former Supreme Court chief justice John Marshall's principle in *McCulloch v. Maryland* (1819) that the power to tax was the power to destroy was put to the test when Congress voted by a narrow margin to impose a tax of 10 percent on all further issues of banknotes other than those authorized by the National Banking Acts of 1863 and 1864. "Tax the banks out of existence," exhorted the *Chicago Tribune*.[77] As expected, the flurry of applications for national charters accelerated. More than seven hundred banks traded their state for national charters in 1865, and many of the remaining banks simply closed their doors.[78]

From 1865 on, national banks had a legal monopoly on banknote issues. Simply put, national banks replaced state-chartered banks at the center of the nation's monetary system. From 1863 to 1866, the number of state banks fell from 1,466 in 1863 to 297; total notes and deposits in state banks fell from $733 million to $101 million. As they maneuvered for a place in an expanding postwar economy, state banks had to keep deposit accounts at national banks, from whom the could "buy" banknotes to redeem their deposits.[79] By late 1866, more than 1,600 banks were functioning under national charters. As banks were not authorized to perform trust functions, trust companies were on their own. In keeping with the preferences of Chase and McCulloch, the National Banking Acts of 1863 and 1864 made no allowance for branch banking, an issue destined to polarize bankers for many years to come. Even though national banking was never universal, it did account for about 75 percent of the nation's banking activity in the late 1860s.[80]

The formative stage of the banking system was more or less complete by 1870. National banks were open for business in about a thousand communities. Bank failures had tapered off considerably since the 1850s, and the screening of charter applications was nipping problems in the bud. Thanks to the punitive tax on state banknotes, the chaos and confusion that had plagued the nation during the era of free banking was yielding to a paper money system that enjoyed the confidence of national banknote holders. Because notes drawn on national banks were in effect backed by the faith of the U.S. government, noteholders were unlikely to panic at the least sign of trouble, stampede to the nearest bank, and convert their notes into other forms of cash. Indeed, as the system matured, no holder of national banknotes suffered losses from bank failures or suspensions. Moreover, now that standardization was slowing the profusion of state banknotes, counterfeiting and fraud were harder to commit. In sum, the currency reforms of the 1860s represented a vast improvement in the nation's finances. From now on, the credit functions of banks, heretofore loosely regulated and prone to abuse, were subordinated to their other key function: regulation of the money supply.[81]

Soon after the original legislation was passed, Comptroller of the Currency McCulloch ordered the publication of a booklet for people who wanted to organize banks under the national banking system. The booklet was allowed to go out of print, and as amendments were made to the original law and applications for national bank charters increased, the decision was made to resume publication. Instructions published in booklet form were no doubt appreciated by bankers who needed to know how to comply with federal regulations. According to the 1884 edition, bankers were required to commence business with $100,000 in capital. In cities with populations of 50,000 or more, the capital requirement shot up to $200,000. The treasury secretary retained the discretion to authorize banks in towns with populations of 6,000 or less to organize with only $50,000. As the author explained, "The design and effect of these provisions is to prevent, as far as possible, the establishment of feeble organizations, unequal to the wants of the communities in which they are located."[82]

The comptroller of the currency was strict about cash reserves. In cities designated as financial centers, banks were required to maintain cash amounting to 25 percent of their deposits. For all other national banks, the proportion was 15 percent. All banks were required to maintain a reserve of 5 percent of their circulation, and it was to be held on deposit with the U.S. Treasury. To discourage shady loans, national banks were prohibited from lending more than one-tenth of their capital to any person, company, corporation, or firm. "They are thus, by law, made conservative in their management, and restrained from granting excessive loans, which would at least lessen their general usefulness to the communities in which they are situated and perhaps impair their safety."[83]

The National Banking Act of 1863 gave bankers a choice: they could opt for federal charters, include the moniker "national" in naming their banks, and cast their lot with the new system; or they could apply for state charters and rely on whatever laws their legislatures saw fit to impose on state banks. Either way, few doubted that competition between state and national banks would be fierce and the road to riches would remain fraught with peril. And although the dual banking system promised freedom of choice to bank customers, it also created a split between two very different banking systems: national banks, answerable to the comptroller of the currency and linked to eastern capital; and state banks, subject to regulations that varied widely from one state to the next. And the closer one traveled toward the frontier, the less likely those regulations were to be strictly enforced—if, that is, there were any banks or banking regulations at all.

Alexander Hamilton's death in history's most famous duel saved him from witnessing the derailment of his vision of centralized banking. But all was not lost. Even though the reforms of the 1860s were by no means a panacea, they hastened the acceptance of sound business principles in ways that were impossible during the era of free banking. Problems and contradictions notwithstanding, commercial banks facilitated economic development in two interrelated ways: (1) they extended credit by creating money in the form of banknotes; and (2) they accepted deposits that became the basis for making loans. Bank deposits furnished the money needed to sustain America's increasingly industrialized economy as it evolved into an intricate pattern of specialization and exchange. By financing capital outlays of business, government, and individuals, bank credit became the engine of wealth accumulation and capital formation. Finally, the gradual expansion of the money supply through bank lending sustained economic development and provided the wherewithal to create markets for the nation's exploding cornucopia of goods and services. Like two precocious boys blundering their way to manhood, the banking system and the country grew up together, molding themselves to changing circumstances as settlers pushed westward and cast themselves into the crucible of the frontier.

With the National Banking Act of 1863 and subsequent amendments, the pendulum swung back in the direction of central banking. Dissatisfaction with bank failures and monetary instability since Jackson's crusade against the Second Bank of the United States had crystallized in support for banking reform. Like it or not, the Industrial Revolution was wreaking havoc with commercial practices, and businesses were finding it hard to survive without the things that banks could provide—machinery, credit, and cash. It is a testament to America's entrepreneurial spirit that so many businesses not only survived but prospered during the free-banking era.

But the pendulum halted in mid-swing. Even though the Treasury Department now had the power to regulate currency and credit and conduct examinations, there was nothing in the legislation to create an institution along the lines of the First and Second Banks of the United

States to serve as a lender of last resort and bring all financial institutions under the same regulatory umbrella. As national banks muscled their way into the financial system, state-chartered and private banks continued to spew out paper money, interest rates on loans remained beyond the reach of effective regulation, and bank panics were accepted as the price of capitalism.

Nor was there a mechanism in the laws of the 1860s to help bankers reconcile their contradictory responsibilities toward credit and money. The former required liberality, while the latter required conservatism. The clash between the two was manifested most painfully with respect to a bank's liquidity—that is, its ability to pay depositors and banknote holders in cash on demand. Banks satisfied the demand for money by stockpiling cash as best they could and adapting the quantity of money to the needs of their local economies. These efforts often led to restrictions on credit that produced an increase in unsatisfied credit needs. At that point, a beleaguered banker might decide to loosen up on credit, only to encounter a heightened risk of monetary disturbance. This oscillation reflected the fact that bankers' responsibilities toward credit and money were too important for one to be subordinated to the other.[84]

Although banks in the early national period failed to provide all the liquidity that businessmen wanted, they were certainly better adapted to commerce than the alternatives. If one had to pinpoint the primary business concern in the Republic's formative years, it would most definitely be liquidity, and it was through the creation of liquidity that banks played their starring role in establishing a framework for economic and community development. Simply put, banks survived politically and thrived economically because they made people's lives easier and their businesses more efficient. In addition to their primary role of supplying liquidity, their success hinged on their ability to perform four basic functions: (1) inject cash into the economy; (2) allow businessmen to diversify their concerns; (3) extend loans or, in the vernacular of the age, "accommodations"; and (4) make investment opportunities available for people who could stomach the nineteenth-century economic roller coaster.[85]

Like the beaks of Darwin's finches, banks in the decentralized era of free banking evolved, or did not, as a reflection of the desires, needs, and whims of local residents. Nevertheless, they were all on the same page when it came to pursuing their fundamental goals—the provision of monetary and intermediation services.[86] Banks monetized the economy, developed credit channels that fostered investment in new regions and new industries, and helped integrate distinct regional markets into a unified whole. Arguably, banks' most lasting contribution to the American economy was to reduce the dispersion of rates of return on financial assets.[87] Thus did banks grease the wheels of commerce. In the process, they provided a surefire vehicle of wealth creation for bank owners and shareholders.

As Congress legislated and bankers navigated the shoals of their profession, Americans continued to push westward—past the Alleghenies and the Blue Ridge and the Great Smokey Mountains and on to the Mississippi. Most scurried across the nation's heartland as fast as they could in their haste to reach the more promising vistas of California and the fertile valleys to the north. Yet even as they abandoned the settled East for opportunities in the West, they were unable to shake the paradox that had bedeviled the Republic at its inception and, arguably, has never quite lost its grip: how to make democracy thrive in a nation committed to free-market capitalism. If America was indeed the new Athens, if the ideals enshrined in Western civilization truly followed the westward course of economic development—then how could the opportunities afforded by unlimited land and resources remain open to everyone?

By the early nineteenth century, the trans-Mississippi West was the newest arena for the paradox to play out. Early on, the frontier was a tabula rasa where resources were produced, acquired, and distributed in an astonishing variety of ways, and where success went to those swift and cunning enough—and, not incidentally, white and masculine enough—to recognize opportunities and exploit them for all they were worth. Yet westward migration quickly turned the frontier into a laboratory where experiments in commerce and banking from the colonial and early national periods were replicated. Barter; commodity money; paper money; merchant banking; territorial, state, and national bank chartering—these and other solutions to the ancient conundrum of resource allocation were adapted from historical precedent and modified to suit local needs. Those needs stemmed from rapid-fire economic development that might have foundered on conservative banking patterns—if, that is, there had been conservative banking patterns to founder on. In the scramble for western riches, conservatism did not count for much, and there was no single pattern of sound banking that bankers could rely on for precedent. What succeeded in one area might fail in another.

Sound banking came not so much from laws or structures as from conservative management that was in short supply in frontier America.[88]

The Indian country destined to become Oklahoma was part of that vast laboratory. It was among the first regions to be explored, among the last to be included in America's networks of commerce and banking, and among the most fascinating in the evolution of a commercial culture. "It is in the West," wrote Tocqueville in *Democracy in America* after his sojourn in the 1830s, "that one can observe democracy attaining its furthest limit. In those states, which were in a sense improvised by chance, the inhabitants arrived only yesterday on the land they occupy. They barely knew one another, and each was ignorant of his closest neighbor's past. In that part of the American continent, therefore, the people escape the influence not only of great names and wealth but also of that natural aristocracy that derives from wisdom and virtue."[89] Little wonder, then, that westerners became the quintessential jacks-of-all-trades. Tocqueville's European upbringing left him ill prepared for a culture in which nobody was obliged to spend a lifetime in a single career or occupation: "You meet Americans who have successfully been lawyers, farmers, businessmen, ministers of the Gospel, and physicians."[90]

Oklahoma's path of commercial development began in the Arkansas and Red River valleys, where French trappers in primitive canoes were the vanguard of a civilization bent on conquering a continent.

PART II

The Indian Territory to 1889

CHAPTER THREE

The Riverboat Frontier

Far' Yo' Well, Miss Lucy!

Steamboat farewell

In December 1915, the U.S. attorney's office in Oklahoma City summoned a most unusual witness to appear in District Judge John Cotteral's court. His name was Joseph Evins, and he was asked to travel all the way from Dardanelle, Arkansas, to testify on the government's behalf that the Arkansas River was not navigable above Fort Gibson. Oklahoma attorney general S. P. Freeling begged to differ, and what was dubbed "the riverbed case" captured a slice of the public's attention in an otherwise bellicose season. One suspects that sandbars and flotsam on an Oklahoma waterway were a welcome diversion from the news emanating from Europe, where the dogs of war were pulling civilization ever further into the abyss.

So who was Joseph Evins, and what did he know about river navigation that warranted a trip from Dardanelle to Oklahoma City? As it turned out, he knew plenty—probably enough to determine the outcome of the case. Born in 1833, Evins was a mature man of twenty-seven at the outbreak of the Civil War. He apparently dodged military service and found his life's calling on America's waterways. By war's end, he was an accomplished riverboat pilot and was familiar with every twist and turn of the Mississippi, Missouri, and Ohio Rivers. Early in 1881 he found himself aboard the *Wichita,* a government snag boat charged with clearing debris (known in riverboat jargon as "snags") from the Arkansas River. Under the command of a Captain Hanberry, Evins spent twenty-one months plying the waters from Fort Smith to locations many miles upriver from the tiny village of Tulsa. Now eighty-two years old and testifying in a city that did not even exist at the time of his nautical adventures, Captain Evins, as he was known in the press, described "innumerable sand bars which clogged the channel of the stream above the mouth of Grand river and how in many cases five or six hours were consumed in backing the boat from mud banks and bars."[1]

On what might have been a cold and blustery day on the flatlands of Oklahoma, Captain Evins's listeners were surely spellbound by tales seemingly ripped from Mark Twain's *Life on the Mississippi.* Unfortunately, not many people were there to listen. "Historians would find a wealth of material in the testimony given at the riverbed hearing," wrote the reporter who covered the case, "but strange to say but very few spectators are ever seen in the courtrooms. Practically the only ones present are the attorneys for the United States and the state of Oklahoma, the clerks and U.S. District Judge John Cotteral."[2]

Judge Cotteral no doubt thanked Captain Evins for his testimony and sent him on his way. One suspects that he exited the courtroom under the withering glare of attorneys for the state of Oklahoma whose case had just become a lot more complicated. Perhaps he was escorted to the Santa Fe station by a bright young clerk who made sure the aging pilot did not slip on a patch of ice, or stumble getting aboard the train.

In due course, the conductor blew his whistle, and the eastbound train pulled out of the station. And then, lulled to sleep by the clattering of steel on steel, Captain Evins might have drifted back to an era that was already slipping from the collective memory of a nation charging hell-bent-for-leather into a world that was far beyond his ken—a world that knew so little about what it was like to stake a claim on the riverboat frontier.

Navigation of the waterways that proved so vexing to Captain Evins dated back to the second decade of the eighteenth century, when French Creoles from Canada and the Louisiana country arrived in their pirogues, or dugout canoes, to wreak havoc on the region's fur-bearing creatures. Beaver pelts ranked first among fashion-conscious consumers on the Atlantic coast and in Europe, but the hides of otters, minks, muskrats, skunks, and foxes would certainly do in a pinch.[3] Realizing that birch-bark canoes suitable for the Great Lakes were far too flimsy for rivers of the South and Southwest, these intrepid trappers settled on cottonwood trees, ubiquitous along the banks of the Arkansas and Red Rivers, to fashion their boats.[4] Thus did the mighty cottonwood tree establish its presence at the dawn of Oklahoma commerce.

Because they rarely ventured into the wild country beyond the river-banks, pilots of these crude vessels were limited in their explorations to wherever the water could carry them. Unlike their British nemeses on the Atlantic coast, the French were less interested in putting down permanent roots than they were in divesting animals of their skins and shipping them to New Orleans and points east. In 1722, Sieur Bernard de la Harpe provided a semblance of structure for the interior fur trade by establishing a trading headquarters at Arkansas Post, said to be the first non-Indian settlement in the Mississippi Valley, some sixty miles above the mouth of the Arkansas River. Another French settlement, Natchi-toches, coalesced about two hundred miles above the mouth of the Red River. Other settlements were probably located further upstream, but neither records nor archaeological evidence have survived to yield their secrets.[5] Although the peripatetic Frenchmen left few signs of their pass-ing, they did manage to sprinkle the American lexicon with exotic place-names for the waterways that sustained them. Even today, the Poteau, Illinois, Verdigris, San Bois, and Saline Rivers bear testimony to the French fur traders who opened the riverboat frontier in Oklahoma.[6]

From the establishment of Arkansas Post in 1722 to the eve of Presi-dent Thomas Jefferson's famed real estate deal in 1803, the French retained control of the interior fur trade. Competition came from Spanish explorers whose travels took them all the way to the Wichita Mountains in their futile search for the mythical El Dorado, and whose mother country held sway over the Province of Louisiana in the latter half of the eighteenth century. Yet governance from faraway Spain meant little in the trans-Mississippi West, where the language, social customs, industry, and commercial institutions pointed straight back to France. Long before American colonists freed themselves from British rule and glimpsed their destiny on the far side of the Mississippi, French trappers were piloting their pirogues across distances beyond reckoning to the European imagination, setting their snares and traps alone or, perhaps, in the company of Indian wives who shared their privations and adopted hybrid forms of their language. Women who stayed behind in crude cabins while their husbands went snaring and skinning for months on end filled their days with curing meat and tending to their mixed-blood children, waiting patiently for their men to return.[7]

Far to the north, nestled between the Missouri and Osage Rivers in present-day western Missouri, were the Osages, semi-sedentary farmers who ventured beyond their riverine villages to hunt bison on the western prairies. Their first contact with the French dates back to the 1690s. Sieur Bernard de la Harpe, the founder of Arkansas Post, penned the first description of them. In 1719, Charles Claude du Tisne made the first official visit to the Osage country. The French wasted little time in cultivating the goodwill of their Osage neighbors, and for good reason: by facilitating links between Canada and Louisiana, and by discouraging British settlement beyond their thin strip of Atlantic colonies, the French found that the Osages were ideally suited to furthering France's commercial interests in North America. It was a short step from supplying the Osages with arms and manufactured goods to encouraging them to mount raids on non-Indian intruders.

The Osages proved to be quick studies, and over the course of the eighteenth century, they complemented their martial skills with business acumen aimed at extracting goods from French and Spanish explorers. The result was a win-win situation: the French prospered by trading weaponry and manufactured goods for furs, livestock, and slaves; and the Osages, the first Plains tribe to acquire both horses and guns, became power brokers who controlled access to the Missouri River. Between the 1750s and 1830s, the Osages used their new technologies not only to slaughter bison but also to dominate their neighbors, including the Caddos, Wichitas, and Pawnees. With a speed that was no doubt shocking to people whose lives were tuned to the rhythm of subsistence agriculture and occasional hunting expeditions, the Osage economy was drawn inexorably into the maelstrom of European commerce and imperial ambitions.[8]

Inevitably, the Osages were also drawn into the orbit of the Chouteaus, a powerful Creole family from Saint Louis. Shortly after founding the village of Saint Louis in 1764, Auguste Chouteau teamed up with his brother, Jean Pierre, to corner the Osage trade. By the late eighteenth century, the Chouteaus' Osage trade represented more than 50 percent of the commerce in Saint Louis. The Chouteau brothers' success was due in large measure to their willingness to live among the Osages and learn their culture from the inside. Between 1794 and 1802, they managed to secure from Spain a monopoly of the Osage trade. Determined to stymie French ambitions and consolidate Spanish power in the trans-Mississippi region, Spain renewed the Chouteaus' monopoly in 1800 for an additional four years. Spanish authorities were prescient enough to recognize the threat posed in the sparsely populated region by westward migration that went into overdrive following Britain's defeat by upstart colonists.[9]

On the riverboat frontier, official monopolies were no guarantee of success. In 1802, a simmering rivalry with the Spanish trader Manuel Lisa caused the Chouteaus to lose their monopoly. With typical frontier ingenuity, Jean Pierre used his clout among the Osages to convince about three thousand of them, representing a third of the tribe, to relocate to the convergence of the Arkansas, Verdigris, and Grand (or Neosho) Rivers, otherwise known as the Three Forks region, near present-day Muskogee and Fort Gibson, Oklahoma. Shortly thereafter, the Chouteaus established a trading post about sixty miles above the mouth of the Grand River, a site that is now within the town limits of Salina in Mayes County.[10]

A lack of documentary evidence has frustrated efforts to determine when the Chouteaus built the trading post that was likely the first non-Indian settlement in Oklahoma. Some historians have suggested that it was up and running by 1802.[11] What is known for sure is that the Chouteaus had been active and influential in the region for many years, as was witnessed by the development of the Osage Trace that served as a conduit for furs bound for Saint Louis. Moreover, Auguste recorded in 1797 that Jean Pierre visited an Osage village near the Three Forks.[12] Perhaps a precise date for construction of the trading post was less important than the commercial culture that was emerging in the Three Forks region in the opening decades of the nineteenth century. Logic dictated that the Chouteaus would never have induced three thousand Osages to abandon their homeland unless a trading infrastructure was in place to satisfy their commercial needs. Likewise, the Osages would not have pulled up stakes and migrated south without assurances that their enviable position in the Missouri Valley would remain in force. In the absence of a chronology, one thing was certain: when Louisiana was formally transferred to the United States on March 10, 1804, the Chouteaus and their Osage customers were in the catbird seat.

Achieving supremacy in the fur trade was one thing; maintaining it was something else altogether, particularly now that Louisiana was open for business. A letter dated July 13, 1806, from John. B. Treat to Secretary of War Henry Dearborn has survived to shed light on just how tenuous monopolies could be on the riverboat frontier. Mailed from "Arkansa," the letter indicates that Treat bore some responsibility for regulating the Indian trade. Clearly on the defensive, Treat assured Secretary Dearborn that control would never be relinquished to the good people of Arkansas and, furthermore, that nobody would be given exclusive trading privileges. Apparently, the secretary of war had reason to be skeptical. Two men, Morgan and Bright, were making no secret of their plan to establish a trading post. Treat knew all about them, and he was awaiting instructions from Washington, D.C., as to how he should proceed. "And whatever they may be," wrote the beleaguered Treat, "so far as is in my power, they shall be strictly complied with."[13]

But that was not the worst of it. Treat's letter went on to report that Bright had ascended the Arkansas River with every intention of establishing a trading monopoly with the Osage Nation. (One can imagine the Chouteaus' response to such temerity.) Moreover, it was well known that Bright was establishing credit accounts with Indians along the White and Saint Francis Rivers and that pelts were being collected from Indians "at exorbitant prices."[14] One Indian (not a chief) had received "upwards of $3000 by which means more than one hundred Hunters are secured to them."[15] Treat closed his letter to the secretary of war on what might have been a hopeful note: "Seven days since Capt. Many (of the artillery) with a party of 20 men left this to ascend and remove from the Banks of White River all Intruders he might there meet with."[16]

The Chouteau brothers probably did not lose much sleep over the likes of Morgan and Bright. Flush from making the real estate deal of all time by purchasing Louisiana from the cash-strapped Napoleon Bonaparte in 1803, President Jefferson appointed Jean Pierre as agent to the Osages and sent his son, Auguste Pierre, to a new military academy at West Point, New York. After his graduation in 1806, the young Chouteau served in the army under General James Wilkinson and took part in several hazardous missions to tribes in the West. On a fur-trading mission on the Upper Arkansas River in 1815–17 with Jules de Mun, Chouteau was captured by Spanish soldiers, lost equipment and furs valued at $30,000, and was imprisoned in Santa Fe by Spanish authorities.[17] As heirs of the Inquisition, the Spanish had no qualms about meting out justice in whatever way they chose to a young and no doubt frightened Auguste Pierre Chouteau.

Colonel A. P. Chouteau, as he was known to distinguish him from his famous uncle in Saint Louis, was eventually released from captivity. He put his death-defying adventures behind him and returned to the Three Forks region in about 1817 to assume control of his family's trading dynasty. For the next twenty years, Chouteau's Trading Post served as Grand Central Station for some two thousand hunters in the Three Forks region. Animals sacrificed to the booming fur trade included deer, bears, beavers, otters, wildcats, raccoons, skunks, buffaloes—in short, anything on four legs whose skins could be shipped downriver to fill the wardrobes of fashion-conscious consumers back east. Eventually, Chouteau's Trading Post was luring thousands of dollars' worth of European goods into the Three Forks region each year.[18]

As his fame spread and fortune skyrocketed, Colonel Chouteau built up a lavish lifestyle and debts to go with it. Travelers in the Indian country who visited Colonel Chouteau and his growing family at La Grande Saline, described as a "two-story log palace," included the missionary Isaac McCoy, English scientist Charles J. Latrobe, Texas promoter Sam Houston, and U.S. commissioners Henry Ellsworth and Montfort Stokes.[19] Among the most illustrious visitors to Chouteau's Trading Post was the writer Washington Irving, who passed through the Three Forks region in early October 1832 on his famed tour of the prairies. His description of the Osage Agency, as it was widely known, provided a glimpse into frontier commerce through the lens of a master storyteller: "The little hamlet of the Agency was in a complete bustle; the blacksmith's shed, in particular, was a scene of preparation; a strapping negro was shoeing a horse; two half-breeds were fabricating iron spoons in which to melt lead for bullets. An old trapper, in leathern hunting frock and moccasins, had placed his rifle against a work-bench, while he superintended the operation, and gossiped about his hunting exploits; several large dogs were lounging in and out of the shop, or sleeping in the sunshine, while a little cur, with head cocked on one side, and one ear erect, was watching, with that curiosity common to little dogs, the process of shoeing the horse, as if studying the art, or waiting for his turn to be shod."[20]

A mile and a half above the mouth of the Verdigris River was another trading post operated by Captain Nathaniel Pryor, a native Virginian who was the first person to volunteer his services in Lewis and Clark's expedition to the Pacific Ocean. Like Colonel A. P. Chouteau, Pryor served in the U.S. Army with distinction before making his mark in the Indian trade. In a letter dated December 15, 1830, to President Andrew Jackson in support of Captain Pryor's bid to become a subagent for the Osage Nation, the famed Sam Houston described a candidate with impeccable credentials. As a soldier, Pryor fought bravely under then General Jackson at the Battle of New Orleans; in his subsequent trading activities, he did "more to tame and pacificate [sic] the dispositions of the Osages to the whites, and surrounding tribes of Indians than all other men."[21] Like Colonel Chouteau, Nathaniel Pryor was the archetypal trader in the Three Forks region—skilled in the arts of war and peace, and uniquely qualified to use commerce as a portal to peaceful and mutually beneficial relations with American Indians. "Capt. Pryor is a man of amiable character and disposition," wrote Houston, "of fine sense, strict honor—perfectly temperate in his habits—and unremitting in his attention to business."[22]

To accommodate the quickening pace of commerce, Fort Smith—named for General Thomas A. Smith of Georgia—was established at the mouth of the Poteau River in 1817.[23] That same year, a contingent of Cherokees from the southeastern United States arrived in Arkansas to become the vanguard of an epic migration. Faced with a juggernaut of non-Indian settlers into their ancestral homelands, members of the Cherokee, Choctaw, Chickasaw, Creek, and Seminole tribes were deciding that relocation to the trans-Mississippi West was the only way to maintain tribal customs, far from the rapacious ways of their unwanted neighbors. Voluntary relocation from the Southeast to the western wilderness hardened into policy during the presidency of Andrew Jackson, the frontiersman-turned-statesman whose martial exploits left him with an enduring hatred for America's original inhabitants.

Between 1817 and 1842, a trickle of Native American immigrants became a flood, and military forts were built to maintain order and regulate trade. Two forts established in 1824 by Colonel Matthew Arbuckle were of special significance for the Chouteaus and their fellow fur traders: Fort Gibson, located near the mouth of the Grand River and named for General George Gibson of Pennsylvania who had distinguished himself in the Revolutionary War; and Fort Towson, located near the mouth of the Kiamichi River some 120 miles to the south of Fort Gibson, and named for Nathan Towson who saw action in the War of 1812 and the Mexican War.[24] Roads built to connect these and other forts facilitated not only military transport but also the flow of goods to and from the increasingly populated country west of Fort Smith.

Strategically situated on the banks of the Grand River, Fort Gibson's future as a commercial center was assured. Early on, most river travel was still limited to canoes and bateaux—small, flat-bottomed rowboats that were uniquely suited to river travel. Heavy loads required keelboats with a carrying capacity of several tons. These craft were sometimes propelled by oars, push-poles, or sails, but usually they were dragged by men on shore with towropes.[25] Flatboats from Missouri also plied the Arkansas laden with pioneer commodities such as bacon, hides, ginseng, sarsaparilla, and snakeroot. Typically, crews floated their flatboats down the Arkansas and Mississippi Rivers, found customers for their boats and cargo, and then returned overland to their point of origin to do it all over again. Following their relocation to the West, Creeks and Seminoles took advantage of quickening business activity and sent dried peaches, pecans, beans, gopher peas, rice, and other commodities down the Canadian River to Arkansas and bustling ports to the east and south.[26]

Yet primitive transportation with its roots in the French fur trade was no match for modern marvels wrought by the Industrial Revolution. Far to the east, steamboats were transforming commerce on the rivers, and it was only a matter of time before they extended their reach to the trans-Mississippi West. One of the first steamboats to dock at Fort Gibson, *The Facility,* arrived in February 1828 under the command of Captain Phillip Pennywit of Cincinnati towing two keelboats that brought three hundred Creek women and children to their new home in the West.[27] Within three years, Fort Gibson was a regular stop for steamboats bound for Saint Louis and other points on the Mississippi and Ohio Rivers.[28] Some Cherokees accustomed to steamboat traffic on the Tennessee River and other waterways in their southeastern homeland no doubt welcomed the arrival of these remarkable vessels and scrambled for jobs aboard ship and on the landings.[29] The surge in steamboat traffic was reflected in a report in the *Saint Louis Republican* on May 16, 1839, noting that until April of that year 378 steamboats had been constructed in eastern boatyards. Pittsburgh reigned as the center of steamboat construction, followed by Wheeling and Cincinnati. Predictably, western boosters wondered when entrepreneurs on the far side of the Mississippi would start fighting for a share of the market.[30]

Inevitably, relentless hunting took its toll on the indigenous fauna, and frontier entrepreneurs had to look elsewhere for opportunities. For Colonel A. P. Chouteau, money-making prospects lay far to the west, near the mouth of the Little River in present-day Hughes County, Oklahoma, where the federal government was erecting a new fort to curtail Kiowa and Comanche raids on their less warlike Creek and Chickasaw neighbors. No less a luminary than Sam Houston promoted Colonel Chouteau as the most likely candidate to sooth relations on the fractious Plains. Trusted on all sides, the popular fur trader did what he could to alleviate tensions that were the inevitable consequence of westward migration.[31]

Following the signing of a treaty on August 24, 1835, Chouteau was rewarded with permission to build a trading post near the newly christened Camp Holmes. During its brief history, this outpost of the Chouteau empire became a destination of choice for Comanches, Kiowas, and other Plains Indians who were acquiring a taste for manufactured goods. Over the next three years, the trader-turned-ambassador acted as an effective intermediary between the U.S. government and various Indian nations, including the Comanches, Kiowas, Osage, Senecas, Quapaws, and Creeks.[32] Some three years after the treaty of 1835, he moved his trading post from Camp Holmes to what was named the Chouteau Creek Crossing of the Canadian River in present-day Cleveland County, Oklahoma. It was said that he moved his operation at the insistence of the Comanche and Kiowa Indians to whom he was fondly known as "Soto."[33]

Word spread in October 1838 that Colonel Chouteau, suffering from an injury to the thigh that prevented him from riding, was ill and not expected to recover. He died at Fort Gibson on December 25, 1838, was honored with a military funeral, and was laid to rest in the fort's cemetery.[34] His assets were sold to creditors, and the debts he had accrued to support his spendthrift ways were left for his heirs to sort out. With

Colonel A. P. Chouteau's death, his family's role in the economic development of the future state of Oklahoma, together with their success in opening the trans-Mississippi West to commerce with the East, faded into the rich history of the riverboat frontier.

Steamboat commerce on the Red River was delayed for more than a decade after it began on the Arkansas because of the dreaded "Great Raft," a monstrous tangle of trees that clogged the channel for dozens of miles and rendered navigation a nightmare. The cause of this natural obstacle course was the soft alluvial soil in the Red River floodplain that gave way during floods and brought trees crashing into the current. Early explorers described a desolate landscape of gnarled and naked branches and bleaching roots lying jagged against the horizon. Unclogging the Red River began in 1830 under the auspices of the U.S. War Department. Progress stalled for a couple of years due to lack of funds, was resumed in 1833, and continued for the rest of the decade at a cost of approximately $300,000.[35]

The results of this engineering feat were dramatic. In 1833, there was virtually no settlement on the Red River from forty miles below the Great Raft to Fort Towson. In 1839, the supervisor of the cleanup, Captain Henry N. Shreve, reported to the War Department that the Red River was open for business: "There are now many flourishing cotton plantations on that part of the river where the raft was located, and where the lands were then nearly all inundated by back-water caused by the masses of timber which formed the raft."[36] Wealthy Choctaws and Chickasaws, many of whom had arrived at their western homes with their slaves and draft animals, rebuilt the cotton plantations they had owned in the Southeast. With their main commercial center at Doaksville and steamboats docking six miles away at Fort Towson Landing near the mouth of the Kiamichi River, planters carved a commercial mecca from the woodlands of what is now southeastern Oklahoma.

Steamboat traffic peaked in the two decades preceding the Civil War. Often named for wives and sweethearts, vessels such as the *Laconia, Violet, Red Warrior, Bull of the Woods, Belle Gates, Napoleon,* and *Arkansas Traveler* brought manufactured goods and an aura of romance to isolated villages along the Arkansas and Red Rivers and their tributaries. Their arrival in port, heralded by blasts from a whistle, was a cause for celebration. People dropped what they were doing and made straight for the landing, where a gangplank was lowered for cargo and African American deckhands, merchants, traders, and government workers bearing supplies for Indians coalesced into a beehive of activity.[37] Huge bundles of buffalo and beef hides, deer skins, furs of all descriptions, bales of cotton, and hogsheads of corn and pecans bound for ports downriver were rolled on board. Traders who had been waiting patiently for the steamboat's arrival jostled for space near the gangplank, anxious to get their hands on weaponry and tools and luxury goods for customers in the interior. The more prosperous ones were accompanied by slaves or hired hands toting crates brimming with Mexican silver dollars, the principal currency at trading posts in the West.[38]

Merchants bound for Saint Louis, Cincinnati, or other points on the steamboat's itinerary to buy goods for frontier trading posts made their way to the deck. Passengers accompanied by servants or slaves were a common sight as they clambered aboard for a trip to exotic Memphis or New Orleans. Less noticeable on the bustling riverbank, but no less significant for the region's economic development, were the bootleggers—known in the common vernacular as "introducers"—who took advantage of steamboat travel to smuggle increasing amounts of liquor into the Indian country. Such nefarious dealings did not bode well for Indians, and they had dire consequences for authorities charged with curtailing the illegal trade in liquor. Determined to outflank officials charged with the impossible task of keeping the Indian Territory dry, steamboat crews sometimes resorted to slinging casks of contraband liquor beneath the hull by means of ropes and nets until the vessel had passed Fort Smith. When the ruse was exposed, frustrated customers had no choice but to smuggle liquor into the Indian Territory by wagon.[39]

Nearby, Indians not quite acclimated to the marvels of modern commerce stared in wonder at the great "fire-canoe" that had shattered the silence of the forests. Finally, with passengers on board and cargo secured, the gangplank was raised and cries of "Far'Yo'Well, Miss Lucy!" followed the craft as it rounded the bend and disappeared from view. With that, village life in all its loneliness and isolation resumed—until the next steamboat put into port.[40]

Even as traders and steamboat pilots were doing their part to push back the frontier, none doubted that Mother Nature was still in charge. In 1844, catastrophic floods wrought havoc on waterways west of the Mississippi. Twelve miles above Fort Smith, the waters at Fort Coffee rose forty-four feet above the low-water mark.[41] At the opposite end of the spectrum, droughts reduced swift currents to a sluggish crawl, and snags just beneath the opaque surface spelled disaster for unwary pilots and their crews. It was not uncommon for steamboats to remain in port for days or even weeks as rivermen waited for the waters to rise. One imagines legions of merchants pacing the banks along the Arkansas and Red Rivers, cursing their bad luck as cargoes languished onshore and future profits slipped through their fingers like water through a paddle wheel.

Tragedy of an entirely different sort struck in faraway New Albany, Indiana, and it served as a cautionary tale for businessmen whose wealth blinded them to the hazards of their trade. During the summer of 1844, the floods that were then raging in the trans-Mississippi West apparently did little to dampen the spirits of Joe Vann, a wealthy Cherokee from Webbers Falls on the Arkansas River whose possessions included vast tracts of fertile farmland and five hundred slaves to keep it productive. His string of racehorses included a prize mare named Lucy Walker whose colts were said to fetch up to $5,000 each.[42] Given his equine interests, it came as no surprise when he christened his steamboat the *Lucy Walker*. Vann was an avid gambler, and when he was not training and racing horses on his private track, he was steaming downriver aboard the *Lucy Walker* with horses to compete with the best that Ohio and Kentucky had to offer.

Flush with victory after one such excursion, Vann and his equine cargo, along with about fifty passengers, pulled out of Louisville, Kentucky. Accounts indicate that seventy or eighty people watched from shore as the *Lucy Walker* pulled out of port. Vann, who was feeling particularly festive on that crisp fall day, plied his passengers with liquor and no doubt regaled them with tales of his horse-training prowess. His listeners included gentlemen in high beaver hats, cutaway coats, and checkered pantaloons, as well as ladies bedecked in the latest crinoline fashions. Rough-cut woodsmen and pioneers were on board as well, perhaps less interested in Vann's boasting than their own tales of entrepreneurship in the wilderness.[43]

The *Lucy Walker* was known as the fastest boat on the Arkansas River, and Vann was not about to let its reputation lapse. As the vessel approached New Albany, another packet pulled up astern and challenged the *Lucy Walker* to a race. Fortified by liquor, the inveterate gambler

Steamboats on the Arkansas River at Webbers Falls, Indian Territory, ca. 1880. The boat in the foreground is the *Jennie May*. Webbers Falls was the port of registry for the *Lucy Walker*. Courtesy Oklahoma Historical Society.

rose to the challenge and ordered more steam. Soon, the boilers were glowing, and the craft's mighty paddles were turning the river into a cauldron of churning foam. Still not satisfied, Vann ordered the furniture to be broken and thrown into the furnace. Next on the list was cargo, including bacon, lard, and tobacco—until, that is, an African American slave clutching a slab of bacon hesitated. Glancing from the roaring furnace to the fodder in his arms, he is said to have protested, "But Massa' Vann, if I done t'rows dat in dere dem boilers is goin' to 'splode and blow us all to hell!"

"If they do," his owner bellowed above the roar of the furnace, "we'll all go together, and if you don't I'll blow you there by yourself!"

The Cherokee gambler drew his pistol, and the hapless slave had only seconds to consider his options. In a single motion, he heaved the bacon into the fire, turned, and dove overboard. As he hit the water, three of the boilers exploded.

Joe Vann's body, along with whatever remained of his passengers and horses and cargo, was eventually recovered from what passed into history as one of the greatest calamities to befall riverboat commerce. Pieces of the *Lucy Walker* sank to a watery grave, and Webbers Falls lost its only claim as a port of boat registry on the Arkansas River.[44]

Steamboat traffic slowed to a crawl during the Civil War. After the guns fell silent at Appomattox in 1865, business roared back to life with vessels that were bigger and faster than ever. In 1870, S. T. Abert, assistant engineer in charge of surveying the Arkansas River, reported to the chief engineer of the U.S. Army that twenty cargo-laden steamboats averaging three hundred tons each were plying the waters between Fort Gibson and ports on the Mississippi and Ohio Rivers. Some side-wheelers landing at Fort Gibson were so large they could not turn around in the channel and had to be backed into the Arkansas. A few were fitted for pleasure excursions that might last two or three days.[45]

Whether traveling for business or pleasure, few passengers aboard those storied craft suspected that steamboats were entering their twilight. Prescient observers must have known big changes were afoot in the early 1870s when the Missouri, Kansas and Texas Railroad extended its line southwestward across the Arkansas River valley. Bowing to the quickening pace of commerce, businessmen opted for faster and more efficient trains to ship their cargoes. Travelers followed suit, trading leisurely excursions on the waterways for the rush and clatter of the railroads. Forts Gibson and Towson, as well as small ports along the rivers, declined as commercial centers as old-time river packets deserted the Upper Arkansas for more alluring prospects on the Mississippi and Ohio Rivers. By the time Captain Joseph Evins embarked on his twenty-one-month adventure in 1881 aboard the snag boat *Wichita* from Fort Smith to Tulsa and points west, steamboat travel was on its way to oblivion.

Yet steamboats did not yield their supremacy in transportation without a fight. As non-Indian settlers trickled into the Arkansas and Red River valleys in the two decades following the Civil War, steamboats remained vital to the frontier economy, and they seared indelible images in the memories of pioneers who grew up near the waterways. Alex Sykes, who was born in 1870 in a log cabin in the Cherokee Nation near Muskogee, recalled the days when steamboats were a regular attraction on the Arkansas River. His memories, along with many others, were captured in the late 1930s by interviewers for the Works Progress Administration, and they open a portal into frontier business before railroads thundered into the Indian country. "In my boyhood days," recalled Sykes, "there was a number of steamboats on the Arkansas river. They came from Memphis, Little Rock, and Ft. Smith. Some of the landings I heard them talk of were at Skullville, Tamaha, Webbers Falls, Nevins Ferry. These were the landings on the Arkansas between Ft. Smith and Nevins Ferry. The cargoes were merchandise of all kinds and they would take back cotton, hay and sometimes logs. I remember seeing the *Border City, Lucy Walker,* the *Memphis Packet* and lots of others I can't name. I did not know any of the captains."[46]

Similar memories seem to have been a comfort to an elderly Bill Swimm, who was born in 1868 in Mississippi and moved in 1883 with his family to the Indian Territory. Swimm remembered spending two days and nights aboard the *Fort Smith* as it steamed from its namesake, Fort Smith, to Webbers Falls. "All along the banks were dense bottom timber and cane breaks," recalled Swimm, "which I soon learned upon my arrival were only dens for wild animals of all kinds." His stop in Skullyville in the Choctaw Nation, where postal service dated back to 1833, was particularly memorable for a teenager who did not need Mark Twain to describe the riverboat frontier: "I won't forget it. The boat sounded the whistle for the landing about a mile down stream from Skulleville [*sic*]. And by the time the boat landed all the people in the village were down to the river bank to meet it. All kinds of people, whites, colored, Indians and half breeds and all. Of course, I could understand the whites and negroes, but I looked and listened with amazement at the Indians. They were a new people in my young life."[47]

A similar scene greeted a young B. M. Palmer. Born in 1873 near Fort Smith, Palmer moved in 1886 with his parents to the Indian Territory and settled in Le Flore County, where he lived for many years before moving in 1927 to Muskogee. As he recounted, "When the boats whistled for the landing the whole village would turn out to meet and to greet it. They carried both passengers and freight. The merchants would cart their merchandise away from the landing about as fast as it was unloaded by the roust-a-bouts."[48] Palmer helped build the *Myrtle B,* operated by a Captain Blakely, at the mouth of the Poteau River. "It had a stern wheel and two side wheels," recalled Palmer, "and was so built that it could land bow first or sidewise with ease."[49] Even though Palmer was clearly dazzled by the technology, he hinted at the drawbacks of shipping by steamboat that hastened its demise with the coming of the railroads: "Some of these boats came from as far as New Orleans, Memphis, and Little Rock when the river was up, this being usually in the month of June. Most of the boats, however, from Little Rock and Fort Smith tried to run on a schedule of once a month. Sometimes some of these boats would steam up the river as far as the Nevins Landing with merchandise for Fort Gibson and Muskogee, Indian Territory. If the river was so that the boats could not get up the river due to low water the freight was unloaded at Webbers Falls and then hauled by freight wagons to Fort Gibson and Muskogee."[50]

The gaiety that greeted steamboats made a similar impression on Louis R. Jobe, a one-fourth Creek Indian who was born and raised in the Creek Nation and whose mother had traveled west from Alabama during the period of forced removal. "It was a gay time when the boats came up, [sic] the river and landed," he said. "People would flock to the docks to greet it. They carried cargoes, of mail and provisions, Feed and dry goods, etc. And the people was always it seemed to be looking for some of their kin in [sic] on the boats."[51] Early on, steamboats tried to operate on a monthly schedule. Later, they tried to bring enough goods in June, when navigation was relatively safe, to last until the next June. Return loads consisted of hay and logs, and log rafting was common. When navigation was impossible past Webbers Falls, freight bound for points east and west was transported by ox carts and wagon trains to Nevins Ferry. Like B. M. Palmer, Jobe might have suspected that the steamboats' days were numbered as railroads muscled their way into the riverboat frontier.

Far to the south of the Arkansas River, Lem W. Oakes, who eventually rose to the position of justice of the peace in Hugo, watched steamboats make their way up the Red River and pass near his home some twenty-three miles from Hugo in the Choctaw Nation. They landed at Pine Bluff Ferry, where a warehouse constructed with split logs that were sunken in the ground and covered with hand-riven boards stored the goods that arrived by steamboat. Merchants traveled as far as one hundred miles to Pine Bluff Ferry to obtain merchandise for remote trading posts. In the absence of money to pay for goods, they resorted to good old-fashioned bartering. "People close around who had money would meet these merchants there and buy some of the goods," recalled Oakes.

"Or if they had anything that they could trade for them they would do that."[52] Even though he welcomed the arrival of goods from distant factories during his youth, an elderly Oakes waxed nostalgic about people accustomed to frontier scarcity and who got along just fine on their own. "If people would live on things produced at home more now, they would be better off."[53]

A dozen years before Captain Joseph Evins testified at the riverbed hearings in Oklahoma City, a sixty-two-year-old widow from Wooster Mound, a tiny hamlet some six miles east of Pawhuska, Oklahoma Territory, was going about her day-to-day activities with little fanfare. "Howdy do, John, folks well?" asked the diminutive woman as she stepped into the Indian trader's store. The woman's face beamed with kindness as she spoke to the proprietor and several others who huddled around a fire, rubbing their hands and warming themselves as best they could against the winter chill. She wore a blanket, moccasins, and the buckskin leggings favored by Osage women of her day. Her black hair was streaked with gray, and her face bore the wrinkles and tan one would expect from a lifetime of exposure to the elements. Yet she remained as vivacious as a girl, which perhaps accounted for her longevity and high spirits on a cold January day in 1904. Her smile no doubt broadened when Josephine, one of her daughters whose sharp features revealed her French ancestry, strode into the store with a baby wrapped in a shawl and strapped to her back.[54]

The older woman had been married twice, first to Che-she-hunka and, after he died, to Little Bear, who was the father of her four children, two boys and two girls. With both husbands gone and well past her prime, the quiet woman known to her intimates as "Aunt Sophy" did little to attract attention from outside her tribal community. Yet there was plenty about Aunt Sophy's past to draw attention, which is why, on this particular day, she agreed to an interview with a newspaper reporter. Aunt Sophy was the daughter of Edward L. Chouteau and a niece of Colonel A. P. Chouteau, and she belonged to the last generation with lived memory of the days when wealth was measured in bundles of pelts, and non-Indian civilization west of Fort Smith hugged the banks of the Arkansas and Red Rivers and their tributaries.[55]

Speaking in a soft, southern accent, Aunt Sophy captivated her listener with memories of the Indian country before the Civil War and how westward migration changed everything—when she and her sister, Mary, festooned themselves in costly silks and jewelry sent from Saint Louis and rode in fine carriages with slaves in attendance to do their bidding. She expressed regret that she had so few relics from a youth spent in regal splendor. "We have few mementoes of our mother," explained Aunt Sophy to the reporter. "Our home, with all its furnishings, was burned during the war and everything in it was lost." She recalled the time three or four years earlier when an agent of the Field Columbian Museum in Chicago came to the Osage country prowling for relics. He was said to have purchased a number of items from Brave, her sister Mary's husband. "Mary Chouteau is the wife of Brave," wrote the reporter for the benefit of his big-city readers, "one of the most obstinate opponents among the Osages against changing to the ways of white men. At the council held here last December to discuss allotment Brave was a leading orator in behalf of the fullblood element that mourned the loss of the hunting grounds in the West, and he fought against consenting to anything that might lead to a more civilized life."[56]

The reporter was almost certainly Frederick S. Barde, whose voluminous reporting between 1890 and 1916 yielded an embarrassment of riches about the Oklahoma and Indian Territories. As he ended his interview and prepared to leave the Indian store to file his story, he asked Aunt Sophy if he could take her picture. She hesitated at first, and then consented at the urging of a friend. "I don't like to have my picture taken wearing a blanket," she said with customary self-deprecation. "I used to wear citizens' clothes, but these are more comfortable, and as we grow older we are not so proud."[57]

Aunt Sophy stood quietly in the morning sunshine. Folding her blanket gracefully around her, she did her best to strike a pose for a reporter who was no doubt racing to meet a deadline. One wonders, as he adjusted his lens and prepared to snap an old Indian woman's photograph, if her eyes gave any hint of the things she had seen and the life she had lived on the riverboat frontier.

CHAPTER FOUR

Crossed over the Range

Each day's travel was increasing the distance between me, my home and my mother, to whom I was most dearly attached; and here amid the solitude, darkness and perfect quietude of the vast plains I began to reflect upon the dangers besetting me, and the uncertainty of ever returning to my home or seeing my relatives again.

W. B. Napton, freighter on the Santa Fe Trail

Save for a smattering of trading outposts operated by the likes of Colonel A. P. Chouteau and Captain Nathaniel Pryor and linked with the East by the riverboat trade, the Indian Territory before the Civil War was populated primarily by the so-called Five Civilized Tribes: Cherokee, Choctaw, Chickasaw, Creek, and Seminole. Their westward migration from the Southeast began in earnest with the Indian Removal Act of 1830, legislation that supported President Andrew Jackson's conviction that whites and Indians could never live together in peace. Unable to withstand relentless non-Indian settlement, these tribes found that their adoption of white customs and integration into an alien economy made no difference to land-hungry settlers and their advocates in the nation's capital. Save for the stalwarts who hid in the hollows of Appalachia and the Smokey Mountains when the troops moved in, most resigned themselves to forced removal to the West and rebuilt their lives as best they could in a region deemed to be of no use to the dominant civilization.

Upon arrival in their new home, tribal leaders were assured that they would be left alone for all time—or, in vernacular aimed at assuring skeptical Indians that the Great Father in Washington was on their side, for as long as the grasses grow and the waters run. Then came the War between the States, and all bets were off. Tribal support for the Confederacy, coupled with non-Indian settlement of the trans-Mississippi West, seemed to justify a thorough overhaul of treaties with the Five Tribes. In a series of treaties drawn up after the Civil War, the United States government relocated Osages, Shawnees, Potatomies, Sacs and Foxes, and other tribes from Kansas to reservations just west of the Cherokee and Creek Nations. Still others—Wyandottes, Miamis, Senecas, and Ottawas, to name a few of the most prominent—were sent to the extreme northeast corner of the Cherokee Nation.

The government's most sweeping change was to abrogate previous agreements with the Five Tribes and acquire rights to their western hunting grounds. During the period of wars and reservations between 1865 and 1890, the short-grass prairie that now constitutes western Oklahoma was divided into reservations for Plains tribes.[1] Nomadic hunters whose ancestors had followed the bison from the Rio Grande to the northern Rockies for millennia found themselves in the span of a generation reduced to wards of the federal government and restricted to the western half of the Indian Territory. Equipped with alien implements of farming and stripped of their cultural heritage, Kiowas, Comanches, Apaches, and other tribes that had stood in the way of Manifest Destiny were on their way to the margins of American society.

Forced relocation of Native Americans to the Indian Territory thus spawned the emergence of vastly different cultural regions. The split between east and west was made even wider by differences in climate and topography. In the east, wooded hills and fertile valleys connected by navigable rivers did not seem all that different from what Native American immigrants from the Southeast had left behind. Supposedly beyond the reach of non-Indian settlers, the tribes reconstituted their governments, rekindled their traditions, and resumed their patterns of farming, hunting, and trading. West of the ninety-eighth meridian, arid plains stretched as far as the eye could see. Bison, the mainstay of the Plains economy, had been hunted to the brink of extinction, and the nomads who depended on them for sustenance had little choice but to wrest what they could from the soil. Yet their traditions left them ill-equipped to assimilate into structures imposed by an alien civilization. Grudgingly, they accepted from government agents what the soil and the great prairies could not provide.

Given their differences in culture, climate, and topography, it was inevitable that eastern and western sections of the Indian Territory would follow different paths of economic development. As we have seen, eastern commerce sprouted from the fur trade and followed the course of the Arkansas and Red Rivers and their tributaries to produce a vibrant commercial culture. Western commerce developed much later and molded itself to the contours of the prairies. To establish commerce in that harsh environment, entrepreneurs relied on frontier ingenuity to deliver goods to forts and settlements. In a tradition that dated back to the earliest days of European colonization, trade became the primary means of forging peaceful relations with tribes more prone to fighting than farming. In those vast and sparsely settled plains, it was the freighters who blazed the trail of economic development.

Unlike the Overland Trail to the north that provided a conduit for untold thousands of pioneers bound for the mountain West and Pacific coast, the Santa Fe Trail was essentially a route of commerce. Its path from Missouri to the Spanish settlements cut through the "Great American Desert," a designation that dates back to Major Stephen S. Long's exploration in 1820 of the eastern slopes of the Rocky Mountains. In his report, Major Long offered the opinion that the region between the Missouri River and the Rockies "is almost wholly unfit for cultivation, and of course uninhabitable by a people depending on agriculture for their subsistence."[2]

Nevertheless, there were enough intrepid souls on the far side of this benighted swath of real estate to spawn the development of trade routes to supply them with the rudiments of civilization. The earliest caravans on the Santa Fe Trail were ad hoc affairs, both in terms of equipment and personnel. One writer called the Santa Fe trade "one of the most curious species of foreign intercourse which the ingenuity and enterprise of American traders ever originated."[3] Commerce between outposts in Missouri and Santa Fe was still in its infancy when the Panic of 1819 roared through the economy. In spite of its distance from eastern money centers, Missouri took a hit in 1819 when the Bank of Saint Louis, founded in 1817, failed. The Bank of Missouri, also founded in

1817, followed suit in 1821 and put a damper on statehood celebrations. Reverting to the time-honored tradition of bartering, jaded frontiersmen had all the evidence they needed that banks and their fancy currencies were not to be trusted.

Reeling from bank failures, Missourians were heartened when the *Independence,* the first steamboat to prove the Missouri River navigable, arrived in Franklin, Missouri, in 1819. Steamboats were quickly enlisted to deliver goods up the Missouri River from Saint Louis to Independence and nearby settlements. It did not take much imagination to envision the pelts and specie trickling into Saint Louis from Santa Fe as a far more reliable source of wealth. By 1824, Missouri governor Alexander McNair's list of benefits from the burgeoning business included not only profits from trade, but also the spread of democracy, friendship with Indians tribes, and a stronger bond between the United States and Mexico after it won its independence from Spain in 1821. Missouri senator Thomas Hart Benton seized the initiative and persuaded Congress to designate the Santa Fe Trail as a highway for international commerce. His bill, signed into law by President James Monroe on March 3, 1825, authorized the president to appoint commissioners to mark a road from western Missouri "to the boundary line of the United States [the Arkansas River] in the direction of Santa Fe."[4] The $30,000 appropriation included $10,000 to survey and mark the trail and $20,000 to buy transit rights from Indian tribes.[5] What Senator Benton called "a highway between nations" was poised to become an engine of economic development.

By 1835, the process of freighting merchandise from Missouri to Santa Fe had become routine, and the influx of Mexican specie was making Missouri banks the envy of the nation. "The State of Missouri is at this day the soundest in the Union in her monetary affairs," wrote Captain A. Harris in 1840 to Representative Edward Cross of Arkansas. "She is filled with specie; and the interior Mexican states have supplied it."[6] A milestone in the Santa Fe trade came with the U.S. victory in the Mexican War and subsequent signing of the Treaty of Guadalupe Hidalgo on February 2, 1848. With the stroke of a pen, the boundary between the United States and Mexico vanished, and trade with the Spanish settlements was no longer subject to international trade restrictions. Fly-by-night freighters accustomed to smuggling contraband, handing out bribes to Spanish officials, and avoiding taxes any way they could suddenly found themselves under the scrutiny of U.S. officials.[7] Soldiers were the first to arrive in the newly acquired territories to establish garrisons, and civilians who decided that Major Long might have been exaggerating were soon to follow. By midcentury, military forts and crude villages dotted the high plains, and the Santa Fe Trail—not so much a neat thoroughfare as a zone of beaten and scarred earth, with lots of deviations and trouble spots—was their lifeline.

Allowing for detours and seasonal variations, the trail began at one of the Missouri River's burgeoning ports and followed the course of the Arkansas River. One of the main river crossings was west of Fort Dodge in present-day Kansas, where wagon trains had the option to continue westward on what was known as the Mountain Branch to Bent's Fort in present-day Colorado and south through the Raton Pass into present-day New Mexico. Travelers could also deviate southward on the Cimarron Cutoff or Cimarron Branch, a path that clipped the northwestern corner of what would one day become Cimarron County, Oklahoma. Freighters knew the southern route as *la jornada del muerto*—a blistering path that was the shortest and most traveled branch of the Santa Fe Trail, even as it confirmed Major Long's dim view of America's heartland.[8] For confirmation that the southern route was aptly named, members of Captain William Becknell's expedition in 1822 were reduced to killing their dogs and cutting off the ears of their mules to slake their thirst with blood.[9] (Interestingly, it was only in the twentieth century that the southwestern route became known as a branch or cutoff. For those who traveled across those arid plains, it was simply the shortest and most direct route to Santa Fe.)[10] Oklahoma's outpost, Camp Nichols, was founded near the present-day town of Wheeless in 1865 by Colonel Christopher "Kit" Carson and Major Albert H. Pfeiffer to protect wagon trains from Indian attacks.[11] The trails converged just north of Las Vegas near Fort Union in present-day New Mexico where the Bent's Fort and Cimarron Routes converged and continued through Glorietta Pass and on to Santa Fe, a place of dark-haired beauties and exotic foods that must have seemed to weary travelers from the East like the El Dorado of Spanish legend.[12]

Constructed in 1851, Fort Union rose to prominence as the region's primary distribution center for food and supplies not only for soldiers, but also for Navajos and Mescalero Apaches who had been reduced to wards of the federal government between 1863 and 1868 and held

Wagon trains at Cheyenne, Oklahoma Territory, ca. 1906. Cheyenne was an important trading center at the western edge of the Cheyenne and Arapaho Reservation. Herrington and Young received most of their supplies from Darlington and Sayre, Oklahoma Territory. Courtesy Western History Collections, University of Oklahoma Libraries, Division of Manuscripts (Uncat., D-9, f-2, TC1-1).

captive at the Bosque Redondo Reservation near Fort Sumner. As its economy had never advanced much beyond the subsistence level, New Mexico depended on supplies from the states long after the signing of the Treaty of Guadalupe Hidalgo.[13] A manifest of goods awaiting shipment in one warehouse in 1858 illustrates the variety of goods that arrived in New Mexico via the Santa Fe Trail: "doors, circular saws, bands, packing, machinery, sashes, whisky, sugar, cog wheels, shovels, wheels, church bells, grind stones, furniture, bedding, brooms, stoves, nail iron, lager beer, fan mills, crockery, crates, saw mill, wagon felloes, bows, spokes, horse collars, cement, soda, syrups, wine, leather, glass ware, preserved fruit, log chains, bacon, flour, emigrant chests, axletrees, rope, and pianos."[14] Wagons often returned to Missouri laden with wool—more manageable than the outbound freight, and certainly more profitable than hauling empty wagons across the prairies.[15]

Freighting was a relatively easy business to enter. Anyone who could scrounge up enough money for a wagon, a few head of oxen, and a two-month supply of vittles could establish a freighting business; with luck, there might even be profits at the end of the trail. As the volume of trade increased after 1848, oxen—cheaper and hardier than mules and less likely to be stolen by Indians, but more easily spooked than their equine counterparts—became the draft animals of choice, and by 1865 they outnumbered mules by six to one.[16] On occasion, several trains traveled together to produce a long string of wagons, or prairie schooners, each one large and sturdy enough to carry three to three and a half tons of freight. As one chronicler explained, we may never know the extent of commercial activity that opened the Great Plains to economic development. "There have never been compiled even approximate statistics of the overland travel and freighting from 1846 to 1860, nor would it be possible to list the vast throngs of emigrants that crossed the plains. Roughly speaking, forty-two thousand people did it in 1849 alone."[17] Another chronicler with a yen for statistics took a stab at quantification and estimated that the value of trade on the Santa Fe Trail increased from $3.5 million in 1858 to $10 million in 1859 to an astounding $40 million in 1862, when some 3,000 private wagons plied the (now national) highway of commerce.[18]

A firsthand description of overland freighting on the Santa Fe Trail survives in the form of a two-part article published in the *Kansas City Star* on January 5 and 12, 1902, by William B. Napton. Well educated and proficient with horses and guns, Napton came from a wealthy family in Saline County, Missouri. At the urging of his father who thought that a trip out West would do his son some good, the eighteen-year-old Napton hired on with a train of twenty-six wagons bound for Santa Fe in the spring of 1857.[19] The wagon master, Captain Chiles, better known as "Jim Crow" to his crew, was the son of Missouri senator and colonel James Chiles. "The wagons were heavy, cumbrous affairs with long deep beds," wrote Napton, "covered with sheets of heavy cotton cloth, supported by bows. A man six feet high could stand erect in one of them, and they were designed to hold a load of seven or eight thousand pounds of merchandise each."[20] Napton's train included two wagons loaded with champagne for Colonel Céran St. Vrain, a Frenchman and onetime mountain man from Saint Louis who became one of the most successful businessmen in Las Vegas, New Mexico Territory. St. Vrain's former partner was Charles Bent, the founder of Bent's Fort in southern Colorado and the first territorial governor of New Mexico.[21] Among Napton's companions in Jim Crow's outfit was the son of a Cincinnati banker, nicknamed "Skeesicks" by unanimous consent and for reasons unknown, whom Napton remembered as "accomplished in penmanship and a good accountant; but he proved to be utterly unfit for an ox driver."[22]

Typically, each wagon required six yoke of oxen—hardier and cheaper than horses or mules, and endowed by nature to endure as many as two thousand miles in a season. In case any became crippled or expired along the way, wagon trains included twenty to thirty extras that could be yoked as replacements. At night, the wagons were arranged in a circle with their tongues facing forward. Chains were attached from a hind wheel of one wagon to a front wheel of another to make a safe enclosure for cattle, typically numbering about 330 head, and the 4 or 5 mules that were used for riding and herding.[23] Shattering the morning stillness with their signature command—*"Stretch out! Stretch out!"*—wagon masters signaled that it was time for teamsters to unwind their serpentine convoy and gird for another day of slogging across the high plains.[24]

Manpower consisted of a wagon master and his assistant, a teamster for each wagon, a herder, and two or three extra men. Teamsters were usually of Mexican descent and got by on a salary of a dollar a day, plus expenses. Trudging beside their teams, bullwhackers were equipped with whips whose lashes were twenty feet long—plenty to slice the hide of a stubborn ox or clip the head off a rattlesnake at ten paces. Bullwhackers were not necessarily cruel. Many boasted that they had driven to Santa Fe and back without "cutting the blood" from an ox.[25] Writing some four decades after the heyday of the wagon trains, an anonymous chronicler in 1897 described the cacophony of battle where there were no enemies: "The cracking of this whip was like the crack of a gun and the crossing of a bad ravine or the entrance to a town was accompanied by a popping of whips that sounded like the fire of a skirmish line."[26]

Overland trains started from the Missouri River in the middle of May to make sure that grazing along the way would be adequate. Even at a distance of four decades, Napton relished the beginning of his great adventure on the Santa Fe Trail: "The weather was perfect, the view of the apparently boundless prairie exhilarating. The road, having been surveyed and established by the government before the country was at all occupied, was almost as straight as an arrow toward the southwest."[27] The thrill that the young freighter felt at the outset of his great adventure resonated in the observations of stagecoach passengers who saw wagon trains from a distance. For one, they merited comparisons with caravans of biblical lore; another characterized them as "poetic, grand, beautiful"; and still another likened them to "lines of white cranes trooping slowly over the prairie, or in more mysterious evening resembling dim sails crossing a rolling sea."[28] Such lyrical depictions probably escaped freighters whose real-life experiences were anything but lyrical. The romance of freighting was surely lacking when thunderstorms, described by veteran freighter Josiah Gregg as frightful tempests that combined "so many of the elements of the awful and sublime," vented their fury on hapless caravans.[29]

Upon reaching the buffalo range, crews took time to provision themselves with fresh meat. Napton recalled an impromptu hunt that nearly turned deadly when he killed a calf and looked up to see a roiling herd heading straight for him. With typical frontier chutzpah, the episode quickly became a source of amusement: "The air was so clouded with dust that I could hardly see more than twenty yards from where I was standing, near the carcass of the calf I had killed. There was danger of being run over by them, but they separated as they approached, passing on either side of me, a few yards distant. After a while the rushing crowd thinned, and up rode Captain Chiles, exclaiming, 'Why don't you kill another?'" All told, the youthful freighter-turned-marksman killed some twenty bison. With practice, he managed to complement his hunting skills with prowess at the campfire. "A good steak, cut from the loin of a buffalo cow, broiled on the coals, with a thin slice of bacon attached to it to improve the flavor, was 'good eating,' and I soon became an accomplished broiler."[30]

Until the late 1850s, there were no non-Indian habitations along the route. But there were plenty of Indians, some of whom were friendly toward the caravans that crossed their hunting grounds. Between Independence, Missouri, and the Arkansas River, encounters with the mighty Osages were common. As freighters proceeded westward, they could also expect to meet Indians of the Pawnee, Shawnee, Pottawatomie, and Kansas tribes. On occasion, they were even welcome: not only did these Indians leave the wagon trains alone, but they also were known to provide protection by driving back the fiercer western tribes, most notably the nomadic Comanches. Such aid was not forthcoming beyond the Arkansas, however, where Indians and "squawmen"—white men married to, or living with, Indian women—stampeded cattle by night and sold them back to their drovers by day, feigning ignorance as to the cause of their flight. Kaw Indians were notorious for such mischief and were known to fleece wagon masters for as much as $500.[31]

The trip from Independence to Santa Fe took about two months. Wagon trains headed home around the first of October. Emptied of their merchandise and loaded mainly with specie (usually in the form of Mexican dollars) as payment for the goods they had delivered and pelts bound for processors back east, lighter wagons could make the return trip to Independence in about forty days. When there was livestock for the herders to contend with, return trips could run a bit longer.[32] The rule of thumb for computing freighting costs was to charge one cent per pound per hundred miles. As ad hoc supply trains yielded to structured commerce, the standard time allowance was twelve days for each hundred miles. But freight bills were not always paid in cash as freighters often accepted all or part of their payment in trade.[33]

Undaunted by challenges posed by man and nature, the Kansas City firm of Russell, Majors and Waddell was formed in 1855 and came to dominate the freighting business by reducing the enterprise to a science. While most of the firm's business came from military contracts, it also serviced civilians and even branched into retail stores. Its business model called for trains of twenty-five wagons each. Through trial and error, Russell, Majors and Waddell developed a system capable of transporting millions of pounds of freight that included a profusion of manufactured goods: furniture, glassware, utensils, tools, textiles, and other marvels that flowed from eastern factories. Business growth is reflected in figures from 1860, when the New Mexico trade included 5,984 men, 2,170 wagons, 460 horses, 17,836 oxen, and nearly 6,000 mules, all supported by capital investment of $2 million.[34] Another indication that business was booming came when Russell, Majors and Waddell's Overland Trail depot at Nebraska City required the expenditure of $300,000 for lots, corrals, warehouses, offices, and residences.[35]

In an effort to keep employees in line, Russell, Majors and Waddell posted rules on the back of its wagons. Upon encountering one of his competitor's wagon trains, Napton did a bit of sleuthing and was intrigued to read the crew's rules of the road. "Both liquor and profanity were absolutely prohibited," wrote the freighter-turned-spy, "but of the strict enforcement of the rules I cannot speak."[36]

Napton was no stranger to strict rules. Everyone in his outfit knew that "no captain of a ship at sea ever wielded more absolute authority than Captain Chiles."[37] Yet it seems that Russell, Majors and Waddell's draconian restrictions pertaining to profanity applied to neither the Jim Crow outfit nor others that Napton encountered along the trail whose employees were known for their colorful language. But on occasion, even trail-hardened freighters exercised restraint, at least until they caught their breath. According to our chronicler, a member of another wagon train named Hagan took a particularly nasty fall from his mule. "Hagan got up, pulled himself together and rubbed the dust out of his eyes, but said nothing, though gifted in the way of eloquent profanity."[38] Maybe Russell, Majors and Waddell's stodginess spilled over into its reputation for integrity. According to one writer, "The old-time freighter had the reputation of being honest and dependable. The frontier merchant and the ranchman knew that they could depend upon them to deliver their supplies in good condition."[39]

One can imagine the excitement attending the arrival of wagon trains in Santa Fe and other Spanish settlements in what is now northeastern New Mexico—an event comparable, perhaps, to the arrival of a steamboat in some hamlet on the Arkansas or Red River. "It was truly a scene for the artist's pen to revel in," recalled Josiah Gregg. "Even the animals seemed to participate in the humor of their riders, who grew more and more merry and obstreperous as they descended towards the city. I doubt, in short, whether the first sight of the walls of Jerusalem was beheld by the crusaders with much more tumultuous and soul-enrapturing joy."[40] Runners from hotels, stores, and saloons often greeted the weary travelers several miles from town to entice them with the prospect of civilized refinements. More often than not, the trip ended with a fandango, a flamboyant mix of music and dancing that lured revelers of all nationalities and social classes into the streets to experience Spanish culture in all its glory.[41] Although many freighters no doubt found the *mujeres* of their dreams as they cavorted through town, some woke up disappointed. As one bullwhacker recalled in a lament that rings through the ages, "Those Mexican girls were not such good lookers when seen on the street in the day time, but they were dolls when rigged out in the dancing costumes."[42]

Although Napton was silent on the subject of his romantic liaisons upon reaching his destination in the Spanish settlements, he did provide insight into the business dealings of his wagon master. He recounts that Captain Chiles found a buyer for about half of his wagon train's cattle at Fort Union. Napton described a simple transaction: "One evening he [Captain Chiles] announced that he had made a sale of about one-half of the cattle. The following morning a prosperous looking gentleman of consequential air and mien rode up to our camp and was introduced as the purchaser of our cattle." A flask of brandy lashed to the front of his handsome saddle was offered to one and all, "and this invitation the common politeness of the plains prevented us from declining."[43] Arrangements were duly made to separate the man's cattle from the wagon train, and Skeesicks offered to drive them—on foot, as he had no horse—to the buyer's property elsewhere in New Mexico. "Skeesicks, with apparent reluctance, accepted the service and wages offered, and in a few moments afterwards left us forever," recalled a remorseful Napton. "I could not avoid feeling sorry for him, as he slowly passed from our view, trudging along on foot behind the herd of cattle. We never heard of him afterwards."[44] The one-time banker from Cincinnati no doubt had plenty of time to ponder his career choice as he trudged across the prairie.

Thus did a seller and buyer meet on a desolate plain in New Mexico to strike a deal on a herd of cattle and swill brandy as a sign of good faith. It is hardly surprising that the youthful W. B. Napton failed to mention the details of the transaction—the cost per head, the currency or coin that was used, the credit (if any) that was extended, or even the actual owner of the cattle for which he and his companions had risked their lives to deliver to nobody in particular in the middle of nowhere. Nor do we know if the thirsty Colonel St. Vrain received his champagne in good condition. But perhaps we have all we need to glimpse the stirrings of frontier business.

Napton's memories of life on the Santa Fe Trail remain poignant, even at a remove of a century and a half. Harrowing encounters with Plains Indians; watching in awe as wolves and coyotes and antelopes cavorted across the flatlands; struggling to stay awake during a night ride as his mount plodded on, mile after mile, "with nothing but the rumbling of the wagons and the occasional shout of one of the drivers to break the silence of the plain";[45] river crossings that could easily have turned deadly—these and other tales too numerous to mention flowed from Napton's pen to open a window into the dawn of commerce on the prairies.

Perhaps what comes through the clearest of all was the intense loneliness that this young man felt under that vast sky. He rode in advance of his wagon train one night, alone, with nothing visible but the stars, and was seized with homesickness and melancholy the likes of which he had never known: "Each day's travel was increasing the distance between me, my home and my mother, to whom I was most dearly attached; and here amid the solitude, darkness and perfect quietude of the vast plains I began to reflect upon the dangers besetting me, and the uncertainty of ever returning to my home or seeing my relatives again."[46]

W. B. Napton did indeed make it back to Missouri. The drivers were paid and disbanded, and our chronicler no doubt partook in a tearful reunion with his mother. Little did he suspect that, more than four decades hence, he would have an opportunity to recount his youthful exploits in the pages of the *Kansas City Star* and share with readers in that western metropolis of 1902 the adventure of freighting on the Santa Fe Trail. Writ large, Napton's adventure is the story of economic development on the southern plains—of stimulating demand for draft animals and wagons and dry goods; of creating a need for banks and warehouses and brokerage firms; and of luring adventurers, and eventually settlers, to the Great American Desert, where lonely villages sprouted into cities.

Like steamboating on the Arkansas and Red Rivers, freighting was a thriving business until the completion of transcontinental railways. After 1865, freighters relinquished their long-haul business to the railroads and continued to serve remote communities until modernity put an end to them. Increasingly, the Santa Fe Trail was seen as a temporary means of transporting goods until industry could catch up with the tide of westward migration.[47] Joyous crowds in Las Vegas, Santa Fe's main commercial rival, greeted the first train's arrival on the Fourth of July, 1879—just shy of sixteen years since the rail route had been envisioned and published in a brochure.[48] In February 1880, the first engine on the Atchison, Topeka and Santa Fe spur line chugged into its terminus about a mile south of the Santa Fe Plaza.[49] The train's arrival marked two milestones in the history of western commerce: it fulfilled the railroad's name; and it sent the Santa Fe Trail into oblivion. Eventually, all that remained to mark the passing of mighty caravans were ruts across the flatlands and names etched into cliffs for future generations to ponder. As far as the *Junction City Union* and, presumably, its readers were concerned, the changes could not come fast enough. "A few years ago the freighting wagons and oxen passing through Council Grove were counted by thousands, the value of merchandise by millions," ran an article in August 1867. "But the shriek of the iron horse has silenced the lowing of the panting ox, and the old trail looks desolate. The track of the commerce of the plains has changed, and with the change is destined to come other changes, better and more blessed."[50]

One wonders what W. B. Napton's readers, sipping their coffee and warming themselves in front of a fire on a quiet winter morning, thought about an old man who, in the vernacular of the freighters, had once "crossed over the range."[51]

Early on his trip, W. B. Napton passed by the ruins of an adobe fort. "The wagon master said it was known as 'Old Fort Atkinson,'" recalled the youthful chronicler, "doubtless named for and established and built by the command of Colonel Henry Atkinson of the regular army, with whose military career I happened to be somewhat familiar."[52] Napton guessed that the fort had been built about 1829. The memory of passing by the remains of Fort Atkinson, its walls already crumbling to dust and melting into the prairie in 1857 and surely vanished altogether by the time he wrote his story for the *Kansas City Star* in January 1902, opens a window into another stage of economic development on the Great Plains, and one that was vital to Oklahoma's commercial history: the establishment of Indian trading posts.

Far to the south of the Santa Fe Trail that W. B. Napton came to know so well, another young adventurer, this one from Northboro, Massachusetts, left his trail in frontier commerce by trading with the Indians in present-day western Oklahoma. Most sources place his post at the mouth of Cache Creek in Cotton County; he might have occupied other posts on Walnut Bayou in Love County and Mud Creek in Jefferson County.[53] His name was Abel Warren, and his adventure began in 1836 when he arrived by boat at Fort Smith in the Arkansas Territory.[54] Residents of that tiny outpost no doubt thronged to the dock when his boat signaled its arrival with the blare of a whistle, anxious to connect with friends and relatives returning from distant cities, and receptive to news from the outside world that was slow to reach their isolated community. The newcomer must have watched in amazement as gangplanks were low-ered and cargo was unloaded and merchants, clutching sacks of Mexican silver dollars and perhaps wads of paper money, muscled their way to the dock to claim their merchandise. Perhaps, before disembarking, the twenty-one-year-old adventurer lingered on the deck and caught his first glimpse of buckskin-clad frontiersmen, Cherokees and Choctaws, Creeks and Osages, who fired imaginations in the East and lured so many adventure seekers to the West. Descending the gangplank to the dock, he would have sidestepped barrels of corn and pecans and heaps of animal hides. Surely, as he navigated through the bazaar to find lodging for the night, the savvy New Englander's nose told him that a few casks were filled with contraband whisky.

As Abel Warren made his way through the throng, he might have bumped into a well-dressed gentleman and his entourage with French-sounding names who had traveled from the Three Forks region to Fort Smith to check out the merchandise coming in from New Orleans and Cincinnati and points east. If so, he was surely glad to spot a gentleman in the crowd. Maybe he stopped for a visit or to inquire about a suitable hotel. Or maybe Warren, who had bidden a tearful good-bye to his first love in New England before lighting out for the frontier, was more the practical sort, oblivious to the sights and sounds and smells of civilization in the making, not in the mood for socializing, and content to conjure up visions of the money he was about to earn in the fur trade.

In short order, Warren gathered volunteers and Indian guides and set out for parts unknown. As there were no government forts west of Forts Towson and Gibson, he and his companions were on their own. They eventually reached Cache Creek in the Choctaw and Chickasaw country, where there was ample timber for building and plenty of Red River tributaries to furnish fish and game. Some records indicate that the post was built as early as 1839; others settle on 1842 as a more likely date. What seems more certain is that the post was abandoned by 1846. When the Kiowa-Comanche country was opened to non-Indian settlement in 1901, newcomers began to discover stones and other signs of habitation. Subsequent research in War Department archives pointed to the likeli-hood that the relics belonged to Abel Warren's trading post—thirty-one miles south and seven miles east of the present city of Lawton.[55]

Correspondence between Warren and his children, together with a smattering of written descriptions, have survived, and they shed light on what life was like at the trading post that was probably the first non-Indian settlement in the region. The occupants of the post consisted of ten to twelve men at all times and perhaps twice as many when packtrains and caravans came through. Packtrains, usually preceded by horsemen to make sure that the way was clear and all was well, traveled to and from the post in the dead of night. Because Delawares were known for their linguistic skills, a few of them were usually on hand to serve as interpreters. One to four sentinels kept watch from four towers erected at each corner of the double-log building. When the coast was clear, squads ventured onto the plains to hunt and fish. At daybreak, cattle were driven from a corral to the prairie, where they grazed under the watchful eyes of the sentinels. At night they were herded back to the corral. Bison numbered in the millions, and whenever they roamed too close to the post, livestock was kept in the corral to prevent stampedes. When trouble came calling, none doubted they were on their own. Construction of military forts was far in the future, the nearest settlement was in the vicinity of Pilot's Point, Texas, and only a few scattered families lived near present-day Sherman.[56]

The business of the trading post was, of course, to trade. Positioned at the edge of the great prairies, Warren built up a profitable business with Comanches, Kiowas, Wichitas, and other denizens of that vast landscape. Typically, three or four Indians were allowed to enter the fort at the same time, and they were asked to remove their belt knives and hatchets. Trading sessions, often lasting for two or three days, made liberal use of sign language. One finger represented one dollar, five fingers represented five dollars, and crossing the forefinger indicated half a dollar. Stretching out the arm and touching the shoulder was a yard measure. The traders came laden with bounty stripped from the local fauna and flora—buffalo robes and tongues, dressed and raw deer skins, beeswax—and sometimes Mexican dollars, the most common coinage of the day. In return, the traders expected blankets, gingham handkerchiefs, hoop iron with which to tip their arrows and lances, brass wire, vermillion, ochre for face paint, strips of cloth and glass beads for ornamentation—in short, products that were already wooing Native Americans from dependence on nature's bounty to the consumer nexus. Calico was sometimes the price for Mexican boys who had been taken captive by Indian bands. Freed from captivity, many of these boys joined eastbound caravans and were eventually adopted by well-to-do citizens of Fort Smith. It seems certain that Cynthia Ann Parker, perhaps the most famous captive in the Southwest, visited Warren's Trading Post with her Comanche captors. In all likelihood, this pale-faced girl's foster mother took extra care to keep Cynthia hidden from the post's occupants.[57]

Disaster struck in 1846 when Abel Warren left his prosperous trading post in the hands of a trusted friend and returned to Boston for the first time in ten years. He was married and decided to spend a few leisurely months with his bride in New England before returning to Cache Creek. And who knows? Perhaps, during the long months he spent back east, the frontier businessman had dealings with state banks whose numbers had skyrocketed since President Jackson's bitter and successful battle with the Second Bank of the United States. Maybe he learned something of New York State's failed attempt to guarantee bank deposits. Surely he heard tales of the Panic of 1837 that never made for much discussion in Indian campsites west of Fort Smith, but that had toppled banks and businesses nationwide to herald the dawn of the free banking era.

But in all probability, those concerns faded when Warren received a letter informing him that the custodian of his trading post had looted the place of its hides and furs and stock and had vanished into the wilderness without a trace.[58] Thus ended a bold enterprise in resource allocation, preserved in the memories of Indians who traded at Warren's Trading Post and in a pile of stones left for pioneers of another generation to trip over.

About ten years before Abel Warren showed up in Fort Smith, a group of twenty frontiersmen and military men departed from the newly erected Fort Gibson on a gold-seeking venture up the Arkansas River and into present-day Kansas, where roving warrior bands of Osages from Missouri and Pawnees from Nebraska had a way of bringing such expeditions to a bitter end. The company was led by Nathaniel Pryor, whose previous experience on the Lewis and Clark expedition and later success as a trader and negotiator with tribes in the Three Forks region were more than enough to qualify him to lead men into danger, especially if profits were involved. The mythic El Dorado was beyond their grasp, and they returned home empty-handed. Yet their mission was not a complete washout, for they had introduced a young adventurer of Scottish and Cherokee descent from Arkansas to his life's calling as a trader and explorer. His name was Jesse Chisholm.

Few icons resonate more in western lore than the cattle trail from Texas to the Kansas railheads that bore his name. Yet Jesse Chisholm's real significance in history lies in his work as a frontier trader who honed his negotiating skills among the Plains Indians and served as a mediator in their dealings with the Cherokee Nation, the Republic of Texas, and the United States. The list of people with whom he did business reads like a Who's Who of frontier history: the aforementioned Nathaniel Pryor; the artist George Catlin; General Henry Leavenworth and Colonel Henry Dodge, whose accomplishments were commemorated in two of the West's most important forts; and Sam Houston of Texas fame.[59] Chisholm conducted much of his trading at Chouteau's Trading Post in the Three Forks region. In 1836, he married fifteen-year-old Eliza Edwards, daughter of Creek trader James Edwards, who operated a trading post situated on the right bank of the Little River about three miles above its confluence with the North Canadian River. From there, Chisholm made trading ventures onto the prairie and earned the friendship of tribal leaders. Eventually, he moved west along the Canadian River and established a trading post near present-day Asher and later at Council Grove on the North Canadian River in what became western Oklahoma City.[60]

Chisholm's travels took him east in 1846 when he was invited to join a delegation of fifty prairie Indians, commissioners, and military personnel on a visit to the Great Father in Washington, D.C. The pilgrims rode on horseback across East Texas, boarded the steamboat *Rodolph* at Port Caddo on the Red River in Louisiana, and eventually wound their way up the Mississippi and Ohio Rivers to Wheeling, West Virginia. Perhaps en route they heard stories of the catastrophe that had befallen the *Lucy Walker* two years earlier near New Albany, Indiana, when a steamboat race ended in a fireball. Maybe the *Rodolph* captain was less inclined to gamble than Webbers Falls' most illustrious citizen, the late Joe Vann. At Wheeling, they boarded stagecoaches bound for the nation's capital. In Washington, Chisholm met with President James K. Polk on three occasions and hobnobbed with other Indians and frontiersmen who happened to be in town. Of special interest was a display of paintings by George Catlin that the artist had sketched during an expedition that had included Jesse Chisholm.[61]

Chisholm's trading activities ran the gamut of frontier commerce. In 1849 and 1850, he took advantage of the demand for Spanish mules, which the Comanches possessed in abundance, and traded them to gold seekers determined to strike it rich in the West. Apparently, he and his friend Abel Warren procured the mules with guns and ammunition.[62] He was sought after by railroad officials who were planning a transcontinental railway along the Canadian River. The leader of the survey expedition, Lieutenant A. W. Whipple, noted in his diary, "Jesse Chisholm is a Cherokee, a man of excellent sense and has travelled far among Mexicans, Americans and various tribes of Indians. He speaks—besides his native tongue—English, Spanish, Comanche, Creek, Kioway [sic], Keechi and I believe Delaware, Shawnee, Chickasaw & Choctaw."[63] As non-Indian settlers showed up in increasing numbers in the 1850s, one Indian agent complained that Chisholm and other traders were bartering guns and ammunition that the Comanches were using in their depredations along the Texas frontier. While the Civil War raged in the East, Chisholm continued to offer his assistance as a negotiator and peacemaker. As one Waco chief declared, "Chisholm heap, heap big chief—Comanche, Kiowas, Apaches and Arapahos."[64] When Texas cattlemen began to direct their northbound herds through the middle of the Indian Territory in the late 1860s, it seemed only fitting to use the famed trader's name to designate the full length of the trail.

Jesse Chisholm died in the spring of 1868. Word on the trail was that he succumbed to a helping of bear grease that had become tainted in a brass pot. He was laid to rest near the present site of Greenfield, Oklahoma, near the banks of the North Canadian River. His funeral procession ended when his blanketed body was unloaded from a wagon and placed on the soft sand of the riverbank where his grave had been prepared. Attendees included Indians and fellow frontiersmen who knew that their friend's passing marked the end of an era. One of them, a bespectacled Comanche chief named Ten Bears, took a gold peace medal from around his own neck and laid it on the chest of his fallen comrade. Wrapped now in a buffalo skin, the body was lowered into the grave and covered with dirt and rocks. An enclosure of freshly cut poles was erected, and a board inscribed with Chisholm's name and date of his death was placed above his head.[65]

Ten Bears mounted his pony and rode in a northwesterly direction to rendezvous with his band. Those who remained at the gravesite held a wake in honor of their friend, swilling whisky and firing salutes with their buffalo guns. Jesse Chisholm's eulogy, written by his friend James Mead, read in part, "He was by nature noble, chivalrous and brave. An arbitrator and peace-maker among the wild tribes of the plains and territory, beloved and respected by all."[66]

From Ireland came two brothers, John and William Shirley, who chose the Washita River valley as the location for one of old Oklahoma's most successful ventures. John, the eldest, was a practicing physician, whose career as a frontier trader began in 1859 when he obtained a license to operate a store for the Wichita Agency. The duo complemented their trade with Plains Indians with large-scale farming and ranching. Among their steadiest customers was Jesse Chisholm, who relied on the Shirleys for large orders of trade goods.[67]

When their store was burned during the Civil War, the Shirleys did what came naturally to frontier businessmen: they regrouped and opened another store, this one at Cherokee Town near present-day Pauls Valley. By 1864, John was the proud owner of a Chickasaw permit that enabled him to establish himself as a trader and rancher in the Chickasaw Nation. His customers included Plains Indians, Caddos and Delawares who needed a new place to shop after the Wichita Agency was destroyed, and refugee Cherokees who gathered in the area at the outset of the Civil War. John Shirley described buffalo hunts in which upwards of three hundred Indians, mainly from the Comanche tribe, slaughtered and skinned their way across the prairie until their ponies groaned under the weight of hides, which they traded to the Shirleys in return for merchandise.[68] When Fort Sill was established in 1869, William Shirley reopened the Wichita Agency store, developed a farm and mill, and secured contracts to supply hay for the United States Army. When the need arose for a road to transport supplies and mail from the Missouri, Kansas, and Texas Railroad depot at Atoka, Indian Territory, to Fort Sill, John Shirley received the government contract and used his business savvy to bring the road past Cherokee Town, which was already near a well-known crossing on the Washita River. It was no coincidence that the Shirleys controlled a toll bridge and ferry across the river.[69]

No strangers to danger, the Shirleys lost two employees and a significant amount of livestock to hostile warriors. During the Red River uprising of 1874–75, William decided that retreat was the better part of valor and abandoned his store. Following John Shirley's death in 1875 at the age of forty-seven, his widow sold the Cherokee Town operations and moved to Silver City on the Chisholm Trail. William remained in business and missed his chance for immortality when he declined to have the business center of Caddo County named for him, preferring that residents name it for his wife's tribe—Anadarko.[70] With William Shirley's death circa 1914, the brothers' legacy in the Indian trade faded into the commercial history of old Oklahoma.

On February 17, 1893, the *Weekly Elevator* in Fort Smith, Arkansas, reported that the federal government had made a payment the previous week of $28,000 to Kiowa, Comanche, and Apache Indians at the Anadarko Agency in western Oklahoma Territory. Pasture money, sometimes known as grass money, was apportioned by the Indian agent and paid twice annually to the Indians for the use of their land for grazing. Protecting themselves as best they could against frigid temperatures that had swept in from the north, a large majority of the three tribes were camped in the vicinity.

They were not alone. Like flies drawn to carrion, gamblers and whisky peddlers were there to siphon off what they could of funds that the Indians depended on for survival. A sixteen-year-old Apache boy and his twelve-year-old sister did not make it to the encampment. Somewhere along their fifty-mile hike to Anadarko to secure their family's share of the money, they collapsed and froze to death. Catastrophe of a different sort survives in the story of an Indian woman who arrived at the agency with an inert figure wrapped in a blanket. Demanding payment for her child, the woman refused to uncover the face of the tiny thing nestled in her arms, claiming that the light would hurt its eyes. She accepted the payment and scurried away—without her precious cargo. Authorities unwrapped the blanket and discovered a dead dog.[71]

At the dawn of the nineteenth century, the Plains tribes of North America were masters of their domain. The Five Tribes from the Southeast learned to fear the warriors who roamed the western fringes of their nations and pillaged their villages with impunity. Freighters on the Santa Fe Trail crossed the Arkansas River with trepidation, keenly aware of marauding bands that might strike at any time. Colonel A. P. Chouteau, Nathaniel Pryor, Abel Warren, Jesse Chisholm, and the Shirley brothers were savvy enough to meet them halfway—to speak their languages and honor their traditions as prerequisites to building trust and its corollary in mutually beneficial trade. By laying his peace medal on the stilled breast of Jesse Chisholm, the Comanche chief Ten Bears paid tribute not only to an old friend, but also to the symbiotic relationship between white and Indian cultures whose differences were mitigated by activities dating back to the dawn of civilization: producing, acquiring, and distributing resources.

As he bade farewell to the feisty old trader, mounted his pony, and rode into the sunset, Ten Bears surely pondered the changes that Jesse Chisholm's death signified. The end of the Civil War in 1865 marked the beginning of the Plains tribes' slide into poverty and degradation. For the next twenty-five years, Indians were systematically rounded up and restricted to reservations, many in present-day western Oklahoma. Deprived of the bison that had been the mainstay of their economy for millennia, the tribes had nowhere to turn but to their erstwhile enemies. In the Kiowa and Comanche country, survival depended on payments of pasture money at the Anadarko Agency and supplies issued twice a month from the government commissary. One wonders if Ten Bears anticipated his people's plight at century's end, when his descendants would be reduced to accepting handouts from the Great Father in Washington, D.C. What would he have thought about two Apache children found frozen on the prairie? What counsel would he have given to a woman reduced to wrapping a dead dog in a blanket to con a government official into doling out a child's meager subsidy?

A portal into those troubling days survives in the form of a paper written by General R. A. Sneed, a native of Mississippi and longtime resident of Tennessee, who operated two Indian stores from 1885 to 1890. Forty-eight years had passed since his first visit to the Comanche and Kiowa country. "It was a land that was good to look upon when I first saw it," wrote the former trader and, at the time of his writing, a director of the Oklahoma Historical Society before he died on March 15, 1936. "The Indians loved it then, as their children's children love it still. Of its people, red and white, who were in their prime when I knew them in those days, few now remain and these few will soon be gone. The legendary and traditional lore, the early history, the songs and the stories of the country and its people are of most fascinating interest and are therefore worthy of careful preservation. Once the field of strife and of many warlike scenes it has long been a land of peace. That it may ever remain the abode of a peaceful, happy and prosperous people, is my most fervent wish."[72]

Sneed's tenure as a storekeeper began in July 1885 when the Honorable J. D. C. Atkins, a congressman from Tennessee until he was named commissioner of Indian Affairs by President Grover Cleveland, appointed him as agency trader for the Comanche, Kiowa, and "Prairie Apache" tribes. He was granted authority to open and maintain two stores, one at the Fort Sill Subagency and the other at the main agency at Anadarko. To prepare for the undertaking, Sneed formed a partnership with Z. T. Collier, also from Tennessee, under the name of Collier and Sneed. Before departing for parts unknown, Sneed wondered how a son of the South would take to life on the prairie. But not for long. "Indeed, there was something about the primitive, unbroken prairie-land that was positively enchanting," he wrote, "and now, from the view-point of a lifetime twice as long as it then was, I want to say that the four years spent in the old Comanche and Kiowa country were among the happiest and most satisfactory years of my life."[73]

When Sneed arrived at his post in October 1885, there was only one railway that crossed the Indian Territory—the Missouri, Kansas, and Texas Railroad—and it deposited him at Henrietta, Texas. From there, he caught a stagecoach to Fort Sill. To his delight, his driver—known to his passengers as "Uncle Jeff"—was also a native of Tennessee. The vehicle, capable of carrying eight to ten passengers and drawn by a team of four mules, was known as a "mountain wagon" because of its four heavy-duty springs. Sneed enjoyed reminiscing with his fellow Tennessean as the coach jostled its way to Fort Sill.

A couple of days after his arrival at Fort Sill, Sneed made the thirty-five-mile trip north to Anadarko. The four trading establishments at the agency were operated by Frank Fred, Dudley Brown, the Cleveland brothers, and Reynolds. Sneed and Collier were to move into the soon-to-be-vacated establishment of Charles A. and William H. Cleveland, who were preparing to open a new store at Doan's Crossing on the Red River just south of present-day Altus, Oklahoma—a ford where northbound cattle on the Great Western Trail rivaled in number the ones that traversed the more famous Chisholm Trail. All together, there were about a dozen families at the agency and included the agent, a physician, clerks, teachers, mechanics, farmers, and traders. Although there were as yet no missionaries, there were two Indian schools in the area: the Riverside School north of the Washita River and the Kiowa School on the south side. Sneed remained at Anadarko for two or three days before returning to Fort Sill. After a day or two, he traveled back to Tennessee, where he remained for the rest of the winter to write his shopping list and prepare to move permanently to the subagency at Fort Sill.

Sneed procured goods for the agency store in Saint Louis and Chicago. Groceries, meat, basic provisions, and other stock items came from Fort Worth. Indians were particularly fond of prunes, figs, dates, raisins, and other fruits. Sneed was careful to procure only the best grade of canned goods. Shortly after returning to his post, he began making preparations for a new building near the old subagency and school located two and a half miles south of the military post. Lumber was hauled from the nearest railroad depot at Henrietta, a distance of sixty-five miles. The building was occupied as soon as it was completed, and the stock of goods was transferred on July 17, 1886. Known in the neighborhood as the "Red Store," it towered above the prairie to a height of two stories. Even though the building was an impressive thirty-six by seventy feet, the stock used up so much floor space that only narrow passageways were left for customers and clerks. The upper floor was reserved as a residence for Sneed's family, who journeyed from Tennessee to join him in November.

The Red Store was a veritable consumer paradise. Foodstuffs included staple and fancy groceries, canned goods, and cured meats. In the dry goods department, aisles were crammed with robes, blankets, shawls, silk handkerchiefs, red flannels, and blue broadcloth. Moving on to hardware, men were surely pleased to find high-grade saddles and bridles and a variety of harnesses. In particularly high demand among Sneed's Indian customers were axes, hatchets, saws, and files. The so-called hunter's ax, made of good metal and with a short handle, was all the rage for trimming and making red cedar teepee poles. For the women, there were kettles made of the best grade of brassware, frying pans, coffee pots, and utensils of every description, all available at good prices. "All had to be of the best quality," wrote Sneed, "as the Indians would not buy cheap imitation or goods of inferior material."[74]

Among Sneed and Collier's most popular items were tanned and dressed buckskins, which, for the most part, were purchased in Chicago and used in making moccasins, leggings, and clothing. The proprietors listed it as "black-tail" buckskin and assumed that it came from the Rocky Mountains. As Sneed recalled, "Practically every Indian had a complete buckskin wardrobe which was kept for ceremonial and state occasions."[75]

Sneed maintained his headquarters at the subagency at Fort Sill and made the three-and-a-half-hour buggy trip to the other agency on the Washita River about once a week. He usually spent the night and returned to Fort Sill the next day. The Anadarko store's manager, Webb Hendrix, was his partner's brother-in-law. Sneed's fastest trip to Anadarko was prompted when Hendrix, fearing trouble from agitated Kiowas, fired off a telegram to the subagency that read simply, "Come at once; important." "That time," wrote Sneed, "I made the drive in three hours—a good record, over roads that were none of the best."[76] The trader leaves us to wonder about the crisis that sent him flying across the prairie at breakneck speed.

Comanche, the lingua franca of the southern plains, was apparently not terribly hard to learn. Yet Sneed picked up little of the language: "While I might have learned to speak Comanche, I did not do so for it was best for the manager of the trading establishment not to speak or understand the vernacular of his Indian patrons, as, otherwise, they would have monopolized too much of his time holding converse with him."[77] He did, however, learn to express monetary values and numbers to such an extent that he earned a reputation for being able to sell as many goods as any clerk in his establishment.

Even though Sneed did not become fluent in native tongues, he learned enough about his customers to gain a respect that transcended the cultural divide. His description of the people who frequented his stores merits quoting in its entirety, for it provides a rare glimpse into Indian ways of doing business on the eve of non-Indian settlement in the Kiowa and Comanche country. If Sneed's paean to Indian integrity seems hard to reconcile with the squalor of the encampment at Anadarko in the winter of 1893, then perhaps we should keep in mind that American history is no stranger to paradox. The twin pillars of westward expansion, democracy and capitalism, were at loggerheads from day one of the great American experiment when making money in the marketplace privileged the few against the many. Paradox in another guise reared its head in the waning days of the frontier as Indians were swept into the capitalist nexus and rewarded with poverty and the suppression of tribal traditions. We are left to wonder if Sneed thought about such things as he scurried around his store, mustering his limited linguistic skills to introduce his customers to the marvels of American manufacturing.

> The Indian people were remarkable for their truthfulness and honesty. I seldom had occasion to go to their camps to make collections—they always came in and settled their own accounts. Their sense of honor and honesty and their regard for their word when they had made a promise were almost universally above question. If an Indian died owing a debt, his relatives always paid it. The lowering of their morale did not come until the white people came to live among them. They were keen traders and did not hesitate to take advantage of the other party to a deal if opportunity was afforded, but once they gave a promise, its performance was regarded as a sacred obligation. Though they were unable to read and write, many of them seemed to be skilled in the art of diplomacy.[78]

In 1887, R. A. Sneed went to Saint Louis and Chicago to buy goods for the agency. On his return trip, he took a detour to his home in Jackson, Tennessee, for a brief visit. He resumed his trip in the company of William Davis, an "industrious and trustworthy young negro" who had worked for him on various occasions and accepted an offer of employment at the store at the Fort Sill Subagency.

The trip was an eye-opener for a young man who had never ventured far beyond his Tennessee home. Upon crossing the Red River, Sneed noticed that his companion was taking a keen interest in the unbroken range. He asked him what was on his mind.

"Mr. Sneed," he replied, "who cleared all this land? It sure must have been during slavery times—there hain't no stumps. It look like oil fields that's been long turn out."[79]

Sneed did not record his answer. Maybe he explained to his puzzled companion that, of all the changes being visited upon that vast landscape, clearing trees was not among them. Perhaps, as they bounced northward toward Fort Sill, he told Davis about the advance of commerce on the prairies, and about the services that the subagency was providing to the one-time lords of the western plains.

One imagines the duo continuing in silence, with R. A. Sneed fretting over the status of his shipments from Chicago and Saint Louis, and William Davis pondering his unlikely position in the vanguard of the businessman's frontier.

CHAPTER FIVE

Territorial Trading

They knew no limit in their hospitality toward each other and exhibited their friendship in the truest sense of the word. It was a pleasure to live among people of this disposition and few there are who would not heartily welcome a return of all the hardships just for the sake of living again among people with such hearts of gold.

W. A. West, Cherokee Outlet homesteader

For all intents and purposes, the economies in the eastern United States and the Indian country west of Fort Smith functioned as parallel universes for the first three quarters of the nineteenth century. Except for slender conduits of commerce through which raw materials were exported and manufactured goods were imported to meet the needs of the Indian trade and military outposts, the land destined to become Oklahoma was a land apart. In a replay of economic development during the colonial and early national periods, trade depended heavily on barter and commodity money, and goings-on back east that roiled lives and rearranged relationships made scarcely a ripple. President Andrew Jackson's assault on the Second Bank of the United States that ended badly for proponents of centralized banking; turf wars between state and national banks; New York State's attempt to protect depositors from penury when their banks failed, which they did with unsettling regularity; the Panic of 1837 that toppled banks and businesses—these and other episodes that shaped American banking and commerce might as well have happened on another planet. Eventually, eastern patterns of economic development would make their presence felt in the trans-Mississippi West in ways peculiar to the frontier. But for many years, producing, acquiring, and distributing resources in the West remained primitive affairs, hardly commensurate with the commerce gaining momentum east of the Mississippi River.

Resource allocation on the frontier might have been primitive by eastern standards, but it was far from moribund, and it survives in the form of memories recorded by interviewers in the service of the Works Progress Administration in Oklahoma in the 1930s. Just as these itinerant scholars captured firsthand accounts of the riverboat trade, so, too, did they record the first stirrings of business in remote hamlets and isolated homesteads. Even though their interviews do not reach back as far as freighting on the Santa Fe Trail or cutting deals at the original Indian trading posts, they provide glimpses into the ad hoc commerce that enabled pioneers to secure a foothold in their new homes.

One of those interviewed for the WPA project was Kate Goodman, born near Marlow in the Chickasaw Nation on August 4, 1891. Her family lived in a one-room log house until the Kiowa-Comanche–Plains Apache Reservation and the Wichita-Caddo Reserve were opened to non-Indian settlement on August 6, 1901. At that point, Kate's father, a farmer and cattleman, registered for land and secured 160 acres near Hobart, a tiny village that became the county seat of Kiowa County. Subsequent cessions in 1906 of tribal grazing lands collectively known as the Big Pasture completed the allotment process for the Kiowa-Comanche–Plains Apache tribes, thereby ending homesteading in Oklahoma Territory.[1]

Kate's earliest memories were of cold and blizzards. "My father was out in the mountains rounding up the cattle," recalled Kate. "The snow came in through the top and other open places in our house and covered my mother's bed. At first she nearly froze but as the snow fell upon her the weight of the snow and the covers became so heavy that she went to sleep and slept until my father came home. She was so used to the cold and rough ways of the pioneer life that she soon forgot the experience."[2] Kate's father took heed of his wife's near-death experience and, in true pioneer tradition, bartered with his Indian neighbors for firewood in return for beef. An entirely different dimension of trading with Indians

was revealed when Kate's father and other cattlemen drove their livestock north to the railhead in Cheyenne, Oklahoma Territory. Cattle had
a way of straying into the Kiowa country, and savvy Indians learned early
on that their owners would pay to get them back.

Exposed on the lone prairie, Kate and her family did not take trips to
the grocery store for granted. "After the first year there my father went
to El Reno and got a wagon load of groceries," recalled Kate. "It took
about one week to make the trip and I remember how afraid we were
when my father left us alone over night."[3] Nor did Kate take consumer
goods for granted. She concluded her interview in November 1937 with
a tribute to her mother's sewing machine that had surely mended many
a garment in the days when new clothes were the stuff of daydreams:
"I am using my mother's Singer sewing machine that she brought from
Texas, in 1888, it is very old-fashioned but makes a very nice stitch."[4]

A far different perspective of the Kiowa and Comanche country
comes to us from Charles E. Boyer. Born in Maryland in 1858, Charles
moved with his family to Philadelphia when he was fifteen. Like so many
young men of his generation, he decided in 1881 "to leave Pennsylvania
and go West, adventuring."[5] Charles eventually joined the army and was
stationed at Fort Sill, where non-Indians were a rarity and government
supplies arrived regularly by wagon and team in a region known simply
as the "Indian Nation." He recalled watching dances in an area of Fort
Sill that was later developed as the polo grounds. Sometimes the Indians danced in anger, and sometimes they danced to celebrate a joyous
occasion.

In Fort Sill's early days, the Indians brought furs to a trading post on
a creek about a mile west of town. "Very little money could be found,"
said Boyer, "so they traded. The white people shipped the furs from the
northern part of the state back east."[6] Later, the Red Store was erected
about two and a half miles north of Fort Sill. As the Indians began to
receive government stipends, old-fashioned bartering yielded to shopping sprees. One imagines the storekeeper, R. A. Sneed, and his assistant
from Tennessee, William Davis, bustling through the Red Store's crowded
aisles to assist Boyer with the purchase of a hunter's ax, or perhaps a set
of buckskins to dazzle friends and family back east.

When he was living in Philadelphia, evidence of western bounty
was not hard to come by: "I have stood on a street in Philadelphia and
watched big shipments of buffalo hides unloaded there. I often tried to

find out where so many furs could be found. 'Out West' was about the best answer I could hear, but when I came here I soon learned that the buffalo hides came from this Indian country." Boyer counted himself fortunate to return to Oklahoma many years after his youthful adventures and help "to build and watch Fort Sill grow."[7]

Far to the east of Fort Sill, Morris Brown, whose family had emigrated from Tennessee, was growing up in Poteau, Indian Territory. Known early on as "Poteau Switch," the tiny outpost had little to offer a young man with big dreams. "It was just a wide place in the road," recalled Brown, "with a general store, depot, hotel, livery stable, blacksmith shop and that's about all."[8] Heeding the lure of adventure, Brown drifted to the Comanche and Caddo country. He described western Indians as wild, fierce, and utterly disinclined to work, seemingly content to draw rations and horses from the Indian agency at Anadarko. The Indians liked people from Arkansas and despised Texans; Brown was mute on their attitude toward people from the Indian Territory and Tennessee. "We got so we always told all the Indians we were from Arkansas," said Brown.[9]

As near as Brown could tell, Caddo and Comanche Indians would trade anything they could get their hands on in spite of the near certainty that non-Indian trading partners would cheat them. But they had an ace in the hole: if they suffered from buyer's remorse, they knew they could count on the Indian agent to enforce a strict returns policy. As Brown explained, "If you traded a gun to an Indian for a horse, for instance, and the Indian decided he was sick of his trade or if his wife was dissatisfied the agent would come and make you give the Indian back his horse and you could not get your gun back, either."[10] These perpetual traders were not without a sense of humor. Brown recalled, "They would come riding up like they meant to scalp a fellow and then they would say, 'Howya John?' They called everyone John."[11]

One wonders what the Indian agent might have said about some fun-loving Comanches who were attending a dance near Caddo. Bell Haney Airington, a Chickasaw from Caddo, was there with her baby in her lap and discovered that commodity money comes in many guises. "They had a young Indian girl all dressed in white with jewels on her arms and limbs and they were offering to trade her for nine cows and calves, but no one traded for her."[12]

While Morris Brown was stretching his wings in the Kiowa and Comanche country, Hoyette North White's father was getting into the retail business on his farm a mile west of Harrah in central Oklahoma Territory. Intending to start a townsite, White built a structure to house a general store. As was customary among pioneer storekeepers, he reserved the back of the store for his family's residence. His ambitions of founding a town came to naught when Frank Harrah beat him to it. Derailed but by no means defeated, White went on to build a thriving business, particularly as the word spread throughout Kickapoo country that he was a fair and even bilingual retailer. "They never came singly," recalled Hoyette, "always several at one time and always wore their native costumes, buckskin beaded jackets, leggings, moccasins, and blankets. Father soon learned enough of their language to trade with them. If he didn't understand, they would walk behind the counter and get it themselves." Hoyette noticed that the Kickapoos were reluctant to pay for everything at once. "Each article bought, they paid for then; it seemed confusing to them to wait until they finished trading to pay for, all at once."[13]

As a young woman destined for domesticity, Hoyette was drawn to the Kickapoos' culinary habits. When her father killed a beef, they asked for the head, feet, entrails, and stomach. They cooked the head in much the same way that Hoyette's family did, by simmering it into a sauce. Entrails and stomach were cut into small pieces and cooked with cracked corn.

Kickapoo friendliness sometimes bordered on what might be perceived today as a lack of boundaries. One day, when Hoyette's mother was making peach preserves, several Kickapoo women were enticed by the aroma and entered the family residence in the back of the store. They promptly stuck their fingers in the preserves and licked them clean. "They ate nearly all of them, just chattering and eating," recalled Hoyette. "Mother didn't try to stop them."[14]

Lucy Sweet Wilson, reputed to be the first white woman to settle in Old Greer County in present-day southwestern Oklahoma, arrived in April 1884 and helped her father, a surveyor, lay out the townsite for Mangum. Old Greer County (present-day Greer, Harmon, Jackson, and a portion of Beckham Counties) was almost entirely occupied by cattle whose owners resented the intrusion of settlers, or "nesters," as they were disparagingly known. Texas's claim to Old Greer County fueled a jurisdictional dispute that was not settled until March 16, 1896, when the U.S. Supreme Court directed that Old Greer County be made a part of the Oklahoma Territory. Residents were relieved to wind up in the

Oklahoma Territory because, as everybody knew, the weather was awful in Texas.[15]

Resolution of Old Greer County's identity crisis was still far in the future when Lucy's father traded for a log cabin. (Lucy was silent on his part of the deal.) Tapping into his frontier ingenuity, Wilson used flattened tin cans to seal the cracks between the logs, thus shedding light (or at least reflection) on cowboys' designation of Mangum as "The Tin City."[16] Until entrepreneurs began hauling wood from the Indian Territory, mesquite roots served as the main source of fuel in the area. Commodity money came in the form of buffalo bones that littered the prairie, which people gathered in wagons for fertilizer and delivered to Mangum and Vernon, Texas, to trade for foodstuffs and manufactured goods. When he was not killing rattlesnakes—a task that some early settlers in Old Greer County accomplished at the rapid-fire clip of three per day—Wilson maintained a general merchandise store in part of his home, where he traded canned food and ammunition to Indians in exchange for furs. Enticed by modern ways, Lucy bought most of her clothing from Sanger Brothers Dry Goods Company in Dallas, Texas, until someone astounded her with a catalog from Montgomery Ward. She made the switch and remained a loyal Montgomery Ward customer for more than fifty years.[17]

A year after the Wilsons laid out the Mangum townsite, Clara Tuton and her husband from Seymour, Texas, endured two weeks in a mule-drawn covered wagon to secure a foothold north of town. They arrived in the area in February 1885 with little more than a camping outfit. Her husband wasted little time in trading a couple of horses for property on the North Fork River, where the family lived in a half-dugout (a home consisting of a dirt cellar topped by a crude, aboveground wooden structure) and established a farm. Kiowas often showed up at their farmstead to beg for provisions. Their persistence escalated when they realized that the Tutons had a cure for a sweet tooth. "One thing, especially, that they liked was syrup," recalled Clara. "We usually kept our syrup in a jug and sometimes we would avoid giving them any. One time we had about half a gallon of syrup in the jug and had it setting on a shelf in the dugout. We told them we did not have any syrup. One of the squaws pointed to the jug on the shelf and said, 'Heap syrup, heap syrup.' We then had to divide it with them."[18] Of greater concern to the Tutons than Kiowas bent on a sugar high were Comanches on the prowl for horses and cattle.

Clara's husband freighted goods from Quanah, Texas, with a four-horse team for the munificent sum of a dollar a day. She recalled, "This was considered good wages. The roads were awfully bad and it usually took him four days to make the trip. Usually he would take a load of wheat to Quanah and bring back furniture or any other kind of merchandise."[19] There was a straw bridge across the Red River, which was fine in dry weather. Yet when the river was up, there was nothing to do but wait.

R. Beaumont, whose father served with the Fourteenth Vermont Volunteers and was wounded at Gettysburg, arrived in what was then Greer County, Texas, in February 1888 in a caravan of five wagons, lured by "cheap land and free range for cattle." Settling near Mangum, his family traded an ox team to Daddy Hays, a neighbor, for a two-room house, which was moved to their place. Additional rooms were added later. Beaumont recalled that supplies were often exhausted before wagons could return from Vernon or Quanah, Texas, with provisions. Such was the extent of frontier scarcity that his mother once gave a stagecoach driver twenty-five cents to purchase a spool of thread in Quanah. "Things of that kind could not be found in Mangum," said Beaumont.[20] Wheat was worth twenty-five to fifty cents a bushel, cotton was worth four cents a pound, and cows could be purchased for three to five dollars a head. Cattle came into circulation as commodity money when the elder Beaumont traded several head for farming tools. To protect his family from Indian predations, Beaumont's father bought a Springfield rifle at a store in the Navaho Mountains east of present-day Altus. Settlers were on high alert during the Indian scare of 1890 that was precipitated by the fatal shooting of Poaline, a Kiowa subchief at Byrd Mountain. Although the dreaded attack never materialized, settlers prepared for the worst by holding weekly drills.[21]

The Indian scare of 1890 had faded into memory by the time J. B. McReynolds arrived in Mangum by covered wagon in 1892. As barter was the main method of resource allocation, his sister traded two yearlings for a sewing machine. Given pioneers' penchant for thrift, the sewing machine was no doubt still in use when the yearlings were long gone. "There was very little money in the country in those days," said

McReynolds. "Ministers were paid by donations, such as a wagon, team or groceries." According to McReynolds, a Presbyterian congregation once bought a new surrey for their reverend.[22] (Western commerce would have been familiar to seventeenth-century ministers in Virginia who received their pay in bales of tobacco and college registrars in New England who accepted old cows for tuition.)[23]

Few settlers became better acquainted with barter and commodity money than physicians. Dr. G. P. Cherry came to Mangum from Garland, Texas, in 1889 and set up his practice in the old Gilland Building on the south side of the square. Instead of paying cash for their doctor bills, settlers usually traded produce and yearlings. Dr. Cherry acquired three hundred head of cattle from his neighbors by ministering to their aches and pains. But the work was not for the faint of heart: twenty-mile trips on foot and horseback, sometimes in subzero weather, were all in a day's work. Dr. Cherry recalled one such trip to Turkey Creek in 1896 that might have brought his career to a bitter end: "I felt more like sitting down than walking but I knew if I ever stopped I'd never be able to make the rest of the trip."[24]

In the absence of dentists, territorial doctors often pulled teeth. The most common ailments were rattlesnake bites (hardly surprising, given the slaughter visited upon those unfortunate creatures) and injuries inflicted by horses and cattle. Bucking broncos inflicted the most damage. "There were no rodeos in those days since the 'real thing' was so common," said Dr. Cherry. In reference to his lengthy trips to treat patients, Dr. Cherry closed his interview with a paean to wellness as the best preventative medicine—sound advice in his day as well as ours. "People, however, were in much better condition physically than they are today, due to their active outdoor occupations," he reflected.[25]

President Andrew Jackson's harsh policy of banishing Cherokees from the Southeast and relocating them to present-day Oklahoma was mitigated to some extent by the Treaty of New Echota (1835), which granted the newcomers seven million acres to the west of their new homeland. The region was known as the Cherokee Outlet, and until buffalo herds were decimated and non-Indian settlers began to cast their covetous eyes on its hardy grasses and fertile valleys, it served as prime real estate for hunting. After the Civil War, the Cherokees paid for their allegiance to the Confederacy in the Reconstruction Treaties of 1866, which stripped them of their hunting grounds and designated the eastern third of the Outlet as surplus, where land was set aside to accommodate smaller tribes.[26] From 1866 to 1893, the Cherokee Outlet served as prime grazing land for Texas cattlemen and was crisscrossed by cattle trails that connected Texas ranches to railheads in Kansas and the northern ranges.

Long before the Cherokee Outlet was opened to non-Indian settlement in the Run of 1893, the region's sparse and more or less permanent population included soldiers, civilians who served the military in various capacities, and overland freighters. That population included Neely Mason. He was born in 1884 in Fort Supply on the western edge of the Cherokee Outlet, where his grandmother was employed as a nurse at the army hospital. Mason's father, a Civil War veteran, migrated to Dodge City, Kansas, after the war and tended bar in some of the cow town's saloons before taking up ranching in No Man's Land (later, the Oklahoma Panhandle). According to Mason, the commercial life of the community centered on Lee and Reynolds (later Lee and Ferguson), a government contractor that maintained large herds of mules and oxen for freighting over the plains. In addition to large cedar-picket buildings and corrals, the firm maintained a store with a large stock of merchandise. Mason recalled that Lee and Reynolds satisfied "every need and requirement of the civilian population of this section of the southwest at that time."[27] Buyers paid for hides and furs with their own circulating specie, and the Lee and Reynolds store accepted it at face value in payment for supplies. Lee and Reynolds also owned and operated the stagecoach line between Dodge City and Fort Killiot, Texas, via Fort Supply.[28]

In the closing decades of the nineteenth century, mule skinners and bull drivers who showed up at Fort Supply usually had no trouble finding work with Lee and Reynolds. The best hands earned as much as one hundred dollars a month for their hard and hazardous work. Yet crossing over the range at century's end was not the same lonely adventure that W. B. Napton experienced in 1857 and wrote about in the *Kansas City Star* in January 1902. Settlements, trading posts, and forts now dotted the Plains. Cheyennes and other Plains tribes that had once struck terror into the hearts of Santa Fe Trail freighters were now receiving annuities at Cantonment (present-day Canton) and trekking to Fort Supply to draw beef, rations, and other supplies from the U.S. government. When railroads came through Woodward, Lee and Reynolds suspended operations, and the freighting business went the way of the steamboats.

Pressure to open the Cherokee Outlet to non-Indian settlement culminated in the Run of September 16, 1893, the fourth and largest land run to date. W. A. West joined the melee near Hunnewell, Kansas, and succeeded in staking his claim. Before long, he was hauling his grain to Ponca City. He was also trading chickens for wood, which he used for fuel, with members of the Ponca tribe. When West approached his bartering partners and inquired about prices, they indicated the amount of "heap wood," as they called it, they would give him by holding one hand about twelve inches from the ground and saying, "two chickens." Then, they raised their hands slightly and said, "three chickens." Four chickens usually sufficed for a full load of wood.[29]

West paid tribute to frontier democracy when he recalled that his neighbors "were all of one class" and depended on their neighbors, borrowing and lending as circumstances warranted and helping one another through the hard times. "They knew no limit in their hospitality toward each other and exhibited their friendship in the truest sense of the word," he reflected. "It was a pleasure to live among people of this disposition and few there are who would not heartily welcome a return of all the hardships just for the sake of living again among people with such hearts of gold."[30]

West was by no means the first to extol frontier democracy. More than a half century before the Cherokee Outlet was opened to non-Indian settlement, the French writer Alexis de Tocqueville was struck by what he called "equality of condition" at the heart of American culture. "The more I advanced in the study of American society," wrote Tocqueville in the 1830s, "the more I perceived that this equality of condition is the fundamental fact from which all others seem to be derived and the central point at which all my observations constantly terminated."[31]

Andrew Oiler Crist's adventure in the Cherokee Outlet began in a coal car with a hundred others. He jumped off the train and staked his lot at Pond Creek, where he assumed the county seat would be located. Crist, his brother D. H., and William McKinley put up a tent on their first night in the Outlet and started business the next day as a grocery store under the no-nonsense name, Crist and McKinley. They lived in the tent for a couple of weeks until construction of a proper building could be completed. They moved into the building in December 1893 and journeyed to the Long Brothers Wholesale House in Kansas City to stock up on goods.

Pioneer optimism soured when the Rock Island Railroad bypassed Pond Creek. Desperate for supplies, settlers faced a stark choice: they could either pack their meager possessions and leave, or they could take bold action to secure a stop on the railroad. Some opted to skedaddle, but enough stayed in the area to spawn an uprising that does not quite square with romanticized images of law-abiding yeoman farmers. While Crist and McKinley was doing its best to secure supplies from Kansas wholesalers and prevent disaster, irate settlers were organizing to tear up tracks, pilfer railroad ties, and wreck the trains. When United States marshal E. D. Nix tried to calm an excited Pond Creek crowd, he found himself facing "a hundred citizens lined up with Winchesters and shotguns in hand."[32] Railroad officials responded by posting guards to protect property, and for six months, the area around Pond Creek was plunged into guerilla warfare. Crist recalled one incident that turned fatal for a shipment of livestock: "One day, a load of cattle from the north was to be shipped south, so the people got together and sent men ahead to warn the trainmen to stop the train, that men were working on the rail. They tried to flag the train down, but they would not stop, so the train was derailed and the cars were turned over, killing some of the cattle. The Railroad Company sent men and guards to rebuild the tracks."[33]

Prairie rebels were vindicated when railroad officials promised to stop at Pond Creek twice a day. With railroad service resumed, the violence ended, and Crist and McKinley's business "grew by leaps and bounds."[34] Throughout the insurrection, the storekeepers accepted the barter of commodities in the form of eggs, chickens, hogs, cattle, and produce from their customers as payment for grocery bills.

Not only was Crist a storekeeper schooled in the ways of insurrection, but he also became a farmer in 1895 when he bought a farm near Pond Creek. In a pattern that typifies frontier multitasking, he worked in his store by day and returned to his farm in the evenings to break sod. Mother Nature worked against him in 1896 but was kinder in 1897, when Crist and his neighbors enjoyed a bumper crop of wheat and good prices for their cattle. Prosperity on the farm meant boom times for retailers, and Crist and McKinley was ready. "The farmers bought drills, cultivators, plows and all kinds of farm implements."[35] Such was the extent of his good fortune in both farming and retailing that, in

1903, Crist sold his farm and added furniture, dry goods, and rugs to his expanding stock of merchandise.

While settlers in western Indian Territory were adapting themselves to the exigencies of frontier commerce, their counterparts in the eastern part were expanding on commercial networks established during the era of riverboat trade and developing new patterns along the way. Economic development in eastern Indian Territory was woven into the histories of the dominant tribes—Chickasaws and Choctaws in the south, and Creeks and Cherokees in the north. Their relocation to the wilderness west of Fort Smith was precipitated by white incursions into their southeastern homelands. A trickle of migration in the early nineteenth century became a flood when President Andrew Jackson launched his jeremiad. Even Supreme Court chief justice John Marshall's ruling in *Worcester v. Georgia* (1832) that Indian nations were distinct and independent political communities endowed with natural rights, and therefore entitled to federal protection of their sovereignty, was not enough to derail Old Hickory in his determination to send them packing beyond the Mississippi.

The first stirrings of the Chickasaw migration were felt in 1818, when tribal leaders ceded their lands in western Kentucky and Tennessee to the U.S. government in the Treaty of Old Town. The Chickasaws managed to avoid the severe privations that other southeastern tribes experienced during the period of forced removal. Nevertheless, they suffered a loss of tribal identity that lasted until the eve of the Civil War, when Chickasaw delegates gathered at a convention in Tishomingo, Indian Territory, in 1856 to ratify a new constitution. During the tribe's prewar period of economic growth, cotton, corn, and other grains constituted the principle crops, and prairie lands became prime pasture for horses, cattle, sheep, hogs, and goats. Already famous for breeding horses, Chickasaw breeders took advantage of their navigable waterways to establish markets for their horses and cattle in Arkansas, Missouri, and Louisiana.[36]

After the Civil War, Chickasaw autonomy and independence were threatened as cattle ranchers, railroads, and non-Indian immigrants encroached on tribal lands. In a pattern replicated with the advance of non-Indian settlement in the eastern United States and then in old Oklahoma after the Civil War, Chickasaw commerce was based on bartering and commodity money. Such was the experience of Zack Redford, who was fifteen when his family moved from Texas, crossed the Red River in a wagon hauled by a yoke of oxen on Brown's Ferry at Gainesville, and settled in the Chickasaw Nation. As a young man, Zack was captivated to find that most people in his environs wore six-shooters: "If you saw somebody without one he was usually a preacher."[37]

Redford provided a glimpse into Chickasaw commerce in his memory of a man who ran a lumber mill: "People exchanged articles instead of using money. They didn't have so very much money but got along pretty well without it. If someone would want to buy lumber from him, but didn't have the money to pay for it, he would pay for the lumber with a hog, yearling or work it out. It was easier to get by then for the neighbors shared anything they had—and they were always paid back what they loaned no matter how small the amount nor how large it was."[38] A corollary of ad hoc commerce on the frontier was the absence of socioeconomic distinctions that caught Alexis de Tocqueville's attention during his American sojourn in the 1830s and that W. A. West discerned in the Cherokee Outlet. "There were only two homes better than ours," said Redford, "so when describe it [*sic*] don't think that I was ashamed of it. Everyone had houses similar and they were all we knew."[39] He went on to describe a two-room log house, complete with a fireplace and a stove that was perfectly suited to his family's modest needs.

Redford contributed to economic development by driving a freight wagon for his father. He typically delivered produce to Gainesville, Texas, in a wagon drawn by eight yoke of oxen, with a trailer fastened behind for good measure, and returned to the Chickasaw Nation laden with provisions. The round-trip usually required eight to ten days.

Coupled with egalitarianism was a business culture based on honesty and fair dealing. C. B. Queid was born in Cook County, Texas, on October 13, 1870, and crossed the Red River near Gainesville on a ferry in 1886. He settled near Tishomingo in the Chickasaw Nation to buy cowhides from the Indians and wound up buying anything they had to sell. Queid praised an ethos that warrants attention in business schools today: "I have been living among the two tribes ever since I came to this country and have had lots of dealings with them; I have found them to be just as honest as they can be and they are all my friends. I never had any trouble with any one of them and they are good neighbors to live by. We did not have to lock our doors every time we left the house when the Indians were our neighbors but I cannot say that much for my own race of people."[40]

J. M. Lane, who moved from Arkansas to the Indian Territory in a covered wagon in 1882, was another of the Chickasaw Nation's earliest non-Indian settlers. In 1886, he secured a job hauling freight for William L. Byrd, who operated a store in Stonewall and became a candidate for governor of the Chickasaw Nation. "Those were turbulent times for politicians," recalled Lane, who was clearly fascinated by the political machinations in his adopted home.[41] According to Lane, Governor Byrd looked after the interests of all his constituents, Indian and non-Indian alike, "regardless of their political beliefs and he also was considerate of the landed rights of the white citizens."[42] Lane and his wife went on to secure work at the Roff Ranch—he presumably as a cowhand and his wife as a cook—in 1888 for the grand sum of twenty-five dollars a month. Even as Lane contended with typical frontier challenges ranging from roving outlaw bands to grass fires, he was witness to the stirrings of a revolution in transportation: "We drove our cattle to Atoka to ship them over the M.K. & T. Railroad, which was the first railroad across the Territory."[43]

Admired for egalitarianism and honesty, Chickasaw culture embraced two elements that did not bode well for inclusion in the dominant civilization's expanding webs of commerce: "queer customs," as Lane described them, and a yen for whiskey. What Lane dismissed as superstition were actually spiritual traditions that are not so different from those maintained by other premodern cultures, but that clashed with Anglo-American culture and its foundation in Christian teachings. Even more ominous for the Chickasaws was their fondness for strong drink. "The Chickasaws were very fond of whiskey," said Lane, "and would give anything asked for a quart of firewater after they began drinking. I have seen them give a horse if they had no money."[44] Neither traditional customs nor a weakness for alcohol served the Chickasaws well when free-market capitalism cloaked in the mantle of Christianity swept them into the consumer nexus.

East of the Chickasaw Nation was the Choctaw Nation, and its history in Oklahoma began in 1820 when tribal leaders in central Mississippi signed the Treaty of Doak's Stand. With the stroke of a pen, Choctaw leaders exchanged their rich cotton lands for approximately

Choctaw Light Horsemen (law enforcement officers) at Antlers, Indian Territory, 1893. Courtesy Western History Collections, University of Oklahoma Libraries (Phillips Collection, No. 1523 SE2-2).

thirteen million acres in the Canadian, Kiamichi, Arkansas, and Red River watersheds. A few settlers made the trek westward in the 1820s, but it was not until President Jackson pushed his Removal Act through Congress in 1830 that most Choctaws bowed to the inevitable. Commercial centers complete with U.S. post offices, blacksmith shops, and retail establishments coalesced at Boggy Depot in the west, Doaksville in the southeast, and Skullyville in the northeast.[45] Law enforcement developed in the form of the famed Light Horsemen whose skills in the saddle and endurance on manhunts won the everlasting respect of U.S. deputy marshals with whom they often cooperated.[46]

Like the other southeastern tribes, the Choctaws paid for their allegiance to the Confederacy by ceding land to the U.S. government for the creation of reservations for Plains tribes and acceding to demands for expanded railroad rights-of-way. During treaty negotiations after the Civil War that opened the floodgates to non-Indian incursions into Indian land, Choctaw chief Allen Wright suggested "Oklahoma"—*okla humma* in his native tongue, which translates roughly as "red people"—as a suitable name for the western territory that was relinquished to the federal government. In spite of its best efforts, the Choctaw government was powerless to prevent the ensuing exploitation by railroads, non-Indian ranchers, coal miners, and entrepreneurs. Even though it was the largest of the Indian nations, the Choctaw Nation in 1890 maintained only a few primitive roads to the "States" and had no banks at all.[47]

One of the Choctaw Nation's first entrepreneurs was Jesse Green Robb. Born in Georgia in 1854, he moved to the Indian Territory in 1880 and settled in what was then Sugar Loaf County. After teaching in the village of Le Flore for four years, Robb engaged in merchandising. He obtained a special permit from Choctaw governor Edmond McCurtain that required him to pay the Choctaw Nation fifteen of every one thousand dollars' worth of business he transacted. Early on, Robb bought his goods at Fort Smith and freighted them by wagon to Le Flore, a distance of sixty-five miles. He later moved his business to Cavanal, a location near the present town of Wister. All traces of Cavanal have disappeared. Like C. B. Queid in the Chickasaw Nation, Robb always felt welcomed by his Choctaw neighbors and safe from thieves, perhaps owing to the tenacious Choctaw Light Horsemen. At the same time, he recognized the danger posed by liquor traffickers who passed easily across the porous border between Arkansas and Sugar Loaf County. Despite the best efforts of the federal government through the courts and federal marshals, "that evil existed then, as now, to an alarming degree."[48]

Hiram Quigley was ten years old when his family came to the Choctaw Nation in 1866 and settled near Boggy Depot, where one Captain Hester operated a retail establishment. Supplies were freighted in from Fort Smith, 160 miles east of Boggy Depot, and sometimes required as many as 10 wagons and teams. Commodity money in the form of hides stripped from deer, coyote, beaver, skunk, and other hapless creatures were sold or traded for groceries. Quigley recalled wagons returning from Fort Smith laden with barrels of flour.

In 1880, Quigley quit farming to work for a cattle outfit for fifty cents per day, plus room and board. Charles Floor owned the toll bridge spanning Boggy Creek, and he operated with a charter that prevented noncitizens (i.e., non-Choctaws) from fording the creek for several miles in each direction. Choctaws crossed the bridge at no charge; everyone else ponied up twenty-five cents for each conveyance. Judging from the traffic across Boggy Creek, Floor had quite a business. "I have seen as many as three hundred northern people cross the toll bridge in one day on their way to Texas," recalled Quigley.[49]

Like Dr. G. P. Cherry of Mangum, E. K. Hargrave's father spent his pioneer days tending to the sick and wounded. From his home in String-town in the Choctaw Nation, Dr. Hargrave traveled as far as Atoka and Muskogee, Indian Territory. Ailments such as malaria, typhoid, and influenza often turned deadly in an absence of timepieces to help patients regulate their medications. The other problem—a lack of money—was more easily solved with bartering and commodity money. "Indians, like the settlers, did not have very much money," recalled Hargrave when queried about his father's experiences as a pioneer doctor, "and father took everything he could in the way of supplies that the family could use, such as; meat, potatoes, chickens, corn, yards of materials issued to the Indians by the Government, beaded gloves, saddle blankets, and soap."[50] On one occasion, Dr. Hargrave mortgaged his saddle horse to pay for an order of medicine, which was shipped to him. His rounds often took a week, and he made them on horseback unless he managed to flag down the Katy (frontier shorthand for the Missouri, Kansas, and Texas Railroad) for a ride. It was not until 1917 that he gave up horseback riding and bought a buggy. His relief from saddle sores was short-lived, because he died the following year.

William Allred's father drove a team of steers into the Indian Territory in 1896, moved into an abandoned log house, and made it his home. By trading and buying cattle, he built an impressive herd of several hundred free-range cattle. Allred's main trading post was at McAlester. He sold cattle to buyers who came through the area, some of whom stuck around for picnics in the summer that sometimes lasted up to three days—plenty of time to enjoy some companionship and scout for cattle to buy. Hog buyers, too, frequented the Choctaw Nation with wagons to transport any swine they deemed worthy of buying. Anyone who has seen Rodgers and Hammerstein's *Oklahoma!* would not be surprised to read Allred's account of traveling salesmen who went from house to house in the fall, "walking and carrying two suitcases of beads, cheap rings, all kinds of cheap trinkets and some bolts of cloth to make dresses out of. There was another peddler who went about in a hack selling cheap cloth and dresses, men's pants and shirts. If they could not sell for cash they would take chickens, eggs, butter, furs and hides."[51] In Rodgers's and Hammerstein's imaginations, peddlers might also be persuaded to take the farmer's daughter for a bride.

The Creek Indians' removal to the Indian Territory followed a familiar pattern: decimation through war and disease and the withering of traditions as non-Indians settled in Georgia and Alabama; accommodation to the dominant culture leading to a grudging assimilation; population pressures and conflicts over land; and, eventually, forced removal in the 1830s. Trudging along their own Trail of Tears, Creek Indians and their slaves and whatever livestock they could muster made the arduous trip to their new homeland north of the Canadian River and west of Fort Gibson. Still split by ancient differences, Lower Creeks settled in the Three Forks region where the Chouteau Trading Post wielded its commercial clout, while the Upper Creeks established communities along the North Fork, Deep Fork, and Canadian River valleys. By midcentury, Creek villages were flourishing, and a national government was seeing to tribal business at Council Hill where Tulsa eventually developed.[52] The tribal treasury benefitted from taxes on northbound Texas cattle, but the minuscule fees were scant compensation for the degradation of land as hungry longhorns gobbled their way through the Creek Nation.[53]

The Creek golden age came to a bruising halt during the Civil War. While many Creeks took up arms in defense of the Confederacy, thousands of others languished in squalid refugee camps in Kansas. Abandoned homes burned and farmlands reverted to their natural state. Cattle herds left untended became prey for marauders who systematically rounded them up and drove them to the Kansas railheads.[54] Creeks returning home at war's end faced an uphill climb to rebuild their shattered economy.

And that is precisely what they did. Cession of their western land to the U.S. government occasioned by the treaties of 1866 did not affect trading patterns established before the Civil War. Between 1865 and 1871, the Creeks leveraged their strategic location in the Three Forks region and access to the Texas Road (a major thoroughfare through the Indian Territory) to increase their markets for produce on an impressive scale. Corn, potatoes, wheat, oats, turnips, peanuts, cotton—these and other crops enabled the Creeks to trade hunting for large-scale agriculture and, except for die-hard traditionalists, not look back. The success story was due in no small measure to competent and committed Indian agents. As Northern Creek agent James W. Dunn observed, "They have surrendered the spoils of the chase for the fruits of agriculture."[55]

Prosperity in the Creek Nation did not mean a sudden assimilation into the modern economy. Trade still depended on the twin pillars of frontier finance: barter and commodity money. A. Faltinson's first husband, Dr. S. S. Kimmons, moved from his native Mississippi in 1897 to become one of Tulsa's first physicians. The conditions that he found reveal a pocket of frontier scarcity in a modernizing nation. "Ignorance, poverty and filth reared their ugly heads at every turn," said Faltinson. "Old wives' remedies, neighbors' suggestions, all had to be handled with the care and policy of a diplomat."[56] In the absence of a bridge across the Arkansas River, Dr. Kimmons braved quicksand that could easily have sucked him and his mount to a frightful death. If he did make it to his destination, he often made do with payment in commodity money or returned home with nothing to show for his exertions. "Sometimes, the Doctor was paid in money but more often in supplies, such as ham, a side of bacon, a jug of cider or bucket of sorghum and sometimes not at all." At times, compensation came belatedly from patients who did the best they could in tough circumstances. Faltinson recalled an unexpected payment of $150.00 from someone who had moved to Texas two years earlier. As she recalled with a touch of pathos, "Honesty and appreciation had flourished in squalor."[57]

Not all ministers were as fortunate as the one in J. B. McReynolds's congregation in Old Greer County, who received a surrey from his flock. Eliza Palmer of Okmulgee and her fellow worshippers did what they could for their tireless shepherd, particularly when he needed to travel in style: "The minister didn't expect money in those days for we didn't have much money but he had to live, so between meetings he farmed. We paid him with lard, chickens, or anything we had. Sometimes we would get together and make a quilt and give to him. When there was to be a conference we all gave what we could and bought him a hat or pair of shoes or whatever he had to have to go."[58]

The Creek Nation's neighbor in northeastern Indian Territory was the Cherokee Nation. During the colonial era, the Cherokees were the largest tribe on the southern frontier and were concentrated in regions that became the states of Georgia and Tennessee. They responded to white incursions into their homeland by developing an impressive national organization, complete with a written constitution, a first-rate school system, and their own native alphabet. Through marriage with tribal members, non-Indian traders earned the right to establish retail establishments, which prompted the opening of supply routes for wholesale goods between Cherokee settlements and Anglo-American communities.[59] Yet adopting the culture and commerce of their white neighbors was scant protection from land-grabbers. The vanguard of Cherokee migration made it to Arkansas and eventually to the Indian Territory as early as 1808. The mass exodus of 1838–1839, precipitated by Andrew Jackson's draconian policy of removal, seared itself into history as the "Trail of Tears," when a quarter of the tribe perished during their westward trek.

Like their Creek neighbors, the Cherokees enjoyed something of a golden age during the 1850s. Their tribal newspaper, the *Cherokee Advocate,* was published in their native syllabary, and public schools were established. General stores that had facilitated Cherokee assimilation into Anglo commerce back east were replicated in the Indian Territory and quickened the pace of economic development.[60] Prosperity spread to all economic levels to produce a standard of living on a par with that of the general population in Arkansas, Kansas, and Missouri. Then came the Civil War and the punishing treaties of 1866, and Cherokees were once again pawns in a white power struggle. Forced to surrender enormous swaths of land, including the Cherokee Outlet, to the U.S. government and open their nation to the railroads, Cherokee sovereignty seemed to be on a slippery slope to oblivion.[61]

Against daunting odds, Indians and non-Indians alike in the Cherokee Nation relied on barter and commodity money to survive. Ellalee Pore was six years old when her family moved to Bartlesville from Kansas in 1876. Her father paid $1.60 a year for a permit to live in the Cherokee Nation. The Pores had no furniture for their double log house, but they did have a cow; a quick trade reversed the equation. Early on, Ellalee's father's luck was all bad: he lost his horses and his crop in a flood. "After our stock died and we lost our crop, our living consisted mostly of cornbread baked in a Dutch oven, sweet milk and hog meat. We only had biscuits on Sundays and special occasions," she recalled.[62] But her father "was an old frontiersman and was not easily discouraged so he took another five year lease on the place."[63] "Emergencies" were available at Jake Bartles's store on Turkey Creek. Whatever the land or Bartles's store could not provide could be found in Coffeyville, Kansas, where the Pores traveled twice a year for supplies.

As a day trader (the old-fashioned variety) and freighter, Ellalee's father hauled freight through the Indian Territory and Texas to Mexico. He returned home not only with provisions but also with harrowing stories that bring to mind W. B. Napton's account of freighting on the Santa Fe Trail: a bison herd that stampeded through his camp and the somewhat puzzling reliance on ropes tied around wagons at night to keep rattlesnakes at bay stood out in Pore's mind to illuminate her father's workaday life. But he wouldn't have had it any other way. "The frontier life was a dangerous one but he liked it," she said.[64] Outlaws posed a man-made threat to commerce in the Cherokee Nation, but they "never molested the farmers and only stopped at the farm houses for something to eat, which we gladly gave them." Pore was clearly proud to have friends in low places. "I knew several of these men, Henry Starr, Cherokee Bill and the Daltons."[65]

Glove Morris came to the Cherokee Nation in 1870 and settled near the Arkansas line. Most Cherokees, whose farms averaged about ten acres, were subsistence farmers who "raised just enough to put their families through the winter."[66] In a spirit of cooperation that belies images of rugged frontiersmen, Cherokees formed "harvest crews" and went from one field to another, helping one another to bring in their crops. Cincinnati, Arkansas, was their main trading point as well as the place where they milled their grain and tanned their cow hides. Old-timers claimed that a distillery was located in Cincinnati before the Civil War. Morris's memory of frontier days includes the prices for store-bought goods, crops, and livestock: "Dress shoes sold at Cincinnati at that time for about one dollar and a quarter. Calico cloth sold at five cents per yard. Corn sold at fifty cents per bushel. Good cows sold at twelve and fifteen dollars; horses at twenty-five dollars; and sorghum at forty cents per gallon."[67]

Even though real money was trickling into the Cherokee Nation, most folks in Morris's community did their trading by barter: "They traded with one another—the things one had that he did not need he traded for the things he needed and which he did not have."[68] He recalled only one ferry in his part of the Cherokee Nation to facilitate commerce—Fisher Ferry on the Arkansas River—and several fords in the Illinois River. Amusements in those rough environs included horse racing and a staple of frontier music, Cherokee fiddling. Little did Morris suspect that Cherokee fiddling would wind its way into American folklore as a symbol of frontier ingenuity.[69]

Ferries and fords were used not only by individuals looking for opportunities to barter but also by retailers who served as conduits for eastern goods. Catering to the needs of farmers and ranchers, Cherokee stores sold nails, cloth, rifles, medicines, dry goods, needles, yarn, farm implements—in short, pretty much everything that American and European manufacturers had to offer. Most were simple log structures, often with a second story in which store managers and clerks resided, and were usually located at crossroads that developed into towns. Tahlequah, the capitol and largest town in the Cherokee Nation, boasted two thousand residents and six general stores in 1894. Vinita, the Cherokee Nation's second largest town in 1886, had a population of six hundred and had three general stores. Smaller towns such as Webbers Falls, Oaks, Claremore, and Bartlesville usually had from two to four general stores. Cherokee merchants relied heavily on the river trade that, by the 1890s, extended into the Indian Territory as far as Tulsa. Beginning in the 1870s, competition from the railroads was sending steamboats on their slide to obsolescence.[70]

From colonial days through the last decades of the nineteenth century, economic development in recently settled areas began with bartering and commodity money. Although these primitive tools of commerce enabled people to establish a foothold on the frontier, they were hardly commensurate with the needs of industry, let alone a global economy. To weave itself into the commercial webs of an increasingly industrialized nation, and to participate in an economy becoming ever more global in scope, the Indian Territory needed financial institutions to provide the two requirements of modern finance: currency and credit.

That, of course, is what banks are for. In the parallel universe back east, banks had been sprouting like mushrooms ever since Old Hickory crushed the Second Bank of the United States. They provided currency and credit and, in the process, spawned controversies that have never loosened their grip on American finance. Yet banks remained at the periphery of the Indian Territory, accessible to the elites via steamboat and arduous horseback rides, and utterly absent in the lives of common folk who seemed to get by just fine on their wits and the kindness of neighbors.

Banks could not simply be imported wholesale into the Indian Territory. Communication and transportation were too undeveloped, and frontier commerce remained too entrenched, to support anything akin to modern financial institutions. But there was an emergent need for currency and credit, particularly as the rest of the nation was charging hell-bent-for-leather into modernity. To provide a bridge to the modern economy, and to hammer the last few nails in the frontier's coffin, the Indian Territory offered up a largely neglected participant in Oklahoma banking before statehood: the merchant-banker. It is in the ingenuity of these quintessential jacks-of-all-trades that we find the genesis of Oklahoma banking.

CHAPTER SIX

Jacks-of-All-Trades

There being no banks in the early days, financing was done principally by the
merchants and in some instances by ranchmen when cattle were involved.

Jake Simmons, Indian Territory settler

In the summer of 1893, a young historian from the University of Wisconsin stood to deliver a paper before a meeting of the American Historical Association in Chicago. The gathering of intellectual heavyweights
coincided with the World's Columbian Exposition, a commemoration of
the four hundredth anniversary of Columbus's arrival in the New World
that celebrated the past even as it showcased the latest in science and
technology. Attendance was light when the thirty-two-year-old Frederick Jackson Turner took his turn at the podium.[1] The professor's youth
and lack of notoriety were partly to blame for the scant attendance, but
there was also competition a few blocks away, where crowds were bask-
ing in reenactments of America's foundation stories offered by Buffalo
Bill's Wild West and Congress of Rough Riders of the World. Turner the
scholar and Cody the showman thus commemorated, each in his own
way, the era that was passing.

Like a good academic, Professor Turner soldiered on. Bearing the
unassuming title "The Significance of the Frontier in American History," Turner's paper included a prophetic passage from the census of
1890, its momentous message buried beneath a pall of bureaucratic dross:
"Up to and including 1880 the country had a frontier of settlement, but

at present the unsettled area has been so broken into by isolated bodies of settlement that there can hardly be said to be a frontier line. In the discussion of its extent, its westward movement, etc., it cannot, therefore, any longer have a place in the census reports."[2]

Nobody could have guessed that Turner's paper would blow through the halls of academe like a prairie windstorm to become the most familiar model of American history. "The existence of an area of free land," wrote Turner in an oft-quoted passage from his chef d'oeuvre, "its continuous recession, and the advance of American settlement westward explain American development."[3] Reduced to its essentials, Turner's so-called frontier thesis begins with the assertion that laws and customs from the Old World had little relevance in the American wilderness, where an abundance of land and dearth of people fostered innovation and put a premium on practical skills.[4] Mobility and its corollary, wastefulness, were all but inevitable in a land of seemingly endless resources. The acquisition of material wealth trumped cultural creativity. "And, most important of all," Turner declared, "men found that the man-land ratio on the frontier provided so much opportunity for the individual to better himself that external controls were not necessary; individualism and political democracy were enshrined as their ideals."[5] Over the course of three centuries, these traits were revitalized over and over again as the frontier receded westward. Those who opted out of the migration experienced the frontier as a safety valve. If push came to shove, disgruntled easterners could always pack up and move. At the very least, they could fantasize what lay beyond the horizon.[6]

Turner and his disciples who framed our approach to frontier history were onto something in their assessment of the character traits fostered by three centuries of pushing back the frontier. Conspicuous by its absence from their analysis was the businessman's role in settling the continent. Turner's historiography, certainly lyrical and satisfying as a national narrative, has clouded our collective memory of westward expansion and earned justifiable criticism. Perhaps because objectivity suffers in the glare of the present, Turner and his ilk turned a blind eye toward economic forces that undermined settlers' independence and self-reliance, converted wants into needs, and promoted consumerism as an antidote to frontier scarcity. Turner was loath to admit that yeoman farmers could be undone by anything other than natural disasters and hostile savages. To learn about the frontier businessman, we rely on anecdotal evidence buried in newspaper articles, biographical directories, county histories, personal reminiscences, and advertisements.

Since Turner's day, academics have continued to eschew banking and business in favor of more compelling themes drawn from America's foundation narratives. With a few notable exceptions, scholars' retreat from the businessman's frontier can be attributed to two factors. First, the fault line between business and scholarship reinforces stereotypes and discourages dialogue, and it has produced a strain of anti-intellectualism that is never far from the surface of American culture. Arguably, anti-intellectualism is most pervasive in western states, where the frontier was late in yielding to civilized refinements and success in business has always trumped other measures of achievement.[7] Second, bankers and business-men drawn to the profit potential of newly opened lands were wary of being perceived as promoters of special interests. Most preferred to work behind the scenes, earning money while focusing in their articles and speeches on the paradise that was open to all.[8] Documentary evidence so prized by historians thus conceals the genuine wellsprings of frontier enterprise. Beneath all the populist rhetoric and paeans to the pioneer spirit, it was hard-nosed practicality that shaped the businessman's persona to produce Jackson's Everyman with an eye on the bottom line.

But all is not lost for readers hankering for a dollars-and-cents perspective of the frontier. Just as interviewers in the service of the WPA in the 1930s captured stories of steamboats and Indian stores and ad hoc business transactions, so, too, did they illuminate the introduction of currency and credit in the Indian Territory. Their stories are corroborated in correspondence, newspaper articles, and archival collections. Not surprisingly in a nation dedicated to free-market capitalism, the businessman's frontier was settled by entrepreneurs—chiefly cattlemen, miners, and farmers—who had the wherewithal to exploit the Indian Territory's considerable resources. To provide these entrepreneurs with financial services, merchants facilitated the flow of currency and credit as a sideline to their retail establishments. In the process, they became merchant-bankers—jacks-of-all-trades who were as adept at extending loans and exchanging currency as they were at selling seed and farm implements, and perhaps a few yards of calico for the missus, to their customers. With improvements in communication and transportation, many merchant banks evolved into financial powerhouses capable of serving local needs even as they linked up with institutions in more settled regions. As the frontier gave up the ghost in the late nineteenth century, so did the merchant-bankers, but not before passing the baton to honest-to-goodness bankers whose increasingly specialized financial services rendered merchant banking obsolete.

Modern finance was far in Oklahoma's future when an enterprising Illinoisan by the name of Joseph G. McCoy, anxious to cash in on opportunities afforded by the booming postwar economy, figured out a way to supply western beef to eastern markets. Already in the cattle business and anxious to get his hands on rugged longhorn cattle that roamed the hill country of South Texas, McCoy cut a deal with the Hannibal and St. Joseph Railroad to supply beef to Chicago. His next task was to select a town along the Kansas Pacific Railway where he could build the facilities needed to handle large numbers of cattle. He chose a nondescript railroad depot at Abilene, Kansas, as the destination for northbound cattle drives and, in the early 1870s, transformed it into a well-equipped cattle capital, complete with a shipping yard, barns, offices, and state-of-the-art scales. He then sent agents deep into the Indian Territory to enlist drovers to bring their herds to the burgeoning cow town.[9] The trails they carved into the prairie from Texas to Abilene and similar cow towns sprouting along the railway—particularly the Chisholm Trail and, slightly further west, the Great Western Trail—became fodder for legend. They also provided frontiersmen with a glimpse of fertile lands in the Indian Territory that would one day succumb to the plow and the barbed-wire fence and sprout mighty cities.

Railroads, too, were snaking their way into the Indian Territory. About the time Joseph McCoy was setting up shop in Abilene, a former Confederate colonel, J. J. McAlester, was setting his sights on coal deposits that fanned out beneath the Choctaw Nation in eastern Indian Territory. Alert to the benefits of marriage to an Indian woman, Colonel McAlester took a Chickasaw bride as the prerequisite to exploiting coal deposits near the Cross Roads, a settlement that took its name from its position at the juncture of the Texas Road and the California Trail. McAlester's discovery caught the attention of officials at the Missouri, Kansas, and Texas Railroad (the Katy). In 1872, the Katy came chugging into the Cross Roads, rechristened "McAlester" in honor of the Confederate colonel who had effectively launched the coal-mining era in the Indian Territory.[10]

Cattlemen had their longhorns and railroad moguls had their coal, but it was not until the end of the Civil War that farmers cast their covetous eyes on the Indian Territory. In the 1880s, pressure to open the region to white settlement coalesced into a political movement. Westbound immigrants had long shunned the nation's midsection as unfit for settlement. Such impressions changed as settlers ventured onto the grasslands to discover that, with a little pluck and an occasional rainstorm, crops could be wrested from those arid plains. Encouraged by the Homestead Act of 1862, which required a settler to live on his or her land for five years to perfect the title,[11] a trickle of pioneers onto the Great Plains became a flood. Into a region of longhorn cattle and hard-riding cowboys came wagons loaded with the accouterments of an alien civilization. They also brought wives and children whose homes, schools, and churches were soon competing with saloons and lonely cow camps.[12] As these settlers' numbers increased, so, too, did the nation's interest in the Indian Territory, still barred to white settlement, where Indians were accused of squandering God's bounty (not to mention the U.S. government's largesse) with inept farming practices, grasslands were waiting to be grazed, and mineral wealth was there for the taking. Like a willing mistress, the great prairies to the west and woodlands to the east beckoned with the promise of untapped resources and wealth beyond reckoning.

As anyone who has started a business knows, the first thing you need is a customer. Indian Territory entrepreneurs might have added a caveat: you need a way for customers to get to you. That was no small task in a region crisscrossed by thirty-one rivers and upwards of two hundred creeks.[13] Although some waterways could be forded, many crossings were rendered dangerous and even impassable by high water and steep banks. To facilitate travel and, not incidentally, enrich tribal coffers, the Five Tribes flexed their sovereignty in the nineteenth century and licensed citizens to establish and operate ferries. The Cherokee Nation charged people twenty-five dollars a year for a license to operate a ferry on the Arkansas and Canadian Rivers. On the Illinois, Verdigris, and Grand Rivers, the licensing fee dropped to ten dollars. Licensing fees were fixed by law, and no one was allowed to open a new ferry within a half mile of an existing one. What is more, boats were required to be in good condition, and only experienced ferrymen were permitted to operate them. Travelers were to be ferried across streams promptly during seasonable hours, always with a high regard for safety, and never on Sunday. Those found in violation of tribal laws were subject to a fine amounting to twice the cost of the license, half to be remitted to the national treasury and half to the informer.[14]

Ferries were often named for the people who operated these lucrative enterprises. For many years, members of the prominent Carey family in the Cherokee Nation operated the Carey Ferry across the Grand River. A post office was established there in November 1873, but it ceased operations in March 1888 when mail was redirected to the community of Echo.[15]

B. F. Colbert, a well-to-do Chickasaw from Mississippi who lived in the Indian Territory north of Denison, Texas, operated a ferry for twenty-two years before C. Baker & Company of Saint Joseph, Missouri, was commissioned to build a wagon bridge across the Red River. A barrel set on a sled was placed on the north side of the river, and people who crossed were required to pitch their silver dollars into it. A man who crossed the river in 1870 said that Colbert's routine was to hitch a horse to the sled at night and haul it to his house. If he was indisposed, he dispatched a black assistant to bring in the barrel. Even though there were other ferries in the vicinity, Colbert's Ferry was said to have brought some 19,000 wagons, plus uncounted horsemen and foot travelers, into Texas in 1872.[16]

Far to the west, Jonathan Doan was doing his part to bring prosperity in the form of cattle herds to Old Greer County. Doan, a native of Ohio, built a picket house near the Red River south of present-day Altus with a roof fashioned from mud and grass and a buffalo hide to cover the doorway.[17] From modest beginnings, Doan's Crossing blossomed into one of the busiest crossings in the West for drovers bound from Texas to the railhead in Dodge City, Kansas. Today, a simple granite marker engraved with the names of cowboys and a few dilapidated buildings are all that remain of Doan's Crossing, where cattle followed the Great Western Trail in numbers that rivaled, and perhaps exceeded, those that traversed the more famous Chisholm Trail to the east.

Crucial though they were to economic development, ferries and fords sometimes worked against internal improvements. In 1873–74, Edward King toured the southern and southwestern United States for *Scribner's Monthly Magazine.* Following their publication in *Scribner's,* his articles were published in a hefty volume in London under the title *The Great*

South. Arriving at the Red River after a ten-day journey from Vinita, Indian Territory, King was surprised to see a long line of cattle fording the stream. Upon inquiry, he learned that neither the Chickasaw Nation nor the State of Texas had authorized construction of a bridge because a Chickasaw citizen had been granted a charter to charge one dollar for each person who crossed the Red River in either direction. For many years, his income ran as high as one hundred dollars a day, while his expenses for maintaining the ford were no more than twenty dollars per week. Such one-sided arithmetic testifies to the quickening pace of commerce in the Indian Territory as well as the gains to be made on the frontier.[18]

Ferries and fords played a crucial role in the lives of the Indian Territory's earliest non-Indian settlers. One of them was B. M. Palmer. Born near Fort Smith in 1873, he came to the Indian Territory with his parents in 1886 and lived for many years in Le Flore County. Early on, his father paid a dollar a month for the privilege of living in the Indian Territory, where he raised cotton, corn, and cattle. Palmer recalled horse-powered cotton gins and gristmills as well as an abundance of wild game, including wild horses and hogs. The horses grazed in the valleys and took refuge in the mountains when winter set in. The Bob Vann Ferry about seven miles upstream from its confluence with the Arkansas River was the preferred means of crossing the Canadian River. The stage running between Webbers Falls, Indian Territory, and Fort Smith, Arkansas, relied on the ferry to cross the Canadian River. Another ferry operated by Bullet Foreman was located near the mouth of the Illinois River. As Palmer recalled, "As to fords they were numerous at different points on the Poteau River but were of no particular name."[19]

W. R. Mulkey was born in 1869, and he was a virtual encyclopedia of ford and ferry lore. His parents, who had Cherokee rights, brought him from Texas to the Rattlesnake Mountains (later called Nebo Mountain) near Warner, Indian Territory. His family raised corn, cotton, wheat, and oats, and the cotton gin and gristmill that they used was located in the vicinity of present-day Checotah. Two Jews, Mose and Ben LaFayette, operated these businesses as well as a general merchandise store. Mulkey's parents did much of their trading at a store operated by John Pierce at Texanna, Indian Territory, but they mainly survived on whatever the land provided. Mulkey recalled, "We made belts and hat bands and pocket books from rattlesnake skins and there was [*sic*] plenty of rattlesnakes here as they were back in Texas and we were used to them."[20] Equally memorable to Mulkey at a distance of several decades were the fords and ferries: Brown's Ferry on the Red River between Gainesville, Texas, and Ardmore, Indian Territory; Foreman's Ferry across the Illinois River, operated by the aforementioned Bullet Foreman; Lynch Ferry across the Arkansas River at Webbers Falls; Vann's Ferry east of Webbers Falls (surely named for Joe Vann, the hapless gambler and owner of the ill-fated *Lucy Walker* that sank to its doom near New Albany, Indiana, in 1844); Nevins, Rogers, and McMakin Ferries across the Arkansas River near Muskogee; the Mud Ford and Alberty Ford east of Warner; and the Rock Ford across the North Canadian River south of Texanna. Mulkey left a glimpse into changing technologies in his account of the Lynch Ferry that began as a pole ferry, was later attached to a cable, and finally operated under steam power.[21]

Louis R. Jobe, who was born and raised in the Creek Nation, claimed that his mother traveled west on the Trail of Tears. Two military roads crossed his neighborhood: the Fort Arbuckle Road, which ran through the Creek Agency and south toward Okmulgee and Fort Arbuckle, and the Texas Road, which passed by Muskogee. Nevins Ferry at the mouth of the Grand and Verdigris Rivers was operated by Julia Nevins and her husband. "This was the ferry which was the main artery between Talequah [*sic*] and Ft. Arbuckle," recalled Jobe. "Freight, mail and passengers going to and fro to all directions used this ferry." The Nevins Ferry was one of many enterprises to fade into history when railroads and bridges rendered them obsolete. Similarly, the Harris Ferry on the Arkansas River was operated by Red Bird Harris until it "was abandoned about the year 1873 or 1874 after the railroad came across. It was no longer needed it seemed."[22]

Stringent laws and licensing of Indian Territory river crossings did not mean much to Mother Nature. Dr. Virgil Berry of Okmulgee in the Creek Nation recalled a harrowing incident on the banks of the Grand River in 1890. Not only was the river at flood stage, but also "old John Charbeneau's small flatboat, that served as a ferry, had been washed away." Turning back was out of the question, so Dr. Berry opted for plan B: he stripped, tied his clothes in a bundle, and lashed them to his horse's head. He then led his steed to the edge of the roiling current and, with a reinforcing whack on its rear end, commanded the beast to swim. Surely pondering the wisdom of his career choice, the naked physician grabbed his mount by the tail and held on tight for his improvised ferry trip across the river.[23]

Anyone who thinks that Oklahoma's turnpike system is a modern idea might be interested to know that the Indian Territory's fords and ferries were linked by a network of toll roads, gates, and bridges. Like river crossings, toll roads were operated under licenses granted by tribal governments. And, just as ferry boats were required to be maintained in good condition, so, too, were roads supposed to be safe and serviceable.

The Garey Lane Toll Gate east of Skullyville, Choctaw Nation, on the Fort Smith Road was named for a white man who lived in the vicinity. When a mudhole made the road impassable, the locals knew what to do: they cut poles and covered it so that wagons could pass. Someone came up with the brilliant idea of placing a bar across the road and building a log cabin to serve as a toll collector's residence. Once the toll gate was put into service, travelers in wagons were charged twenty-five cents to proceed.

Lavina Beal of Tushka was born too early to serve on the Oklahoma Turnpike Authority, but she did leave posterity her opinion that the only passable roads in the Indian Territory were toll roads. One such thoroughfare across the Poteau River bottom earned the lyrical appellation, "Pull Tight," because of the difficulty it posed to travelers.[24]

The toll gate on the Butterfield Overland Mail Route consisted of a large trimmed log that was laid across the roadway. Each end was supported by a stone pier to provide a barrier that could be swung open to permit the passage of wagons and stock. More elaborate toll gates featured stout crotched posts to support the bar. A stone was attached to one end of the bar to function as a counterweight.[25]

Membership has always had its privileges. On October 26, 1892, the Muskogee National Council approved a fifteen-year charter for Dick Greenwood to build and maintain a toll gate on the public road between Eufaula and South Canadian. Greenwood was privileged to collect tolls from all travelers except citizens of the Creek Nation, and nobody else had the right to build a gate within a mile of his location. Similarly, Joe and Mike Hilderbrand did not charge "Indians and Negroes [sic]" to pass through their toll gate northeast of Fort Gibson. All others had to cough up $1.50 for a wagon and team, 25¢ for a man on horseback, and 10¢ for a head of stock. In a prime example of horizontal integration, the Hilderbrands owned the gristmill on Fourteen Mile Creek, and—no surprise here!—the only access was across their toll bridge.[26]

Villages destined to blossom into mighty cities sometimes owed their good fortune, at least in part, to the payment of tolls. The first wagon bridge across the Arkansas River at Eleventh Street and Riverside Drive in Tulsa was built by private citizens in 1903, and tolls were charged until 1913. The bridge was a godsend for anyone who needed access to the burgeoning oil fields southwest of Tulsa. But what business giveth to one, it taketh from another. Lee Clinton, president of the Tulsa Stockyards, was the first person to cross the Eleventh Street Bridge when it was opened to traffic on January 4, 1904. He declared that the bridge put him out of business because he was part owner, with A. F. Antle, of a gas-driven ferry at the Eleventh Street crossing of the Arkansas. As Clinton recalled, "The old ferry was a sidewheeler that held four wagons. But before this ferry numerous smaller pole-driven boats crossed the Arkansas."[27]

Clinton was in good company. Modernity was coming on like a freight train, and there was not much room for ferries.

The surge in business activity in the Indian Territory after the Civil War spawned a need for currency and credit. In the absence of banks, entrepreneurship offered a solution in the form of the merchant-banker. Early on, Indians and non-Indians alike found opportunities to hold money for, and lend it to, other people. Traders, shopkeepers, farmers, and even missionaries occasionally found themselves in the role of rudimentary bankers.[28] With their shelves stocked and customers in need of supplies, merchants facilitated transactions by setting up what passed for banks in the corners of their stores. Eugene P. Gum, a director of the Oklahoma Bankers Association whose career lasted from 1918 to 1952, provides a glimpse into these crude institutions that sprouted along the fast-fading line of frontier settlement: "There were no banks so these merchants set up a bank in a little nook in the store. Sometimes it consisted of a crude table and a lock box. It later became dignified by cutting off a space surrounded by chicken wire through which a window was cut to permit the transaction of business. The funds were protected by an old-fashioned, square-door safe that could have been blown by a thin smear of soup. If a customer wanted a year's supply of merchandise he was directed to the chicken wire enclosure to make his note to the bank for the money to make the purchase."[29]

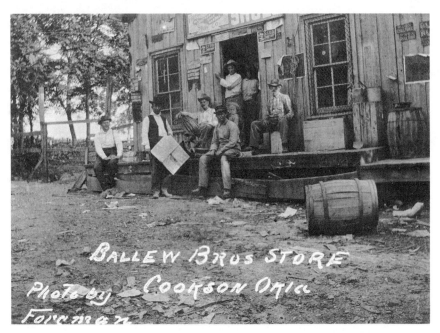

The Ballew Brothers Store at Cookson, Cherokee County, Indian Territory, ca. 1905. Note the wire covering on the windows. Country stores served as service centers in rural areas and performed a wide variety of functions, including banking. Courtesy Western History Collections, University of Oklahoma Libraries (Kobel Collection, No. 4, Exhibit 530).

Gum's account of merchant banking is certainly descriptive, but it does not quite capture pioneers' hankering for real banks. Mrs. Tom B. Ferguson (in all likelihood, the wife of future territorial governor Thompson B. Ferguson, 1901–1906), a settler of Watonga in the early 1890s and clearly a finance major at heart, claimed that the romance of the Nile and mystery of tropic isles were no match for building banks on the arid plains of the Oklahoma Territory. "Very few people associate romance with the banking business," she recalled with a flair for understatement, "but it is there, especially in the banks of pioneer days and particularly is this true of banks in small towns. They register the life, hopes, and deeds of the community." Mrs. Ferguson could scarcely contain herself "when, after being bankless for over two years after the town was established at the opening of the Cheyenne and Arapaho Reservation, we found that a bank was to be established."[30]

In nearby Okarche (a name derived from the first letters of "Oklahoma," "Arapaho," and "Cheyenne"), Franz Loosen, whose family had emigrated from Germany and founded the First Bank of Okarche on October 28, 1892, still relied on bartering to fatten his bank's loan portfolio. "There was a large black community outside of Okarche," said Franz's granddaughter, Patricia Loosen. "My grandfather would go to loan money to these people, and they would pay him with chickens, and rice, corn, meat—and there was a gentleman's handshake."[31] For those who could neither read nor write, a simple *X* was all Herr Loosen needed to know that his loan was secure.

In an address to the Oklahoma Bankers Association, J. W. McNeal gave his own take on the swashbuckling bankers who paved the way for civilization. "Pioneer banking is a graveyard," asserted McNeal to his colleagues in the fall of 1902, "in which lie buried the capital assets, hopes, and ambitions of many an embryo Napoleon of finance. Darwin may have discovered here his doctrine of the survival of the fittest."[32]

If Darwin had made his way to the Indian Territory instead of the Galapagos, he would have found a growing cadre of merchants in stiff competition to furnish basic banking services. Their establishments also became beehives of activity for entertainment-starved settlers. "The places of amusement were the country store and the post office," recalled A. T. Lowman, a pioneer who came to the Oklahoma Territory from Nebraska in 1893 and settled near Watonga after a twenty-two-day trek with his wife and six children. He continued, "Saturday afternoons every one who could would knock off working and go to the store. There the crowd would play ball, pitch horseshoes, run horse races and exchange the gossip of the neighborhood. Many picnics were planned for Sundays and there were fishing parties and dances."[33]

A similar story comes to us from Arthur Bynum, who described Tulsa in 1885 as "a little struggling settlement, hardly large enough to be called a village," where Indians from as far west as the Sac and Fox Agency flocked to trade.[34] They set up teepees west of Elwood, just north of the Saint Louis and San Francisco Railroad (Frisco) tracks, and generally stayed a week or two. Except for a few scattered frame shacks that housed businesses on Main Street, there was not much to block the view of the Osage hills to the north and woods and river bottoms to the south. As banks and places of entertainment remained far in the future, early settlers made do with what they had, including water that came in a peculiar hue. Bynum recalled, "There being no banks as yet, the merchants acted as bankers and naturally the stores became meeting places to pass the time. There was also a good well of water at the back of the store. The tin cup attached took on a permanent reddish tint from the Jamaica ginger that was consumed in quantities at that time."[35]

With little money in circulation, many merchant-bankers operated on a credit system that allowed customers, Indians and non-Indian settlers alike, to pay for supplies with the proceeds of their hunts, farming activities, and government annuities. One wonders whether merchant-bankers had enough schooling under their belts to reflect on the etymology of "credit"—*credo,* or "I believe" in Latin.[36] Given the hazards of frontier lending, their belief in eventual repayment was surely tempered with something akin to faith, or maybe just optimism that the odds would somehow accrue in their favor. When merchant-bankers managed to get their hands on currency, they used it to pay creditors and restock their shelves.[37] When customers came to buy supplies, they often left their money on deposit and used it as collateral for revolving lines of credit. In the absence of impressive buildings and swank lobbies to instill confidence in their customers, merchant-bankers relied on their most important assets: honesty, integrity, and accountability. On the businessman's frontier, success often hinged on whether or not a man could be trusted to handle another man's money.[38]

Thus did banking become an important sideline to territorial merchants, and as their clientele increased, so did the time they spent in accepting deposits and making loans. As industries muscled their way into the region, companies often issued scrip (paper vouchers, often spelled "script" by their users) in lieu of currency to their employees. Such was the case in the Choctaw Nation, where Colonel McAlester's discovery of coal deposits and the subsequent arrival of railroads in the early 1870s to carry it out spawned company towns populated largely by European immigrants whose hard-earned scrip was redeemable only at company stores.[39]

Jake Simmons, a black cattleman near Muskogee who was born in 1865 and whose descendants rose to prominence in the oil industry after statehood in 1907, knew all about merchants who served as bankers. "There being no banks in the early days," said Simmons, "financing was done principally by the merchants and in some instances by ranchmen when cattle were involved."[40] Farmers and ranchers who wanted to borrow money went to a nearby merchant and offered security, such as crops or cattle, in return for scrip ranging in value from five cents to ten dollars. Merchants were accustomed to accepting scrip as a medium of exchange as long as its source was not too far away. Eventually, the person who issued the scrip would issue a recall and pay cash for it. But before its recall, scrip fostered what amounted to a game of chance. "There was a great deal of bartering in this script," recalled Simmons, "for oftentimes parties who had the script would need the real money when he was going to Okmulgee or some other point where the script would not be recognized and naturally he had to suffer a loss to get the real money by discounting it."[41] Such complex financing spilled over to his and other ranches, where tending cattle was simple compared to the bookkeeping: "I remember that if I did not have cash to pay my help at the ranch I would give to the employee a strip of paper about the size of a bank check and show thereon the amount I desired to pay him. This employee would take it to town and as he purchased his food, clothing or what not the merchant would write on the back thereof his name and the amount purchased and on his books he would charge this to me. When the amount on the front of the paper was taken up, the last merchant would retain it and would deliver it to me showing that it was fully paid. By this method it required considerable bookkeeping, but that was the only alternate [*sic*]. Other ranch men like F. S. Severs did as I."[42]

One merchant decided to add a bit of pizzazz to otherwise bland scrip and printed his picture on one end and the note's value on the other. Henry Vogel, a native of Switzerland who came to the Indian Territory in 1887, recalled, "It rather resembled money and was about the size of our present paper money, all the other firms had script but it was just ordinary pieces of paper."[43] This might have been the same scrip that caught the attention of Alex Sykes. Born in a log cabin in the Cherokee Nation in 1870 and captivated by the steamboats that came whistling by his home, Sykes's interest in money began at an early age, when his father found him playing with "green back confederate money" and told him it was of no value. Surely the youthful Sykes was disappointed to learn that such colorful pieces of paper could fetch nothing in the marketplace. But "Spaulding script" was something else altogether. "I well remember the Spaulding script," said Sykes. "It was about four and a half inches long and two inches wide. This script was issued by H. B. Spaulding in the city of Muskogee, Oklahoma. It had H. B. Spaulding's picture on one end and the amount on the other end. This script ranged in amounts from five cents to ten dollars. People wanted sure enough United States money and would sell this script to scalpers at a discount ranging from ten to twenty-five percent on the dollar. The time soon came when they insisted that Spaulding take up his script and they insisted so strongly that he finally recalled all of it and quit. It came near, if it did not, bankrupt him."[44]

A. E. Dixon arrived via train in Okmulgee and promptly opened a two-story grocery and hotel at a location later occupied by the Rhea Department Store. "Our store was the first cash store in town," recalled the modernizing Dixon. "The other merchants still used script and tokens. We did a good business with the Indians here."[45] In all likelihood, Dixon carried glass in his store's inventory, or at least knew where to procure it. If so, he was ready when disaster befell the Citizens National Bank. "Ed Grayson, a negro, was breaking a horse when both of them crashed through the front window of the Citizen's National Bank. This happened about 1905 or 1906," Dixon recalled.[46] Thus did banking crash its way into Okmulgee lore.

For Bill Swimm, frontier financing represented a blend of subsistence agriculture, bartering, and merchant banking. Most people raised "only enough for home use," he said. Nothing was produced for the market. Cotton, hogs, and cattle were the main products, and money was reserved for clothing and household necessities. In the absence of money, people relied on "furs and hides from wild varmints and animals that we would trade or sell."[47] Oxen and horses served as draft animals and pulled plows constructed of wooden teeth. As a harbinger of consumerism, wooden teeth were replaced with iron teeth that could be purchased from the store in Webbers Falls or ordered from Fort Smith, a veritable mecca for trade before railroads pushed steamboats into obsolescence. Swimm recalled, "As modern farm tools came into being the people kept abreast with the times until we had plows, cultivators, wagons, mowing machines, etc. Corn and cotton was produced extensively and became the money crops along the Arkansas River valleys."[48]

Swimm did not recall scrip in the Webbers Falls area. Instead, farmers and ranchers went to merchants to borrow money. Rather than require them to sign a note or offer collateral for a mortgage, merchants charged the amount they were borrowing to their accounts and recorded debits for whatever they purchased. Cash was sometimes used for small purchases. Coupon books eventually came into use in amounts ranging from five cents to one dollar and five dollars and were accepted only in establishments where they were issued. Primary issuers of coupon books included Gibson Brothers, Hays Mercantile Company, and Bob Blackstone. "Of course, this curtailed a lot of bookkeeping," recalled Swimm.[49] Until the First National Bank was opened in Muskogee in 1889 and dropped the curtain on frontier financing, the closest bank to Webbers Falls was in Fort Smith.

Patrons of merchant-bankers who were familiar with banking in the frontier fashion had little choice but to put up with a defining feature of nineteenth-century finance: usurious interest rates. Lenders justified the staggering cost of money with basic laws of supply and demand and the risks they assumed in extending credit. Customers muddled through with currency (if they had any) of dubious value and annual interest rates on borrowed money of 15 to 35 percent, and sometimes as high as 60 percent.[50] Clearly, it was not only outlaws who put the wild in the West.

Citizens of the Choctaw Nation were fortunate to count on the services of M. W. Maupin, a merchant-banker in Durant who offered not only reasonable interest rates but also lunch for his hungry customers. Maupin was ahead of his time in offering a wide range of services under one roof to accommodate men who were laying track for the Missouri, Kansas & Texas Railroad. "I had a short-order counter in my store and fed many people," recalled the entrepreneur about what might have been Oklahoma's first food court. "I also served as a banker for the working men cashing their checks, charging them ten percent."[51] Not a bad deal in a land of rampant usury.

In the absence of banks, residents of the Cherokee Nation satisfied their depository needs at four general merchandise stores in Tahlequah: John W. Stapler and Sons; J. T. Parks Grocery Store; John Thompson's Mercantile Store; and the Lawrence Wyly Mercantile Company. As a rule, store owners never charged their customers for taking deposits. Holding deposits for brief time periods was simply customer service with a frontier flair—akin, perhaps, to layaway plans in modern department stores. People flush with cash sometimes took it to a merchant bank just before closing time and left it there until the next morning, when they would return to pick it up. Deposits of three hundred to four hundred dollars of this nature were not uncommon. John W. Stapler, who moved from Delaware to Tahlequah after his sister, Mary, married Cherokee chief John Ross in 1844, went a step further by safeguarding customers' cash and allowing them to write checks against the balance, much as a bank carries regular checking accounts. Interest charges were noted on the checks, and customers paid their interest at the end of each month in the same way that consumers today make payments on their charge accounts. Checks issued by John W. Stapler and Sons resembled regular checks, but with a major difference: the name of the merchant rather than a bank was printed above the signature line.[52]

The Staplers' store and nearby residence burned in the 1890s. Soon thereafter, a brick building was built to accommodate the store. On December 11, 1891, one of John W. Stapler's two sons, James S., established a private bank, the Bank of Tahlequah, with capital stock of $20,000. In the time-honored tradition of merchant banking, the first depositor, J. T. Parks, showed up at the bank on the first morning it opened with a sack of money that he had been keeping at home. Meanwhile, the Staplers' corner building continued to function as a dry goods store until 1911 or 1912 when the Bank of Tahlequah, rechristened the First National Bank of Tahlequah on June 5, 1900, took it over. At the time of the conversion, the bank's capital stock was increased to $40,000. In 1902, capital stock was increased to $50,000.[53]

Merchant banks typically had a sturdy safe to prevent losses to outlaws who roamed the Indian nations. When what we might call preferred customers wanted to borrow money, merchant-bankers extended the needed funds and charged interest to their accounts. Loans were sometimes as much as $200 and $300. Federal money bound for the Cherokees, largely in specie and sometimes amounting to $50,000 or more, arrived from Saint Louis at Gibson Station (not Fort Gibson) aboard the Katy Railroad. The Cherokee chief then sent a party accompanied by armed guards to bring it to Tahlequah, where it was placed in an iron safe and kept under guard until it was spent.[54]

Few merchant-bankers left a more lasting legacy than Frederick Drummond. Born in Ardrosson, Scotland, in 1864, Frederick and his two brothers, George and Charles, immigrated to the United States in 1884 with a grand total of $3,000 that represented half of their mother's holdings. After a brief stay in New York, Frederick lit out for Texas, where he acquired what passed for a fortune in the cattle business. Unfortunately, drought and a dearth of financial skills left him broke and looking for a second chance.[55] He worked his way to Saint Louis, where fortune appeared in the person of John R. Skinner, owner of the Osage Mercantile Company, who offered the young Scotsman an opportunity to test his mettle in the Indian trade. Drummond took the bait and headed west once again, this time to become a clerk in the Osage Mercantile Company in Pawhuska. After taking up residence in the Osage Nation in 1887, Drummond courted Addie Gentner of Coffeyville, Kansas. They were married in 1890.[56] By then, Frederick was becoming fluent in the Osage tongue and was known among his customers as Ts'o-Xe, which translates from Osage as "green persimmon" or "tart." A cousin who helped out in the store claimed that his nickname stemmed from his tendency to pout.[57]

His alleged moodiness notwithstanding, Frederick and his bride rose to prominence in the Osage Nation. Eager to expand his business and confident that his customers would follow him, Frederick sold his interest in the Osage Mercantile Company and moved in 1903 to Hominy, a small town some twenty miles south of Pawhuska, where he bought out the Price Mercantile Company as the basis for his new enterprise. Known far and wide as the Hominy Trading Company and, in later years, the Pioneer Store, the store functioned as the Wal-Mart of its day as a purveyor of everything from groceries and hardware to farm implements, clothing, and shoes. At one time, Drummond's store was the nation's largest dealer of Pendleton blankets, a product favored by the Osages.[58] As the largest furniture dealer in the area, the Hominy Trading Company became the go-to place for custom-built coffins—a role that, so far, has escaped the top brass at Wal-Mart.[59] But it did not escape the attention of other merchants in the territorial and early statehood periods. Three hundred and twenty miles west of Hominy, George H. Langston plastered a sign on his hardware store in Guymon to entice customers to Langston Hardware's cornucopia of goods and services: "windmills, well casing, stoves, ranges, harness, saddles, furniture, pianos, undertaking."[60]

Like so many merchants who felt marooned without a real bank, Drummond became connected with the First National Bank and served as president of Farmers State Bank in Hominy.[61] "So the family has been, more or less, in the banking business ever since," explained Frederick's grandson and namesake, Frederick Ford Drummond, during an interview in the spring of 2011.[62] Frederick's grandfather also served as Hominy's first mayor after the town's incorporation on March 3, 1908. The home that he and Addie built in Hominy, completed in 1905, remains

a model of Victorian architecture and taste. It was deeded to the Oklahoma Historical Society in 1980 and placed on the National Register of
Historic Places in 1981.[63]

The Drummond family patriarch died on August 22, 1913, in Stillwater. When he was laid to rest in Hominy, the line of buggies and wagons
at the cemetery was said to have stretched out for a mile, and more Indians attended his funeral than that of any other non-Indian.[64] By then,
the Hominy Trading Company and Drummond's banking interests had
become the foundation for a family dynasty whose interests extend to
three of Oklahoma's iconic enterprises: cattle, oil, and banking. As of this
writing in 2013, the fourth generation of Drummonds in Osage County
is represented by Frederick Ford Drummond II's son, Ford, a graduate of
the University of Virginia Law School who came home from Charlottesville to extend his family's legacy into the twenty-first century.

From Muskogee, Indian Territory, comes the story of the Patterson
Mercantile Company, a merchant-banking establishment in the classic
mold. The story begins in the early 1880s, when the Patterson Mercantile Company was operating as an unincorporated bank and relied on
word of mouth rather than advertising to publicize its banking services.
For the convenience of out-of-town customers and cattlemen, the store
began accepting coin and currency and sealed it in heavy canvas bags
for safekeeping. When cattle deals and other transactions failed to make
much of a dent in the store's cache (mainly because deals usually resulted
in changes in ownership rather than cash payments), someone came up
with the idea of opening a bank. Eventually, the bags were bursting with
some $30,000 in cash and coin, and the prospect of bank robberies com-
pelled the reluctant bankers to put their de facto bank into operation.
The words "The Patterson Mercantile Company, Muscogee, Ind. Ter."
were emblazoned in large print on both passbooks and checks, but the
word "bank" was nowhere to be seen.[65] Everyone knew it was a bank, so
why bother? No sense wasting ink.

The Patterson Mercantile Company's journey from merchant bank to
consumer paradise survives in a WPA interview, subsequently published
in the *Chronicles of Oklahoma,* with Ella Robinson, an employee of the
firm.[66] The company's founder, James A. Patterson, was born in Tennessee in 1819 and arrived in the Creek Nation in 1854 as an employee of
Colonel William H. Garrett, the Creek Indian agent. After a series of

adventures in the mercantile business that typifies frontier commerce, Patterson took advantage of the M.K. & T. Railroad's decision to build a line through the Indian Territory in 1872 and opened the first dry goods store at the present site of Muskogee. He formed a partnership in 1876 with Andrew W. Robb that ended with Patterson's death in 1897. In 1889, a stock company was formed. Stockholders included A. W. Robb as president and Herbert J. Evans as secretary. Shortly thereafter the store, located initially at the corner of Main and Broadway, was divided into departments to become what might have been the first department store in the Indian Territory.

Experienced businessmen, all of whom became stockholders, were appointed as heads of the various departments, which included dry goods, clothing, shoes, and groceries. The company also operated a mill and gin in Muskogee and employed more than sixty people with an annual payroll of $30,000. A catastrophic fire compelled the company to move a block west, where an impressive brick building was constructed and additional employees were hired to handle the company's burgeoning stock of goods.

Robinson joined the Patterson Mercantile staff in 1897, just in time to help with a midsummer sale in the last two weeks of July. The aspiring retailer admitted to being a bit nervous—it was to be her first experience of standing on her feet all day. But Robinson was anxious to demonstrate her aptitude for the male-dominated arena of commerce. On-the-job training came in the form of a retail extravaganza that shines across the decades like a blue-light special at K-Mart: "In the mad rush for bargains the store was filled with customers all day, standing and almost fighting for bargains. Sometimes the goods was [sic] badly damaged in the fray. I remember one dozen fine napkins that were so badly damaged that they were charged to the woman who fought for them and would not take them. They were delivered to her the next day."[67]

Robinson returned home after her first day on the job in a state of exhaustion and declared to her mother that she was through with the retail business. Her mother knew what to do, and after a good meal, a hot bath, and a sound night's sleep, her daughter reported to work the next day with a new resolve. Robinson quickly earned a reputation for getting along with the store's black patrons, and her career in retailing was assured. She even learned to cope with the semiannual sales in January and July, when people from a radius of seventy-five miles descended on Muskogee for orgies of buying. "They were real sales," recalled Robinson. "High class merchandise at little above cost prices. Long before the doors were opened in the morning the sidewalks would be crowded with people and the grand rush began when the doors were open. The people would look forward with much interest to the sales realizing that they could secure fine merchandise at little cost."[68]

Many patrons shopped until they were ready to drop, spent the night in a rooming house or hotel if they could afford it, and showed up early the next morning to resume their shopping marathons. When they had had enough, they left for home in buggies laden with merchandise that had wound its way to Patterson Mercantile Company from wholesalers in Saint Louis, Chicago, and New York. Less well-heeled customers camped out in the wagon yard at the corner of Cherokee Street and East Broadway. On many days, Robinson sold as much as $250 worth of merchandise in a single hour; cash sales in her department alone sometimes ran as high as $1,000 to $1,500 in a day. Clearly proud of her position in the vanguard of frontier consumerism, Robinson described dresses and table linens and damask whose quality was second to none: "A dinner arrayed in the best linens from Pattersons, french china and cut glass from the Turner art department and sterling silver from a leading jewelry house, presented a setting at a dinner party fit for a King, and as dinner parties was [sic] one of the most popular social occasions, the demand for our linens never slacked."[69]

It seems utterly incongruous that this beehive of retailing operated in its early days without a bank. Yet by all accounts, the owners succeeded as merchant-bankers. Out-of-town customers and cattlemen were invited to leave their money in stout canvas bags that were placed in the store's safe until they came for it. "Later," said Robinson, "a real banking system was organized with real checks and was carried on exclusively for the benefit of their customers and with no profit for themselves."[70] And, like other merchant banks throughout old Oklahoma, the Patterson Mercantile Company served as a meeting place, much like the agora of ancient Athens, but without the togas. "Just stand around Patterson's store awhile," said the savvy Robinson, "and the fellow you wanted to see came along."[71]

By the 1880s, the Indian Territory was surrounded by bona fide states (with the exception of No Man's Land, the present-day Oklahoma Panhandle) and none doubted that the sparsely settled country between Texas and Kansas would be next. Once derided as a wasteland fit only for Indians and outlaws and useful only for products that could be exported and fashioned into something useful back east, the area was beginning to shed its pariah status. Cowboys who drove herds north along the great cattle trails realized the potential of its rich grasslands; miners knew about the vast coal deposits beneath its eastern woodlands; and nesters were clamoring to sink their plows into its fertile soil. With lawmen few and far between, outlaws were finding plenty of opportunity to ply their trade and providing more reasons to hasten the Indian Territory's inclusion in the national polity. Simply put, the time was approaching when demands for non-Indian settlement would have to be addressed. Promises to the Indian tribes notwithstanding, land that was supposed to be theirs for as long as the grass grew and the rivers ran had a role to play in America's economic development.

The first stirrings of economic development in present-day Oklahoma were felt in the early eighteenth century, when French fur trappers piloted their slender crafts along the Arkansas and Red Rivers and their tributaries in search of creatures to butcher and skin. Even as their initial thrusts into the wilderness were bearing fruit in the riverboat trade, commerce on the western plains was taking shape in the form of freighting companies that delivered supplies to remote settlements and military outposts. In their wake came pioneers who relied on bartering and commodity money to carve precarious livings from the wilderness and, in the process, develop mutually beneficial relations with their Indian neighbors. Trading posts and merchant-bankers served their needs and, at the same time, greased the wheels of commerce by facilitating the flow of currency and credit. Like streams flowing into a mighty river, these smatterings of economic activity paved the way for modern methods of banking and commerce.

With the notable and tragic exception of the dominant culture's treatment of Native and African Americans, democracy and capitalism got along reasonably well in old Oklahoma. There was more than enough land and its bounty to go around. Survival depended more on cooperation than competition. Class distinctions that had hardened back east meant little in a land where a man's worth was measured by what he could accomplish with crude tools and determination. If the Indian Territory was not quite the yeoman's paradise envisioned by Jefferson as he gazed westward from the heights of Monticello, neither was it mired in systems of status and privilege. Pioneers were free to make their fortunes and equally free to lose them. As long as the gods of good fortune were smiling, and as long as one's skin was a proper shade of white, the race went to the swift and the skilled. Those who failed had only themselves to blame.

In the waning days of the frontier, the relationship between democracy and capitalism began to fray. In a replay of economic development in the East, America's promise as a land of opportunity butted up against free-market capitalism, with dire consequences for anyone caught in the squeeze. Frederick Jackson Turner's paean to frontier values certainly resonates in America's foundation myth, and it lingers in the collective memory of a nation that seems to suffer from a perpetual identity crisis. But with the closing of the frontier and the onset of modernity, the bell of freedom was ringing a bit hollow to farmers crushed by tenancy, investors brought to ruin in speculative schemes, and bank depositors whose meager savings disappeared in brazen robberies and insider shenanigans.

In May 1890, the Indian Territory was split into the Oklahoma Territory in the west and the Indian Territory in the east, and the process of integrating them into the nation's commercial networks began. Known from May 1890 to Oklahoma statehood in November 1907 as the Twin Territories, they became the latest cauldron of power struggles and conflicting visions about maintaining democratic ideals in the white-hot crucible of capitalism. It comes as no surprise that the struggle between democracy and capitalism crystallized in territorial banks, where businessmen with an extraordinary license to shape community development were empowered to lead the charge from frontier scarcity to the consumer nexus. For better or worse—and always for entertainment—it was bankers' turn to chart the course of banking in Oklahoma before statehood.

PART III

The Twin Territories, 1890–1907

CHAPTER SEVEN

Twilight of the Frontier

What a relief it was to those who had anything to deposit to be able to walk into a bank and transact their business and feel that the risk of long distance banking was over.

Mrs. Tom B. Ferguson, Oklahoma Territory settler

Following the Civil War, demands to open the Indian Territory to non-Indian settlement made their way to Congress. Throughout most of the nineteenth century, present-day Oklahoma (minus No Man's Land) was known as the Indian Territory; it was not until May 1890 that the region was split into the Oklahoma Territory in the west and the Indian Territory in the east. In a preview of controversies to come, the earliest bill aimed at opening the area to settlement ran afoul of the "Indian ring" whose members were more interested in exploiting tribesmen than bowing to political pressure. Stories of politicians on the take became grist for reformers who wanted to balance the fruits of capitalism with the fairness of democracy, and the Indian Territory was at the red-hot center of the debate. Aided and abetted by congressmen whose moral compasses were clearly out of kilter, cattle barons and railroad moguls plundered public lands with impunity and used Indians as pawns in a rich man's game. "If the glaring frauds, the vile and corrupt schemes of the monopolies who hold millions of dollars' worth of property in the Indian Territory, upon which they pay not a dollar's worth of taxes, could be exposed, it would furnish sufficient material to write another history," declared A. P. Jackson and his coauthor, Kansas real estate promoter E. C. Cole, who had made several excursions into the Indian Territory in search of promising townsites. "There never was a more open and glaring swindle upon the face of the American continent. It is in the interest of the rich to enrich the rich, and all efforts by petition after petition to the capital at Washington, D.C., though sent to our representatives, seem to be lost in oblivion when they reach there. They simply lie on file in the office of the Interior Department and there remain. In the meantime the poor home-seeker is thrust aside by the cold heart of these cattle-kings and their partners at Washington, and, when requested, the United States army is at their command."[1] In short, monopolists owned vast and valuable acreage, paid no taxes, and leased land from the federal government at two cents per acre that was supposed to belong to Indian tribes in perpetuity.

"The cattle-kings, the land-grabbers, and their followers must go," continued the reform-minded polemicists. "Oklahoma shall be the home of the free, where, almost at the doors of the capitalist and the poor man, lies a country whose native richness invites, whose fertility will reward the honest farmer with abundant harvest, whose genial climate invigorates and promises long life at small cost to man, and succulent grasses for his cattle, almost the year round."[2]

Efforts to open the floodgates to non-Indian settlers routinely went down in flames.[3] It was not until Elias C. Boudinot, a prominent Cherokee who did double duty as a clerk for the House Committee on Private Land Claims and an attorney with the Missouri, Kansas, and Texas Railroad (Katy), published articles on unoccupied land in the Indian Territory that inchoate lobbying hardened into politics. Boudinot cited four areas that were ripe for settlement: fourteen million acres of unoccupied public land in the middle of the territory; the Cherokee Outlet along Kansas's southern border; Old Greer County, still claimed by Texas, in the southwest; and No Man's Land between Kansas and the Texas Panhandle, west of the one hundredth meridian and east of New Mexico Territory.[4] Like a modern-day realtor eyeing a fat commission, Boudinot offered additional information and maps to potential homesteaders.[5]

Some of those potential homesteaders were becoming increasingly vocal in their demands. A Kansas farmer expressed the views of many when he suggested that the good Lord had created the Indians' land to be cultivated and improved. As the natives were clearly not up to the task, the farmer declared, "Why damn 'em, the government ought to let them have it that *will*."[6]

Predictably, railroad moguls added their voices to the rising chorus. Their rhetoric was matched by construction: just as the Katy was roaring into the Choctaw Nation to haul off its coal, the Atchison, Topeka and Santa Fe Railway was completing a line to Wichita.[7] The most strident advocates of opening the Indian Territory to non-Indian settlement came to be known as "Boomers" and, a bit more lyrically, "Oklahomaists." Their movement coalesced under the leadership of C. C. Carpenter. Fresh from similar agitation to seize Sioux lands in South Dakota, Carpenter saw no reason to hesitate down south. Yet when Carpenter and his Boomers threatened invasion, President Rutherford B. Hayes called their hand and ordered troops to the Kansas border. Gunplay was more than the Boomers had bargained for, and their movement lost its traction.[8]

But not for long. Following the Boomers' stillborn invasion, a former soldier from Indiana stepped into the breach to play one of the most dramatic roles in the settlement of the West. The latter-day Moses was David L. Payne, and to follow his trail is to revisit the seminal events in the closing of the frontier. His namesake might have been his mother's cousin, Davy Crockett, whose stubborn and ultimately fatal defense of the Alamo was his ticket to immortality. Or perhaps he was named after David of biblical lore who slew Goliath to become a symbol of victory against daunting odds.[9] What we know for sure is that Payne, born in Indiana in 1836, left home with his brother in 1858, bound for Kansas. After an ill-fated stint as a sawmill operator, he took to hunting and scouting and found himself in the company of luminaries who were even then taking up residence in America's pantheon of culture heroes: Kit Carson, Wild Bill Hickok, California Joe, Buffalo Bill Cody, and George Armstrong Custer, under whom Payne served after the Union's attention shifted from Confederates to Indians.[10]

Political and military service, including membership in the Kansas State Legislature and even a brief posting as assistant doorkeeper in the U.S. House of Representatives, strengthened Payne's allegiance to his adopted state of Kansas and drew his attention to the Indian Territory, where Boomers were trying to claim soil that, in his estimation, was rightfully theirs. Citing the treaties of 1866 as justification for opening up the fourteen million acres that Boudinot had singled out for settlement and that was entering the common vernacular as "the Oklahoma country" and "the Oklahoma district," Payne seized control of the Boomer movement in 1879. He and his followers let it be known that the quest to settle what came to be known as the Unassigned Lands in the middle of the Indian Territory transcended the moneymaking potential of free land.[11] At a Boomer camp six miles southeast of Hunnewell, Kansas, religious services opened with the patriotic tune "America" and were led by a chaplain whose sermon, delivered with the passion of a true believer, was drawn straight from Exodus: "The Lord commanded unto Moses, go forth and possess the promised land."[12] Such folks were not to be denied—for very long, anyway.

Funding problems followed Payne into the Indian Territory where he set up, if only temporarily, what might have been the first bank in the Cherokee Outlet. Within two months of pitching his camp on the Chikaskia River south of Hunnewell in the summer of 1884, Payne's settlement mushroomed to four box houses, hundreds of tents, an underground workshop, a printing office, and a well for water—but no bank. Drawing on his thin reserves of fiduciary acumen, the Boomer in chief got his hands on a cast-iron safe to store valuables, thus launching a form of purse-and-package banking. The "bank," broader and longer than it was deep, resting on wooden horses, and concealed with a table cloth, served as a desk. Certificates of membership in the colony were attached to each purse, with the owner's name affixed. No ledgers were kept, and deposits and withdrawals were always in whole, never in part. When federal troops showed up and prepared for their customary dispersal of the trespassers, the bank was broken and purses were returned to their owners. Other valuables were left in the safe, which was caulked, tossed into the water well, and concealed with brush. When the troops rode into camp on August 7 and set fire to the village, Payne and six others were arrested, but the purse-and-package bank was overlooked. A few colonists who still had possessions in the bank eventually returned to the campsite and, with block and tackle, hoisted the safe from its hiding place and liquidated the bank.[13]

David L. Payne's sister, Mrs. J. E. Brower of Kay County, Oklahoma Territory, described the circumstances leading to her brother's death in an interview in December 1903 with reporter Frederick S. Barde. Payne's repeated invasions into the Unassigned Lands and subsequent expulsions by U.S. soldiers eventually landed him in court in Fort Smith, Arkansas, where he pled his case before Judge Isaac Parker, known far and wide for his propensity to hang people. In the fall of 1884, he was exonerated of his crime. Elated and eager for another foray into the Oklahoma country, Payne went to Wellington, Kansas, to make a speech. "He had just written me a letter from Wellington," recalled his sister some nineteen years later, "where he had gone to make a speech, and told me of his grand success and was coming home to pay me a visit before he 'marched his colony to the promised land.' But at 11 o'clock, November 28, 1884, I received a telephone message that D. L. Payne dropped dead at the Hotel Barnard, at Wellington, Kas., while sitting at the breakfast table."[14]

Following Payne's death, the Boomer mantle was taken up by William L. Couch who, according to one ardent admirer, could "be trusted to carry out the plans of the dead, so nobly begun and nearly completed."[15] The erstwhile leader had been in his grave all of two weeks when Couch led a procession of Boomers to the vicinity of modern-day Stillwater, Oklahoma, where they showed their resolution by erecting cabins. Predictably, soldiers were right on their heels. A pitched battle was avoided when the commander, Colonel Edward Hatch, wisely decided to withdraw his troops and wait for hunger to set in. Couch managed to contain the hotheads in his camp who were spoiling for a fight, but time was clearly not on his side. On January 30, 1885, the disappointed settlers loaded their wagons and headed back to Kansas, flanked on either side by what must have been a very relieved cavalry.[16]

Even as Couch and his Boomers were exiting the Stillwater valley and mothballing their "On to Oklahoma!" banners, there were indications that politics in Washington, D.C., were changing with respect to settling the Oklahoma country. Secretary of the Interior Henry M. Teller was recommending the opening of Indian lands to non-Indian settlement, partly to satisfy the stubborn Boomers, but largely to address the ruthless exploitation of Native Americans that plagued the Oklahoma country through the imposition of federal laws. One cynical chief from the Indian Territory made reference to "the land shark problem— that is, how to get Congress to pull the land sharks through the Indian treaties."[17] President Chester A. Arthur, who had assumed the presidency when James A. Garfield was assassinated in 1881, was inclined to agree with Teller's recommendation.

On March 3, 1885, the day before President Arthur's term expired, Congress passed legislation authorizing the president to negotiate for cessions of the Creek, Seminole, and Cherokee surplus lands in western Indian Territory. Although President Arthur did not have time to do much about it and his successor, Grover Cleveland, would be satisfied with a leisurely pace, the handwriting was on the wall.[18] Officialdom was about to preempt the Boomer cause, thus setting the stage for the final act in America's westward expansion.

What Boomers had failed to achieve through audacity would be accomplished with the stroke of a pen. Yet the Boomers left their mark by compelling a reluctant federal government to hasten the inevitable. Through their obstinacy, the Kansas groups had given form to an extreme form of frontier boosterism that would reappear long after the dust settled and Boomer land lust was satisfied.[19] But it was the federal government, and not the renegade Boomers, that would fulfill the promise of the Promised Land.

To facilitate communications in the Indian Territory, a post office was established at the so-called Oklahoma Station in the middle of the Unassigned Lands on December 30, 1887.[20] C. E. Bennington, a conductor for the Gulf, Colorado and Santa Fe Railway, recalled the origins of the diminutive outpost: "At the time the Santa Fe was building through Oklahoma I was conductor of a construction train sent out to build switches. When we came to where Oklahoma City now stands an argument arose as to where the siding should be built, one saying that it should be further north and another insisting that it should be closer to the North Canadian river. As a compromise I suggested that the siding be built immediately east of a big cottonwood tree, that stood until lately at the corner of Broadway and Grand avenue. This was agreed to and Oklahoma City grew from the suggestion."[21]

The story continues with A. W. Dunham, who was appointed by the Atchison, Topeka and Santa Fe Railway to take charge of Oklahoma Station on February 20, 1888. Upon his arrival, he was accompanied by the company's traveling auditor and the route agent for Wells Fargo and Company to a ramshackle building across from the station that was used to house and feed "'mule skinners,' tenderfeet and other transients."[22] After stepping over a few Indians curled up on the floor in bright, colorful blankets, Dunham made his way to a stairway to find his accommodations. "Upstairs," wrote Dunham more than three decades later, "each of us was furnished a blanket, and, although the bed was spread with a thin cover, the weather was so cold we all slept with our clothing on and utilized our overcoats as well. Breakfast next morning was served on a long pine table at which we sat on benches, the bill of fare consisting of the usual sow belly, soggy biscuits, molasses and black coffee."[23]

From such inauspicious beginnings, Dunham launched an eleven-year career with responsibilities ranging from railroad agent, express agent, and manager of the Western Union Telegraph Company to stagecoach agent in what was to become Oklahoma City.[24] At the time of his posting, Oklahoma (as the outpost was then known)[25] was the only reporting or agency station between Arkansas City, Kansas, and Purcell, Indian Territory—a distance of 154 miles. Not long after his arrival, Dunham was joined by his mother, two sisters, and a brother, and the family moved into a cottage that the company provided for its agent. Despite military warnings and frequent evictions at bayonet point, the Dunhams' neighborhood included Boomers hunkered down in tents and dugouts, maintaining as low a profile as those windswept plains could afford, and determined to get a jump start on the impending landgrab. Like the rest of the Indian Territory, Oklahoma Station was short on banking facilities. The express company took care of money orders and transporting money and valuables, and frequent transfers of money were necessitated by the payroll at Fort Reno and activities at the far-flung Indian agencies. Government money was supposed to be guarded by cavalry, but mistakes were made and shipments sometimes went without protection. Keenly aware that "a vast number of criminals of every description"[26] roamed the Indian Territory, Dunham recalled an incident that might have turned ugly when a cavalry escort failed to show up: "I distinctly remember one occasion that the Government failed to provide an escort, and we were obliged to hold approximately forty thousand dollars almost a week. The little safe we had offered no real protection, so I concealed the money in old rubber boots and rubbish underneath the counter, close to my sleeping place. Not even the night operator knew we were taking so great a risk. Many bad men were known to be in the country at the time; trains were being held up and robbed at other places, but we were not molested in the least."[27]

The pace quickened after March 2, 1889, when Congress, blissfully unaware that Oklahoma Station's finances depended on a pair of old rubber boots, provided for the disposition of the Unassigned Lands to settlers pursuant to homestead laws. As the primary author of the so-called

Oklahoma bill, William M. Springer of Illinois, remarked in November 1888, "There is an irrepressible conflict between barbarism and civilization. The result of that conflict is not a matter of doubt. No portion of this continent can be held in barbarism to the exclusion of civilized man."[28] With full title to the Unassigned Lands in federal hands, a bill was rushed through Congress, and President Grover Cleveland signed it in the waning hours of his administration. President Benjamin Harrison had been in office less than three weeks when, on March 23, he issued a proclamation that the Unassigned Lands—1,887,796 acres in all—would be eligible for homesteading at noon on April 22.[29] Although homestead laws were to be in effect, there was a caveat: people who entered before the designated time would be denied the right to take a homestead.

President Harrison's proclamation that the Oklahoma country would be opened for settlement echoed across the country. Homesteaders flocked to the borders and spent frantic days securing their cargos, cleaning their weapons, and greasing the axles of their wagons. Journalists from coast to coast came to report on what was sure to be the scoop of their lives. Reporting for *Cosmopolitan,* Hamilton Wicks described what it was like to be caught up in the maelstrom in that spring of 1889: "I had been sojourning during the early part of April for a brief period in New York, when the Oklahoma question loomed up in the horizon of popular discussion. The Springer bill had been introduced and rejected in the Forty-ninth Congress, and the proclamation of President Harrison had been issued, declaring that one million eight hundred and eighty-seven thousand seven hundred and five acres of the richest agricultural lands in the West, situated in the very centre of the Indian Territory, would be thrown open to settlement at twelve o'clock high noon, on April 22, 1889. In common with many others in every part of the land, I was seized with the Oklahoma fever."[30]

Wicks threw a couple of flannel shirts into a suitcase stuffed with maps and charts of "the new Eldorado" and boarded the Penn Limited. We can only imagine his thoughts as the train clattered past the farms of Pennsylvania, beneath the peaks of Appalachia, across the prairies of Illinois and Iowa, and onto the Kansas flatlands, where westward expansion was lurching to its denouement. "Now," he wrote at journey's end in Arkansas City, "for the first time, I became conscious of the conditions among which I must struggle in this enterprise directed against a wild and unoccupied territory. From the peace and reserve of a mere traveler I was at once hurled into the conflict for personal supremacy with a seething mass of 'boomers.' A foretaste of what I might expect was presented to me at Arkansas City. It was as though I had suddenly been interjected into a confused Fourth-of-July celebration, where the procession had resolved itself into a mob."[31]

The three-hundred-mile boundary of the region open to homesteading had already been set, and negotiations with tribal leaders had given clear title to the government to dispose of the land as it saw fit. The same act of Congress that provided for settlement of the Unassigned Lands contained a clause authorizing President Harrison to appoint a commission to negotiate with tribes in the western Indian Territory to open their surplus lands for settlement. Over a period of five years, the three principals of the so-called Jerome Commission (named for its chairman, David H. Jerome, a former governor of Michigan) made arrangements with most of the tribes that still held lands in western Indian Territory. Their modus operandi was to secure agreements with tribal leaders to assign individual allotments to every man, woman, and child listed on official tribal roles. The U.S. government would purchase remaining land and open it for homesteading. Their groundwork paved the way for subsequent land runs and lotteries in the early 1890s.[32]

At high noon on a bright and clear Monday, April 22, 1889, a drama forever etched in the American consciousness roared to life when mounted soldiers fired their guns and blew their bugles to signal the big bang of Oklahoma history. Horses straining at the bit and rearing in anticipation shot forward. Contraptions of every description lurched into a kaleidoscope of horses and buggies and wagons. Trains packed to overflowing, their smokestacks belching thick black smoke, chugged toward the Santa Fe station as riders perched in precarious positions on top of and between cars did their best to avoid being crushed between pistons or dismembered beneath wheels. Curses filled the air in a cauldron of spilled cargo and dust and noise the likes of which nobody had ever seen. Cries of pain as wagons careened into ditches and horses threw their riders mingled with whoops of triumph when those fortunate enough to make it unscathed through what came to be known as Harrison's Horse Race staked their claims to a new life.

A. W. Dunham saw them coming. The land run was still fresh in his mind some thirty-five years later when the former Oklahoma Station master shared his memories with attendees at the Oklahoma Historical Society's annual meeting. "On that memorable day, April 22d," explained Dunham to what must have been a rapt audience, "in order to get a better view, I stood on a box car along side the depot at the zero hour of 12 o'clock noon. My astonishment was complete—people seemed to spring up as if by magic as far as the eye could reach. I could see them racing in every direction, some on horses, some in vehicles, and a greater number on foot. They were carrying all sorts of impedimentia [*sic*]— some had spades, some stakes, some clothing, some had hand-bags, some had pots and pans, or other cooking utensils. My words are not adequate to describe the scene. I then commenced to realize that history was in the making."[33]

By the end of the day, nearly every townsite and homestead claim was occupied. In the ensuing days, the dust settled to reveal bustling communities—Guthrie, Kingfisher, Norman, Oklahoma City, and Stillwater— scrambling to put their affairs in order.[34] It would be left to courts of law to determine who had staked their claims legally, and who had jumped the gun to earn everlasting infamy as a "sooner," sometimes called a "moonlighter," and always held in contempt by settlers who had played by the rules.[35] Under the headline "A Brighter View," a *Los Angeles Times* reporter who took the train from Guthrie to Purcell, Indian Territory, captured the essence of the post-run panorama: "The ride tonight from Guthrie to Purcell reveals strange and beautiful pictures. All over the level lands approaching the Canadian River bottom the lights of camp fires burning in the open air or the lights of lamps glimmering through canvas tents give the entire country a weird but pleasing look. Three [*sic*] was no timber line to obstruct the view for miles of distance. It was a fine spectacular scene."[36]

One of those lights glimmered from a campsite near the railroad depot, where T. M. Richardson and his two sons had staked out a lot. The elder Richardson, a native of Mississippi and resident of Texas, was a lumberman whose holdings included properties in his native state to Texas and in what would eventually become Oklahoma. For ten days before the run, he and his sons had been in Purcell, Indian Territory, where he had opened a lumberyard and prepared to join the stampede into the Oklahoma country. "There were about ten thousand people there," recalled his son, T. M. Jr. "We slept on the floor of the Lumber office. People there slept on the ground, in the open, on wagons in our lumber yard, in tents, or any way they could, all awaiting the day of the opening."[37] The Richardsons were fortunate to secure seats on the northbound train; many of their fellow travelers were packed like sardines in the aisles and piled high on the coaches, the back of the tender, and even on the engine. One woman described the train as a huge centipede with hundreds of arms and legs and heads protruding from its body.[38] At the end of their harrowing ride, the Richardsons were greeted by troops who kept what order they could and, to mitigate the chaos with ritual, dropped the flag in the evening and sounded "Taps." Apparently, that was about it for entertainment. "There was no amusement of any kind conducted when we were first here," recalled T. M. Jr. who, at the age of fifteen, was no doubt scouting for diversions. "I never saw any dogs in town the first night and there were only a few women, but they came in later."[39]

T. M. Jr.'s father, meanwhile, was about to add banking to his résumé. His partners from the little town of Albany, Texas, included George T. Reynolds, a wealthy banker and cattleman who contributed capital to the venture but remained in Texas, and J. P. Boyle, the cashier and designated handler of day-to-day details. The elder Richardson had already obtained stationery, checks, passbooks, and other tools of the trade in Dallas. He had also purchased a safe and some heavy oak desks, chartered a boxcar, and filled it with his acquisitions and lumber that he planned to use to erect a temporary building. The car was routed on the Santa Fe Railway to Oklahoma Station and rested on a siding for several days before the run.

Having applied for a national bank charter a few days before the run, Richardson was determined to beat competitors to the punch.[40] Within an hour of his arrival at the Santa Fe depot, he had staked a claim on the northeast corner of the intersection of Clarke Street (later named Grand Avenue and eventually Sheridan Avenue) and Harvey Avenue, three blocks west of the depot.[41] It was not long before Richardson was trading lumber for greenbacks, gold coin, silver dollars, demand notes, due bills, two-cent pieces, and even wooden nickels.[42] Plagued by second thoughts about his location, he paid three hundred dollars for a lot just east of Broadway at 106 West Main Street, which was a block north and two blocks east of his original claim and closer to the business district.[43] A tent was erected, and a sign was placed in front bearing the inscription "Oklahoma Bank."[44]

New arrivals were still panting from their exertions when, sometime in the afternoon of April 22, E. E. Elterman from Bloomer, Wisconsin, spotted Richardson's sign. Elterman's pockets bulged with drafts on New York banks. Scrutinizing Richardson and deciding that the Texan was trustworthy, Elterman said simply, "I understand you folks are going to start a bank. I am going to start a dry goods store here and I want to be your first depositor. I wish you would take this New York exchange and give me credit as soon as your books are opened up."[45]

Apparently, Richardson decided that the fellow from Wisconsin was trustworthy as well, and the transaction was completed before the sun set on a dusty, crowded road in the middle of nowhere. Like the Jews of medieval Venice and the Medici money changers of Renaissance Florence, T. M. Richardson and his ilk began with modest accommodations—perhaps not much more than benches, or *banci* in Italian, from which they extended credit and thereby greased the wheels of commerce.[46] Like the merchant-bankers whose role they were usurping, territorial bankers had reason to think about "credit" as a derivation of *credo,* Latin for "I believe." One suspects that their belief in repayment was similarly challenged as they conducted their business on a lawless frontier. But even as chaos reigned, there were glimpses of good times to come. "The early business men were honest and capable," recalled stationmaster A. W. Dunham. "They wanted only what was right and were willing to co-operate for the best interests of the town. It was a pleasure to know and do business with them."[47]

T. M. Richardson's experience was far from unusual. Contrary to images of yeoman farmers who staked their claims in the countryside, the most aggressive settlers were drawn to towns, where men anxious to exert leadership and amass fortunes found a ready stage for the drama of community building. The town was thus the focus for public energies that gave flavor and substance to Oklahoma's territorial experience.[48] Myron R. Sturtevant, whose youthful exploits included participation in the Alaska and Yukon gold rushes, received his appointment as national bank examiner from Comptroller of the Currency Charles G. Dawes in March 1901. Sturtevant explained how those energies were manifested at the genesis of Oklahoma banking.

> Those expecting to open a bank, were ready usually with a pair
> of horses (no autos in those days) and dray carrying a small Cor-

liss safe and a tent, which tent was pitched with some stakes holding down the ends, then the flap of the tent was cut, some chicken wire was installed for the cashier cage, plus two or three loaded rifles and a chair inside of tent, then business was started. In most towns a frame building about the size of a modern hen house were [*sic*] ready for business two to six days after opening. In one town, tents blew down, checks blew away and the banks capital was impaired about Nine Hundred Dollars, quite a sum to make up out of profits in those days; especially at that time when new banks were not required to put up any surplus.[49]

Quick though he was to open his bank, T. M. Richardson missed out on bragging rights to Oklahoma Station's first bank. That distinction goes to the Citizens Bank, which was the first financial institution to be organized in those rough environs. Capitalized with $25,000, Citizens Bank opened for business about a week after the land run in a false-front, one-story frame building on the southeast corner of Main and Broadway. Founders included James Geary as president, L. A. Gilbert as cashier, and Fox Winnie as a director.[50] Within ten minutes of opening for business, the bank's coffers were bursting with aggregate deposits of $20,000. As deposits slowed in the ensuing months, the Citizens Bank appealed to depositors by branding itself as a bank that had grown rapidly from day one.[51] A more permanent structure was soon to follow.

Up north, the First National Bank of Guthrie was staking its claim as the first real bank in the Unassigned Lands. With J. W. McNeal as president and A. W. Little as cashier, the institution sprang into existence as a private bank under the no-nonsense name, the McNeal-Little Banking Company. Such was the pace of Guthrie's economic development that, on May 1, 1889, the newly designated First National Bank of Guthrie reported total resources of $108,728.48—not bad for a bank that had been in business less than two weeks! McNeal and his associates moved into one of Guthrie's original brick buildings, where it remained until 1923. The First National Bank of Guthrie received the first charter granted to an Oklahoma bank (charter number 4348) and quickly became a commercial hub of the Oklahoma Territory.[52]

But the Oklahoma Bank was not far behind. Dissatisfied with his location east of Broadway, Richardson purchased two lots from John R. Tanner of Illinois for $2,500 on the southwest corner of Main and

Broadway. It was a win-win situation: Richardson had his corner lots, and Tanner had $2,500 in his pockets—not bad for a few days' excursion into the Oklahoma country. Tanner returned to Illinois and was later elected as governor. Richardson stayed in Oklahoma City to build his empire.[53]

George T. Reynolds, who remained in Texas, served as the Oklahoma Bank's president. With T. M. Richardson as vice president and J. P. Boyle as cashier, the Oklahoma Bank boasted capital stock of $50,000. Its no-nonsense ads in Oklahoma City's first community newspaper, the *Oklahoma Times,* touted the bank's principals as businessmen who meant business. "The officers of this Bank are substantial and practical business men," ran an advertisement on May 9, 1889. Citing Reynolds's business connections back in Albany, Texas, and promising "liberal and courteous treatment" to all, the Oklahoma Bank was fully prepared to compete with the upstart bank on the opposite corner. For readers who needed a bit more convincing, the Oklahoma Bank concluded its advertisements with an unambiguous message: "We cite the above in order to show you that we are not a wild-cat bank, but have come to stay."[54]

The Citizens Bank was similarly committed to the long haul and used the power of advertising to publish references from leading businessmen. Combined deposits of the Citizens Bank and the Oklahoma Bank were approximately $100,000 when they opened, and their combined capital-ization was about $75,000.[55] But business was business, and bankers did what they had to do to stay afloat. As journalist Frederick Barde noted, "Real estate titles were flimsy and merchants had a shaky financial stand-ing. Small loans were made, however, and for the accommodation only 3 per cent a month interest was charged. If the amount was large and well secured, the monthly interest was reduced to something 'reason-able'—perhaps 15 or 16 per cent a year. But this rate was the lowest."[56]

While nascent banks in the Unassigned Lands of present-day central Oklahoma were vying for customers and justifying high interest rates as the unavoidable cost of risk, merchant-bankers throughout the region were passing the baton to specialists who still had to contend with the ad hoc nature of their enterprise. Pioneer banker Tom J. Hartman recounted the genesis of banking in the Indian Territory, when banks chartered under the laws of Arkansas opened for business with little or no capital and charged whatever interest rates the market would bear. Punishing interest rates were to be expected in scrappy little Oklahoma Station and other outposts in the Indian Territory. Denied credit from eastern financiers who were leery of risking their money in the Indian Territory, capital-starved settlers fortunate enough to have access to banking facilities had no choice but to mortgage their livestock and crops to the hilt, and they could expect to pay interest rates ranging from 2 to 5 percent per month.[57] Even in more settled areas of America's midsection, the cost of money smacked of usury. In Nebraska, for example, interest rates of 4 to 5 percent per month were not uncommon.[58] But before bankers could make loans of any kind, they needed capital, and the ways in which they procured it became fodder for western lore. "About thirty years ago," recalled Hartman to what must have been an incredulous interviewer,

> I heard one of our earlier bankers, in addressing a meeting, state that during the first banking experiences in the Indian Territory, he did not put up any capital whatever. He bought a safe and printed the word "Bank" on a piece of cardboard, and tacked it up at the side of the door. In a little while, a "Nester" dropped in and said, "So, this is the new bank" and deposited $150.00. A little later, in came another "Nester" and deposited $200.00. He said, "I got to thinking it over and decided that maybe my bank was going to be a success after all, so I had $100.00 in cash and thought if the other fellow had confidence in a bank, I had better deposit my $100.00 to show my confidence." This bank prospered in a small way, and after a few years we paid in what was considered very substantial capital—$5,000.00.[59]

In a land where being the first carried a lot of cachet, it is hardly surprising to find a swirl of controversy about who, exactly, were the first honest-to-goodness bankers in the Indian Territory. Hartman gave the nod to P. S. Hoffman, J. B. Charles, and E. L. Conklin. With due deference to the Patterson Mercantile Company and perhaps other businesses whose foundation stories languish in forgotten scrapbooks, Hartman's 1937 interview for the WPA includes a passage from a letter that he received from Conklin that probably comes as close as we can get to the genesis of Oklahoma banking. At the very least, Hartman opens a portal into a typology of frontier banks that were unique in their particulars, but similar in the ways they were founded and managed in their infancy:

In 1887, located as traders at Sac and Fox Agency, Messrs. P. S. Hoffman, J. B. Charles, and Myself, operating as Hoffman, Charles and Conklin, often found ourselves in great need of banking facilities, especially to obtain the cash wherewithal to pay Government checks to the Indians. We practically operated as a bank, but did not formally organize ourselves into a bank until September 1892. As a trading Company we extended credit, accepted deposits and cashed checks. However, we seldom had very much cash on hand at one time. The Dalton boys and others who sometimes happened along would make themselves free with the cash and fail to leave a check for the same. For about five years we conducted a bank somewhat grocery-store fashion, patterned after farm work, open for business early after breakfast, closing late in the evening, were liberal with accommodations to customers at off hours and part of Sunday.[60]

Hoffman and his partners received a certificate for the Bank of Hoffman Charles & Conklin in January 1898, and their bank was eventually chartered as the Union National Bank of Chandler.[61] Meanwhile, banks were popping up like proverbial mushrooms all over the newly settled region. The Guthrie National Bank, operating under charter number 4383, was giving the First National Bank of Guthrie a run for its money. The First National Bank of Muskogee was organized by Robert L. Owen—who went on to represent Oklahoma in the U.S. Senate—and chartered on August 1, 1889, under charter number 4385. This bank had the unique reputation of being a dividend-paying bank; according to Tom Hartman, "there is no question but that the dividend record of this bank exceeds that of any other bank ever organized in the State of Oklahoma."[62] Down in the Chickasaw Nation, J. F. Anderson in Ardmore organized the J. F. Anderson and Son Bank on August 17, 1889. Paid-in capital was $3,200, and deposits on the first day of business added up to $203.75. Anderson's bank was eventually chartered as the First National Bank of Ardmore to become the fourth national bank established in present-day Oklahoma.[63] A couple of years later, the First National Bank of Vinita (charter number 4704) and the First National Bank of El Reno (charter number 4830) extended the federal banking system's reach into the Twin Territories.[64]

Okarche's claim to the first territorial bank charter in the Oklahoma Territory dates back to October 28, 1892, when Julius Loosen, a recent arrival from Polk County, Nebraska, founded the First Bank of Okarche in a small frame building. Family tradition has it that, during his first few years in America, Loosen's reliance on loans from a bank in Osceola, Nebraska, made him wonder what it would be like to sit on the other side of the loan officer's desk. His opportunity to find out came when the Cheyenne and Arapaho country was opened for non-Indian settlement on April 19, 1892. Okarche was a cattle-loading station on the Rock Island Railroad at the eastern boundary of the reservation before the area was opened in a land run. The station blossomed overnight into a village of primitive shelters and enough residents of German origin to earn its moniker as Oklahoma's "Little Germany."[65]

Short on both capital and banking experience, Julius and his wife, Adele, relocated to the newly opened country, scraped together $3,000 in capital, and enlisted B. F. Buffington from the Osceola bank to serve as cashier in a bank they christened, appropriately enough, the First Bank of Okarche. Loosen's son, Franz H., was brought in as assistant cashier. On January 11, 1893, the territorial secretary issued a charter authorizing the four incorporators—the three Loosens and Buffington—"to do a general banking business."[66]

The First Bank of Okarche's capital was quickly increased to $5,000. Within a year, the upstart bank was off and running with $10,000 in capital. After spending about a year with the bank, Buffington resigned as cashier, and Franz was elevated to his position. When Julius died in 1896 during a visit to his native Germany, his other son, Emil C., was elected president and his widow, Adele, was elected vice president. Family lore is replete with stories of depleted deposits and crop failures during the bank's formative years. But, as a First Bank of Okarche publication commemorating the bank's fiftieth anniversary attested, "The settlers were rugged individualists, the bank was well capitalized, and the management was full of confidence in the future of the country. These facts made it possible for the institution to survive and for the community to prosper."[67]

Some banks opened for business with unusual charters and histories that stretch the imagination. In the treeless and lawless expanse known as No Man's Land that eventually coalesced into Beaver, Texas, and

Cimarron Counties in the Oklahoma Panhandle, the 101 Ranch near Kenton carried on banking functions for some thirty years. Caldwell, Kansas, served as a reserve center. In 1889, geographically challenged officials in Washington, D.C., placed No Man's Land under the jurisdiction of a court in Muskogee, Indian Territory, a mere five-hundred-mile jaunt from Kenton on horseback.[68]

In case they wanted to make a quick getaway and take their bank with them, a group of bankers in Wichita Falls, Texas, set up shop in Lawton and mounted their bank on rollers. "Because they didn't have permission to have a bank, they could roll it out of town," said City National Bank of Lawton chairman Roma Lee Porter, whose family has been involved with the bank (no longer mounted on rollers) since 1931. "They slept in the building," she continued, relishing the opportunity to share a favorite story. "And then every weekend, they went back to Wichita Falls and took the money back to Wichita Falls. And when they were crossing Cache Creek, they tied it to their heads, while they swan across the creek, and Indians were sitting on the other side, just laughing at them."[69] It turns out that banks were not the only businesses to follow their customers. From 1912 to the 1920s, Earl and Ewel Dixon piloted their horse-drawn cookshack to feed harvest and threshing crews in the North Flats area north of Guymon.[70]

A similar tale comes from Blaine County where three banking brothers—Clay, Oliver, and Gene Willis—were preparing for the arrival of the Kansas City, Mexico and Orient Railroad in the newly designated town of Cantonment by relocating the Bank of Fay, which they had recently purchased and which was supposed to be located in the town of Fort, to the new community. But there was not a moment to lose. Vexed by banks that moved—or, as the case may be, rolled—with the dollars, the territorial legislature was considering a bill that would prohibit banks from relocating at their owners' whims. Clay, the most politically savvy of the brother bankers, made his way to Guthrie and quickly schmoozed his way to the inner circle. Yet another brother, Bert, whose own career in Blaine County banking spanned a half century, recalled what happened next in his unpublished memoir—written in 1953 at the urging of state bank examiner E. H. Kelley, and tucked away in the Oklahoma Historical Society's archives ever since: "He politicked around until he got in a favored spot with a few of the members and also the governor and the bank commissioner, so he had a member tack on an amendment to the bill that exempted the banks that were then in the process of being moved, and that was the position of the Bank of Fay, and the bill went through that way and the Bank of Fay became the Bank of Cantonment. He had the charter amended accordingly and for several years it was the Bank of Cantonment, but in due course of time the charter was again amended to Bank of Canton."[71]

When the first engine "poked its nose into the townsite," the Willis brothers were there to welcome newcomers with open arms and a brand-new bank. Willis claimed that the bank was the first business in town. The second and third were saloons, the fourth was a Methodist Church and, at the risk of redundancy, the fifth was another saloon. "I believe that they all believed in reciprocity," wrote Willis, whose humor tended to the dry side. "From the bank to the saloon to the church to the saloon. It was rather a queer setup and I wouldn't know how to set them up in order of importance. The saloons were quite popular in those days."[72]

The Chickasaw Bank was chartered on November 8, 1889, to transact business in Cowley County, Kansas, for ninety-nine years. Cattlemen in the Chickasaw Nation, together with bankers and businessmen from Arkansas City, Kansas, ponied up $50,000 in capital, and they rented a post office box to establish residence—in Arkansas City, that is. H. P. Farrar, cashier of the First National Bank of Arkansas City, was responsible for checking the post office box and forwarding mail. The bank eventually jumped over to "The Oklahoma Country" and opened for business in Purcell, Indian Territory, where it battled for its share of business in a region where success was anything but guaranteed.[73]

Tom J. Hartman's reference to the "Dalton boys and others who sometimes happened along" to relieve him and his associates of their cash serves as a reminder that the safety of money was often a state of mind. John Lloyd of Bennington, Indian Territory, was a teenager in the 1880s when his mother rode to the home of Governor Wilson N. Jones, principal chief of the Choctaw Nation, to visit his family. As she bade her goodbyes and prepared for the seven-mile-trip back home, Governor Jones walked up to her horse and tied a small, heavy bag to her saddle. Mrs. Lloyd was shocked to learn that the bag contained $10,000 in gold. Governor Jones quickly explained that, as the wife of a well-known missionary to the Choctaws, she would be the perfect steward of such a vast sum, and that he would come for the money when he needed it. Even in those hardscrabble environs, what thief would stoop so low as to rob a preacher's wife?

Surely masking her skepticism, Mrs. Lloyd rode home with the loot and hid it at the foot of her feather bed. Shortly thereafter, five horsemen rode up to the Lloyds' home and asked if they had any chickens to sell. As soon as Mrs. Lloyd pointed out the birds she was willing to part with, the men drew their pistols, blasted the chickens' heads off, paid for them, and rode away with the headless chickens. Young John was impressed with the men's marksmanship. Years later, he was traveling through Paris, Texas, when he recognized one of the men who had ignited his youthful imagination. The chicken killer turned out to be none other than one of the West's most notorious outlaws, Frank James, long since pardoned of his manifold depredations. James confessed that he had indeed taken part in the avian slaughter and, moreover, that his companions on that day were his brother, Jesse, and the Younger brothers. John then told the onetime bank robber about the $10,000 that his mother had hidden in her bed. In the classic mold of robbers who preyed only on those who deserved it, James replied that he and his companions would never have stolen it, even if they had been alerted to its presence.[74]

Thus did Mrs. Lloyd's feather bed enter into banking lore. Like David L. Payne's brush-covered water well in the Cherokee Outlet and A. W. Dunham's rubber boots at Oklahoma Station, Mrs. Lloyd's bed had to suffice for financial security until a proper bank could be established.

For thirteen months (April 1889–May 1890) after the Run of '89, residents of Oklahoma Station and its environs muddled along in a legislative vacuum. Prospects for law and order dimmed in April 1890 when the celebrated Boomer leader and Oklahoma City's first mayor, W. L. Couch, took a bullet to the knee in a shoot-out with J. C. Adams, a notorious sooner and rival land claimant. Adams was arrested and sent to prison. Couch, who had left office in November 1889, lingered in agony for several days before succumbing to gangrene.[75] Things took a turn for the better when Congress passed the Oklahoma Territory Organic Act of May 2, 1890. With the stroke of a pen, the territory had the government's blessing to put its affairs in order. The Organic Act followed the model of state formation articulated in the Northwest Ordinance of 1787. Its provisions thus predated the U.S. Constitution, and it guaranteed that the federal government's expansion into the Oklahoma country would be democratic in character.[76] Under the auspices of the Organic Act, President Benjamin Harrison appointed a governor and a supreme court of three judges who also served as district judges. Voters were invited to elect twenty-six representatives to a bicameral legislature, thirteen representatives to an executive council, and a territorial delegate to Congress. The laws of Nebraska were in force until the legislature could draw up a legal code. County and township governments were to be organized, but until elections could be held, the governor was authorized to fill posts by appointment.[77]

To accommodate territorial growth, the Organic Act provided that all reservations in western Indian Territory would automatically come into the Oklahoma Territory at such time as they were opened to settlement. Old Greer County was technically included within the territory's boundaries but was specifically exempted from the application of homestead law or further settlement until the Red River boundary dispute with Texas could be settled.[78] Future controversy was assured when the capital was located temporarily in Guthrie. Seven counties were designated—six in the Oklahoma district and one in No Man's Land. In the Oklahoma Territory's first election on August 5, 1890, voters participated in a name-that-county contest and came up with the following names: Payne, Logan, Kingfisher, Oklahoma, Canadian, and Cleveland, all located in the Oklahoma district; and Beaver in No Man's Land, later split into Beaver, Texas, and Cimarron Counties.[79]

President Harrison appointed George W. Steele of Indiana to serve as territorial governor and Robert Martin of El Reno as secretary. Other appointments included Horace Speed of Guthrie as U.S. district attorney, Warren S. Lurty of West Virginia as U.S. marshal, and Abraham J. Seay of Missouri, Edward B. Green of Illinois, and John B. Clark of Wisconsin as supreme court justices. Justice Seay stepped down from the territorial supreme court when President Harrison appointed him as Governor Steele's successor. Seay's tenure as governor began with an inauguration on October 18, 1891, and ended when President Cleveland appointed William C. Renfrow of Norman as the territory's third governor.[80] In a pattern that typifies the revolving door between politics and business, Seay's exit from politics in 1893 gave him the time he needed to make his fortune. At one time, Seay owned two hotels in Kingfisher, was president of three national banks, and owned considerable stock in at least four others. He was also an investor in Oklahoma real estate and Missouri mining operations. Through wise investments, his fortune peaked at more than half a million dollars. By the time of his death in 1915, distributions and losses occasioned by poor health had diminished the value of his estate to approximately $200,000.[81]

When the legislature gathered for its initial session on August 29, 1890, in Guthrie, lawmakers spent more time squabbling over the location of a capital city than deliberating more pressing concerns.[82] Wrangling over the location of the capital and other plums—county seats and colleges, to name the most contentious—signaled that a politician's ideology was less important than his ability to bring home bounties for his constituents.[83] As territorial delegates and their successors in the state legislature often learned the hard way, assertiveness trumped experience, and certainly education, every time.

If designating a permanent capital had hinged solely on population, then Guthrie would have been the clear winner with 5,884 citizens. Lesser towns included Oklahoma City with 5,086; Kingfisher, 1,234; Norman, 764; Stillwater, 625; and El Reno, 519.[84] Oklahoma Territory's second election, held on November 4, 1890, named a Republican, David A. Harvey, as the first territorial delegate to Congress.[85]

The Organic Act signaled the formal separation of Oklahoma and Indian Territories, which would be known throughout their tortuous journey to union as a single state in 1907 as the Twin Territories. Henceforth, governance in the Oklahoma Territory would be separate from the hodgepodge of tribal, territorial, and federal laws that governed the Indian Territory. The territorial governor and legislature were instructed to follow the laws of older states in framing their legal codes. The Organic Act was also a watershed in terms of banking insofar as it authorized the extension of the National Banking Acts of 1863 and 1864 into the Oklahoma Territory. In the absence of formal codes, territorial officials were compelled to follow the banking laws of Arkansas. Integration into the national banking system meant that banks could receive a federal charter if they had $30,000 in paid-in capital and invested one-third of it in United States banks. Under a federal charter, banks could receive federal deposits, conduct the nation's business, and issue currency in amounts up to 90 percent of the value of their capital.[86]

Inclusion in the federal banking system was certainly a milestone in Oklahoma's economic development. Yet the National Banking Acts of 1863 and 1864 were highly restrictive insofar as they compelled bankers to maintain a high capital base, invest in U.S. government bonds, and adhere to tight loan regulations. Not surprisingly in a region so recently hewn from the frontier, few bankers had either the desire or ability to accept such onerous restrictions. Oklahoma's first banks were therefore private enterprises, subject to no controls, and dependent on limited resources and the integrity of their principals.[87]

Between the passage of the Organic Act in 1890 and statehood in 1907, national banks chartered in Washington, D.C., competed with Oklahoma Territory banks chartered in Guthrie. Private banks to the east, where land was held in common and governance emanated from a complex stew of tribal and federal authorities, were left more or less to their own devices until 1901, when Congress extended provisions of Arkansas statutes pertaining to corporations to the Indian Territory. Even then, the Indian Territory did not have a banking department, and general corporate law provided the only means of oversight and control over banks.[88] In such towns as Muskogee, Ardmore, McAlester, and Tahlequah, banks sprouted up with little more than a strongbox and a few sticks of furniture—not the most auspicious formula for commercial development. Bank chartering thus became a defining issue in Oklahoma's economic development, and it spawned decades of raucous debates that lead straight back to the dawn of the Republic, when Alexander Hamilton and Thomas Jefferson nearly came to blows over centralized banking.

The Organic Act of May 2, 1890, put bankers on notice that their freewheeling days were numbered, and it provided access to the federal system to those with national banking ambitions. Yet it did not preclude the addition of more colorful chapters to an already colorful history of banking and business. Like many banks in the Twin Territories, the First National Bank of Weleetka opened in a tent. Relying on frontier ingenuity and whatever odds and ends were at hand, the proprietor kept money in an old telescope bag and transacted business over a table until he managed to construct a box house. By then, he had upgraded to "a crude cashier's window and a cash box"; a year later, "a nice brick bank was built with modern improvements."[89]

A similar tale comes from Pottawatomie County, opened to non-Indian settlement in a land run on September 22, 1891. Willard Johnston, a fiery Scotch-Irishman from New York State who participated in the land run and whose descendants built one of America's largest mortgage companies, Midland Mortgage Company of Oklahoma City, as a prelude to establishing MidFirst Bank in the early 1980s, served as cashier under J. H. Maxey at the Bank of Shawnee. The bank opened in a small, wooden building, and the safe was placed so that it could be removed in case of fire. When construction began of a more permanent structure, Johnston moved the safe to the back of the lot and put it under a tree. Many years later, the frontier banker explained his odd arrangement: "As the safe weighed more than two tons and was burglar proof I was not afraid of anyone running off with it, but I know it looked strange to see me carry the currency out there and put it in a safe setting on the back end of lots under a tree, and expecting to leave it there all night."[90] Johnston reorganized the Bank of Shawnee in November 1898 to create the First National Bank of Shawnee. In 1902, he moved across the street to launch the State National Bank, which he presided over for many years, presumably with the safe inside.[91]

A founder and onetime president of the First National Bank of Enid told the story of his bank's genesis in the Run of '93. He and several other young men made the run into the Cherokee Outlet in hopes of staking out lots in what was to become the town of Enid. Equipped with weapons as well as a tent, groceries, cooking utensils, water, and bedrolls, they dashed across the line at the signal shots and found a promising location in which to put up their tent. Just as they were adding the finishing touches to their modest establishment, a friend dropped by with a considerable sum of money and declared that he was afraid to go to sleep for fear of being robbed. He asked the newcomers if they would take care of his money until he could become more comfortably settled. The young men agreed to help out their friend, and, before long, the word was out that a group of well-armed young men could be trusted with other people's money. Legal tender began to pile up at their tent in such quantities that one of the men, clearly a visionary, asked his companions, "Why don't we establish a bank?"[92]

That seemed like a good idea. The group placed sums that had been left in their safekeeping in separate envelopes and found a nail keg to serve as a depository, all the while taking turns as round-the-clock security guards. As the dust settled in the upstart metropolis, the young men found some paint and created a banner to hang over their tent with the simple inscription "Bank of Enid." From these modest beginnings arose the First National Bank of Enid.[93]

Whatever the exact circumstances of their formation and extent of their regulation, there is no doubt that real banks heralded the dawning of a new era. Mrs. Tom B. Ferguson of Watonga described the relief that she felt when a real bank opened up for business. Carved from the Cheyenne and Arapaho Reservations in western Oklahoma Territory, Watonga went bankless for some two years. Businesses, the county treasurer, and even the post office were forced to send their money to a town thirty miles away for deposit. "With outlaws and bandits in the offing," recalled a relieved Mrs. Ferguson, "it was always a gamble as to whether their precious cash would ever reach its destination. What a relief it was to those who had anything to deposit to be able to walk into a bank and transact their business and feel that the risk of long distance banking was over."[94]

Yet the risks of life on the edge of civilization were far from over. Throughout the fall of 1890, headlines blared with reports of restive Indians in the northern plains who were allegedly massing for attack. "They were all well armed with Winchester rifles, had plenty of ammunition and were well equipped with ponies," ran a riveting account in the *Oklahoma City Evening Gazette.* "They were uniformly insolent and reticent."[95] Trouble was brewing down south as well, where Captain Jack Hayes of the Fifth Cavalry at Fort Reno was fielding requests for protection from settlers along the western boundary of the Oklahoma Territory. Ominously, an Indian prophet known as the Messiah was fanning the flames of revolt among the Cheyenne, Arapaho, Ponca, and Caddo tribes, urging them to take up the ghost dance "with a great deal of religious and war-like fervor." The word on the street was that one of the Messiah's minions from the Shoshone reservation near Fort Messick, Wyoming, was responsible for the excitement. Tensions throughout Indian country were rising to a fever pitch. They would culminate soon enough near a tiny hamlet in South Dakota called Wounded Knee.[96]

In the Oklahoma Territory, rumors morphed into reality when settlers learned that Cheyenne Indians who had taken up the ghost dance near Fort Reno had gone on the warpath, eluded federal troops, and were bearing down on Oklahoma City (as it was now known) "for the massacre of the population."[97] Alerted to the danger, citizens mustered in the center of the city, where hardware merchants W. J. Pettee and Gilpin & Frick were doling out weapons and ammunition. As a small child, Myrtle Hill Allen was " paralized [*sic*] with fright" when a man rode into town from Yukon shouting, "The Indians are coming." As she recalled many years later, "All women and children in our neighborhood were sent word to go across the street from our home to the two story brick home of Judge Allen in case the Indians came. We later learned it was a joke some one had played, but it was very real to we children."[98]

The threat was also very real to T. M. Richardson, Sr. In a replay of countless dramas—real and imagined—that frame our understanding of the West, the banker-turned–Indian fighter rose to the occasion and invited neighbors to take refuge in his house.[99] Avenues entering the city of five thousand from the north, west, and south were guarded by a contingent of citizen-soldiers. "During all this time," recalled one of the city's original settlers, C. A. McNabb, "a constant stream of farm wagons (no automobiles then) was pouring into the city from the west, laden with farmer families and some household equipment. It was reported at the time that several farmers brought the family cow and the pigs."[100]

Rifle shots rang out along the advance guard, and settlers braced for attack. "It was thunderous, hair-raising, gore-inspiring to those who were called upon to defend the city and its precious populace," wrote McNabb. "Everybody was on tiptoe, awaiting the arrival of the Indian advance guard."[101] Relief mixed with disappointment when the would-be Indian fighters realized that the advancing fires and commotion were not from Cheyennes on the warpath, but from "a charivari party, some ten miles west of the city, indulged in by a hundred, more or less, young people. The noises were such as only young minds, charivari bent, can devise." The eighty-niner McNabb concluded his account of the Indian scare of 1890 with a dose of bravado: "Most of us remained up for the balance of the night, hoping, perhaps, that some savage redskins might show up. There has never existed in my mind the least doubt of the successful ter-mination of that battle. Had it been fought as anticipated, the Cheyenne Indian tribe would today have been extinct."[102]

Maybe so. But now that the frontier was entering its twilight, the good people of Oklahoma City might have come up with a better way to settle their differences with their Cheyenne neighbors. And who knows? Maybe T. M. Richardson spent a few moments of that sleepless night wondering if the Cheyennes who were allegedly bent on laying waste to Oklahoma City might one day become customers of his bank. Maybe the gun-toting banker had seen enough of the passing of frontier ways to know that nothing lasts forever, and that a new day was dawning in the Twin Territories.

As settlers across the West rose to the defense of their communities, it is safe to assume that Richardson and his comrades-in-arms were too preoccupied to reflect on the possibility of peaceful and mutually beneficial relations between Indians and businessmen. And surely, as they locked and loaded their weapons and waited for the worst on that awful night, they gave nary a thought to what such a relationship might mean in the tug-of-war between democracy and capitalism.

Such musings would have to wait for another day.

CHAPTER EIGHT

Bust and Boom

If you have any money deposited in a bank that you do not absolutely need, leave it there. You will find no other place so safe for it. By letting your deposit remain intact you will be doing your part toward strengthening the public confidence which it is so important to maintain at a time like this.

News brief, *Daily Oklahoma State Capital*

The prospect of Indian attacks was not the only thing that kept territorial bankers up at night. In the summer of 1889, T. M. Richardson and his colleagues at the Oklahoma Bank decided to equip their little one-story wooden building on the corner of Main and Broadway with the latest in security technology. In the absence of telephones, electric call bells were placed in the Wand Drugstore, the Gerson Brothers Clothing Store, and the Gerson Drugstore, all just west of the bank. Push buttons were also placed around the bank, some under the counters, and others on the floor. The bank went so far as to supply merchants with rifles with the understanding that, if robbers came calling, they were to push or step on their call buttons to summon help and charge to the bank, ready to teach bank robbers a lesson about frontier justice.

Just after a four o'clock closing, an Oklahoma Bank employee accidentally stepped on a button. Within seconds, the bank was surrounded by armed merchants spoiling for a fight. This and subsequent false alarms desensitized neighbors to the likelihood of a robbery, and bank officials dismantled their elaborate system. As fate would have it, bandits left the

Oklahoma Bank and its successor, the First National Bank of Oklahoma City, alone, even though they plied their trade throughout the Oklahoma Territory, all too often with impunity.[1]

Even if they were fortunate enough to dodge Indian attacks and bank robbers, territorial bankers were not immune to chicanery within their own ranks. On the day of the land run into the Unassigned Lands, J. M. Ragsdale and C. R. McLain launched the Commercial National Bank of Guthrie. Building on a small amount of capital, their bank grew until they controlled institutions in Norman, Stillwater, Kingfisher, and El Reno. Boasting that his bank had been the first in the territory to receive a national charter, Ragsdale advertised $300,000 in paid-in capital, an enormous sum requiring a generous stretch of the imagination. But on November 22, 1890, depositors choked on their coffee when they read in the morning paper that bank president Ragsdale, vice president McLain, cashier C. W. Blueler, and other bank officers had fled the territory. Under the shocking headline "Gone to the Wall," a newspaper reported that "the Commercial National Bank, heretofore supposed to be one of the most substantial institutions in the Territory, had made an assignment and would not open at the regular hour."[2] Anxious creditors gathered in front of the bank to find writs of attachment plastered to the doors.

Using flour barrels to stash coins and currency, the rascals left depositors throughout the Oklahoma Territory penniless. The newspaper did its best to unravel the conspiracy: "The banks affected are the Commercial [National Bank] of Guthrie, the Bank of Norman and Ragsdale & Co. of Kingfisher and El Reno. It is not known exactly what the liabilities and assets are, but it will seriously affect the small depositors, whose money was recklessly squandered."[3] A few prescient souls might have seen it coming—Ragsdale was later accused of being a "sooner"![4]

Embarrassed by this return to the Wild West, the legislature wasted no time in strengthening banking laws. In December 1890, legislators made it unlawful for insolvent institutions to accept deposits. Officers of insolvent institutions were held individually liable if they broke the law, and usury was forbidden in a decree that limited interest rates to 12 percent per year. With typical frontier ingenuity, bankers skirted around the law by withholding a portion of the principal. Where appropriate, corporate laws were applied to financial institutions. Still, the territory had to wait until 1897 for comprehensive bank codes. Some institutions dealt with the dearth of codes by applying for charters in Kansas, Texas, or another nearby state and establishing territorial branches.[5]

Inured to the perils of frontier banking, T. M. Richardson and J. P. Boyle received a new charter as the First National Bank of Oklahoma City on August 20, 1890. Still insisting in their newspaper advertising that theirs was "not a wild cat Bank" and they had "come to stay," Richardson and Boyle decided in late 1890 to build a more substantial building. In January 1891, their modest, one-story frame building was replaced with a three-story, cut-stone structure on Main Street that was later known as the Huckins Estate Building. The bank took over part of the first floor, and its lobby was a wonder to behold, complete with a marble floor and mahogany fixtures on a par with the most renowned banks in the country.[6] Their decision to upgrade to nicer digs made sense in an era of self-regulation, when depositors accustomed to frontier scarcity needed lots of convincing to entrust bankers with their money. Richardson and his ilk learned the hard way that there were two secrets to successful banking: the personal reputation of the banker, and architectural features that radiated the twin virtues of safety and permanence.[7]

A busy intersection in Oklahoma City's business district, 1893. Just four years after the Run of '89, brick buildings were already replacing frame structures. The three-story building at the extreme left is the First National Bank. Courtesy Western History Collections, University of Oklahoma Libraries, Division of Manuscripts (Collection No. 461, Exhibit No. 49).

Historians tend to gloss over the cultural and economic significance attached to a bank's physical characteristics. But one has only to read advertisements and correspondence from the Twin Territories to appreciate the importance of architecture and bank vaults in fostering confidence. Ornate design, rich woods, marble, brass, and other ostentations were not simply extravagances aimed at stroking someone's ego. On the contrary, they served as symbols of safety insofar as they were tangible evidence of a bank's investment in its community.

Rich ornamentation and a prominent location were especially attractive to customers when bankers proved themselves trustworthy. A prime example of constructive self-promotion comes from Altus in Old Greer County, Oklahoma Territory, a rough village in the short-grass country some 150 miles southwest of Oklahoma City. In an effort to enhance the reputation of its banks, the *Altus News* spared no hyperbole in convincing readers that Altus bankers were of the highest caliber. Its inaugural edition of March 15, 1900, sought to allay anxieties about J. A. Henry, president of the People's Bank of Altus, who had come all the way from Vernon, Texas, to handle the people's money. Just in case readers were slow to catch on, the newspaper invoked several of Altus's founding fathers who had already won the town's respect to testify to Henry's integrity: "We call the attention of the readers of the News to the ad. of the People's Bank of Altus. This institution will be of great benefit to the people of Altus and Greer county. The most [*sic*] of our people are well acquainted with Messrs. Hightower, McMahan and Baker. Mr. Henry has been the cashier of the Waggoner National Bank of Vernon, and is regarded as a good financier and clever gentlemen. He is a safe, conservative man, one in whom the people can place the utmost confidence."[8]

Bank vaults, architecture, and accoutrements, reinforced by the good name of people who worked in the financial sector, were potent symbols of safety in the Twin Territories. They became less potent as frontier banking gave way to a regulatory environment that shifted the burden of proof from individuals to government and from personal assurances to reports written by examiners, agents, and state bureaucrats. But as bankers in the Twin Territories knew all too well, frontier ways would not go quietly into the night. For many years, posh surroundings and a sterling reputation were about all bankers had to assure their customers of a good night's sleep. Just as bankers spared no expense to signal their long-term vision, so, too, did communities rely on posh banking houses as evidence of their permanence.⁹ (One can practically hear our hopeless romantic, Mrs. Tom B. Ferguson of Watonga, whooping in agreement.)

Then again, piles of cash did not hurt. Comfortable in their new offices in the summer of 1891, Richardson and Boyle noticed a significant uptick in deposits. Several times during that toasty summer, deposits in the First National Bank of Oklahoma City hovered in the neighborhood of $150,000. "If we could just get up to the $150,000 in deposits we would go from there," said Boyle.¹⁰ Perhaps stress was taking its toll. The cashier became ill and sought relief in the balmy climes of Corpus Christi, Texas. In his absence, T. M. Richardson Jr. was adding up the deposits one evening and found that they had rocketed past $150,000. He bolted to his father's office to proclaim the good news. "Get off a telegram to Mr. Boyle right away and tell him about it," said the elder Richardson to his son.¹¹ The young banker quickly complied. Their subsequent means of celebration is anyone's guess.

Boyle said later that the telegram had done him more good than his trip to Texas. The First National Bank thus became the first bank in Oklahoma City to reach $150,000 in deposits—surely as reliable a symbol of safety as a banker could have in the Twin Territories.

When they were not contending with restless natives and thieves and insider tomfoolery, bankers in the Twin Territories were learning the hard way that inclusion in the nation's financial network was a mixed blessing. In an age when contentious issues were never in short supply, none caused more commotion than the debate over free silver or, more specifically, coinage at a weight ratio of sixteen ounces of silver to one ounce of gold. Since the Civil War, financial panics and a chronic shortage of currency endemic to a boom-and-bust economy seemed to indicate that monetary policy was the key to prosperity. Greenbacks, the first national paper money, were issued during the Lincoln administration. The argument for issuing paper money arose from simple necessity: soldiers in the field wanted to be paid, and the only alternative to legal-tender notes was to borrow money at high interest rates.¹² Even though greenbacks helped finance the Northern cause, they also stimulated inflation. After the Civil War, Republicans sought to alleviate inflationary pressure by withdrawing greenbacks from circulation until each dollar was fully backed by metal reserves—primarily gold, which was notoriously hard to find. Gold-backed currency became a defining issue among Republicans, and it pitted the moneyed elite against laborers, farmers, and small merchants who never seemed to have enough cash in their wallets or coins in their pockets. For angry debtors with cupboards to fill and mortgages to pay, inflation was a small price to pay for solvency.[13]

Opposition to the gold standard coalesced in a series of third parties that were highly critical of the Republicans' policy of constricting the money supply for the sake of stability. For heirs to the Greenback Party of the 1870s, salvation lay in issuing paper money. But with the opening of silver mines in the West, and particularly Nevada's Comstock Lode, a more moderate solution to the currency problem came in the form of the so-called free coinage of silver. Rallying around the slogan "16 to 1!," currency reformers steered a middle path between potentially ruinous paper money and the gold standard to advocate bimetallism, made possible by an expanding supply of silver. Frustrations reached fever pitch when Mary E. Lease, leader of a grassroots movement that careened into history as populism, is said to have challenged farmers at an exploratory meeting in Topeka in 1890 "to raise less corn and more Hell!"[14] Banks vied with the railroads for first place on the populists' list of bloodsucking enterprises. As one Nebraska editor put it, "There are three great crops raised in Nebraska. One is a crop of corn, one a crop of freight rates, and one a crop of interest. One is produced by farmers who by sweat and toil farm the land. The other two are produced by men who sit in their offices and farm the farmers."[15]

What Lease, the Nebraska wordsmith, and their irate sympathizers wanted was not buckets of paper money raining down from Washington, D.C., but silver-backed currency that would expand along with the nation's galloping economy. Buried in Lease's oratory and the editor's wisecrack was an appeal for justice in an unforgiving economy that often made a mockery of America's promise.

President Grover Cleveland added fuel to the fire when he began his second term in March 1893 by demanding that the U.S. Treasury suspend silver purchases. Trouble was already brewing on several fronts: the Philadelphia and Reading Railroads tumbled into receivership with debts totaling a whopping $125,000,000; wary British investors were unloading American securities; and gold reserves dwindled to a paltry $96,000,000 after the Treasury Department's redemption of notes issued in 1890. Full-blown disaster came in June 1893 when the price of silver went into a tailspin and jittery folks back east, convinced that the entire financial problem stemmed from the coinage of silver, went into panic mode. At the other end of the spectrum, westerners were convinced that the panic was deliberately planned and created by eastern "gold bugs" who wanted to discredit silver. The Panic of 1893 was on, and nobody was surprised when the comptroller of the currency's year-end report included the failure of 158 national banks, 172 state banks, 177 private banks, 47 savings banks, 13 loan and trust companies, and 6 mortgage companies.[16]

Troubles back east quickly made their way to the Twin Territories, where upstart banks had their first taste of a nationwide panic. In Oklahoma City, the First National Bank's survival was due in no small measure to quick thinking on the part of its officers. When T. M. Richardson felt the first shock waves, he brought in several shipments of money until the safe bulged with gold, silver, and currency. Wary of banditry, he assigned a black janitor named Douglas to spend the night in the bank and ordered him to sound an alarm at the first sign of trouble. One evening, a ne'er-do-well with too much red-eye in his gut heaved a brick through a window. Startled from his slumber, Douglas inexplicably dove through the jagged hole. His howls of pain summoned the city's night watchman who determined that the assailant was not a would-be thief, but rather "one of the boys" out to have some fun. The next morning, Richardson asked Douglas why he did not simply use the front door. "Boss," replied the bruised janitor, "you told me if anything happened to sound an alarm and that's just what I did and lost no time doing it."[17]

But the worst was yet to come. About 11:00 A.M. on July 19, James H. Wheeler, cashier of the Bank of Oklahoma City at the southwest corner of Grand and Robinson Avenues, stepped outside and nailed a notice on the door portending dark days to come: "This bank has suspended payment owing to lack of money at hand to meet the heavy run now being made upon it. Depositors will be paid in full. Ample assets to pay all liabilities." The *Oklahoma Daily Times-Journal* of July 20, 1893, revealed a bank on the brink of insolvency: "The run became very heavy yesterday at the Bank of Oklahoma City as soon as the doors were opened in the morning, and up to the time of closing $11,000 had been paid out. Since the run began a month ago the bank has paid out $70,000 more than was deposited. A month ago the deposits were $150,000. The deposits now are $80,000."[18]

Skeptical depositors who flocked to the town center found that the Oklahoma National Bank, whose deposits had plunged from $120,000 to $50,000, was in even worse shape than the Bank of Oklahoma City. The notice posted on its door read simply, "Bank Closed." In a show of confidence in the city's financial institutions, prominent merchants posted and signed a notice indicating that they would accept certificates of deposit on the Bank of Oklahoma City at par for goods at cash prices in their stores. Among those who signed the notice was T. M. Richardson, not in his capacity as vice president of the First National Bank, but rather as the head of T. M. Richardson Lumber Company, which he had founded at the time of the Run of 1889 and which was by now a sprawling enterprise.[19] Such assurances failed to prevent citizens in the city of five thousand from pouring into the streets. As the crowd swelled, bankers prepared to reap the whirlwind.

At the First National Bank, Richardson and his staff were dishing out money to depositors as fast as they could and continued to do so after the bank's usual closing at 4:00 P.M. By nightfall, employees' nerves were frayed, and Richardson decided to call a halt to the drain on bank deposits. Mounting the front steps of the bank, he held up his hand to call for silence and told the crowd that twelve hours of banking was enough for one day. "We're going to close up now, folks," Richardson announced to the milling throng. "We will be open in the morning and all of you who haven't been waited on today can have your money if you want it. But I want to tell you that there is enough money in our safe to pay off every depositor in full. If any man loses a dollar in this bank," he concluded, pointing to a nearby telephone pole, "I want to be hanged to that telephone post over there."[20] In support of the beleaguered bank vice president, a Colonel Johnson spoke to the crowd and advised everyone to keep their money in the bank. D. C. Lewis put his money where his mouth was—he held up a $1,000 certificate of deposit and vowed to keep it in the bank. According to the *Oklahoma Daily Times-Journal*, "The doors were kept open until 6 o'clock, but no money was drawn out after 3 o'clock. Plenty of money was still in sight at close of business."[21]

What people in the crowd did not know was that the First National Bank was running dangerously low on cash. Even as Richardson was doing his best to forestall disaster, bank employees arrived with bulging bags and marched conspicuously into the building. Satisfied that they might not wake up destitute the next morning after all, the anxious customers disbursed, blissfully unaware that they had been duped: the bags were full of washers.[22] Having bought some time, Richardson worked through the night, contacting other banks and making arrangements for an infusion of cash.

Among Richardson's confederates was Henry Overholser, a well-known civic and cultural leader whose only interest was commercial progress. As one chronicler, Albert McRill, noted in his classic account of the city's beginnings: "Whatever added to the number of business houses, or put money into the tills of merchants was, in his thinking, good for the city."[23] Overholser's paean to free enterprise captured the spirit of Oklahoma City in its infancy. That spirit flourished to the extent that public infrastructure has often taken a backseat to profit-driven projects. Although there have certainly been challenges to the elevation of business interests over the public sphere, Overholser's commitment to business-building enterprises has echoed through the years in a culture wary of government intervention, and captivated by the wonders that blossom from a free and unfettered marketplace.

Not only was Henry Overholser a forceful and consistent spokesman for the business elite, but he was also well connected. His father-in-law, Samuel Murphy, was the territorial treasurer, and he agreed to deposit $5,000 in territorial funds to prop up the bank.[24] Additional funds were pledged by Guthrie bankers M. L. Turner and Joe McNeil, who drove to Oklahoma City that night with cash. When morning dawned on July 20, the immediate crisis was fading, and the lines that formed outside the bank consisted not of frightened customers but depositors anxious to get their money back in the vault.[25] The previous day's withdrawals of $22,000 were almost equaled by the $17,110.96 that was deposited, leaving the bank with almost as much cash as it had before the panic began.[26] The First National Bank's symbols of safety, buttressed by T. M. Richardson's bravado and an infusion of cold cash, had prevented a tense situation from spinning out of control.

Other banks were not so fortunate. The Panic of 1893 forced two banks to close their doors as early as April: the Oklahoma National Bank, an outgrowth of the Citizens Bank; and the Bank of Oklahoma City. To their credit, the two failed banks paid off every dollar they owed their depositors.[27] It is also to the credit of the territory's entrepreneurial spirit that a new bank was established in 1893: the State National Bank. Its founders included Edward H. and George Cooke, Will Henry, and Whit M. Grant.[28] State National Bank was destined for a long and successful run in Oklahoma banking, capped by a historic merger with its erstwhile competitor, the First National Bank of Oklahoma City, in 1927. But that is a story for a subsequent volume.

The media responded to the national financial crisis with typical frontier chutzpah. "The territory of Oklahoma, since it was opened to settlement a little over four years ago, has made remarkable progression," ran a story in the *Oklahoma Daily Press-Gazette* just a couple of months after the panic had passed. "Oklahoma is a country of young men, full of the ideas, energy and courage that make countries great." Not surprisingly in a region so recently hewn from the frontier, politicians were seen as serpents in the garden whose wiles were the only impediment to unending prosperity. "The territory is in a very prosperous condition, everything considered, but is handicapped by territorial government."[29] A corollary of prosperity was the safety of money. Determined to promote the safety and soundness of banks, opinion leaders relied on the territorial press to calm whatever jitters remained from the recent panic. "If you have any money deposited in a bank that you do not absolutely need, leave it there," admonished the *Daily Oklahoma State Capital* in August 1893. "You will find no other place so safe for it. By letting your deposit remain intact you will be doing your part toward strengthening the public confidence which it is so important to maintain at a time like this."[30] Readers were further counseled to maintain perspective toward what had entered the common vernacular as the "Panic of 1893." The suspension of banks and the closing of mills and mines were bad news, to be sure, but they had to be balanced with the opening of new businesses and the strong demand for labor. As always, humor was an effective antidote to financial woes, particularly when the White House offered such a compelling target in the person of the corpulent Grover Cleveland. "If worrying over the country's condition would reduce the president's pompous self-conceit instead of swelling his big toe," quipped an anonymous wordsmith in the *Daily Oklahoma State Capital,* "there would be a little something to feel thankful for."[31]

Financial doings back east, and even banking and commerce in the Twin Territories, meant little to settlers who were still trying to figure out how to survive. One did not have to travel very far beyond the metropolitan areas, such as they were, to realize that the lack of currency remained a major impediment to economic development in the 1890s. As one old-timer from western Oklahoma Territory recalled with a flair for oratory, "Times were hard, and it took lots of rustling to get enough to eat. Money was the scarcest thing in the country. To tell the truth, nobody had any money to speak of, and such money as there was in the country was mostly in nickels, dimes and quarters. A $5-bill was a curiosity. Gold was rarely seen. I doubt if the little bank that was run in a tent got enough gold in a month to plate a brass ring for a man's little finger."[32]

A. T. Lowman of Dewey County agreed. With a nod to frontier egalitarianism that would have rung true to Alexis de Tocqueville of France and W. A. West of the Cherokee Outlet, Lowman suggested that everyone's finances were pretty much the same; high- and lowborn alike spent money as fast as it came in. He reflected, "If I made $5.00 and got groceries with it I had to start thinking where I was going to get the next $5.00 as I knew that what I had would not last long." Lowman's most memorable financial coup came when he cleared $84.00 for four loads of posts that he hauled to his homestead from Kingfisher: "I put most of that money into things that would keep and things that we needed, like fruit jars and flour, leather for shoe soles, coal oil, etc."[33]

Long before he rose to prominence as a historian at the University of Oklahoma, Edward Everett Dale learned to survive in a cashless economy. Born near present-day Denton in Tarrant County, Texas, on February 8, 1879, young Edward moved with his father to Old Greer County in 1889. "Money was almost unbelievably scarce," he recalled in his autobiography, *The West Wind Blows.* "The ranchmen had money, of course, and so did the cowhands to whom they paid twenty to forty dollars a month. Most of the settlers, however, seldom had more than a few coins in the pockets of their faded jeans and many never had as much as fifteen dollars all at one time during an entire year. Prices were extremely low, but this meant nothing to the man who had no money at all and no means of getting any."[34]

Even when banks managed to muscle their way into the hinterlands, they were not always to be trusted, and money remained as elusive as ever. The Kickapoo lands, opened for settlement by a land run in 1895, quickly gained a reputation for "wildcat banking." This dubious distinction was matched in the Cherokee Outlet, opened by a land run in 1893, which was likewise known for its fly-by-night bankers. Scouting for easy profits, wildcat bankers went into business with little or no capital, issued scrip that quickly became worthless, accepted deposits with no intention of redeeming them, and closed within a year or so of opening. Unscrupulous shysters moved from one community to another and left legions of disillusioned depositors in their wake. Such nefarious doings made it nigh impossible for honest bankers to maintain their reputations, let alone build their communities.

A classic tale from the school of hard knocks comes to us from Shawnee, a scrappy little town that blossomed after land runs in 1891 opened the Pottawatomie and Sac and Fox reservations to non-Indian settlement. "Shawnee is a typical new town, such as are born of booms and unusual happenings," wrote the journalist Frederick S. Barde. "Down the street on both sides are brand new buildings, many unpainted and some, more ambitious, covered with a priming coat of paint—plenty for the prevailing weather. On every hand is the sound of hammers and saws, everyone is putting up a building in town and sleeping in a tent or a covered wagon on the outskirts."[35]

But not everybody shared in Shawnee's prosperity. Barde told the story of an old-timer who stepped out of a crowd of gamblers as they loafed in front of a short-order restaurant called the Golden Buck and asked for alms to help him "git back to Missourah." Chided for wanting to leave the territory and asked for an explanation, the old man shook his head, bared his two remaining teeth, and told a tale of shattered dreams to reveal the underbelly of America's promise: "I come here with a good span of Missourah mules, a wagon, $60 and my woman two years ago. An' I waited. An' now that saloon's got my $60, and the banker down yonder has got my mules an' my woman has quit me fer another man. Guess I'll go back to old Missourah."[36]

To promote sound business principles on the rapidly fading frontier, President Grover Cleveland appointed William Cary Renfrow as the fourth governor of the Oklahoma Territory. A native of North Carolina, Renfrow served in the Civil War as a sergeant in the Fiftieth North Carolina Infantry. After the war he moved to Russellville, Arkansas, where he started a family and established a mercantile business. In a pattern that typifies the frontier businessman, Renfrow caught wind of opportunity farther west and relocated to Norman, Oklahoma Territory, in 1889, where he added ownership of a livery stable to his resume. Such was Renfrow's success in the livery business that he opted for a career in banking, a route that led many territorial businessmen into politics.

It was not long before Renfrow became a majority owner of Norman State Bank, a position that he used as a platform for real estate investments and involvement in the Democratic Party. In 1890, his admiration for President Cleveland prompted him to suggest naming the county surrounding Norman after him. The president returned the favor in his appointment of the now wealthy W. C. Renfrow to the governorship, a position that began with his swearing-in on May 7, 1893.[37] Governor Renfrow's treasurer, M. L. Turner, was also a wealthy man, and he engaged in the bond and brokerage business after his service to the good people of Oklahoma Territory. On the eve of his retirement from public service and return to the private sector, Turner commented somewhat enigmatically, "I believe that the spoils belong to the victor"—seemingly a reference to the wealth that would be his after a stint in politics.[38] During a term of office that lasted longer than those of his three predecessors, Governor Renfrow applied his business expertise to campaigning for statehood (a frustrating experience for all concerned!) and promoting settlement in the Oklahoma Territory.

Governor Renfrow was sworn into office just as the Panic of 1893 was gathering steam in the East and preparing to unleash its fury in the West. Yet the impending storm was not enough to dampen businessmen's enthusiasm for opening banks. The days when entrepreneurs could pitch an IOU into a safe, or perhaps assign value to a hodgepodge of furniture and fixtures, and declare that they had enough capital to open a bank and start accepting deposits and making loans were fading into western lore. But in the absence of formal banking codes, businessmen still had an astonishing amount of leeway in opening banks and structuring their transactions. And in the absence of either territorial or federal agencies to keep accurate records, there was no way to know how many banks there were. By one historian's reckoning, about 175 territorial, national, and private banks were doing business in the Twin Territories in 1895 and 1896.[39] Whatever the exact number of banks, we can be sure that their number fluctuated wildly as chartered and unchartered banks alike—most undercapitalized and all under-regulated—opened, merged, consolidated, moved, and went bankrupt, leaving depositors to fret about their nest eggs and borrowers to struggle with high interest rates.

Shawnee was a typical boomtown whose need for reliable banking services was satisfied in February 1895 when territorial secretary Thomas Lowe granted a charter to the Bank of Shawnee.[40] Capitalized with an impressive $50,000, the Bank of Shawnee was managed by three of the Oklahoma Territory's most illustrious bankers: J. H. Maxey, president; Willard Johnston, cashier; and J. H. Maxey Jr., assistant cashier.[41] Just below the Bank of Shawnee's newspaper advertisements were announcements that the T. M. Richardson Lumber Company (the Lowe's of its day) was the place to go for lumber, shingles, sashes, doors, blinds, laths, and building paper—pretty much everything settlers needed to build their homes on the prairie.[42]

Like any boomtown, Shawnee had its share of busts, including the failure in August 1896 of the Farmers and Merchants Bank. "The bank did little business and carried but small deposits," ran an account of the bank's demise in the *Daily Oklahoman*. But there was more. The article continued, "There was an ill feeling sprung up between the bank and the merchants of Shawnee on account of the refusal of the bank to contribute to the fund to secure the Choctaw shops to that town. Consequently, the merchants withheld their patronage and the failure followed."[43] Thus was go-it-alone individualism, enshrined in collective memory as the sine qua non of the frontier, revealed as more myth than fact, particularly when it came to handling the people's money.

Bankers with the savvy to participate actively in community development had much to be grateful for as agricultural enterprises sprouted from the prairies. Between 1896 and 1920, a steady rise in farm prices created the basis for the golden age of American farming.[44] Farmers in the Oklahoma Territory who cast their lot with the dairy business were shipping huge quantities of creamery butter to Texas and Mexico by the mid 1890s. Dairymen who lived near railways discovered that it was far more profitable to sell raw product to a creamery than it was to make and sell their own butter. A creamery at El Reno obtained raw milk and cream from nearly 500 farmers who were fortunate to live along the Chicago, Rock Island and Pacific Railway and Choctaw, Oklahoma and Gulf Railroad and shipped some 1,500 pounds of creamery butter each week to Mexico. "It is needless to say that we have the finest pasturage in the world," declared one creamery booster, "and that our cows yield milk in abundance. Each farmer owes it to himself as a business proposition to visit his nearest creamery and learn whether he can afford to waste money by making his own market butter and feeding his milk to the pigs. The El Reno creamery has induced the farmers to buy better cows and otherwise improve the breed of their live stock. Our mild winters and splendid forage make it possible for cows to produce milk in larger quantities during the colder months than when further north. Our farmers could make the winter milk one of their most profitable revenues."[45]

Albert Leonard, Oklahoma Territory agent for a Kansas City packing firm, estimated that it would take only five years for income from eggs and poultry to exceed that from any other agricultural product except cotton. "The growth of the industry has been truly marvelous," beamed Leonard in June 1897. As recently as 1895, raising chickens was a haphazard business and was practiced for the most part by pioneers whose sole ambition was to feed their families. "The country was new, and the women were burdened with the duties incident to a new home," Leonard said. "The market increase in 1895 over 1894 was noticeable, and the poultry output of 1896 was five times greater than the preceding year." Leonard estimated the total value of eggs and poultry in the most recent year was three quarters of a million dollars, reflecting, "That may not seem an immense sum when compared to other states, but Oklahoma, it must be remembered, is in its infancy."[46]

The poultry business was particularly strong in Guthrie, Oklahoma City, Perry, and Edmond. Smaller towns such as Shawnee, Norman, El Reno, Kingfisher, Hennessey, and Newkirk, together with many smaller trading points, were doing an aggregate business in the hundreds of thousands of dollars. Even though most poultry was raised east of the Atchison, Topeka, and Santa Fe Railway, Leonard saw no reason why other areas could not join in the chicken boom. As he saw it, the only real impediments to success were New York's control of poultry pricing and the lack of cold storage facilities in the Twin Territories. To facilitate inclusion in national distribution networks and, rather ambiguously, to "encourage intelligent chicken raising," a territorial poultry association was organized. One farm at Perry covered a quarter section, and its extensive buildings were stocked with birds from Massachusetts, New York, and Canada.[47]

Fruit growers, too, had plenty to crow about. In the late summer of 1897, peach farmers were producing the finest crop ever in the Oklahoma Territory. Peach trees were finally big enough to produce fruit "of a superior size and flavor." The most splendid varieties were Elbertas and Crawfords. "It is seldom that a blemished peach is found," ran an upbeat newspaper article, "and such a thing as a wormy peach is almost unknown."[48] Logan, Oklahoma, Canadian, and Kingfisher Counties led the territory in peach production. Farmers were getting up to fifty cents a bushel, and buyers claimed that Oklahoma peaches surpassed even those of California. To consume Logan County's surplus, a distillery was established in Guthrie to make peach brandy—good news for the cocktail set, but surely the road to perdition as far as territorial teetotalers were concerned. All that was needed was a fruit-evaporating plant to guarantee the Oklahoma Territory's position as a hub of peach production.

Territorial creameries, poultry farms, and peach orchards were doing a fine business, but cotton was in a league of its own. "Cotton is as good as money in the bank," ran one of many articles in the territorial press extolling the value of cotton. "There are buyers in every town who fall over each other in their rush to overtake the grower as he drives along the street. They climb upon his wagon, dig down into his bales of cotton, test its quality, and then begin bidding."[49] Cotton growers in 1896 produced about 50,000 bales. Conservative estimates placed the crop in 1897 at 100,000 bales, and some buyers predicted a bonanza of 150,000 bales. The most productive counties were Custer, Blaine, Roger Mills, Washita, and Greer Counties. The average yield went from one-third of a bale per acre in 1896 to one-half of a bale in 1897. At an average price of 6½ cents per pound, cotton in 1897 was expected to yield the princely sum of nearly $5,000,000.[50]

In a tribute to King Cotton that would have rung familiar to Rodgers and Hammerstein, a newspaper article gushed with pride over a crop that had advanced considerably since the days when slaves and their mules wrested plants once derided by northerners as "a lazy man's crop" from the land. Like other farm products, cotton was benefiting from scientific techniques, high-tech cultivators, and high-powered seeds, and the result was a wonder to behold: "The fields are a beautiful sight. The plants are waist high and stretch away in undulations of dark green, crested with waving blossoms of white, shading down through delicate pinks to a deep red. The plants are trees in miniature, and the fields are Lilliputian forests. . . . It swells and expands in the sunshine as if it were conscious of its importance in the world. Some day its contents may help to make the sails of a mighty ship or help in the fight of civilization by clothing the heathen in the furthermost isles of the sea."[51]

As farmers did their part for community development, communication technology struggled to keep pace with demand. On August 20, 1897, Western Union Telegraph Company, in conjunction with the Atchison, Topeka and Santa Fe Railway, announced that it would begin stringing a wire for its exclusive use between Arkansas City, Kansas, and Purcell, Indian Territory, the next week. The announcement came not a moment too soon. The existing wire was so over burdened that newspaper dispatches and other important messages were not sent until long after they were filed. "The right of way belongs at all times to the railway company," explained a newspaper brief, "and other messages are not sent until the railway company releases the wire."[52]

Statistics, often born with a generous dose of skepticism, confirmed what all could see with their own eyes and feel in their own wallets: the Oklahoma Territory was on a roll. "The hypochondriac has been proven a false prophet, an ignoramus who belongs on the staked plains, but not in Oklahoma," ran one giddy account of prosperity in the late 1890s. It continued, "Conservative estimates . . . early in the year showed a wonderful wealth in store for the people. These estimates have been fulfilled. More than that, they have been exceeded in actual results by millions of dollars. It is no longer a matter of conjecture; it is a reality."[53] Fair weather, fertile soil, and hard work produced crops with impressive values: wheat, $11 million; cotton, $5 million; livestock, $3 million; and miscellaneous crops, $2,500,000. The aggregate value was $21,500,000: "This is $86 for every man, woman and child in the territory. Oklahoma claims that this record never has been beaten in as new a country."[54]

Prosperity on the farm was reflected in a 25 percent increase in territorial bank deposits in only two months in the late summer of 1897. "The misfortune of the Oklahoma farmer has been that he was poor, and not that he was in debt," continued the newspaper account. More-over, the influx of money did not seem to be "turning the heads of the people. They are building barns and fences, adding comforts to their homes, sending their children to school, getting farm machinery for next year, investing in live stock which heretofore they were unable to buy, purchasing farm machinery and in every instance doing what they can to correct the false idea among people of other states that Oklahoma is not a law abiding, progressive and prosperous country," the article continued. There was less talk about free silver and gold and more about the right time to plant corn, wheat, and cotton. The article reflected, "The tirade against the 'money kings' is weaker; the farmer is getting into the business a little himself." Further evidence of the good times was evident in county fairs; a half-dozen or so were slated for the fall of 1897. Planned as old fashioned "pumpkin rollers," organizers decided it was preferable "to give Mrs. Jones a prize of $10 for the best display of preserves than it is to go in debt for race horses."[55]

Bountiful harvests and burgeoning bank accounts signaled that a new era was dawning in the Twin Territories, and it fell under the gaze of one of the late nineteenth century's most notable intellectuals: James Bryce, 1st Viscount Bryce. Combining the analytical prowess of an Oxford law professor with the global vision of a historian, Bryce followed in the footsteps of Tocqueville to examine the temper of the American West—its vastness, its exceptionalism, and its peculiar contradictions. After extensive travel in the United States and two visits to the West in 1887, Bryce merged his understanding of history and constitutional law in *The American Commonwealth*. Like Tocqueville, Bryce was fascinated by Americans' fixation on material development. And, like Turner, he acknowledged the role of the frontier in molding the American character: "The very similarity of ideas and equality of conditions which makes them hard to convince at first makes a conviction once implanted run its course the more triumphantly. They seem all to take flame at once, because what has told upon one, has told in the same way upon all the rest, and the obstructing and separating barriers which exist in Europe scarcely exist here. Nowhere is the saying so applicable that nothing succeeds like success."[56]

Bryce's chapter in *The American Commonwealth* titled "The Temper of the West" describes a pattern of settlement that was without precedent. Economic development, wrote Bryce, "which might not have seemed a glorious consummation to Isaiah or Plato, is preached by Western newspapers as a kind of religion."[57] Wary of painting with too broad a brush,

Bryce was sensitive to regional characteristics, and he was quick to key in on the Oklahoma Territory's susceptibility to new ideas and penchant for experimentation. He reflected, "Oklahoma, into which settlers have swarmed from all parts of the North West as well as the South West, is pre-eminently the land of sanguine radicalism and experimental legislation."[58]

Impressed though he was with the American experiment, Bryce had misgivings about the unique temper of the West. Although his western sojourns predated the Run of '89 by a couple of years and the Oklahoma Territory's bumper crops of 1897 by a decade, the patterns that he discerned were far from outdated. If anything, they were crystallizing, and nowhere more clearly than in the Twin Territories, where advances in communication and transportation were pushing the pace of change into overdrive and economic development was molding itself to the contours of capitalism on steroids.

For Tocqueville in the 1830s, constant striving did not lead to happiness. Americans "encounter good fortune nearly everywhere," he wrote after a visit to Ohio, "but not happiness. With them the desire for well-being has become an uneasy, burning passion that keeps on growing even while it is being satisfied."[59] The 1st Viscount James Bryce saw much the same at century's end when he put his own spin on a commercial juggernaut that was steamrolling its way across the West: "Politically, and perhaps socially also, this haste and excitement, this absorption in the development of the material resources of the country, are unfortunate. As a town built in a hurry is seldom well built, so a society will be the sounder in health for not having grown too swiftly. Doubtless much of the scum will be cleared away from the surface when the liquid settles and cools down."[60]

The Panic of 1893 was short-lived. Within a year of T. M. Richardson's heroic stand outside the First National Bank of Oklahoma City, banks in both territories were already in a growth mode. Four years into the recovery, the First National Bank boasted capital of $60,000, and the bank's advertisements promised "Courteous and Liberal Treatment" to merchants and farmers alike.[61] Gus A. Gill set the pace for bank expansion in the Indian Territory by establishing a private bank in McAlester, the hub of the region's booming coal-mining industry. Opened in 1894, his bank operated with $25,000 in capital and received deposits, made loans, and performed other functions that his customers no doubt thought were long overdue. Two years later, C. C. Hemming organized a second bank in McAlester and secured a national charter as the First National Bank of South McAlester. Other banks were established shortly thereafter in Miami and Tulsa.[62] Even though they responded to a wide variety of business environments, territorial bankers had two things in common: they wanted to put the Panic of 1893 behind them, and they wanted to cash in on the opportunities afforded by a rapidly expanding economy.

By the time county assessors in the Oklahoma Territory submitted their reports for 1897, whatever memories lingered from the Panic of 1893 were submerged in a rising tide of prosperity. In the spring of that fecund year, two shrewd Pennsylvania farmers took the president of the Deming Investment Company on a tour to check on the safety of his company's mortgages. What he saw astounded him. "Did you ever see such wheat?" asked the awed easterner as he surveyed amber waves of grain stretching to the horizon. He certainly had not, and his reports to the home office were enough to send the mortgage business into overdrive. Two years later, Bradstreet reported "a great commercial awakening" in the Oklahoma Territory and opened an office to handle the inquiries that were pouring in from other parts of the country. By then, the railroads were running regular excursions for people who wanted to see for themselves what the territory had to offer.[63]

Although assessors' reports for 1897 included the usual tally of wins and losses, aggregate figures showed substantial gains in taxable property. Of particular interest to bankers in search of collateral were gains in livestock. Increases since 1896 were as follows: hogs, 72,969; horses, 16,367; mules, 3,124; cattle, 22,819; and sheep, 5,115. Assessors' reports excluded figures from the Kiowa-Comanche–Plains Apache, Kaw, Osage, and Wichita Reservations.[64]

Still, the news was not altogether rosy. "The amount of money in each county is represented as ridiculously small," ran a newspaper account. Some counties reported no money at all in circulation. Most noticeable in this regard was Lincoln County which, paradoxically, was known as one of the most prosperous counties in the Oklahoma Territory. One suspects duplicity among reluctant taxpayers. D County, long since rebranded with a more inspired name, reported an abysmal $75.00 in circulation. At the other end of the spectrum was Oklahoma County, which was awash in cash and coin—$171,359, to be exact. The total showed a per capita circulation in Oklahoma Territory of $1.00. "But," asserted the newspaper with typical prairie pride, "the cry of 'hard times' is seldom heard here."[65]

Tangible property reported to the indefatigable assessors revealed a territory groping from frontier scarcity to consumer abundance. Defunct Day County, one of the most remote counties in a territory that was itself rather remote, reported two pianos. The aforementioned D County was slightly more musically inclined with three pianos. Oklahoma County, whose pianos were valued at $15,735, was a veritable conservatory. For reasons known only to its canine lovers, Kingfisher County reported dogs worth $272. A taxpayer in Logan County set the standard for patriotism by reporting three United States bonds.[66]

For bankers looking to fatten their loan portfolios, any sign of taxable property was something to celebrate. One imagines a banker with a linguistic flair lifting his glass, perhaps sloshing over with peach brandy, and regaling his comrades with that favored toast from the Old Southwest: *Laissez les bons temps rouler!*[67]

CHAPTER NINE

A Happy Medium

There is a happy medium between the extremes of recklessness and penurious conservatism. You may increase your business by keeping within this happy medium. No profession demands a stricter standard of moral integrity than ours. Lawyers and doctors may get drunk and violate the entire decalogue and still do business, but bankers and ministers are required to keep the straight and narrow way, or lose standing and go out of business.

J. W. McNeal, president, Guthrie National Bank

Bankers were not the only ones rejoicing over the quickening pace of commerce. From the first land run in April 1889 to statehood in 1907, communities hewn from the frontier were the destination of choice for rascals of every description. Like hawks in search of prey during the fall migration, they flocked to the Twin Territories to line their pockets with ill-gotten gains. Journalist Frederick Barde, who, for all we know, might have succumbed to their wiles during a moment of weakness, wrote that "gamblers, crooks and confidence men of every kind came from every State to fleece the new settlers and such strangers and visitors as might fall into their nets."[1] Scoundrels were nothing new on the frontier, but in the Oklahoma and Indian Territories, they lifted perfidy to an art. To the everlasting frustration of bankers and businessmen who sought a legitimate path of economic development, gamblers and con men that swarmed into the Twin Territories between 1889 and 1907 confirmed the region's reputation as a haven for outlaws.

Favorite venues were trains, where experienced shysters kept their eyes peeled for potential targets. The stretch of the Santa Fe Railroad between Guthrie, Oklahoma Territory, and Arkansas City, Kansas, was especially popular. Conductors who were familiar with con artists and their nefarious ways made them promise not to harass passengers. A few of the more ethical ones complied, paid their fare, and spent their time scouting for easy targets between stations. But most had no qualms about breaking whatever promises they had made to the conductor and swindled whomever they pleased.

Al Glazier operated the first regular passenger train through the Oklahoma country several years before it was opened to non-Indian settlement, and he enjoyed reminiscing about his career after retiring to Ardmore, Oklahoma. "He knew most of the crooks in the west," wrote his interviewer, "and his inviolable rule was that no jobs should be pulled off on his trains. He had served in the Union Army, knew how to use a gun, and would not hesitate to shoot if necessary to serve his company." Three of Glazier's unpreferred passengers lived in Guthrie: "Big Ed" Burns, "known all over the United States"; Harry Faulkner, an English crook and onetime justice of the peace in Guthrie; and one known alternately as "Scarface Charley" and "Crazy Horse," whose real name was known only to those who knew him best, and maybe his mother.[2]

Those who made it to Guthrie with their wallets intact might have visited the Reeves brothers' gambling house, operated by Dick and Bill Reeves. Opened on the day of the Run of '89 in a big tent "where there was room enough for 1,500 men and women to gamble and drink and carouse," the Reeves brothers ran their business in Guthrie for twenty years. Barde's description of the famed honky-tonk confirms an image of the western saloon that has never yielded its place in our collective memory: "Gamblers from every State tackled the game that ran night and day in that sleepless place. Hundreds of thousands of dollars passed over its tables. The six-shooter and the dirk settled many a dispute, and the dead man was hauled away and the blood scrubbed from the floor as a part of the day's business. Outlaw gangs that infested Oklahoma in those days risked their loot against the faro bank and the roulette wheel—and usually lost."[3]

Within a few years of the Run of '89, law and order was putting a civilized veneer on the territory's most notorious saloons and honky-tonks, particularly in the larger communities. By the time Barde's article was published, most of the people "who gave evil reputation to the Reeves Place" had vanished. "Most of them are dead," continued the journalist. "Only a part of the building remains—vacant, gruesome, and abandoned. Rain beats in at the open windows on stormy nights. Tattered curtains, visible from the street, sway in the gloomy interior, as if moved by ghostly hands." The original two-story frame building was located on the northwest corner of Second Street and Harrison Avenue. A two-story brick building, complete with a stage and rows of curtained boxes, was added to accommodate "a free-and-easy variety show." The fire department eventually condemned the frame building and tore it down to reveal sodden soil, "black with the accumulated seepage of sin. Boys scrambled in the debris and found corroded coins—but only a few, for the claws of the slathering tiger that kept watch over this gambling hell, let little escape their clutch."[4]

Mrs. Joseph Willis, a lover of flowers who lived within sight of the building, coaxed a garden from the detritus of Guthrie's past. Her efforts spawned a community project; eventually, plants nurtured in the putrid loam of the Reeves Place were winning prizes at flower shows. Thus did memories of poker and faro and roulette wheels, of freewheeling cowboys in town to gamble away their wages, of drunken brawls and ignominious deaths, give way to more pleasant ones, more in keeping with Guthrie's determination to put the frontier behind.

Those who continued on to Oklahoma City might have slaked their thirst, and perhaps lost their shirts, at the Blue Front, a two-story frame building at 7½ Grand Avenue known far and wide as "the southwestern rendezvous of many of the most noted professional crooks and thieves in the United States, who came this way in search of plunder." The establishment was operated by Johnny Kingston and his wife, Aunt Betsy, "a giant-like woman" who was known far and wide as a force to be reckoned with. Unlike the Reeves Place, the Blue Front was not known for mayhem: "Johnny Kingston was too smart for that; it was a place where swag was divided, where 'mobs' were organized to work confidence games, to blow safes, and to get money in the various gentlemanly ways known to professional crooks."[5]

On the eve of Oklahoma statehood, Barde interviewed an old-timer who was "almost tearfully reminiscent" as he described the Blue Front as a mecca for global gamblers—where homegrown rogues mingled with foreigners from Cairo, Monte Carlo, Nice, Budapest, Paris, and London.

Kingston, a native of Birmingham, England, once belonged to a mob that ran three-card monte games openly for three or four years at Coney Island. His route to the Oklahoma Territory took him through Omaha, Nebraska, and Ogden, Utah, where there was no shortage of miners to fleece. Kingston went on to ply his trade between Saint Joseph, Missouri, and Atchison, Kansas, the gateway to the southwest. "Atchison was filled with crooks and grafters of all kinds," explained the wistful old-timer to his interviewer, "with numerous roadhouses and hang-outs for their entertainment. The trick knife and the trick lock men were as thick as bees in a clover patch."[6] It was here that Johnny Kingston met his future bride, Aunt Betsy, who was operating a roadhouse that was the forerunner of the Blue Front.

Johnny Kingston operated the Blue Front until about 1905. None knew him and his gang better that Al Glazier, the conductor who spent thirty years shuttling passengers between Kansas and the Oklahoma Territory on the Atchison, Topeka and Santa Fe Railway and warning villains to leave them alone. Glazier's rules of etiquette might have had some traction on his trains, but not at the Blue Front. "We had rich pickings in the old days," said Barde's wistful interviewee. "All we had to do was to throw salt on 'em and eat 'em alive. I have seen four and five thousand dollars taken from a single immigrant. The graft was easy, and seemed naturally to belong to the atmosphere of the country."[7] It was not unusual for grafters to go in cahoots with a local banker to hasten the collection of checks. For services rendered, bankers received from 10 to 20 percent of the proceeds as a sort of commission. By the time someone realized he had been fleeced, the capper (the hustler) was long gone.

Like J. M. Ragsdale and his fellow fleecers at the Commercial National Bank of Guthrie, early-day gamblers often posed as pillars of their communities until they lit out from the territory with other people's money. Barde's profile of the art of grafting has a familiar ring. Then, as now, some men rob with a gun, while others prefer to do so by other means: "Its qualified exponents were men of wit, cleverness, and even gentleness, knowing the ways of men, their weaknesses and their strength, as they knew the letters of the alphabet. They employed both art and science in their undertakings, and were philosophers and psychologists. They held lint for the surgeon and lifted a glass of cold water to the lips of their victims, the latter imagining all the while that another had struck the blow. If possible, there was no violence, and good fellowship reigned in place of the icy mitt."[8]

In an editorial for the *Oklahoma City Times,* Dell B. Kell wrote what amounts to an obituary for the days when Oklahoma City was wide open for cappers and con men to build their businesses. For reasons he might have taken to the grave, Kell was acquainted with many of the gamblers and drifters who helped to maintain the Oklahoma Territory's reputation for lawlessness. What is more, he knew (or at least claimed to know) what became of them: "Bud" Cox went to Texas and was killed; Dick Hawkins was killed in Wyoming; Bill Sparr was still following the races in Wichita, but was broke; "Whitey" Rupp died a drunkard; the Arkansas Kid wound up in the penitentiary; Bud Mitchell was similarly housed for horse stealing; the "Butterfly Kid" "went bughouse from morphine" and probably died; Obe Hathaway was arrested as a bootlegger; "Cincinnati Red" was killed while working a shell game in Colorado; and Jim Furber was killed in the Kiowa and Comanche country for reasons unknown. "Boots" was still a familiar sight around Oklahoma City, "but he looks like he had been dragging a long sack between two cotton rows." All three Shawcross brothers were dead—Sam went insane in Chicago, Bill was shot in a saloon brawl in Shawnee, and John was killed in a mining camp in Colorado. Bert Hurst, once known as the swiftest dice man in the country, became addicted to dope and was digging postholes in Kansas, "and his mind is a wreck." Kid Monnahan was one of the fortunate. At the time Kell penned his tribute to the bad old days, Kid Monnahan "was the only man in Oklahoma City rich enough to own a bicycle." Perhaps Monnahan enjoyed soirees in the company of Frenchy Lebritton, who became respectable and rich and lived in a palatial home in El Reno.[9]

We leave the final word on the Twin Territories' shady past to Dutch Jake, who was "no doubt in the penitentiary, at least he should have been years ago." In response to a merchant's query, the outlaw waxed poetic to describe his life's journey: "I am an outcast from society. I dare not darken the sacred portals of my father's house, I wash my face in a barbershop, eat French fries off a high stool, and call the red-light district my home—I am a gambler."[10]

The eastern press took to Oklahoma lawlessness like a duck to water. However, the stories that might have attracted readers on their own merits in popular magazines such as *Puck* and *Judge* were spun into tall tales until nobody could tell fact from fiction. As though they did not have enough challenges to keep them up at night, legitimate business-men and bankers found themselves on the losing side in a war of words. Stereotypes were inevitable, including Oklahoma Ike—a broncobuster who rode with the reins in his teeth, a Winchester in each hand, and a dozen six-shooters and a bowie knife strapped in his belt, who sent outlaws scampering for cover by hollering to all within earshot, "Every coyote has got to git in his hole, for I'm going to wash this town away in a river of blood. Whoop! Watch the river begin to rise!"[11]

Bankers and businessmen reserved special opprobrium for Amos Fitts of Perry in Noble County. Relying on his territorial citizenship to build credibility, Fitts hoodwinked news editors with outrageous stories, con-fident that primitive communication would make it all but impossible to verify his whoppers. Fitts employed his most outrageous hyperbole to raise the outlaw Bill Doolin—in real life, "a sick, emaciated man, hardly able to walk, with rheumatism"—to America's pantheon of antiheroes. "Doolin was killed on an average of three times a week for months," ran an exposé of Fitts in the legitimate press. "There were running fights daily between his gang and United States officers. It was the easiest thing in the world to arrange for a train robbery on the Santa Fe railway, even though the alleged robbers were known to be in hiding 100 miles away."[12] Travelers who bypassed Oklahoma lest they perish in the cross-fire meant fewer customers for businesses and fewer deposits for banks.

Fed up with such nonsense, one reporter sympathetic with Oklahoma's plight vented his spleen under the headline, "Busy Liars in Oklahoma":

> More injury has been done to Oklahoma by false newspaper stories than by all actual misfortunes combined. Since the open-ing of the country to settlement mercenary and irresponsible scribblers have originated every conceivable kind of fiction, which they sold to Eastern newspapers as facts. The country was described as the birthplace of crime and the mother of famine, droughts, tornadoes and floods. It is almost impossible to con-vince strangers that the population of Oklahoma is composed of law-abiding people from every state in the Union, who came here to take advantage of the healthful climate and the produc-tive soil.[13]

Amos Fitts and his ilk remind us that media's power to shape reality is nothing new. Even as they were titillated by tales of hair-raising adventure, readers gained an impression of the Twin Territories that was certainly spawned by the frontier experience, but that became ever more preposterous with the passage of time. Subsequent generations of Oklahomans have learned the hard way what it means to be on the receiving end of misperceptions cultivated by mass media. Worse yet, wild-eyed exaggerations did more than hurt people's feelings; they actually slowed the pace of economic development. In March 1898, an eastern insurance company ordered its agencies in the Twin Territories to assume no risks on persons living within twenty-five miles of an Indian agency or west of the ninety-eighth meridian. As the reporter covering the story noted under the headline "Their Idea of the Wild West," "This order is amusing when it is known that it cuts out some of the best towns and villages in Oklahoma, where an Indian outbreak is no more to be feared than an invasion of Cossacks from Siberia."[14]

McMaster's Weekly, one of the first territorial magazines to abandon religion and settlement promotion as its raison d'être and publish articles of general interest, suggested as early as April 1896 that modern ways were putting an end to frontier mayhem, particularly the variety embodied in the badman of western lore and popularized by the likes of Amos Fitts. "In the evolution of modern civilization the bad man, namely, the desperado and tough, who gloats over killing his fellowman, disappears," asserted Colonel F. B. Jenkins of California in an interview for *McMaster's Weekly.* He continued, "A few years ago we heard a great deal of characters like Sam Bass, Jesse James, Ben Thompson and Rube Burrows, but to-day there is not in the United States a single individual with a national reputation for wickedness and dare-devilry such as any of these acquired."[15]

U.S. marshal Patrick Nagle of Guthrie chimed in with his own obituary for the badman. "The desperado business in Oklahoma is practically a thing of the past," claimed the lawman in an interview in March 1897. "This is very evident when I tell you that since I have been in office—about a year—there has not been a train held up, not a bank or postoffice [*sic*] robbed and only one 'bad man' killed in the territory. Our greatest trouble is with bootleggers, who sell whisky to the Indians." Marshal Nagle claimed that the only outlaw gang still in business was the Christian boys, and their depredations were confined to the Indian country southeast of the Oklahoma Territory. "I am told that they are preparing to leave the country," concluded the marshal on an upbeat note.[16]

Marshal Nagle was right—laws were certainly taking a bite out of crime. But there were still plenty of run-of-the-mill bandits doing their best to keep the tradition alive. In an effort to downplay their threat to legitimate commerce—or, perhaps, because there was too much to cover—the territorial press gave them scant attention. On January 26, 1894, the *Edmond Sun-Democrat* sandwiched a few lines about a bank robbery in Pawnee between a promotion for De Witt's Witch Hazel Salve as a "perfect remedy for skin diseases, chapped hands and lips" and the same company's Little Early Risers, "famous little pills" that promised relief from poor digestion, dyspepsia, billiousness [*sic*], and constipation. (Incidentally, the bank robbers got away with one hundred dollars. The bank's cashier, Mr. Barrett, was taken hostage and delivered to an undisclosed location about three miles from Pawnee, where he was turned loose.)[17]

The *Daily Oklahoman* devoted only fourteen lines, albeit on the front page, to the Reverend C. L. Berry, a Presbyterian preacher who was convicted in October 1897 of wrecking the Farmers and Merchants Bank of Perry. In his former career as president and cashier of the aforementioned bank, Berry had presided over his bank's failure that cost citizens of the Pawnee and Osage Nations between $40,000 and $50,000. He was definitely not accused of being slipshod in his thievery—at the time of its demise in early 1897, the bank "only had 60 cents on hand." The story of the minister gone astray ended with speculation that "Mr. Berry will probably be sent for several years to the penitentiary."[18] If *Oklahoma City Times* editorialist Dell B. Kell is to be believed, Reverend Berry could expect plenty of interesting companions during his forced penance.

In December 1898, scoundrels at Earlsboro made front-page news in the *Oklahoma Champion* by orchestrating "one of the boldest attempts at a bank robbery ever perpetrated in Oklahoma." In what was described as a well-planned but poorly executed strategy, three armed men entered the State Bank of Earlsboro and ordered customers and staff to raise their hands and fork over their money. What the men did not count on was a combination of advance intelligence and modern technology: "The bank had wind of the intended raid and was not caught napping altogether, for the double time lock on the safe played a pretty and timely part." Still, the victims did not emerge unscathed from their ordeal. Bank principal Eugene Arnett "received several welts over his head with a six-shooter, and probably would have been handled pretty roughly had not several citizens entered the building just at that time." The frustrated robbers absconded with only about three hundred dollars. Their pillaging continued when they held up S. O. Welbourn near the Seminole line and forced him to accompany them to the outskirts of Wewoka, where they relieved him of his horse and loose change. At press time, the bandits were still at large. The State Bank of Earlsboro and the Choctaw, Oklahoma and Gulf Railway were expected to offer a reward for their capture.[19]

Three episodes in 1897 served notice that frontier lawlessness would not pass quietly into the history books. In the spring of that year, it came to light that deputy U.S. marshals were plotting to rob a bank in Guthrie. Such was the magnitude of the alleged conspiracy that the Department of Justice in Washington, D.C., planned to launch an investigation. Sifting through the murky details that some dismissed as fabrications, Barde reported in the *Kansas City Star* that Samuel Wisby, an office deputy under U.S. marshal Patrick Nagle, made a written statement that deputy U.S. marshal Samuel Large of Shawnee and other ex-deputies had asked him to participate in robbing a Guthrie bank. Deputy Wisby told the bank president about the plot, but he neglected to tell Marshal Nagle about it. Upon questioning, Wisby expressed no doubt that Deputy Large would have killed him for betraying the plot. Apparently, the alleged scheme got no further. Wisby was dismissed for keeping Nagle in the dark. Large, who was ill at his home in Shawnee, was to be questioned about his role in the stillborn conspiracy.[20]

The second episode was an unpleasant reminder of wildcat banking, which had branded the Twin Territories as a risky place to do business. In early November, the press reported that receivership of the defunct Commercial National Bank of Guthrie had ended the previous day in Logan County District Court. The bank had failed in November 1890 when its principals, including J. M. Ragsdale and C. R. McLain, absconded with some $150,000. Creditors eventually received about $70,000. The National Bank of Newton, Kansas, was on the hook for about $50,000.[21] An obituary of the Commercial National Bank published in the territorial press shortly after its failure in November 1890 still resonated in November 1897 when the bank's term of receivership came to a close: "The Commercial National Bank was a poor man's bank, and with many depositors it swept away all. This bank has been a blue day for the Territory, as the company of Ragsdale & Company who have banks in Guthrie, Norman, Stillwater, Kingfisher and El Reno, failed to open their doors this morning. The bank has been running since the settlement of Oklahoma, and has received on deposit something like one million dollars, which was spent in erecting a magnificent bank building and in wreckless [sic] loans on undeeded lots in Guthrie."[22]

The third piece of bad banking news in 1897 came in early December with the failure of the Stock Exchange Bank of El Reno. The bank's principals were subsequently arrested for accepting deposits after knowing that their bank was in failing condition. Included in the roundup were Gustav Thelan, president; Michael Eichhoff, cashier; Charles A. Newman, assistant cashier; and Louis Eichhoff, a member of the bank's board of directors. Their arrest came on the heels of a meeting of about seventy-five depositors, mostly poor, and all furious that their meager savings had been vaporized in the collapse. Seething with indignation, depositors delivered fiery speeches and demanded that the officers be taken from their homes and hanged. Frontier justice was thwarted by the voice of reason, but there remained strong public sentiment against allowing them to post bond. The bank had about $66,000 on deposit when it failed. The word on the street was that depositors would be lucky to receive as much as twenty-five cents on the dollar.[23]

Somewhere between the wild-eyed exaggerations published back east and mundane criminality that was downplayed in the territorial press lay the true condition of Oklahoma banking. In terms of sound banking principles, it was not a pretty picture, and legislators in Guthrie were building a consensus that something had to be done. In January 1897, Councilman Johnston of Noble decided to put an end to wildcat banking, once and for all. In the absence of laws regulating private banks, failures were all but inevitable. Since the Panic of 1893, there had been one to three bank failures in every county. Complaining that private bankers were under no obligation to make sworn statements, Johnston proposed a bill to require bankers to file quarterly statements with the registrar of deeds and the territorial secretary in Guthrie. Fired by populist sentiments, Councilman Johnston further proposed that a territorial officer be placed under heavy bond and charged with the duties of bank examiner. Penalties for violating his proposed law included fines of $1,000 to $50,000 and a ten-year prison sentence. Johnston's colleagues in the legislature had reason to be skeptical: as of early 1897, every banking bill had been lobbied to oblivion.[24]

Meanwhile, "Pop" May in the House of Representatives was setting his sights on national banks. In a concurrent resolution aimed at putting "the national banks through a fiery roasting," Representative May hurled four accusations at national banks and the big (i.e., eastern) money they represented: (1) national banks wanted to issue and regulate all paper currency; (2) national banks were "controlling to a large extent our elections and dictating national legislation to a degree that makes it impossible to secure any reforms in the interest of the people"; (3) national banks were complicit in the shrinkage of monetary volume, which had drained the country's wealth by more than $20 billion; and (4) by ensuring a chronic shortage of circulating medium, national banks hampered the exchange of products "to the extent that there is great poverty and idleness on the one hand, and opulent plenty on the other." Calling on all patriots to rally to the defense of liberty and the Constitution, May ended his resolution with a not-so-subtle summons to rebellion: "Resolved: That the Oklahoma general assembly recommends the boycotting of the national banking currency in every territory and state favoring free silver, and that they shall issue bonds in the denominations of $5, $10 and $20, bearing interest at the rate of 5 per cent annually, redeemable at pleasure and receivable for all dues to the state and its subdivisions."[25]

Pop May's resolution favored sending delegates to a free-silver convention in Denver scheduled for September 10, 1897, where ways would be devised to purge the banking system of its alleged evils. Owing to its populist membership, the House was expected to adopt the resolution. Even as Representative May and his cohorts girded for battle with national banks, a lawsuit was pending over an Oklahoma statute aimed at punishing officers of insolvent banks who accepted deposits when they knew their banks were in failing condition. Opponents of the law said it was void because of the first legislative assembly's failure in 1890 to properly enact it. "The legislature of 1890 was notorious for its inefficiency," ran a newspaper story on the stillborn anti-bank wrecking law, "and its record was blackened by many stories of boodling."[26]

In early March 1897, the council committee of the whole decided it was high time to drive wildcat banks out of the territory and recommended passage of Representative D. S. Rose's banking bill.[27] A native of Ohio with a diploma from Mount Union College and a law degree from Cincinnati Law College, Rose was known as "a brainy fellow with an excellent education." As a free-silver Democrat who favored an expansion of the money supply through a more liberal coinage of silver, Rose made a name for himself by introducing several bills aimed at banking reform. In a newspaper profile, the bachelor from Blackwell and author of the "anti-wild cat" banking bill was characterized as "a close reasoner" who could "dissect a bill and find its defects with apparently little effort." Rose's potential as a statesman and bank reformer apparently held more promise than his prospects for marriage. Poised between Victorian traditions and modernity, Rose clung to old-fashioned attitudes toward the fair sex that did not bode well for a prospective mate. The profile continued, "Rose would make a good husband for some worthy young woman, but he injured his matrimonial chances by his able but ungallant fight against the woman's suffrage bill, the defeat of the bill being attributed mainly to his opposition. He has introduced a number of good bills, among them being a banking bill that will become a law and will protect the people from 'wild cat' banks. Rose could hold his own in any legislative assembly."[28]

Numerous amendments were made to Rose's banking bill, but not enough to block its passage on March 12, 1897, in the House of Representatives. Under its provisions, private banking was abolished, and banks were prohibited from engaging in trade or commerce and investing depositors' money in "speculative margins" on stocks, bonds, and commodities. Three people, two of whom had to be citizens of the Oklahoma Territory, were required for incorporation, and the corporate life of a bank was lengthened from twenty to fifty years. Shareholders and directors were to be liable for twice the amount of the par value of their shares. The minimum required for paid-in capital was set at $5,000, a third of which could be in the form of furniture and equipment. Oversight of territorial banks fell to a banking board consisting of the governor, secretary, treasurer, auditor, and attorney general. Each bank had to have a reserve fund amounting to 15 percent of its deposits, 10 percent of which had to be in cash. The maximum legal interest rate was set at 12 percent, but enforcement was spotty at best. Statements of financial condition were to be given to depositors every ninety days, and examiners who erred in reporting on banks' conditions were to be liable for the amount of their bond. Heretofore based on corporation law drawn from

Nebraska, banking in the Oklahoma Territory was finally coming into its own. Wildcat banking, RIP.[29]

Anyone who expected smooth sailing for the bank bill were in for a shock. On March 12, Representative Rose caused a sensation in the House of Representatives when he announced that five of the most important sections of the engrossed, or official, copy of his banking bill had been stolen. The bill had already passed both houses and needed only the territorial governor's signature to become law. As Rose was wondering if the bill could be restored, the original bill, including its amendments, was found in possession of the chief clerk of the House. The missing sections were promptly engrossed and sent to Governor Renfrow for signing. The theft was believed to have taken place during the evening of March 11 when the bill was in the custody of Chief Clerk Mackey, who was sick and unable to attend to his duties. Apparently, it was an easy matter to take the bill from his desk and remove the sections "which the banking lobby had failed to have stricken out by the corrupt use of money." Understandably miffed, Representative May "declared that somebody should be put in the penitentiary for such infamous actions."[30] Members of the House wanted to investigate, but there was not enough time to produce convicting evidence before the fourth legislature's adjournment on March 13.

Realizing how easy it would be to highjack bills on their way to the governor's office, legislators took precautions to prevent other bills from suffering the same fate. Representative Johnson detailed J. H. Hightower, "who has the reputation of being a fighter," to carry the bills, and both houses posted guards at the chief clerk's desk. Yet as one investigative reporter—surely the indefatigable Frederick Barde—noted on March 12, banking reform was not out of the woods: "It was discovered this afternoon after the repeal of the old banking law that the Rose bill contained no provision for the prosecution of nearly fifty persons who had been indicted under the old law and are now awaiting trial for receiving deposits after their banks were known to be in a failing condition. An attempt will be made to remedy the defect."[31]

The theft was seen by many as conclusive proof that something was rotten in Guthrie. A House committee's failure to uncover evidence of boodling (or bribery, in modern and slightly less colorful vernacular) prompted Representative Doyle to object to what he called "a stealthy attempt to assassinate the character of legislative members." The war of words escalated when Representative Rose, author of the banking bill and chairman of the committee appointed to investigate stories of boodling, accused fellow legislators of corruption. "My only regret is that the committee did not have time enough to go to the bottom of this matter," declared Rose. "I am satisfied that money was used here and I feel that the honest members of this assembly have been subjected to an unjust contest in having to fight for the passage of needed and wholesome laws against the opposition of those who were bribed to defeat them." Rose made specific reference to $2,750 deposited in "a certain Guthrie bank" for the purpose of influencing votes on an appropriation bill. "It is a disgrace to have to work with men who accept such money," concluded the irate legislator. "There is no whitewashing in this report. I am not in the whitewashing business."[32]

A few days after the infamous theft, the press weighed in on the most important legislation to emerge from the contentious fourth assembly. Topping the list was Rose's banking bill, cited by Oklahoma Territory governor Renfrow as a valuable and necessary measure that would accrue to the benefit of depositors.[33] Under the new law, oversight of territorial banks fell to a banking board consisting of the governor, secretary, treasurer, auditor, and attorney general. To examine banks and issue reports on their conditions, the banking board appointed T. M. Richardson Jr. as territorial bank examiner.[34] The son of pioneer banker T. M. Richardson, Richardson Jr. was working alongside his father at the First National Bank of Oklahoma City at the time of his appointment. Somehow, the younger Richardson managed to avoid the taint of scandal that surrounded his father, who had recently been acquitted of wrongdoing in the failure of a bank in Perry in which he was involved. The elder Richardson had been charged with receiving deposits when he knew that his bank was in failing condition. In all likelihood, the leniency shown the elder Richardson after the Perry bank failure had something to do with the fact that, for many years, he had been "a warm friend of Governor Renfrow."[35]

T. M. Richardson Jr. was twenty-two years old when he shouldered his new responsibilities. In spite of his youth, he came equipped with "good technical knowledge of his position." The job paid $1,000 annually, plus expenses, and derived from fees levied on banks. As banks were not required to comply with the new law until January 1898, Richardson was in for several months of work without remuneration.[36]

The new bank examiner quickly filed a bond in the amount of $25,000 with territorial secretary Thomas Lowe. His sureties included two of his bank's principals: T. M. Richardson Sr., vice president, and J. P. Boyle, cashier.[37] Thus did the First National Bank of Oklahoma City take its place at the vortex of territorial commerce and politics.

On May 18, 1897, territorial governor William C. Renfrow returned to Guthrie from a visit to Hot Springs, Arkansas, carrying "a mysterious bundle." It turned out to contain a bicycle, "fully equipped with all the latest devices." Up to now, Renfrow had been branded an "old fogy" on the subject of bicycles. "Such foolishness is all right for young people," the governor once quipped, "but when it comes to middle aged persons, dignity should be considered, before men and women make public spectacles of themselves."[38] Clearly, old-fashioned attitudes were loosening their grip on the soon-to-be ex-governor of Oklahoma Territory, but not entirely. Having learned to ride a bike in Hot Springs, Governor Renfrow promised not to ride in public until his successor assumed office. Politicians on bicycles, it seems, was more than the modernizing governor could stomach.

Governor Renfrow did not have to wait long to indulge his new passion. In May 1897, Cassius M. Barnes returned to Guthrie from Washington, D.C., where he had received his appointment as governor of the Oklahoma Territory. Flags and streamers were everywhere. Perched on a car platform at the train station, Governor Barnes clutched a bouquet of roses as he bowed to the multitude. He was met by Guthrie mayor B. F. Berkey and Guthrie club president C. G. Horner and escorted to an open carriage drawn by four beautiful black horses. Seated in the carriage next to Mayor Berkey, President Horner, and Captain D. F. Stiles, who had commanded a company of soldiers at Oklahoma Station during the Run of '89, the governor was whisked from the train station to his new home. Trumpeters from the territorial militia, a military escort, marching bands, and a line of carriages were on hand to announce his arrival. After an informal luncheon, Governor Barnes made a five-minute visit to the office of former governor Renfrow, who was sporting a big white carnation on his coat.[39] Perhaps his bicycle was parked out back for a quick getaway.

While Governor Barnes was settling into his new job, territorial bankers gathered in June 1897 for a historic meeting. Summoned to

Guthrie to discuss the new banking law by Bank of the Indian Territory President U. C. Guss, delegates commended the new banking law and organized the Oklahoma Territory Bankers Association, forerunner of the modern-day Oklahoma Bankers Association. Oklahoma Territory's five national banks had been invited to attend. In a foretaste of the contention to come, nearly one-third of the territory's private banks were unrepresented.

Upon the recommendation of the committee on permanent organization, the following officers were elected: U. C. Guss, president; W. S. Search of the Shawnee State Bank, vice president; J. C. Smith of the People's Bank of Kingfisher, second vice president; Otto A. Shuttee of the Citizens Bank of El Reno, secretary; and D. W. Hogan of the Bank of Yukon, treasurer. The executive committee included B. S. Barnes of Ponca City as chairman and four members-at-large: L. D. Freeman of the Farmers and Merchants Bank of Perry; J. W. McNeal of the Guthrie National Bank; John Grattan of the Grant County Bank of Medford; and R. T. Drennan of the Bank of Hennessey. The president and secretary were ex-officio members of the executive committee. The group's constitution extended membership to national as well as territorial bankers. Members could be expelled by a two-thirds vote of those present at any meeting. No voting by proxy was allowed, annual dues were set at five dollars, and annual meetings were to be held between November 15 and December 15. El Reno was selected as the location for the next meeting.[40]

Four decades later, frontier banker Tom J. Hartman recalled the genesis of today's Oklahoma Bankers Association in an interview for the Works Progress Administration: "The early bankers, realizing the necessity for organization, met in Guthrie, in June 1897, and organized the Oklahoma Bankers Association."[41] With populism still raging across the West, people were clamoring for regulations. Pressures came not only from progressive reformers but also from federal agencies bent on regulation, and they were fueled by business mergers and financial panics that compelled bankers to join forces in associations to lobby for their interests.[42]

Even as bankers were celebrating their union in a formal organization, bank examiner T. M. Richardson Jr. was learning what it meant to pay for the sins of the father. His appointment as bank examiner by Governor Renfrow had met with resistance from bankers who resented his youth as well as his connection with the defunct bank at Perry through his father. Some claimed that the younger Richardson knew his day of reckoning was coming and was scrambling to earn his year's salary in a few months by hastily examining banks and drawing his fees. Whatever his degree of prescience, the bombshell fell quickly. He was ordered to cease his examinations, which meant that he had to remain idle until a successor was appointed.[43] The young bank examiner's fall from grace is reflected in his terse, one-line letter of resignation to Governor Barnes: "I hereby resign my position as territorial bank examiner, and am ready to turn over to my successor when appointed."[44]

Speculation that J. N. Pugh of Woodward would be appointed as Richardson's successor turned out to be accurate. Pugh was duly sworn in and posted his $25,000 bond on July 22. The Banking Board promptly formulated new rules to govern examinations of territorial and private banks and directed Pugh to pick up where his predecessor had left off. A report was expected on the condition of the Oklahoma Territory's forty-nine territorial and private banks as of July 23, 1897.[45]

As the new bank examiner hustled to collect his data, Guthrie banker J. W. McNeal was regaling the press with encouraging news about the circulation of coin and currency. "I had a striking illustration to-day of how money has been brought from its hiding places and put in circulation," said McNeal in early August 1897. "There was a run on our bank during the panic in 1893 and a large amount of the deposits were withdrawn. Two packages of $500 each, which were taken out at that time were brought in to-day. They never had been broken and apparently had been buried. I find a constantly increasing confidence in a good business future among all our patrons." McNeal further claimed that most bank loans were small because farmers only wanted enough money to tide them over until their crops came in. The Guthrie banker anticipated heavy demand for speculative money in the fall, when stockmen would be looking for money to invest in cattle.[46]

Further evidence of the territory's prosperity is found in Governor Barnes's reply to an inquiry from a newspaper in New York about the state of the territory. Barnes's letter gushed with enthusiasm over the territory's bounty of wheat, corn, cotton, peaches, and grapes. "Oklahoma will market 40 million dollars' worth of these things this season," wrote the governor, "which, at the present increased prices, will bring prosperity to the farmers of the territory, and through them to all lines of business and trade. Already a very prosperous state of trade is noticed on

An oil well being spudded in front of the Citizens Bank in Lawton, Oklahoma Territory, August 20, 1901. Courtesy Oklahoma Historical Society.

every side, with strong indications of a steady increase. Money is becoming more plentiful and obligations of every kind are promptly met." Governor Barnes went on to assert that real estate dealers were fielding inquiries at a level not seen "since the early boom days."[47] Wheat took top billing as Oklahoma's ticket to prosperity.

No sooner did Governor Barnes enlighten New Yorkers on the state of territorial commerce than official reports added the stamp of legitimacy. On August 23, the comptroller of the currency in Washington, D.C., issued a statement indicating that national banks in the Oklahoma Territory carried an impressive aggregate reserve of 70.28 percent. National banks in the Indian Territory reported reserves of 37.07 percent.[48]

Less than three weeks later came the first complete statement of the condition of the Oklahoma Territory's forty-nine territorial and private banks. Bank examiner Pugh, who had examined twenty banks during his brief tenure in office, reported total resources at the close of business on July 23 of $2,294,263.64. The minimum cash reserve allowed by law was 15 percent, but the actual cash reserve was an impressive 51 percent. Deposits had increased 25 percent in two months. Practically all deposits were owned by farmers and businessmen in the Oklahoma Territory and not, as many suspected, the property of grain and cotton buyers from other states. At the same time, the Oklahoma Territory's five national banks were reporting total capital of a quarter of a million dollars. As of May 1897, national banks had nearly $600,000 in deposits, $44,800 in surplus and undivided profits, and $370,000 in loans.[49]

Pugh's next report, published in mid-October under the giddy head-line "The Banks Full of Money," showed continued growth in the Oklahoma Territory's banks. At the close of business on September 30, 1897, total resources of territorial and private banks were $2,598,197.61. Since July 23, deposits had increased by 20 percent, or $350,000. The reserve fund had increased another 11 percent and was now 62 percent of deposits, even though the law required a reserve fund of only 15 percent. Inexplicably, loans were down by 10 percent, or $100,000. Two new banks, one in Ponca City and the other in Mulhall, had incorporated since the bank examiner's first report.[50]

In his annual report to the Department of the Interior for the year ending June 30, 1897, Governor Barnes shared the good news with officialdom in Washington, D.C. In only seven years of existence, the Oklahoma Territory had become one of the most talked-about and read-about regions of the United States. Its population exceeded 300,000, rendering the Oklahoma Territory more populous than a dozen states. Moreover, the territory included fewer people of foreign birth than any state in the Union, rendering it "distinctly an American community" whose residents were "the embodiment of courage, thrift, energy and enterprise, an optimist of optimists, a conqueror of a new world." Governor Barnes relied on facts and statistics to support his sanguine report: property carried an assessed value of $32,034,752, compared to $19,937,940.86 in 1894; university attendance was 172, with an expectation that the number of students would soar to 200 in 1898; and 131 students were enrolled in the Agricultural and Mechanical College, which was "richly endowed by the government" and "well equipped in all its departments." Taking aim at journalists whose wild-eyed exaggerations of Oklahoma lawlessness were a brake on economic development, Governor Barnes asserted, "There is no border ruffianism, no every day open outlawry, no semi-savage barbarity, such as is depicted in some unreliable journals or has found belief in the minds of misguided and uninformed individuals in unprogressive communities." The governor assured his readers that, contrary to public opinion, Indian tribes were flourishing and even increasing in population. Perhaps most remarkably in that oppressive age, educational opportunities were even available to the territory's blacks, "who are given the same advantages as the whites."[51]

Governor Barnes reserved special praise for the banking law slated to go into effect on January 1, 1898, which promised to put an end to wildcat banking. "The last legislature passed a law which amply protects depositors in banks," crowed the governor, "and affords them a redress not heretofore possessed in Oklahoma." The governor went on to cite bank examiner's Pugh's recent report on the splendid condition of territorial banks. Building and loan associations, too, were doing their part to lift the Oklahoma Territory from frontier scarcity to material abundance. The governor wound to a conclusion with an invitation to investors to bring their money to the Oklahoma Territory. He bragged, "The people are congratulated that notwithstanding predictions to the contrary, the interests of corporate investments have been accorded liberal recognition by the legislature, and investments of capital are as safe in Oklahoma as anywhere."[52]

Ironically, the rising tide of prosperity spelled trouble for lenders whose customers suddenly had enough cash to pay off their notes. After years of hardship for small borrowers, the supply and demand curves were finally shifting in their favor. As one lender complained, "Last year my patrons were paying only the interest, and getting extensions on the principal. All this is changed now, and I am collecting $2 where I collected $1 last year. The difficulty at this time is to place my money." Another money lender said simply, "The day of 2 and 3 per cent a month money in Oklahoma is gone." Confessing that he had once enjoyed interest rates of 5 percent per month, the lender summed up the small banker's lament at century's end: "Three years ago it was almost impossible for the small borrower to get money from the banks. The times were uncertain and panicky and the banks were holding their cash. As a result, many persons with good collateral went to the 'money sharks,' and the competition pushed up the rate of interest. These borrowers are now going to the banks and getting all the money they want at from 8 to 10 per cent a year on real estate. The small money lender will be forced to do business at from 12 to 15 per cent a year. This will do away with the man of small capital."[53]

While small lenders scrambled for customers, large ones scrambled to stay out of jail. The failure of the Stock Exchange Bank of El Reno in

A bank under construction in Crescent, Oklahoma Territory. Courtesy Oklahoma Historical Society.

December 1897 was foreshadowed in bank examiner John Pugh's report of August 17, 1897, when he informed the territorial banking board that the bank was crippled. One of Pugh's criticisms was that the bank's officers were not diligent in monitoring their loan portfolio. Moreover, "the directors are using too much money, but promise to make it up at once. Cashier and management do not pay enough attention to making collections and are not particular enough about loans."[54] Pugh was also concerned to find too much responsibility vested in the cashier.

But there was more. Officers owed the bank a substantial amount of money, and the cashier had a substantial overdraft. The bank's loan portfolio actually violated banking laws of 1897 that prohibited banks from lending more than 10 percent of their capital stock to a single corporation, partnership, firm, or association. Additional troubles included the bank's $5,832.45 in overdue paper and a reserve of 8 percent of aggregate deposits when the law required a minimum reserve of 15 percent. Pugh concluded his report on a note that was, in hindsight, too optimistic: "This bank should, by careful management and close attention to business, pull through all right. They have plenty of notes secured by chattels on wheat which they will be able to collect within thirty days to make reserve good and place them in good circumstances."[55]

As depositors took to the streets outside the defunct Stock Exchange Bank of El Reno in December 1897 to demand that its officers be hanged from the nearest tree, Pugh went on the defensive. Denying allegations that he shared responsibility for the failure, Pugh claimed that he had given ample warning to the territorial bank board. He also questioned the board's authority to close a bank that was incorporated under laws that would become obsolete on January 1, 1898, when the new law was to take effect. Meanwhile, odd things were happening in El Reno. Reports surfaced that one depositor was allowed to withdraw all his money—"a large amount"—late on Saturday night before the failure was announced on Monday. Another, whose deposit was received an hour before the bank closed, "has had it mysteriously returned to him."[56]

On November 26, 1900, Guthrie National Bank president J. W. McNeal delivered a speech at the annual meeting of the Oklahoma Territory Bankers Association in Enid. The thrust of McNeal's presentation was to suggest ways that bankers might increase their business—ways that apparently did not include overzealous promotion but, rather, a fixation on the bottom line. "My advice to all is to look after your profit account," began the Guthrie banker. "Never undertake to boom your town. Do your part as real estate owner and let that be your limit. Do not be deceived into thinking that you can secure business based on the size of your subscription to public enterprises. Gratitude as a banking asset might as well be charged off."[57]

Clearly, a new day was dawning in the Oklahoma Territory. Wildcat bankers and community boosters who had gone into business with little more than a stack of IOUs and a lockbox were fading into a past that many would just as soon forget. Hellholes such as the Reeves Place in Guthrie and the Blue Front in Oklahoma City were succumbing to a tide of law-abiding citizens. Civic leaders were becoming ever more intolerant of media that branded the Oklahoma and Indian Territories as havens for outlaws. Thanks to Representative D. S. Rose and other responsible lawmakers, banking laws were providing a proper foundation for economic development. And thanks to the territorial banking board and bank examinations that were now mandated by law, irresponsible bankers—including those who led the Stock Exchange Bank of El Reno to its demise—were getting the message that get-rich-quick schemes would no longer be tolerated, and that regulations would henceforth confine them to the legitimate pursuit of profit. Bankers had a forum to consider these issues in the Oklahoma Territory Bankers Association, a group destined to wield considerable influence on state and federal legislation and in promoting sound business principles among Oklahoma bankers.

"There is a happy medium between the extremes of recklessness and penurious conservatism," concluded McNeal in his address to his fellow bankers in Enid. "You may increase your business by keeping within this happy medium. No profession demands a stricter standard of moral integrity than ours. Lawyers and doctors may get drunk and violate the entire decalogue and still do business, but bankers and ministers are required to keep the straight and narrow way, or lose standing and go out of business."[58]

But somewhere between the extremes of recklessness and penurious conservatism, between frontier lawlessness and rules and regulations that were coming on like a freight train, there was still plenty of room for old-fashioned ingenuity. J. W. Schaff, a contractor in Holdenville, Indian Territory, was short on checks when he received a fifty-dollar load of lumber. So he picked up a board, scratched out a check order, directed it to the Bank of Holdenville, signed it, and sawed it off. In due course, the check was returned to Schaff along with other canceled checks, presumably of the paper variety.[59]

Just another day of banking in Oklahoma before statehood.

CHAPTER TEN

The Scramble

Will you please send us by earliest return mail a blank application for a charter for a State Bank? We will take it as a personal favor if you will send this to
us by first mail as we are in something of a *rush* for it.

T. J. Ballew, assistant cashier, Bank of Geary, Oklahoma Territory,
to William Grimes, secretary of Oklahoma Territory

Perhaps one day evidence will come to light that a banker, or bankers,
played in the first golf game in the Oklahoma Territory in the early
spring of 1899, when a group of sportsmen gathered at "the Havighorst
pasture" north of Guthrie. The group included Robert W. Ramsey and
J. A. Milne, both natives of Scotland, and the Right Reverend Francis
Key Brooke, bishop of the Episcopal Diocese of Oklahoma.

In all likelihood, Reverend Brooke began the first territorial tee up
with a prayer. Although he might have implored the Almighty for fair
weather and safe passage over the nine-hole course, there was not much
he could do about the shortage of "golf sticks." But Ramsey, who had
grown up playing golf with his father at the "Royal and Ancient Golf
Club of St. Andrew's," was prepared. His father had brought his sticks
with him when he emigrated from Scotland to Pittsburg, Kansas. The
younger Ramsey, lugging what was surely some unusual cargo in those
days, brought them to Guthrie. "Thus," wrote the journalist Frederick S.
Barde, "golf sticks that had swept the St. Andrew's green were the first to
be used in Oklahoma."[1]

Although a few territorial sportsmen had learned the game back east, most needed lessons, and Dr. John W. Duke was there to provide them. Teaching beginners to scramble across rough terrain would have been hard enough. Yet Dr. Duke's challenge was compounded by conditions that did not bode very well for the future of golf in Oklahoma. "The game in Oklahoma is rather peculiar to itself, because of local conditions," wrote Barde in one of the Oklahoma Territory's first sports columns. "The wind has a free sweep across the Oklahoma prairies, especially in the golf season, and in making his drives the player in Oklahoma must count upon angles of resistance not met with commonly in eastern states."[2]

Thus did golf make its arrival in the Oklahoma Territory—a milestone not only in sport, but also for bankers interested in closing their deals somewhere other than stuffy offices and boardrooms.

But it was money, and not golf, that captured the public's attention at the turn of the twentieth century. On January 8, 1898, bank examiner John M. Pugh reported on the condition of Oklahoma Territory's forty-seven state and private banks for the quarter ending December 31, 1897. Since September 30, the gain in deposits was $600,000, or 33⅓ percent. Cash increased by $640,000, or 50 percent, and the reserve fund was up 7 percent to a remarkable 70 percent of deposits.[3] A couple of weeks after his report was published, Pugh sent a letter to stockholders and directors of territorial banks admonishing them to attend to their duties under the new banking law. Apparently, many of them had been derelict in their accounting when it came to declaring dividends and writing off bad loans. "As a stockholder," chided the bank examiner, "remember that your interest is a trifle compared with that of the many depositors, whose money you are using, giving them for security only the honesty of your officers and the strict compliance of the law. It being my duty to look after the interests of the depositors, I shall make special effort to see that the requirement of the law is complied with, which will not only protect them but your interests as well. I hope that you will see the responsibility and co-operate with me in enforcing the law."[4]

Pugh's report on the territory's forty-nine territorial and private banks at the close of the fiscal year ending on June 30 was even rosier. "The record of the banking business in Oklahoma for the fiscal year was the most brilliant in the history of the territory," said the bank examiner.[5]

Numbers told the story of economic growth on steroids: deposits were up 75 percent; the reserve account, which exceeded that of any state or territory in the United States, never dipped below 49 percent (July 23, 1897), peaked at 74 percent (December 31, 1897), and averaged 62 and ³⁄₇ percent when only 15 percent was required by statute; cash holdings were 110 percent higher than a year earlier; loans were up 25 percent; and average earnings were 23 percent. Only one bank—the Stock Exchange Bank of El Reno—failed during the fiscal year, and that was "due to bad management."[6] Six new banks were started, two banks were consolidated, and real estate holdings were reduced by 25 percent. In addition to the forty-nine territorial and private banks, there were six national banks, and their reports to the comptroller of the currency in Washington, D.C., showed that they were prospering as well.

Examiner Pugh was upbeat about the banking law of 1897, claiming that it was stringent enough to satisfy the most careful depositor. Nevertheless, he suggested in a statement to Governor Barnes that the Territorial Banking Board consider several changes: (1) banks should be permitted to loan 15 percent of their capital rather than 10 percent as allowed by the current law; (2) a bank's capital should be commensurate with the size of its town and the volume of its business; and (3) banks should not be able to invest more than four times the amount of their capital. Pugh concluded his report with the prediction that the banking business in fiscal 1898 would be even more robust than it was in 1897.[7]

While the bank examiner was issuing glowing reports and reminding bankers to keep their priorities straight, Representative D. S. Rose was fending off criticism of his banking bill. The controversy arose when John W. Shartel, a business leader and attorney who guided Oklahoma City through its formative years, criticized the new law in a speech before the Oklahoma Bar Association. Admitting that the banking law was far from perfect, Rose suggested that Shartel, who was a former president of the Oklahoma Bar Association, was either unfair or uninformed in claiming that the law was poorly conceived:

> While the law was not gotten up or passed by practical bankers, it was, prior to its passage, submitted to them for their criticism and suggestions, and also to lawyers as able as Mr. Shartel. It is granted that some blotches were left in the law by the inconsiderate amendments made by the council, both in provisions

and wording, but it may be improved. On the rigid rules of law, learned through familiarity with court decisions and text books, Mr. Shartel's knowledge may be considerable, but such training cramps originality, rendering him incapable of realizing results of valuable innovations, and for this reason, he must wait to see the good in the legislation he criticizes.[8]

The wheels of commerce were greased by advances in communication and transportation. In late January 1898, G. C. Lofland of Kansas City, a traveling auditor for the Missouri and Kansas Telephone Company, was inspecting offices in the Oklahoma Territory. Forecasting improved service in the coming year, Lofland predicted that the line from Oklahoma City to Guthrie would be completed within days. By summer, the line would be continued to Arkansas City; eventually, it would reach all the way to Kansas City. More lines were planned from El Reno to Kingfisher, Oklahoma City to Norman, and probably Oklahoma City to Chandler. There was even talk of building a line from Guthrie to Chandler. "The American Long Distance Telephone Company will build from St. Louis to Kansas City this summer," said Lofland, "which will enable Oklahomans to talk with New York City, Chicago, in fact, almost any of the big eastern cities."[9] Lofland was pleased with the territory's flourishing economy and expressed no doubt that his company's investment would pay off.

Encouraging reports from the bank examiner and improvements in infrastructure were complemented by testimony from farmers and businessmen. "Practically all the wheat and cotton and other products have now been sold and the money used in making improvements and removing obligations," ran an April 1898 newspaper story on territorial prosperity. The article continued, "Merchants, farmers and bankers who were grumbling and dissatisfied, after the general reverses of several years ago, are quick to say now that the prosperity in Oklahoma was never exceeded in any other state in which they have lived."[10]

The territorial secretary asserted that charters issued to businesses in the preceding twelve months were up 50 percent from the previous year. Many of those charters were issued to corporations in other states that planned to do business in the Oklahoma Territory. Ignoring dire predictions in the yellow press of annihilation by Indians, insurance companies flocked to the territory and established profitable businesses. A leading insurance agent said that the insurance business in the spring of 1898 showed an increase of 25 percent over a similar period in any previous year. A real estate man chimed in with his assessment: "There has been a wonderful amount of emigration here this spring and last fall. From my personal knowledge I can say that one hundred farms in the territory adjacent to Guthrie have been purchased by strangers during the last six months. This condition is true of the entire agricultural district of Oklahoma."[11]

Meanwhile, out-of-state capitalists were finding fertile fields for their money. Over a period of four years, a Topeka capitalist made loans totaling $150,000 to Oklahoma businesses, and he was gradually putting all of his money in securities issued in the Oklahoma Territory. A newspaper account of his investments reported "that he has not lost $20 in defaulted interest." Another capitalist in Milwaukee loaned $30,000 and had "not lost a cent in defaulted interest." The same was true of a capitalist in Mansfield, Ohio, whose loans aggregated $100,000. The manager of one of the largest small loan agencies in the territory summed up the situation: "These men are anxious to place their money, but I am unable to supply customers rapidly enough. All kinds of territorial, county and city warrants are being bought, among the investors being capitalists in Canada."[12]

Bankers were both the cause and effect of the rapid pace of economic development. Across the board, territorial bankers reported plenty of money on hand. One banker claimed that legitimate loans were being made as usual. Even though the Spanish-American War was causing a constriction in the eastern money market, he "had not found it necessary to decrease the business latitude which he had observed for the last six months." The same banker expected large outside investments to be suspended during the war, but he expected them to resume at its conclusion. "Our loans are fewer in number, but larger in amount," he said. "Formerly loans were secured for domestic purposes; they are now invested in improvements and speculations."[13]

It was one thing to convince citizens of the Oklahoma Territory that investments were safe and businesses were thriving; it was something else altogether to spread the word to the rest of the country. Horace Hagan of Guthrie tried for three years to convince a wealthy acquaintance "that Oklahoma was not the desolate, lawless place which sensational newspaper stories alleged it to be. He laughed at me and said that he could be induced more easily to build a street railway or a gas plant in the middle of the Sahara desert than to put a single dollar in Oklahoma." Hagan persisted, and in late 1897 or early 1898, his skeptical friend dropped in for a visit. But he remained wary as he stepped off the train: "His little son had warned his father to carry a pistol to resist attacks from Indians and robbers, and had asked him to bring back a collection of Indian relics."[14]

Wariness turned to perplexity when the man learned that Indian relics were more readily available at the Union Depot in Kansas City than in the Oklahoma Territory. But there were more surprises to come. "What he saw was a revelation to him," said Hagan. "The well established farms and the large number of farm houses in sight at almost any point along the road appeared miraculous to him. He said that he had seen generally no better farming communities in Missouri, Kansas or Illinois." The man wound up purchasing $20,000 worth of bonds issued by an Oklahoma county and contracted for $20,000 more. Even though he was thinking of investing in a cotton gin in another state, the man "admitted that he never knew what cotton really was until he saw Oklahoma's splendid crop that is now coming daily to market." Hagan ended his parable of the Oklahoma convert with a flourish that typifies frontier boosterism: "We've got the stuff to show them, whether they come from Missouri or Kalamazoo."[15]

Oklahoma City mayor J. P. Allen, a native of northern Mississippi and an attorney who was destined to become one the most influential leaders of the young state, delivered the welcoming address at the second annual convention of the Oklahoma Territory Bankers Association on December 7, 1898, in Oklahoma City. Delighted to host territorial bankers in the "metropolis and railroad center of the territory," Mayor Allen yielded the floor to Shawnee banker W. S. Search.[16] Search began his remarks by expressing his pleasure (relief?) that the 1897 banking law had caused so little friction. His wide-ranging speech included the federal government's decision to offer $200 million in U.S. war bonds to finance the Spanish-American War and the receptive market that they found; an increase in the gold reserve—surely as accurate an indicator of public confidence as there was—of $20 million since April 3, 1898; a level of bank deposits that was unmatched in U.S. history; and a steady rise in exports.

Search went on to praise the territory's contingent of Rough Riders, "whose achievements at San Juan heights are historical," and the farmers who kept them supplied with wheat, corn, cotton, cattle, and hogs. He also marveled at the things bankers had accomplished in an era when ingenuity made up for material scarcity: "Without any material increase in banking facilities the deposits in territorial banks as shown by the reports of the bank examiner, were increased from $1,499,149.69 June 13, 1897, to $2,560,485.18 June 30, 1898, at which date the report further states, that not a bank in the territory carried a rediscount." The territory's six national banks were in similarly good shape. Statements issued on May 5, 1898, showed their aggregate deposit was $1,027,893.61, and their rediscounts were nil. "The settlement and subsequent growth of our territory has indeed been remarkable," continued Search; "its material prosperity has exceeded all expectations; the events of its history followed closely in the wake of the boom days and yet we have inherited little of its consequences. The panic of 1893 only hastened the failure of institutions whose unbusiness-like methods would, by a slower process, have accomplished the same results."[17]

Search complimented his fraternity of bankers, two-thirds of whom were members of the association, for maintaining the honor of their profession. He was less enthused about the banking law of 1897 and the competence of its creators. He reflected, "Owing to the hasty manner in which our banking law was enacted, or the incompetency of the legislative body that passed upon it, it could not and did not receive the careful discussion so important a subject demanded, and is, therefore, necessarily imperfect and in many ways conflicting in its terms." Revealing the classic dichotomy between legislators and businessmen, Search urged his brethren to make recommendations for reform to ensure the safety of their depositors and the growth of their communities: "The recommendations of this body, if they be reasonable and right, will have much to do in the formulation of an enactment more perfect and better adapted to the wants of a growing community like ours."[18]

Attendees reconvened on December 8 to listen to bank examiner Pugh's history of banking since the Run of '89. In April 1890, there were three national banks in the Oklahoma Territory with combined capital of $200,000, deposits of $169,000, and loans and discounts of $133,000. The next year, bankers reported loans of $206,000 and deposits of $242,000. By 1892, the territory's four national banks were reporting combined capital of $325,000, loans and discounts of $185,000, and deposits of $682,000.[19]

Then came the deluge. Pugh spoke of "a veritable black Friday" when the Panic of 1893 forced several banks into failure.[20] Even though the number of banks increased to six, capital rose to $115,000, and loans increased to $133,000, bankers suffered as deposits in the national banks dropped to $592,000. Deposits in national banks reached a low ebb of $449,000 in 1896, a decline of $213,000 since early 1893. Yet even in those dark days, well-managed banks summoned the financial where-withal to promote economic development.

Supervision and reporting requirements came with the banking laws of 1897—flawed and long overdue, to be sure, but indispensable to instilling sound banking principles in the financial system. "Since that time the progress made in banking in Oklahoma has been marvelous; in fact, unequaled and unapproached by that of any state or territory in the Union," Pugh noted. Since enactment of the territorial banking law, one bank (the Stock Exchange Bank of El Reno) had failed, two banks had consolidated, and nine territorial and two national banks had been organized. As of December 1898, there were sixty-one banks in the territory with total capitalization of $925,000 and loans and discounts of $1,835,000. "I know of nothing that can more fully demonstrate to my hearers what these figures disclose," said Pugh. "The bankers of Oklahoma are to be congratulated upon this showing, growïng out of the untoward conditions with which they have been brought face to face and, in most cases, have admirably surmounted. The people, too, should be congratulated upon the character of these men who have been practically the mainstay of the territory. For with a solid condition of affairs of the banks of a state or territory, there is a degree of satisfaction which in itself conveys confidence, and when this is once established the success of a banker is practically assured."[21]

O. J. Fleming of Enid was not present at the meeting, and his paper, carrying the unambiguous title "The Country Banker," was read by J. H. Wheeler of Oklahoma City. First and foremost, Fleming admonished bankers to obtain solid collateral by understanding farming in all its dimensions. Climate, seasonal variations, marketing, animal husbandry, soil conservation—knowledge of these and other factors were the sine qua non of successful lending in a region so heavily dependent on agriculture. Fleming went on to insist that speculation was the road to perdition: "Neither the 'country banker,' nor any banker, has a moral right to speculate. It is his duty in all cases where applications are made for loans, to decide in favor of the bank, if the slightest question of doubt exists regarding the repayment of same; he should remember his 'trust.'" In addressing the porous boundary between business and politics, Fleming based his counsel on rock-solid ethics, declaring, "If the bankers of this territory contemplate the buying, selling or the loaning of money on warrants, territorial, county, city or school, I challenge your attention to the fact that you must be able to accurately determine long in advance the political character of the incoming officers."[22]

J. C. Post's paper on the relationship between private, state, and national banks addressed the divide between national banks and their orientation toward eastern capital and state and private banks, which were perceived as more rooted in their communities. Animosity between state and national banks dated back to the National Banking Act of 1863, and intensified in the Twin Territories during the 1890s when prairie populists denounced the money power back east as the source of their tribulations.

While bankers were airing their issues and grievances, editorials in the territorial press blared with resentment toward the money powers. An editorialist in the left-leaning Oklahoma Champion had had enough. "Our country," he wrote as bankers were gathering in Oklahoma City in December 1898, "has grown great, powerful and rich, in spite of the most faulty financial system ever devised by the wit of man—a system which has devastated the country with periodical panics more destructive than warfare, involving in wreck and ruin its tens of thousands in each case—and yet the country has survived and recuperated, and our people quickly forget, and go on repeating the same ruinous policy."[23] Spokesmen for the laboring classes promoted the referendum (submitting important legislation to a popular vote) as the only way to circumvent the influence of big money and return power to the people. "The power of money to control legislation," declared an impassioned advocate for the referendum in the same newspaper, "and to the extent to which such power has been and still is being used, are too well known to require illustration here. Under our present political system wealth has become greater than humanity; the creature, by a seeming perversion of natural law greater than its creator. Money is now absolute king."[24] Others took a simpler approach, particularly when it came to ruinous interest rates: take Saint Paul's advice and owe no man anything.[25] For readers who were slow to get the point, editorial cartoons brought a touch of humor to a serious subject with images of portly and nattily dressed bankers, their attire festooned with dollar signs and pockets bulging with cash and coin, as personifications of the money power.[26]

Animosity over finances flared in the scramble for deposits that could make or break a fledgling bank, and it was destined to exacerbate tensions between state and national banks in the years to come. Another attendee at the Oklahoma Territory Bankers Association meeting in December 1898, J. C. Post, saw no difference between these institutions, "each being safe, sound and solid, one providing equally as much safety as the other for its depositors."[27] Maybe. But there were plenty of bankers with territorial and, later, state charters who resented what they perceived as unfair competition from bankers with national charters and links with eastern capital.

Another item of interest at the bankers' conference was the increasing competition from express money companies. D. W. Hogan of Yukon was outspoken about "this menace to the exchange business of banks" and called on his colleagues to rally to the defense of their industry. "Let us agitate the subject at our state associations," thundered the banker, "and when the American Bankers' association meets next year we will insist on a high commission of able and learned bankers being appointed to devise ways and means for a reciprocal bank draft, the excellence of which will so far overshadow the express money order that it will sink into harmless disuse."[28]

There was also a consensus that bankers should have legal protection from borrowers who did not pay for their money. U. C. Guss, president of the Bank of Indian Territory in Guthrie, expressed the need for safeguards against deadbeat borrowers: "If the banks are public servants and subject to police surveillance, I think they should have the benefit of a law that would protect them against borrowers who do not pay for money borrowed. Money borrowed from a bank should be a first lien without any exemption on the property owned by the borrower, subject to execution and sale, and such property should not be subject to mortgage indebtedness."[29]

Few issues were more vexing to territorial bankers than the safety of deposits. Guss was ahead of his time in suggesting the creation of a fund to bail out depositors in the event of a bank failure. He explained, "I would suggest that each bank pay into the treasury one-fourth of 1 per cent a year, payable quarterly, on the average deposits of such bank, to create a fund to be used only for the purpose of paying off the depositors in a failed bank. This would create a fund sufficient for all needs, and when the fund reaches $200,000, no more calls shall be made until the fund is below that amount." In case of a bank failure, losses would be recouped from the liquidation of assets, the guaranty fund, and stockholders' double liability. "I believe," concluded Guss, "that if this plan were adopted and a bill carefully prepared and passed by the next legislature, it would be a very great advantage to the territorial or state banks of Oklahoma."[30] Little did the Guthrie banker suspect that, ten years hence, legislators in the brand new state of Oklahoma would make deposit guarantee one of their first items of business, thus distinguishing their state as a pioneer in the guarantee of bank deposits.

Following the election of officers and agreement to convene the following year in Shawnee, the meeting adjourned. That afternoon, citizens of Oklahoma City toured their visitors around town to show off "the improvements and advantages."[31] Various clubs hosted smokers that evening as a parting, nicotine-saturated gift to the Oklahoma Territory's moneymen. Surely energized by two days of deliberating on the perils and promises of their profession, attendees returned to their communities with a renewed commitment to sound banking principles.

In 1899, the legislature amended the banking law of 1897. Whereas the original law required paid-in capital of $5,000, the new one linked capitalization to the size of the community where a bank was located. The banking board was abolished and replaced with the position of bank commissioner. The commissioner's powers were reduced from those of the banking board insofar as he had no control over the organization of a bank as long as it met legal requirements. Moreover, the bank commissioner lacked the authority to weigh in whenever the convenience or necessity of a bank was called into question. The bank commissioner was also required to administer a bank's affairs in the event of insolvency. If he became convinced that a bank could not resume business, he was required to institute proceedings for the appointment of a court receiver. Meanwhile, the territorial secretary had his hands full processing incoming correspondence, accepting fees, and granting charters. And all the while, the bank examiner charged with examining every bank in the

Oklahoma Territory did his level best to make his appointed rounds. Banking laws passed in 1897 and amended in 1899 remained in effect until statehood in 1907.[32]

Passing laws was one thing; putting them to work was something else altogether. As the sun set on the Oklahoma frontier, laws passed in Guthrie were scant protection from abuse by undercapitalized banks in communities that were sprouting like mushrooms in the Oklahoma Territory. They had no bearing whatsoever in the Indian Territory, which remained under federal and tribal jurisdiction and where the comptroller of the currency in Washington, D.C., had the final say on banking. All too often, unscrupulous bankers continued the frontier tradition of tossing IOUs in a cashbox and declaring their bank to be amply capitalized. Usurious interest rates, often set at an annual rate between 24 to 36 percent, continued to be extracted from customers who needed money to grow their farms and communities. Like bees drawn to the sweet scent of nectar, businessmen could not get into the act fast enough.

The new century dawned, and the scramble was on. A sampling of news briefs in the territorial press in the spring and summer of 1900, some only two or three lines in length, reveals a veritable stampede of bankers anxious to cash in on the burgeoning economy. On April 12, the Bank of Watonga increased its capital stock from $5,000 to $10,000.[33] A charter was granted to the Citizens Bank of Manchester, capitalized at $5,000, on April 21.[34] Two days later, the Bank of Cashion and the Bank of Glencoe, both capitalized at $5,000, were granted their charters.[35] Before the month was out, charters were issued to the Exchange Bank of Glencoe (capital stock $5,000) and the Home Savings and Loan Company in Stillwater (capital stock $100,000).[36]

On May 7, the Bank of Pawhuska, whose charter had been granted on April 13, opened for business as the first institution of its kind in the Osage Reservation. Capitalized at $10,000, the bank's management team included D. T. Flynn of Guthrie as president, P. S. Hoffman as vice president, and J. B. Charles as cashier. In addition to Flynn, the incorporators included Hoffman and Charles as well as E. L. Conklin and Roy V. Hoffman—all of Chandler, and all affiliated with the Sac and Fox Indian Agency, which operated as a merchant-banking establishment before receiving its charter as the Union National Bank of Chandler.[37]

The Cattle Exchange Bank of Cordell, capitalized at $5,000, received its charter on May 19. Oddly enough, all of its directors were named

Rival banks in Anadarko, Oklahoma Territory, 1901. Banks were among the first businesses to open in frontier towns. Courtesy Western History Collections, University of Oklahoma Libraries (Phillips Collection, No. 3486 TC2-6).

Rowley.[38] Territorial charters were issued to the Bank of Kremlin (capital stock $5,000) and the Bank of Granite (capital stock $10,000) on May 21.[39] Ambitious officers at Lexington State Bank filed a certificate in the territorial secretary's office on June 1 to increase their capital stock from $10,000 to $25,000.[40] A territorial charter was issued to the Farmers Bank of Lamont in Grant County (capital stock $5,000) on June 6. Its directors were J. W. Yeoman, D. W. McKinstry, and Fred S. Gum.[41] Two territorial charters were issued on June 13, one to Custer County State Bank in Arapaho (capital stock $10,000), and another to Kildare State Bank (capital stock $5,000).[42] Cleo State Bank (capital stock $5,000) got into the act on June 14.[43] Businessmen in Tonkawa clearly had big plans on July 21, when they filed articles of incorporation with the territorial secretary for the First International Bank of Tonkawa (capital stock $5,000).[44]

Not to be outdone, national banks in the Indian Territory issued some impressive numbers to the comptroller of the currency in Washington,

D.C. At the close of business on April 26, 1900, their resources and liabilities had increased about half a million dollars, from $3,276,449.49 to $3,728,698.70, since April 5, 1899. During the same period, capital stock increased from $815,500 to $980,320, and individual deposits went from $1,917,046.83 to $2,008,522.19, an increase of nearly $100,000. "A number of new banks have begun business in Indian territory within the last sixty days," ran a newspaper report filed from Muskogee, Indian Territory, "and altogether the financial outlook is exceedingly bright."[45]

News briefs about banks—their charters, directors, capitalization, and other routine aspects of the banking business—were published with numbing regularity at the turn of the twentieth century, and they signify the key role banks played as catalysts of community development. Similarly, reports on the conditions of banks issued by the bank examiner in Guthrie for territorial banks and the comptroller of the currency in Washington, D.C., for national banks functioned as report cards on the Twin Territories' financial well-being. An increase in key indicators such as deposits and lending from one reporting period to the next meant that bankers were doing their part to regulate the flow of currency and credit. It also reflected rising confidence in bankers as trustworthy stewards of the people's money—no small feat in a region where feather beds, rubber boots, telescope bags, and brush-covered water wells served as de facto banks, and where bank robberies and failures and insider tomfoolery were a constant drag on economic growth. In short, a daily dose of good banking news assured depositors and borrowers that wildcat banking was yielding to rules and regulations.

News briefs and reports on banks' conditions are complemented by a third source of information: correspondence between businessmen and the territorial secretary in Guthrie. Whether handwritten, typed, or sent via Western Union telegrams, these documents reveal a communication style that was direct and unambiguous. Businessmen wanted their bank charters, and they wanted them fast. News briefs and official reports are vital to understanding the fundamentals, but they fall short of describing the fiercely competitive marketplace that was the crucible of Oklahoma banking. Judging from the volume of correspondence flooding in and out of Guthrie, one thing is certain: the territorial secretary had his hands full as charter applicants scrambled for a piece of the action.

The sample begins with a letter dated May 18, 1900, from O. B. Kee, president of the State Exchange Bank of Weatherford, to Secretary

William M. Jenkins (1897–1901): "Please find enclosed application for bank charter at the new town Granite, O.T., as I wish to be first if possible. Kindly notify me by return mail if there are any other applications filed for bank at this point." As an added inducement for the secretary to process his application quickly, Kee closed his brief letter with a reference to his and the secretary's good old days in Kansas politics: "Thanking you in advance for the kindness and touble [*sic*] and assuring you that the same will be greatly appreciated by your old Republican freind [*sic*] from Kansas."[46] Some folks did not even bother to buy new letterhead before joining the scramble. M. Whitacre was apparently in the wagon and buggy business in Paris, Iowa, before relocating to Chandler, Oklahoma Territory. (To be accurate, he was also a dealer in Jewel stoves and ranges, Glidden wire, and "high grade foot wear.") In a hastily written note to territorial secretary W. M. Grimes (1901–1906) of May 5, 1902, Whitacre slashed through his old letterhead, crossed out "Paris, Iowa," replaced it with "Chandler O.T.," and wrote, "Please send me the necessary blanks and instructions for the organizing of Ter. Bank."[47]

As it turned out, Granite was a magnet for bankers. In a letter to Secretary Jenkins dated May 31, 1900, J. A. Henry, president of the People's Bank of Altus, requested a blank application with the expectation of opening a bank in Granite. Next to Henry on the People's Bank letterhead were his fellow officers: C. C. Hightower as vice president and J. R. McMahan as cashier. Few businessmen figure more prominently in the history of Old Greer County than Henry, Hightower, and McMahan.[48] On the other side of the territory, George E. McKinnis, a buyer and seller of Indian lands in Shawnee, was likewise determined to be the first banker in town—in his case, the town of Bridgeport. His typewritten missive of November 8, 1901, to Secretary Grimes was brief and to the point: "Please send me application for bank charter. Has any one applied for Bridgeport, Okla?"[49]

Some applicants were vague about their intentions. H. K. Bickford, cashier of the Woods County Bank in Alva, requested several blank applications from Secretary Jenkins, or perhaps the bank commissioner—evidently, he was not sure who was in charge of bank chartering, so he hedged his bets and addressed his query to both men—on February 4, 1901, with no indication of which towns had caught his fancy.[50] A. N. Leffingwell was similarly unschooled in the ways of bank chartering, but he is to be forgiven: his letterhead indicates that he was employed with

Trekell & Rounds Lumber Company, a Cropper, Oklahoma Territory–based dealer in lumber, sashes, doors, cement, and building paper. The company maintained additional yards in Enid, Garber, Billings, Granite, and Mangum. His one-line, handwritten letter of April 13, 1901, to the territorial secretary is a polite plea for direction: "Will you kindly send to my address the necessary blanks with instruction for encorporation [sic] and chartering of a bank and oblige."[51] A week later, Leffingwell remained confused; one imagines a blizzard of applications strewn about his office. "If there is anything lacking in these papers," he wrote to the territorial secretary on April 20, "please notify me and corrections shall be made."[52]

J. A. Mays, president of Elk City National Bank, did not mention where he wanted to open a bank, but at least he was specific about the number. "Please send us blanks for organization of three Territorial Banks," he wrote to the secretary on July 22, 1902. "Mail them to Cheyenne, Oklahoma."[53] J. J. Hughes, president of Farmers State Bank of Cleo, was willing to give the secretary some leeway in answering his query of March 24, 1903: "Will you be kind enough to send me three or four blanks for applications for charters?"[54] Similarly, an applicant from the Mangum Land and Loan Company whose scrawl is not entirely legible and whose grammar needs polishing wanted to be prepared for the opening of the Kiowa and Comanche country. "Will you please mail us three or four charter blankes [sic]," reads his hasty note to the territorial secretary on July 2, 1901.[55] Might as well have some extras—you never knew when you might happen upon a corner lot without a bank on it.

C. H. Brand, cashier of the State Bank of Carnegie, wanted to test the waters before committing his $10.00 in a crowded marketplace. In a reasonably legible letter of March 19, 1903, to Secretary Grimes, Brand wrote simply, "Will you kindly enform [sic] how many banks are chartered for Lathram or Carnegie Okla and what are the names."[56] Brand was wise to be cautious. Just six days later, on March 25, W. T. Clark, cashier of the Bank of Apache with "cash capital $15,000.00," threatened to foil Brand's plans. His brief, typewritten note to Grimes reads, "Will you kindly advise me if there are more than two banks chartered for Lathram or Carnegie, Caddo Co. O.T. and the names of them."[57] The bank sweepstakes in Caddo County went into overdrive when J. P. Whatley, cashier of the Citizens Bank of Lathram, wrote to the secretary on April 4, 1903, to find out what, exactly, was happening in his backyard.

"Has there been a bank chartered for Lathram or Carnegie to be called The Farmers and Merchants Bank? If so what is the amt of the capital and who are the incorporators?"[58] One imagines citizens running for cover as bankers squared off in the streets of Lathram to see who would get to handle the people's money.

Enclosing the $10.00 application fee sped up the process. I. C. Thurmond, cashier of the First National Bank of Elk City whose brother, E. K., was president, penned a note on October 10, 1901, to Secretary Grimes and stuffed money inside for good measure. "Encl. find Articles of Incorporation," wrote Thurmond in a barely legible scrawl, "please send charter to me here at once. Encl. find draft 10.00 fee."[59] Hugh M. Johnson, a recent arrival from Kosciusko, Mississippi, who had transformed himself from a small-town southern journalist into the president of the First National Bank of Chandler, was only slightly more conversant, and apparently more adept as a typist, in his letter to Grimes of January 31, 1903: "I enclose you herewith articles of incorporation of the Firsst [sic] State Bank, of Agra, Okla. which I trust will meet with your approval. I also enclose draft $10.00 which I understand to be the cost of such incorporations."[60] Included on the bank letterhead is a relative, H. H. Johnson, the bank's cashier and one of many Johnsons who had lit out from Kosciusko for the territories and settled into the banking profession.

While territorial bankers jockeyed for position, businessmen from other states were scouting for opportunities. From neighboring Missouri, H. Shelby Mason, manager of the National Orchard and Nursery Company of Saint Louis, wrote on December 16, 1901, that his company was thinking of opening a bank in the territory. But there was a caveat: "Would thank you to advise the lowest capital you can incorporate Under in the Ter. We mean a state or private Bank."[61] Like a latter-day Ebenezer Scrooge, Mason revealed on Christmas Eve that he was not only frugal, but also in a hurry. As his copy of territorial banking laws had not yet arrived at his office, he wrote that he would thank Secretary Grimes for sending a second copy.[62] From the other side of the state, J. F. Cox of the North American Crude Oil Company in Kansas City, Missouri requested on May 23, 1902, "the laws and rules for organizing a state bank in Oklahoma."[63]

The bank scramble was also making the news down south. J. W. McLoud, general solicitor for the Choctaw, Oklahoma and Gulf Rail-

Residents of Crescent, Oklahoma Territory, gather outside the local bank. Courtesy Oklahoma Historical Society.

road Company, wrote from Little Rock on April 2, 1901, to inquire if Secretary Jenkins would be kind enough to send him "about half a dozen blanks for the incorporation of banks under the laws of Oklahoma Territory."[64] In a letter dated April 21, 1904, from Jacksonville, Florida, Thomas A. Davis of the National Turpentine and Lumber Company expressed interest in obtaining territorial laws governing not only banks, but also insurance companies.[65] Six days later, Davis remitted fifty cents to the territorial secretary for a copy of the territory's corporation and banking laws. With an eye on the future, he wanted to know if statehood "will in any way effect [sic] these laws."[66]

Northerners, too, were anxious to cash in on the bonanza. In a handwritten letter to the secretary of state dated January 4, 1901, J. L. Blanchard of Allerton, Iowa, requested a copy of the territory's banking laws. "I am thinking of starting a Bank in that country," wrote Blanchard.[67] In nearby Davenport, Iowa, N. C. Kohl of the Eureka Paste Machine Company was thinking much the same thing. "Will you have the kindness to send me at your earliest convenience a copy of the Banking Laws of your territory or any literature you may have on the subject?" he wrote on October 25, 1900, to the territorial secretary. "I have a desire to familiarize myself with the laws with a view to going into the business if a good city can be found."[68] On December 4, 1900, C. H. Holmes, an agent for the American Mason Safety Tread Company in Minneapolis, wanted to know about territorial banking laws as he expected "to locate a bank there if a suitable opening can be found."[69] More wannabe bankers whose correspondence flooded into Guthrie included a realtor in Milwaukee; a farm machinery jobber in Peoria, Illinois; a lawyer in Equality, Illinois; and a gentleman who preferred to keep his professional affiliation to himself from Edgerton, Wisconsin.[70]

Some entrepreneurs gravitated to building and loan associations that found a niche in extending loans to people of modest means. Typically, these associations solicited contributions from their members. When enough money was accumulated to fund construction of a house, a member was selected to build and live in it. Building and loan associations operated until all of their members were housed. Many associations allowed a continuous increase in their memberships. Members used their homes as collateral for loans to buy their homes from their associations and were expected to amortize their repayments over a specified period of time.

In the Oklahoma Territory, requests for building and loan association applications came from such diverse sources as Beam & Mott, dealers in "Staple and Fancy Groceries" (and, to be thorough, queensware, glassware, dry goods, notions, boots, and shoes) in Navina; the Business Men's Club and J. O. McCollister, a purveyor of loans and abstracts, both in Mangum; Bulow & Lambert, a law firm in Arapaho; B. B. Blakeney, attorney for the First National Bank of Tecumseh; H. E. Shaffer, an attorney, and the law firm of Crossan & Crane, both in Shawnee; and H. A. Noah, a partner in the law firm of Sample & Noah in Alva.[71] Out-of-territory interest came from J. D. Ford and W. J. Alder of the American Mutual Building and Savings Association and E. M. Ellsworth of the Atlas Savings & Loan Association, both in Chattanooga, Tennessee; B. F. Griffith, profession unknown, from East Las Vegas, New Mexico Territory; Homer J. Kendall of the Aetna Building Association in Albuquerque, New Mexico Territory; George H. Hunker of what must have been an affiliate of the Aetna Building Association in Las Vegas, New Mexico Territory; Charles B. Rogers, an attorney in Vinita, Indian Territory; Will E. Lower, profession unknown, of Council Bluffs, Iowa; and George

Lord, an official in the Building and Loan Division of the Michigan state government in Lansing.[72]

Busy as he was, Secretary Grimes was scrupulous in his accounting. In a letter dated September 22, 1902, he informed A. L. McPherson that he had received his articles of incorporation for the Bank of Beaver City. Grimes reminded McPherson that the fee for chartering a bank was $10.00. As McPherson had sent a check for $12.00, Grimes enclosed a check for $2.00 in his letter, leaving a Panhandle banker with an extra two bucks and future generations to ponder a government official who set the standard for fiduciary responsibility.[73]

Our final glimpse of the bank scramble comes in a series of letters pertaining to the Bank of Geary some fifty miles northwest of Oklahoma City. The first hint that the citizens of Geary were about to enter the fray comes in the form of a Western Union telegram dated April 18, 1898, from the aforementioned J. W. McLoud, then writing from South McAlester, Indian Territory, to Secretary Jenkins. McLoud's terse, grammatically challenged message that typifies telegraphic communication reads simply, "When can I expect charter for the Bank of Geary Answer."[74] A subsequent typed letter on railroad stationery to Secretary Jenkins dated April 26, 1898, was enclosed with papers, "executed in duplicate," for the Bank of Geary. Apparently, even a general solicitor needed help with the paperwork, particularly as the territorial legislature had seen fit to provide banking codes just a year earlier, in 1897, and protocols were not altogether clear. "I suppose one of these is to be held by us," wrote the befuddled railroad lawyer, "but I am not sure, and hence send both to you. If one belongs to us, please return it and send Charter to me here, together with the amount of the fee and I will remit. I send this by Wells Fargo Express."[75]

Under the headline "Two New Banks Chartered," a newspaper brief dated May 14, 1898, indicates that the territorial banking board had authorized the issuance of charters to two banks: the People's Bank of North Enid, and the Bank of Geary.[76] On May 20, J. H. Maxey Jr., one-time assistant cashier under Willard Johnston at the Bank of Shawnee, got into the act with a handwritten letter to territorial secretary Jenkins. Enclosed with his letter was a draft for $11.00, drawn on a Kansas City bank, "as payment of fees for Charter of this Bank"—that is, the Bank of Geary. The letterhead indicates that the Bank of Geary had a capital stock of $15,000 and was under the management of Beeks Erick as president, John W. McLoud as vice president, and J. H. Maxey Jr. as cashier.[77]

Correspondence between the Bank of Geary and officialdom in Guthrie continued on March 1, 1899, when John H. Dillon, now serving as cashier, requested a certified copy of the Bank of Geary's articles of incorporation, for reasons unspecified. A draft was enclosed with his letter for $2.20. The letterhead now indicated a shakeup in the bank's management, with Beeks Erick and John W. McLoud still serving as president and vice president, respectively, but with John H. Dillon in the cashier's position.[78] Less than a year later, on February 1, 1900, Dillon sent a handwritten, one-line request to Secretary Jenkins for a blank charter application. "Dear Sir," wrote the seemingly harried cashier, "Please send me blank application for Bank charter." By then, the officers included Willard Johnston as president, John H. Dillon as cashier, and T. J. Ballew as assistant cashier.[79]

On April 2, 1901, under letterhead announcing that the Bank of Geary had capital and surplus of $10,000, assistant cashier T. J. Ballew sent a typed letter to Secretary Jenkins requesting a blank application for chartering a state bank. Clearly, Ballew and his associates—Johnston as president and Dillon as cashier—were in no mood to dawdle: "We will take it as a personal favor if you will send this to us by first mail as we are in something of a rush for it," wrote a feverish Ballew, underscoring "rush" in case the Honorable William M. Jenkins was slow to get the point. Yet Ballew closed with a tone of civility that has gone out of favor in business correspondence: "Thanking you in advance for your kindness in the matter we are, Yours very truly, T. J. Ballew, et al."[80] Later that month, on April 17, Bank of Geary officers indicated in yet another letter to the territorial secretary, a position now occupied by William Grimes, that one blank charter application was not enough for their budding banking empire and that, perhaps, two more applications would do the trick: "We wish to organize a couple of new banks within the next two weeks, and wish to have the blanks ready."[81]

More sleuthing in the archives might yield additional details about the Bank of Geary, but the pattern is clear from this and similar scraps of correspondence that kept territorial secretaries busy: banks were easy and inexpensive to organize; supervision was lax, but improving; shakeups in management were common; and haste in acquiring charters was of the utmost importance in the race to be the first bank on the block.

Individually, businessmen were looking for lucrative opportunities. Collectively, they were creating financial institutions commensurate with the needs of the new century.[82]

Back in Guthrie, politicians were undergoing a scramble of their own. In early July 1900, territorial bank examiner John N. Pugh tendered his resignation to Governor Barnes, effective as soon as his successor could be appointed. Pugh insisted that there was no friction between him and Governor Barnes and that he had simply found "better employment."[83] The bank examiner's notion of better employment surely included a higher salary. At the time of his resignation, the position of bank examiner paid $1,800 a year, plus $600 for incidental fees and traveling expenses. The day after Pugh resigned, the press reported that Governor Barnes had appointed W. S. Search, former president of the Shawnee National Bank, as the new bank examiner. Search had recently sold his stock and retired from the bank. Having served as president of the Oklahoma Territory Bankers Association, Search was "well known in Oklahoma financial circles."[84]

On October 24, 1900, Search published his first report on the condition of the territory's eighty-two state and private banks at the close of business on September 29, 1900. Unlike previous reports based on the average percentage of a limited number of banks, Search reported on all banks, rendering his totals somewhat lower than the totals in previous reports. Nevertheless, his numbers indicated that banks were in "a remarkably prosperous condition": total resources were $4,971,008.79; average deposits were $47,225.00; and the average reserve was 53 percent when only 20 percent was required by law. Twenty-six new banks had been chartered in the Oklahoma Territory since January 1, 1900, "all in small country towns."[85]

Even as bankers celebrated and citizens transferred their hard-earned money from mattresses to banks, trouble was brewing in Kingfisher. A notice was posted on the Bank of Kingfisher on August 13, 1900, announcing that the bank was in the hands of the bank commissioner. Its liabilities of $61,000 fell short of its assets, which were $51,000. The bank's capital stock was $20,000, and the county treasurer had $13,000 in deposits.[86] The next day, the press reported that bank examiner Search was refusing to allow access to the bank's books pending appointment of a receiver. As depositors met to review their options, the word spread that whatever remained of the bank's beginning capital of $10,000 consisted of the bank's building, furniture, and fixtures, all of which was reported as part of its $51,000 in assets. There was also talk of organizing a new bank that would purchase the old bank's business.[87]

And then came the finger pointing. Within two days of the Bank of Kingfisher's failure, the laws governing territorial and private banks were coming under attack. "Bankers in Oklahoma had been distrustful of the Kingfisher concern for several years," ran an account of the debacle. Some alleged that its reports to the bank examiner had always been suspect. Others wondered why the bank examiner waited so long to close its doors. There was a consensus that the amendments made in 1899 to the banking laws of 1897 were a step in the right direction, but there were still problems that needed to be addressed. The most grievous flaw was that too much authority was vested in the bank examiner. To inspire confidence, the old law of 1897 placed banks and the bank examiner under the control of a banking board consisting of the governor, secretary, treasurer, auditor, and attorney general. The examiner was required to file reports in a timely manner, and false reports were punishable as a felony.

Revisions to the law made in 1899 had no such limitations on the bank examiner's authority. The problem was summarized in a press report under the decidedly uninspiring headline "A Defective Banking Law": "The present banking law has no provisions for a banking board. The bank examiner absolutely controls in every particular and is responsible to no person except his bondsmen, who guarantee his faithful performance of duty in the sum of $25,000. The examiner is required to make a showing of his work only once in two years." A banker who apparently preferred anonymity was unequivocal in his assessment of laws that were spawning an imperial bank examiner: "The only protection to the depositor is the integrity of the banker and the bank examiner. Should the latter prove unfaithful to his trust the depositor is left in bad shape. What Oklahoma needs is a bank examining department patterned after that of Kansas or some other good state, where the examiner is as responsible an official as the state treasurer. An effort will be made at the next legislature to cure the defects of the present law."[88]

Far more significant than the Bank of Kingfisher's failure was the failure on April 4, 1904, of the Capitol National Bank of Guthrie. Bank president Charles E. Billingsley admitted that half a million dollars had

Capitol National Bank of Guthrie, Oklahoma Territory, banknote. Courtesy Andrew Shiva Banknote Collection.

been drained from the bank's coffers over several days. As a depository of federal and territorial deposits, the bank was better equipped than most to fend off a run. But heavy withdrawals in the morning and early afternoon were more than even this titan of territorial banking could withstand, and by 2:20 P.M. it was game over. In all probability, Billingsley saw trouble coming. He was also president of the National Bank of Holdenville, Indian Territory, which had failed recently "as the alleged result of carrying bad paper." The *Daily Oklahoman* reported that Billingsley's foibles were to blame for the debacle in Guthrie: "Bad investments is given as the primary cause of the failure."[89]

With deposits in excess of $1 million, the Capitol National Bank's failure was destined to cast a long shadow. It was quickly identified as the most serious breach of fiduciary responsibility in the territory's history. As federal and territorial officials scrambled to recoup their losses, the *Daily Oklahoman* rallied to the support of rank-and-file depositors: "Many men had in the bank their entire capital and others can ill afford to lose their deposits."[90] The Capitol National Bank's failure came on the heels of two others in the Indian Territory: the aforementioned National Bank of Holdenville, in which Billingsley was heavily invested; and the Bank of Duncan. Following the Capitol National Bank's demise, two more banks toppled in rapid succession: the Citizens Bank of McLoud; and the Citizens Bank of Ponca City.[91] Many years later, national bank examiner Myron R. Sturtevant asserted that the Capitol National Bank was liquidated with no loss to depositors.[92] But at the time, five failures in a single month left many citizens of the Twin Territories wondering when the next shoe would drop, and if their feet would be in it.

Further along the spectrum of banking woes was J. S. Crosby's attempted murder of M. L. Turner, president of the Western National Bank in Oklahoma City. Crosby, "a victim of the cocaine habit," entered the bank on the morning of November 7, 1900, and asked Turner for a loan on a farm. When Turner refused, Crosby reached for his gun and fired. He missed, and the bank president sprang into action. Then, an article reported, "Turner grappled with the man and overpowered him before aid came."[93] The assailant was taken to jail and later identified as the same man who had held up two farmers the previous evening as they were bringing in election returns. Crosby's take from the holdup was a horse and buggy and five dollars in cash.

Less than two weeks after J. S. Crosby opened fire on a bank president, William Thomas Phillips, a bookkeeper at the Guthrie National Bank, was arrested on a federal warrant for embezzling $3,900. The thirty-one counts charged against him ranged from making false entries to embezzlement. President J. W. McNeal had suspected trouble since August and dismissed Phillips on September 1. The bookkeeper remained under surveillance until his arrest on November 19. Phillips, formerly of Rock Island, Illinois, and whose brother was a bond broker in Kansas City, was twenty-eight years old, single, and "prominent in society." The press turned the banker's fall from grace into a morality tale: "Gambling and dissipation was the cause of Phillips's downfall."[94]

Continuing banking troubles seemed to confirm the Oklahoma Territory's reputation as a lawless land. On November 22, 1900, robbers entered the Farmers Bank of Orlando, blew up the vaults with dynamite, and made off with about $1,700 in cash. Money was brought in from Guthrie to tide the bank over until the loss could be replaced.[95] On December 17, it was the Bank of Cashion's turn. Its vault was blown with dynamite at 2:00 A.M. and robbed of about $3,200. Many people, including bank president J. W. Wilson, heard the explosion, but nobody investigated until it was too late. Tracks behind the bank indicated that a wagon had been parked for a quick getaway. Two men who commonly slept in a nearby barbershop opposite the bank reported seeing three men just before the explosion. A railroad section toolbox was broken, and a crowbar taken from it was found at the bank.[96] At the end of

December, mutilated currency and coins were circulating in and around Cashion and led locals to suspect that the Bank of Cashion had been cracked by homegrown talent. "A number of badly twisted coins were taken over the counter by a merchant," ran a news brief on the robbery. "The cash box taken from the safe was found in a hay stack about a mile south of town."[97] Fewer signs of the perpetrators remained when robbers drilled a hole in the top of a safe at Dixon's Store in Catoosa, Indian Territory, and filled it with explosives. The blast blew both doors off the safe and left books and papers badly damaged. Sixty-five dollars and a Confederate twenty-dollar bill were taken. A news brief of the robbery was succinct and downbeat: "There is no clue."[98]

Alarmed by the spate of bank robberies, small-town bankers looked for new ways to safeguard their deposits. One bank was advised to replace its square safe with a screw safe to make it harder for robbers to crack. The hope was that target hardening might reduce rates on burglar insurance. But surety companies knew better. A leading surety company responded to a banker's query with a disturbing assertion: "We are not accustomed to discriminate in the determination of our rates between styles of safes where the safes are the product of any of the standard makers and are of their best grade and are of modern construction." Why? As the surety company explained in its letter to a very disappointed banker, "there is not a safe on the market to-day and probably never will be that is absolutely burglar proof, provided that the right methods of attack are employed." Some bankers were surprised to learn that the surety company preferred safes to be located in the open rather than enclosed in a fireproof vault because "entrance thereto can be secured in a very few minutes and when once inside the burglars are screened from view while working upon the safe and the noise of the explosions on the safe is so muffled as not to attract attention on the outside."[99]

Clearly, banking woes would not yield easily to rules and regulations that attended the closing of the frontier. But there was another feature of the western landscape that was apparently more vulnerable to modern ways. One wonders if anyone took time from their labors to notice that modernity was dropping the curtain on what is arguably the most potent symbol of the frontier: the cowboy. "The genuine cowboy," ran a feature story in October 1900, "one of the kind that would rather ride in the

Interior of the Woodward Bank, Woodward, Oklahoma Territory, ca. 1900. Cuspidors are provided at each teller window for customers' convenience. Courtesy Western History Collections, University of Oklahoma Libraries (Woodward County Collection, No. 145, Exhibit No. 368).

rain all day in a 'slicker' on a good pony than to snooze across the country in a sleeping car, has almost gone out of business in Oklahoma."[100]

Not quite. Denver Boggs was practically a legend in northwestern Oklahoma. To know him was to understand the nature of what was passing. "Instead of bumping along the trail with a cow outfit," as had been his youthful habit, Boggs at century's end was operating his own ranch. "There are few men who have a wider acquaintance in the cow camps of the Southwest," wrote his chronicler, "and none who has seen more of the wild, hilarious life which, twenty years ago, was the ambition of every schoolboy to follow."[101]

Born on January 25, 1856, Boggs claimed to be the oldest native of Denver. Slowed by age and circumstance, the cowpuncher made do as a farmer, stockman, and songwriter near Winchester, Oklahoma Territory. Songs "came to his lips as naturally as the daisies blossomed on the prairies in the spring."[102] Bankers and their customers were surely among the fortunate few to gather at Winchester, Woodward, Alva, or some other burgeoning town at the dawn of the new century to hear Denver Boggs recite his poetry and croon such melodies as "The Dying Cowboy," "The Grave by the Old Rock Corral," "The Old Dutch Oven," and "The Line Rider's Dream"—classic tunes from the old cow trail that were fading from memory as commerce steamrolled its way across the prairies.

CHAPTER ELEVEN

The New Land of Promise

There will not be much noise about the development of the Indian territory and little of the picturesque action that was associated with the sudden
unfolding of the land adjoining it. But its growth will be little slower and
some day the people in the states about it will wake up to find a prosperous,
well established neighbor, rich in farms and mines.
    "Indian Territory: The New Land of Promise," *Kansas City Star*

The fourth annual meeting of the Oklahoma Territory Bankers Association opened in an opera house in Enid on November 26, 1900. In review-
ing the progress of Oklahoma banking, bank examiner W. S. Search of
Shawnee reminded his colleagues (as though they needed reminding)
that the first banking laws dated back only three years, to 1897. Prior to
that time, banks were operated much as any other business—organized
under general corporation laws, and lacking any requirements regarding
capitalization. It was not uncommon for depositors to furnish virtually all of the resources for a start-up bank. Since the office had been
established, the territorial secretary had issued charters to 140 banks.
Eighty-three remained in operation, nineteen had nationalized (i.e., had
taken out national bank charters), six had failed, and thirty-two had
either gone into voluntary liquidation or had never organized. According to records in the territorial secretary's office, the earliest charter was
issued on January 10, 1891, to the Bank of Kingfisher, recently closed
due to insolvency. The Citizens State Bank of El Reno, whose territorial

charter was issued on September 26, 1892, had the distinction of being "the oldest bank in continuous business in the territory." Citizens State Bank of El Reno also distinguished itself by having "the largest volume of business of any territorial bank." In the absence of information on the condition of banks prior to the passage of the first banking laws, 1897 was the baseline for comparisons.[1]

Search went on to cite the 1900 census, which put the population of the Oklahoma Territory at 398,245, meaning that territorial banks had eighteen dollars on deposit for every man, woman, and child. "We are informed that the increase in Oklahoma's population for the decade was unprecedented in the history of our nation," said Search. "Its material growth has kept pace with its population and certainly, the splendid showing of our banks out distances all these."[2]

History does not record whether or not Frank P. Johnson, one of Oklahoma City's rising stars, was in the Enid opera house that day. Before immigrating to the territory in 1895, Frank and his brother Hugh had operated the *Kosciusko Star* in northern Mississippi. Thanks to Frank's thoughtful editorials and Hugh's business acumen, their small-town newspaper became known as "the Official Organ of Attala County."[3] A falling-out over the contentious issue of free silver prompted first Frank and later Hugh to abandon the *Kosciusko Star* and seek opportunity elsewhere.[4] Frank's father-in-law and the fifth mayor of Oklahoma City, J. P. Allen (1897–99), had begun the Johnson migration from Kosciusko when, with the best wishes of the Kosciusko Bar Association, he traded a successful law practice for new opportunities in the Oklahoma Territory in 1895.[5] With a wife and baby to take care of and upward mobility stymied in his hometown, Frank Johnson weighed his options and decided to follow in his father-in-law's footsteps. Hugh and several other members of the family followed suit, and by the late 1890s members of the Johnson family were making their mark in the Oklahoma Territory.

Although Frank Johnson's decision to strike out for the Oklahoma Territory was unique in its particulars, it typified the choices made by other businessmen, many of whom were attending the banker's convention in Enid, to test their mettle in frontier business. Johnson's route to territorial business was captured in a condolence letter penned by F. T. Raiford, a fellow cadet from Mississippi A&M College in Starkville, to Johnson's widow, Aida Allen Johnson. At the time of Frank Johnson's death in October 1935, Raiford was editor and publisher of the

Selma Times-Journal in Selma, Alabama. In a writing style that captures a sense of the adventure upon which his friend was embarking, Raiford explained how he accepted Johnson's invitation to see him and his family at a train station on their way from Kosciusko to Oklahoma City: "Well do I remember when I received a wire from him to meet the train at Senatobia and go West with him. You had your infant daughter lying upon a pillow in the seat of the railway coach. Each of you were eager to tackle the beckoning opportunities in the new country to which you were bound."[6]

The Alabama editor offered words of condolence that might have taken some of the sting from Mrs. Johnson's grief. Frank Johnson, wrote Raiford, "had the stuff out of which real men are made—ambition, courage, a fine mind and a lovable personality." In a passage seemingly ripped from a Horatio Alger novel, Raiford recalled walks that he and Johnson took before they graduated from college and went their separate ways, pondering the possibilities that lay ahead: "I recall many long walks we had up and down the rail road tracks, dreaming dreams about how to meet that kindly stranger, Fate, and wondering about how best to get a grasp on the big world which then looked so forbidding."[7]

Settled in their new homes in the Oklahoma Territory, Frank and his brother Hugh resumed the partnership that had proven so successful in Kosciusko. Their ventures in the late 1890s included publishing another newspaper and selling fire and mortgage insurance. When Hugh moved to Chandler to become one of Lincoln County's best-known bankers, Frank remained in Oklahoma City, where he struggled to support his family as a teacher at Irving High School before finding his life's calling as a banker.

While bankers were convening in Enid in November 1900, the Union Trust Company of Oklahoma City was establishing a People's Savings Bank, the first of its kind in the territory. As the moniker implies, trust companies, or, as is often the case, trust departments in banks, act as trustees—that is, they administer financial assets on behalf of clients. Assets held in the form of a trust are subject to legal limitations on their use and are exempt from certain taxes. As is the case with insurance policies, trust owners designate beneficiaries to inherit their trust assets. Officers in the People's Savings Bank included H. D. Price of Oklahoma City as president, R. K. Wooten of Chickasha, Indian Territory, as vice president, and Frank Johnson of Oklahoma City as treasurer and secretary.[8] In all likelihood, Johnson was too preoccupied with his new position to attend the bankers' convention in Enid.

Less than two months later, a territorial charter was issued to the Oklahoma City Savings Bank. Directors included Frank Johnson and his father-in-law, J. P. Allen.[9] Johnson expanded his banking portfolio in February 1901 when he joined four other businessmen to establish the Bank of Busch in Roger Mills County with $10,000 in capital.[10]

The Oklahoma City Savings Bank grew quickly. Pioneered in Europe in the eighteenth century and up and running in the United States in the early nineteenth century, savings banks allowed customers to set aside a portion of their liquid assets and earn interest on their savings. Because money in a savings account could not be withdrawn immediately on demand, savings banks were not obligated to maintain reserves, and cash was available to make interest-bearing loans. But in the absence of laws governing savings banks in the Oklahoma Territory, the Oklahoma City Savings Bank was incorporated under territorial banking laws and was subject to examinations, publication of statements, and restrictions pertaining to loans and cash reserves that applied to other banks.

Under the leadership of Frank Johnson as president, G. B. Stone as vice president, and L. C. Parmenter as cashier, the savings bank was capitalized with $15,000 and located in a small frame building on Main Street that later became the home of Dean's Jewelry Company.[11] In early April 1903—just over two years after the bank was chartered—the *Daily Oklahoman* published a stunning announcement: "At a recent meeting of the directors and stockholders it was unanimously decided to double the capital of this bank. The new capital has now been fully paid in cash, and we have a capital of Fifty Thousand Dollars with a surplus of Eight Thousand. This, with the double liability of stockholders imposed under the law, makes a total guarantee to depositors of $108,000.00. We therefore have by far the largest capital of all the State Banks of Oklahoma and are exceeded only by a small portion of the National Banks."[12]

By the time of the bank's increased capitalization, Frank Johnson was already waxing nostalgic about his bank's rags-to-riches history. "The bank was started over two years ago," he said in an interview with the *Daily Oklahoman,* "and has had a steady and solid growth ever since. We began in a small frame building when one man could do all the work; now we occupy one of the handsomest brick buildings on Main street and employ five men."[13]

The savings bank boasted two departments: a commercial department, which received deposits and made loans based on approved collateral and personal security; and a savings department, which serviced accounts of one dollar and upward and paid interest at the rate of 5 percent per annum, compounded twice a year. Deposits could be withdrawn wholly or in part at any time upon presentation of a bank book. The bank also issued certificates of deposit for large and small sums alike, all of which bore interest. Other features included safety deposit boxes and escrow services. As a Democrat to the marrow of his Mississippi bones, it was probably Frank Johnson who insisted that the bank remain open for deposits from 7:00 to 8:30 on Saturday evenings for the convenience of working people.[14]

Yet even bigger doings were afoot. In July 1903, just over three months after Johnson announced his bank's capitalization, the Oklahoma City Savings Bank and the nearby American National Bank agreed to consolidate.[15] The Oklahoma City Savings Bank was to close immediately, and the consolidated institution, slated to remain the American National Bank, opened for business in the Lee Hotel Building on North Broadway where the original American National Bank had been operating since its inception in January 1901, and where it had opened for business on April 24, 1901. Officers elected at a stockholders meeting on the afternoon of July 24, 1903 included E. F. Sparrow, president; G. G. Sohlberg, founder in 1904 of the Acme Milling Company (the city's first flour mill), vice president;[16] and Frank Johnson, cashier. Directors elected that evening included E. F. Sparrow, G. G. Sohlberg, Frank Johnson, C. B. Ames, E. M. Jones, J. W. Ripley, G. B. Stone, J. M. Owen, and Guy E. Blackwelder. Listed among the out-of-town stockholders was none other than Frank's brother, Hugh, president of the First National Bank of Chandler and now, as evidence of his entrepreneurial drive, president of the First National Bank of Stroud.[17] A brief biography of Frank Johnson appearing in the *Daily Oklahoman* at the time read as follows: "F. P. Johnson, the cashier, was president of the Oklahoma City Savings Bank until yesterday. He came to this city five years ago [*sic*] from Mississippi and organized the Union Trust company, which later became the Oklahoma City Savings bank. Mr. Johnson's abilities in financial affairs, coupled with remarkable enterprise and endless energy, have placed him in the front row in local enterprises, and there is no limit to his prospects."[18]

First National Bank of Chandler, Oklahoma Territory, banknote. Courtesy Andrew Shiva Banknote Collection.

In keeping with the pro-business boosterism of territorial newspapers, the *Daily Oklahoman* did its part to emphasize the bank's impressive credentials and promote business growth. It declared, "Several of the most influential and wealthy citizens of Oklahoma City will shortly become identified with the new institution, which commences business today with a capital of $100,000 and deposits amounting to more than $600,000." At the age of thirty-one, buoyed by a wealth of experience and honed to the rhythms of business, Frank Johnson affixed his star to the American National Bank and found his life's work in banking. The *Daily Oklahoman* was describing the cashier as well as his institution in its concluding paean to the American National Bank: "With the prominent capitalists and commercial men here and elsewhere interested in the enterprise, a successful career is assured and it promises to become one of the strongest financial institutions in the two territories."[19]

Predictions of success were quickly realized. In June 1905, several days of quiet negotiation resulted in a merger between the American National Bank and the Bank of Commerce. The Bank of Commerce vacated its quarters and relocated to the Lee Hotel Building, where the merged banks operated as the American National Bank. With James H. Wheeler as president, Frank Johnson as cashier, and H. B. Carson and Oscar Avey as assistant cashiers, the combined institution boasted capitalization of $100,000 with a surplus of $18,000. Deposits totaled some $800,000, "making it the fourth bank in the territory with deposits amounting to near one million dollars." The *Daily Oklahoman* reported as follows: "The consolidation while highly advantageous to the stockholders will also be looked upon with favor by the patrons of both banks, and the American National bank as now constituted will rank as one of the most stable and largest institutions in Oklahoma City and the territory."[20]

The slate of directors included a recent arrival to Oklahoma City: R. A. Vose. Vose was born in Maine and was living in Clinton, Iowa, when he accepted an offer from his uncle, W. W. Bierce, to visit him in Oklahoma City. Bierce, a member of the American National Bank's board of directors, was also involved in the cotton business. Vose's visit and participation in his uncle's Southwest Cotton Oil Company, together with his purchase of American National Bank stock in 1904 and subsequent invitation to join the bank's board of directors, launched the career of one of Oklahoma City's most influential citizens and laid the foundation for a historic relationship between the Johnson and Vose families, converging from Mississippi and Maine in the Oklahoma Territory.[21]

In September 1906, Frank's "kindly stranger, Fate," proved to be very kind indeed, and the future seemed a bit less forbidding. Citing personal reasons, J. H. Wheeler resigned as president of the American National Bank, and Frank Johnson was promoted from cashier to the top job. An announcement in the *Daily Oklahoman* suggested that his rise to the presidency was "very gratifying to those persons who have been watching his progressive career and realize that his business ability and integrity of character merit the promotions which have been awarded him from time to time."[22]

A decade after his departure from the *Kosciusko Star,* Frank Johnson reached the inner circle of his adopted city's business elite. Surely he had opportunities to visit with his brother Hugh in Chandler to compare their routes to success, and to speculate on what else lay in store for the brother bankers.[23]

Bankers' good fortune meant more work for bank examiners whose annual appropriation of five hundred dollars for office expenses and travel was hardly adequate to fund their wide-ranging activities. To examine notes, examiners often found themselves in remote locations, eyeballing horses and mules and crops to make sure they constituted legitimate collateral.[24] Between 1900 and 1902, 124 banks opened for business. According to the *Third Biennial Report of the Territorial Bank*

Commissioner, 1900–1902, "The banks have been increasing in numbers so rapidly that to visit each one personally and conduct the large correspondence of the department, attend to the opening of the new banks under proper requirements, is rendered a matter of great difficulty, and to give to the business the attention and care it demands and ought to receive is practically out of the question."[25]

Bank examiners' challenges were compounded when banks packed up and moved without notice. One examiner's report omitted seven banks because he couldn't find them![26] Failures of the Capitol National Bank of Guthrie, the Citizens Bank of Enid, and the Bank of Beaver City prompted the *Beaver Herald* in western Oklahoma Territory to rally to the defense of bank examiners who did the best they could in the face of frontier hardships and nefarious goings-on in territorial banks. The paper argued, "The bank examiner must not be blamed too strongly for these conditions, for there is four times as much work to do as it is possible for him to attend to with his present force. The safety and solidity of banking institutions is absolutely necessary, not only to the general welfare, but for the ordinary daily transactions of business."[27]

Given the job's onerous requirements, it came as no surprise when W. S. Search announced his intention to resign as territorial bank examiner at the end of the 1901 legislative session. The press reported that he was going into the banking business, more than likely in Oklahoma City. Search attributed his decision to the salary that "was too small to recompense him for time and work."[28] Three days after his announcement, the speculation ended: Search had already applied for a national bank charter from the comptroller of the currency. Dubbed "the new Search bank," the institution was to be capitalized at $100,000. With the former examiner as president, the bank was slated for opening in March 1901.[29]

Meanwhile, Myron R. Sturtevant was serving his stint as national bank examiner in the Twin Territories and Arkansas. He closed seven banks, including the Capitol National Bank of Guthrie, before rising to prominence at the First National Bank of Saint Louis. During a visit on a warm summer day with one-time bank examiner Eugene P. Gum, Sturtevant wiped perspiration from his brow and entertained his friend with a tale from Asher, Indian Territory, that was hardly unique in the Twin Territories, and that surely made bank examiners think twice about their chosen profession.

They had attempted to move a heavy, square-door safe into the bank. When the dray arrived in front of the bank one wheel dropped into a mudhole and the safe rolled off into the mud. It fell on its back and was submerged all except the door and a small margin around it. It had been raining for several days. I donned rubber boots and a slicker and waded out to the safe to count the currency. This safe remained in the mudhole for several days before it could be installed in the bank. The comptroller criticized me severely for allowing this. I wired him, "I am hired to examine safes and their contents, not move them." I examined banks in tents, guarded by vigilantes.[30]

Closing failed banks was rarely a smooth operation. After closing a bank in Elk City, Sturtevant discovered that the stockholders owned some pigs that were being kept in a pen at the depot stockyards in preparation for shipment. "I sold the pigs," wrote Sturtevant in an unpublished account of his adventures in banking, "knowing it would take several days before authority could get through, then I hot-footed it to the judge, who was a good smart understanding judge." Then holding court at Chickasha, the judge threatened to throw him in jail. "Then judge,"

Residents navigate the muddy streets outside a Postal Savings Bank. Note the dentist's office on the second floor. Courtesy Oklahoma Historical Society.

said the defiant bank examiner, "I will be out of my trouble and wont [*sic*] have to face any scally wags coming to Oklahoma."[31]

As it turned out, the judge was having a bit of fun at the examiner's expense. He smiled, put his hand on the young man's shoulder, and congratulated him on doing the right thing to cancel out his liabilities. A week later, Sturtevant must have experienced déjà vu when he sold a stud horse for fifty dollars. Apparently, a bank president had absconded with his depositors' money and left behind not only a group of irate

Commercial National Bank of Muscogee, Indian Territory, banknote. Courtesy Andrew Shiva Banknote Collection.

First National Bank of McAlester, Indian Territory, banknote. Courtesy Andrew Shiva Banknote Collection.

depositors but also a horse worth three hundred dollars. Again the examiner hightailed it to the judge, now presiding in Norman, to justify his actions; again the judge joked that he would send him to jail before admonishing him to sell whatever assets he could to recover assets. Even then, the examiner's troubles were not over. The horse was costing him twenty-five cents a day to feed, and there was no telling how long he would have to wait to receive permission from the comptroller of the currency in Washington, D.C., to sell it.

The examiner's travels eventually took him to the Osage Nation, where he was scheduled to conduct his first examination of the Bank of Pawhuska. He drove a pair of horses from Pawnee to Cleveland, where he examined the First National Bank and, somewhere along the way, met the great Osage Indian, Black Dog. Continuing on toward Pawhuska, he spent one night "in a two-bed bedroom" in Ralston and awoke to the alarming realization that his roommate had smallpox. "I was not worried," recalled the bank examiner, "as in those days Oklahoma Territory smallpox patients were not quarantined."[32]

Apparently, Sturtevant could not be bothered with something as mundane as the scourge of civilization. He had banks to examine.

Bank failures and swindlers and scourges of civilization were not what Tams Bixby, chairman of the Dawes Commission, discovered when he toured the Indian Territory in the spring of 1903. Created by an act of Congress on March 3, 1893, the commission consisted of three commissioners appointed by the president to negotiate with the Five Tribes for the surrender of their tribal land titles in exchange for allotments in severalty. Under the chairmanship of Henry L. Dawes of Massachusetts, the commission was responsible for preparing the Indian Territory for eventual statehood. Whether they wanted to or not, Indians were about to become citizens of the United States.[33]

When Henry L. Dawes died in early 1903, Bixby, a Virginia native whose family moved to the Minnesota Territory in 1857, was elevated to chairmanship of the commission that continued to carry the original chairman's name. Bixby was known as a conservative businessman who knew a good thing when he saw it, and what he saw in the Indian Territory made his head spin: bumper crops of wheat, corn, and cotton; coal, natural gas, oil, granite, and timber in abundance; and a climate perfectly suited to growing fruit. At the time of his travels, the Indian

Territory encompassed 19 million acres and boasted 250 towns ranging in population from 200 to 9,000. As near as he could tell, the only drawbacks were a lack of good drinking water and the prevalence of malaria in the summer and fall. The water supply would certainly be improved as settlements increased, and cases of malaria would decrease as people became acclimated to their new environs. "One thing we do know," said the new chairman of the Dawes Commission, "people are coming into this country every day and they are as a rule good people. The deposits in the banks are rolling up and there is no lack of banking facilities."[34]

In spite of formalities that were devised to transfer land from tribal to non-Indian ownership, Bixby insisted that it was becoming as easy to acquire a recorded deed to land in the Indian Territory as it was in Massachusetts. Even though the Indian Territory was only two hundred miles from Kansas City, few were aware of its potential. Bixby reported, "To most people it is still the Indian country, where the new settler and the outside business are not sought." The Creek Nation was the most advanced in making land easy to acquire, but the other Indian nations were not far behind. "Land that has been given up to grazing or to desultory farming is opening to cultivation and before long this will be a country settled as thickly as Oklahoma is to-day—a country of farms and mines,"[35] the chairman reflected. The federal government's policy was to discourage the sale of large tracts of land to individuals and to encourage ownership by farmers. Ultimately, the Indian Territory would consist of midsized farms that would be worked by the farmers who owned them. There was plenty of room for open-range ranching in western Oklahoma Territory, Texas, New Mexico Territory, and western Kansas.

Infrastructure—or rather, the lack thereof—remained a problem. Under tribal governments, there were few provisions for roads and bridges. As national bank examiner Myron Sturtevant found when he bogged down in the streets of Asher, mud often made the roads impassable, and streams were dotted with toll bridges and ferries operated by tribal citizens who had obtained charters from their tribal governments and merchants in towns who defrayed expenses to enable customers to get to them. Crossing waterways went from routine to nightmare when rains turned placid streams into raging torrents. Increasing settlement and, eventually, statehood were expected to bring the Indian Territory into the twentieth century. At the time of Bixby's promotion to chairmanship of the Dawes Commission in early 1903, however, the Indian Territory lagged far behind the Oklahoma Territory and neighboring states in building an infrastructure to facilitate inclusion in the nation's expanding webs of finance and commerce.

A particularly vexing problem, with dire implications for economic development, was the lack of schools for non-Indian settlers. Tribal schools operated under the supervision of Indian agencies and were on a par with schools in other states, but children of noncitizens were barred from attending. Their only options were to attend subscription schools or leave the territory. As the *Kansas City Star* put it, "Nothing can be done under the present status of the territory to give free schools to the children of non-citizens until territorial or state government comes, unless Congress passes a law to give temporary relief to white settlers who do not want their children to grow up without the educational advantages offered the youngsters of Zululand."[36]

Poorly developed infrastructure and the lack of schools did not stop settlers from coming. Towns were growing, and merchandise began showing up in their stores that visitors were surprised to see. "The business men are not overlooking opportunities and seem to manage their affairs with up-to-date business methods. In fact, the enterprise and activity of the territory business man is a feature that impresses itself soon," the *Kansas City Star* reported. It was by no means unusual for traveling men to "quit the road" and apply business experience they had acquired elsewhere to a new venture in a favorite Indian Territory town. As one person explained in an interview for the *Kansas City Star,* "Young men have traveled through here until they 'got stuck' on a town and backed their selection with their money. They seem to prosper, and I don't know any that are sorry for it."[37] Those towns were beginning to issue bonds to pay for water and sewers. Taxes, beyond imagining in the unsettled conditions of the frontier, were now feasible. Citizens accustomed to frontier scarcity looked forward to schools, paved streets, and other marvels of the modern world that people in other states had long taken for granted.

Four years before joining the Oklahoma Territory to together become the forty-sixth state, the Indian Territory was a commonwealth of 80,000 Indians and 400,000 non-Indian settlers just seven hours by train from Kansas City. Its opening to non-Indian settlement was the result neither of a land run, as was the case in the Unassigned Lands, nor a lottery, as was the case in the Kiowa-Comanche–Plains Apache Reservation. Rather, it was opened gradually as settlers trickled in from other parts of the country and abroad and secured the right from tribal governments to stay. Based on his experiences with the Dawes Commission, Tams Bixby endorsed the *Kansas City Star*'s prediction that the Indian Territory was facing a very bright future. The story concluded, "There will not be much noise about the development of the Indian territory and little of the picturesque action that was associated with the sudden unfolding of the land adjoining it. But its growth will be little slower and some day the people in the states about it will wake up to find a prosperous, well established neighbor, rich in farms and mines."[38]

In the first decade of the twentieth century, the Indian Territory remained a land of contrasts. Prospering towns and nascent industries that so impressed Tams Bixby existed side by side with activities that had changed little since Frenchmen plied the waterways of Louisiana. The traffic in furs, for example, was still a brisk business. One buyer in South McAlester reported paying an average of $1,000 a week for furs. Buyers prowled the countryside in search of farmers who relied on old-fashioned trapping to supplement their incomes. Farmers' sons laden with coon and possum skins were a common sight in towns, where they hoped to earn money for their handiwork. Hunters earned as much as five to six hundred dollars every winter by trapping wild animals for their pelts. Prices depended on the condition and size of pelts and the cost of curing them. Skunk, coon, and possum pelts were the most common. Skunk pelts brought 25¢ to $1.25 each. The highest prices went for black skunk pelts, as long as they were in good condition. Pelts with white streaks were cheaper because furriers had to cut them out to produce marketable capes and collarettes. Other animals in danger of losing their hides included wildcats, minks, otters, wolves, gray foxes, bears, badgers, and deer. Most pelts marketed in South McAlester were procured in the Choctaw, Creek, and Seminole Nations.[39]

While trappers were divesting woodland creatures of their skins, the surge in business activity was wooing bankers into the Indian Territory. Authority to open national banks dated back to the Organic Act of May 2, 1890, when Congress extended provisions of the National Banking Acts of 1863 and 1864 into the Indian Territory. The first national banks were opened in Muskogee, Ardmore, McAlester, and Tahlequah.

Restrictions imposed by the National Banking Acts—the relatively high capital base, the obligation for banks to invest in U.S. government bonds, and restrictions on loan policies—initially discouraged businessmen from opening banks in the Indian Territory. Prospects improved in 1901 when Congress extended to the Indian Territory some of the laws of Arkansas pertaining to corporations. Merchant-bankers who had been providing banking services quickly applied for national bank charters, and federal judges were only too happy to apply the laws of Arkansas to grant them.[40]

Such was the pace of activity that, on June 7, 1901, bankers came together to form the Indian Territory Bankers Association (ITBA). Under the leadership of Edmund McKenna, founder of the Bank of Poteau, the ITBA sought to help its members become better acquainted with banking regulations and to promote pro-banking legislation. Beginning with a membership of 16, the ITBA boasted 147 members by 1904.[41] Like its sister organization in the Oklahoma Territory, the ITBA provided its members with a forum to share ideas and influence legislation.

Predictably, the growth of commerce caught the attention of bankers. A sampling of newspaper briefs between 1902 and 1903 reveals a replication of the scramble for bank charters in the Oklahoma Territory. The main difference was that applications in the Indian Territory were by definition for national charters and went to the comptroller of the currency in Washington, D.C. On April 22, 1902, a charter was granted to the Muskogee State Bank at South McAlester. Plans were in the works to build a two-story bank. The new bank was capitalized at $25,000, and its officers included Bert R. Greer, president; F. W. Hirchman, vice president; John B. George, cashier; Morgan Caraway, secretary; and Thomas J. Farrar, position unknown.[42] Less than three months later, the incorporators changed their minds, sold their property, and announced that they would not use their charter. A news brief reported simply, "The directors state that they have decided it would not be a paying proposition."[43]

A week after officers of the Muskogee State Bank called it quits, the press reported that stockholders in the National Bank of Commerce in Saint Louis who composed the Hamilton Trust Company were buying stock in national banks in the Indian Territory. Some of the Hamilton Trust Company's initial investments were in the First National Bank of Checotah and the Commercial National Bank of Muskogee.[44] It seems likely that the entry of a powerhouse from Saint Louis into territorial banking persuaded Muskogee State Bank incorporators to seek their fortunes elsewhere.

On April 25, 1902, the Citizens Bank of Grove, capitalized with $10,000, announced that it would be open for business in thirty days. Officers included Samuel J. Salyer, president; A. A. Hampton, vice president; and Walter Charlesworth, cashier.[45] The porous boundary between banking and politics was revealed in July 1902 when Muskogee mayor H. B. Spaulding resigned from his position as vice president of the Territorial Trust and Surety Company and announced that he was launching a private bank under a charter issued to the Spaulding Mercantile Company.[46] In late September 1902, articles of incorporation were filed in the district clerk's office for the State Bank of Broken Arrow. Launched with $10,000 in capital, the new bank's incorporators included L. Marr of Tulsa, president; M. S. Fife and S. M. Marr of Blackwell; and J. R. Dominick of Kansas City. For the benefit of the geographically challenged, a news brief stated, "Broken Arrow is a new town, twenty miles from Tulsa, in the Creek nation."[47]

In March 1903, the Weleetka National Bank was authorized to open its doors with $25,000 in capital. R. L. McFarlin was president, and E. L. Blackman was cashier.[48] In early April, the comptroller of the currency approved the application of G. W. Barnes Jr. and his associates to organize the Barnes National Bank of Muskogee with capital of $100,000. Its incorporators included Barnes, three members of his family (more than likely, his sons), and E. D. Nims.[49] Later that month, four more charter applications were approved: the National Bank of Coalgate with capital stock of $50,000; the Muskogee National Bank with capital stock of $50,000; the Citizens National Bank of Wagoner with capital stock of $25,000; and the First National Bank of Indianola with capital stock of $25,000.[50]

On May 1, G. W. Barnes and E. D. Nims purchased the Commercial National Bank of Muskogee. Barnes of Toledo, Ohio, and Nims, who was president of the First National Bank of Roff, Indian Territory, represented the men who received a charter to open the Barnes National Bank in Muskogee. The Commercial National Bank, whose principals included D. H. Middleton, C. W. Turner, and D. N. Fink, was established three years earlier with capital stock of $100,000. Capitalization was slated to be increased to $150,000 with the purchase. Middleton planned to open another bank in Muskogee on September 1 with capital stock of $100,000.[51]

Down in the Choctaw Nation, the Bank of Stigler was incorporated with capital stock of $25,000. Stigler was a new town located south of the Canadian River on the Muskogee Southern Railway. Samuel Rose of Okmulgee was president, W. E. Rowsey of Muskogee was vice president, and W. B. Hudson of Joplin, Missouri, was cashier. The bank was scheduled for opening on June 1, 1903.[52] In all probability, this was the same bank that John Nance, a non-Indian settler in the Choctaw Nation, described in an interview for the WPA on April 13, 1938. Assuming that discrepancies between Nance's interview and press reports can be attributed to an imperfect memory, we turn to Nance to describe a nascent bank whose founding was replicated throughout the Indian Territory in the early 1900s: "The first bank to open was in 1904. It was started in a tent by C. C. Sloan; the money was kept in a steel vault inside the tent and it was necessary to guard this rag bank day and night for about four months. A building was constructed after four months service in the tent and the bank moved in the building and became the First National Bank of Stigler."[53] Even though Milo Starr, a cousin of the infamous bank robber Henry Starr, prowled the area, Nance was adamant that there was never a bank robbery in Stigler—not even when the bank was housed in a tent.

The bustle continued unabated when the second annual meeting of the Indian Territory Bankers Association convened in South McAlester on May 14, 1903. Approximately 150 bankers from the Indian Territory and surrounding states were on hand to listen to W. M. Tomlin of the Chickasaw National Bank in Purcell describe what everyone already knew: phenomenal growth over the past year had caused the number of Indian Territory banks to double. Following a morning of speeches and self-congratulations, a special train over the Missouri, Kansas and Texas Railway took bankers through the coal mining district, where about twenty mines could be seen in operation. Bankers returned to South McAlester for a ball in the new Elk clubhouse.[54]

Delegates to the ITBA convention reconvened the next morning to hear H. P. Hilliard, cashier of the Mechanics National Bank of Saint Louis, promote the Louisiana Purchase Exposition slated for 1904 in Saint Louis. Known informally as the Saint Louis World's Fair, the exposition aimed to commemorate the one hundredth anniversary of the

Louisiana Purchase (albeit one year late) even as it celebrated the latest in science and agricultural production.[55] At Hilliard's suggestion, delegates passed a resolution pledging national banks to contribute one-half of 1 percent of their capital stock to the Indian Territory World's Fair fund. The combined capital stock of national banks in the Indian Territory was an astonishing $4 million, more than enough to finance an exhibit at the world's fair.

Prior to adjournment, delegates elected officers and agreed to gather for the next ITBA convention in Holdenville.[56] As they climbed aboard trains and buggies and mounted their horses and prepared for their journeys home, some might have predicted greater attendance at the next convention now that telephone lines were crisscrossing the land. A year earlier, a franchise had been granted to R. C. Acuff to build a telephone line from Wagoner to Clarksville, a distance of forty miles.[57] Even in the Osage Nation, where modernity met with stiff resistance, tribal members were beginning to see the benefits of rapid communication. In May 1902, the first telephone line on the reservation had been completed to link Pawhuska with Elgin, Kansas.[58]

Back in Oklahoma Territory, bankers closed the eighth annual convention of the Oklahoma Territory Bankers Association (OTBA) in El Reno on November 18, 1904, by adopting a resolution in favor of joint statehood. By then, the movement to unite the Oklahoma and Indian Territories as a single state was gaining momentum, and bankers wanted to voice their approval. Their resolution was direct and to the point: "WHEREAS, the logic of events is rapidly forcing the conditions by which the ultimate destiny of Oklahoma and the Indian territory will be one state of the American union; therefore, be it *Resolved,* That the business welfare of the two territories would be advanced by the immediate extension of the Oklahoma laws over the Indian territory, and we respectfully urge the delegate to Congress from Oklahoma to use his best endeavors to secure the passage of such a law."[59] As evidence that bankers in the Oklahoma and Indian Territories agreed on single statehood and other issues of importance to commerce in the Twin Territories, committees from the OTBA and ITBA agreed in December 1904 to consolidate their organizations at the next annual convention of the Oklahoma Territory Bankers Association in June 1905. Uniting in a single organization was long overdue. With the exception of press associations, practically all the organizations in the Twin Territories with similar goals and objectives had already consolidated.[60]

While bankers rallied behind the banner of joint statehood, business-men from twenty-two towns in the Oklahoma Territory did their part to promote commerce by contributing goods to a cross-country trip to New York. Laden with corn, wheat, broomcorn, cotton, flour, and other samples of the land's bounty, two trains pulling twenty-five cars pulled out of Enid at noon on October 19, 1904, to the blaring of trum-pets and clashing of cymbals. Passengers were quartered in a sleeper car and included the promoters of the advertising scheme, speakers anxious to extol Oklahoma's progress to anyone within earshot, representatives from every town that had contributed products, and brass bands. The plan was to stop at every city and town on the Frisco line. Four days would be spent at the fairgrounds in Saint Louis, where the Louisiana Purchase Exposition had been drawing crowds from all over the world since its opening on April 30, 1904. From Saint Louis, the trains would proceed to Chicago and New York over the Michigan Central Railway. A newspaper article read, "At each stop the people will be invited to visit the cars, listen to the band and hear the speakers who will tell of the ter-ritory and its farming products."[61] Upon its arrival in New York in early November, the cornucopia would be sold to customers who had surely been dazzled by emissaries from the storied West.

The speed of commercial development ramped up a notch when bankers from both territories gathered in Muskogee on May 25 and 26, 1905, for the ninth annual convention of the Oklahoma–Indian Ter-ritory Bankers Association. As the moniker suggests, the union of the OTBA and ITBA was now complete. As the association's president, H. A. McCandless with the Exchange Bank of Perry, said in his introductory remarks, "The present meeting is one which marks an epoch in the his-tory of our Association. It should probably be called the First Annual Convention of the Oklahoma–Indian Territory Bankers' Association, as it is the first held since the consolidation of the Association of the two Territories into the present one. However, having reverence for age, we call it the Ninth Annual Convention, as this is the ninth time the bankers of Oklahoma have met together as an association since the organization, and would be the Fourth Annual Convention of the Indian Territory Bankers' Association."[62]

After expressing optimism that the "imaginary line" separating the Twin Territories would be erased within a year, McCandless did the numbers: there were 95 national banks and 256 territorial banks in the Oklahoma Territory, and 118 national banks and 138 territorial banks in the Indian Territory. This added up to a total of 607 banks in both territories. Of this number, 321 banks were members of the association, which accounted for more than 50 percent of the total number. "This is indeed a very large percentage," said McCandless, "and one of which an old state might be proud."[63]

Turning to comparisons with national banks in various states, McCandless claimed that only eight states had more national banks than the Twin Territories. In the absence of statistics for banks organized under state or territorial laws, he could only surmise that "the showing would be equally favorable" for the Twin Territories. With the exception of a small number of bank failures a dip in deposits due to a partial crop failure, the past year had been one of widespread prosperity. "No depositor has lost a dollar through the failure of national banks within the two territories during the past year. In fact," continued McCandless as knowing heads surely nodded in agreement, "in the banking history of Oklahoma and Indian Territory, the only national banks, wherein depositors have suffered any loss are the Capitol National of Guthrie and the National Bank of Holdenville."[64] Nothing more needed to be said about their disgraced colleague, Charles E. Billingsley, who had presided over the demise of both institutions.

McCandless suggested that few sections of the United States with a similar number of national banks, with the possible exception of the New England states, could make as impressive a showing, adding, "This, notwithstanding that a celebrated, if not eminent jurist, has recently informed the world that our business people are grafters, thieves and ruffians."[65] Apparently, there was no need to mention the offending jurist by name. One imagines much nodding of heads and clenching of jaws as attendees reflected on the unfair treatment that their territories received in the national press by Amos Fitts and like-minded journalists who preferred titillation to factual reporting. McCandless went on to praise National Bank Examiner Myron R. Sturtevant for his business sagacity: "No doubt there are more prosperous banks today, which would have been failures, but for the exercise of the same correcting hand."[66]

Bankers' good fortune in the Indian Territory was all the more remarkable because, McCandless said, "there is absolutely no law for the supervision of banks." It was still possible for anyone to start a bank "who has sufficient credit to purchase a safe and necessary stationery and sufficient cash to pay his first month's rent." The Oklahoma Territory was fortunate to have laws on the books to ensure at least a modicum of supervision of territorial banks, but, even there, poor compensation rendered bank examiners unable to perform their duties as thoroughly as they might have liked. Paul F. Cooper was then serving as territorial bank examiner; according to reports from the field, he was providing "an excellent service in spite of scant compensation."[67]

McCandless braved a firestorm when he addressed a common concern that there were too many banks: "Many towns hardly large enough to support one bank have two or more struggling for an existence, none of them making proper returns to their stockholders on the capital invested."[68] This and other issues—methods of accounting for profits and mercantile collections, for example—still needed to be resolved. Nevertheless, the tone of McCandless's address was entirely upbeat. He concluded with praise for the convention's host city, Muskogee—risen from a "bleak prairie" to become a testament "to the pluck and energy of the sturdy manhood, which is building and shaping the destinies of the new commonwealth soon to be admitted to the Union as the State of Oklahoma."[69] The roar of approval was surely deafening as delegates applauded their association's president before turning their attention to the next speaker.

The march of commerce that captivated delegates at the bankers' convention in the spring of 1905 was sending the pace of social change into overdrive, and none other than the German sociologist Max Weber was on hand to observe it. Less than a year before bankers from both territories convened for their first joint convention in Muskogee, Professor Weber, perhaps best known for his seminal work, *The Protestant Ethic and the Spirit of Capitalism,* traveled with a group of German scholars who had been invited to present lectures in Saint Louis in conjunction with the Louisiana Purchase Exposition. He and his wife, Marianne, left Germany in mid-August 1904 and arrived in New York in September. After several days in New York, the Webers and their party set out for Saint Louis, passing through Niagara Falls before reaching Chicago, "the monstrous city which even more than New York was the crystallization of the American spirit."[70]

In Chicago, Professor Weber was struck by the vast disparities of wealth and the ubiquitous smoke from industry. "It is an endless human desert," he wrote. "There is a mad pell-mell of nationalities. . . . With the exception of the better residential districts, the whole tremendous city—more extensive than London!—is like a man whose skin has been peeled off and whose intestines are seen at work."[71] He was awed by the intensity of work, and especially the " '*stockyards*' with their 'ocean of blood,' where several thousand cattle and pigs are slaughtered every day." But even as modernity rushed on in its "magnificent wildness," the Webers marveled at outposts of serenity—churches, colleges, and quiet neighborhoods— that testified to "a tenacious desire for beauty and tranquility."[72]

The party continued on to Saint Louis, where Professor Weber delivered his lecture ("German Agrarian Conditions, Past and Present") to a disappointingly (but perhaps understandably) small crowd. It is unlikely that his listeners included three other luminaries, likewise drawn to the bustle of the Louisiana Purchase Exposition, and all caught in the maelstrom of changing times: Henry Adams, on hand to observe the "dynamos of power," as he had a decade earlier at the World's Columbian Exposition in Chicago; Geronimo, or Goyathlay ("one who yawns"), an Apache warrior reduced to a curiosity, and whose earthly remains became a source of controversy a century after his death when members of Yale University's Skull and Bones Society were alleged to have stolen his skull from his grave in Fort Sill, Oklahoma, to augment their collection of oddities back east; and Ota Benga, a Pygmy from the Mother Forest of Africa who was selling photos for ten to twenty-five cents a pop, and who captivated tourists with music from a sacred horn, the *molima,* that his ancestors had sounded for 40,000 years.[73] It is also unlikely that any bankers from the Oklahoma Territory opted for a lecture on German agriculture. They were too busy promoting the produce from their fertile fields to bother with the minutiae of farming in a faraway land.

Lecture delivered and obligations fulfilled, the Webers headed south, partly to visit stepcousins who had been cut off from their fatherland and friends, but above all to witness firsthand things that Europe could not offer. As always, Weber sank into his surroundings and penetrated to the heart of things—in this case, "the conquest of the wilderness by civilization, a developing city and the developing state of Oklahoma in an area that had until recently been reserved for the Indians. Here it was still possible to observe the unarmed subjugation and absorption of an 'inferior' race by a 'superior,' more intelligent one, the transformation of Indian tribal property into private property, and the conquest of the virgin forest by colonists."[74]

Weber and his wife rode the train from Tulsa to McAlester, where old Indian romanticism blended with modernity. He marveled at the silence of the forest. Larger streams such as the Canadian River reminded him of the romanticism of the *Leatherstocking Tales.* "They are in an utterly wild state, with enormous sandbanks and thick, dark greenery on their banks," he said of them.[75] He saw the death knell of the virgin forest in crude cabins and modern factory-built houses, in vast cotton crops, and above all in the stench of petroleum from "the high, Eiffel Tower-like structures of the drill holes in the middle of the forest."[76] Crazy towns and camps, railroads under construction, primitive streets, and tangles of telegraph and telephone wires extended "into the unbounded distance."[77]

Professor Weber predicted that McAlester would soon assume the character of Oklahoma City, "that is, that of any other western city," where immigrants arrived as poor wretches and became rich within a few years.[78] He was both attracted and repelled by the birth pangs of civilization, with its fabulous bustle alongside the reek of petroleum and racket of trains. At the same time, he reveled in the free-and-easy atmosphere, friendliness, and mutual respect; "and the humor," he wrote, "is nothing short of delicious."[79]

Weber concluded his description of the Indian Territory three years before its union with the Oklahoma Territory to form the forty-sixth state with unease about the juggernaut of modernity that suffuses his sociology: "Too bad; in a year this place will look like Oklahoma [City], that is, like any other American city. With almost lightning speed everything that stands in the way of capitalistic culture is being crushed."[80] After a tour of Fort Gibson on the Canadian River, Weber was nostalgic and, at the same time, dismissive about his sojourn in the Indian Territory: "But enough of this trip 'to the old, romantic land.' The next time I come here, the last remnant of 'romanticism' will be gone."[81]

The romantic allure was indeed fading. For better and worse, civilization and its discontents were coming on fast and entwining east and west in an ever-tightening embrace, and the Twin Territories were caught in the middle. Like Tocqueville, whose travels in Ohio convinced him that Americans' restless energy was no guarantee of happiness, and the 1st Viscount James Bryce, whose travels in the American West in the 1880s had alerted him to the perils of rapid economic development, Weber saw contradictions brewing in the Indian Territory's headlong lurch into modernity. A dearth of law, lax supervision of banks, the complexities wrought by the dual banking system, panics and failures endemic to the boom-and-bust economy, wildcatters and outright thieves masquerading as bankers—these and other conundrums had shaped banking in Oklahoma before statehood, and they were unlikely to go away when the statehood celebration ended and the speeches faded into memory.

Nor were capitalism and democracy any closer to striking a balance. If anything, the conflict between these pillars of civilization was deepening as more and more settlers staked their claims in a new land whose promise was never open to everybody, and where opportunity all too often lured its seekers into the abyss.

CHAPTER TWELVE

Taking Stock

You're doin' fine, Oklahoma!
    Refrain from Richard Rodgers and Oscar Hammerstein, "Oklahoma!"

There are several ways to measure the Twin Territories' economic development on the eve of statehood in 1907. The most straightforward mea-
surements are found in territorial and national bank reports published in
newspapers. A sampling of reports between 1902 and 1906 tells a story
of steady and sometimes astonishing growth. The frequency with which
banks' conditions were published reflects the fact that banks were seen
as barometers of financial well-being. Increasing amounts for loans and
deposits meant that finances were in good shape; declining numbers
usually pointed to the cyclical nature of an overwhelmingly agrarian
economy and were dismissed as temporary. Insofar as media reflect and
reproduce cultural norms, bank reports published in the mass media of
their day reassured people that their money was in good hands. At the
same time, they instilled in readers an assumption that growth would
continue—perhaps, even, that economic growth was their birthright.
The more people came to accept economic growth as the new normal,
the more they rejected frontier scarcity and scrambled to join the consumer bandwagon. In the territories' transition from frontier scarcity to
consumer abundance, bankers were winning the battle of public opinion
by demonstrating their fitness to manage the people's money.

Territorial bank commissioner Paul F. Cooper's report on the condition of the Oklahoma Territory's 152 territorial and private banks at the close of business on March 12, 1902, showed some impressive increases since September 30, 1901: deposits were up $836,189.64; the average reserve was 54 percent; loans and discounts increased by $577,898.70; and total resources were $9,456,098.96.[1] Cooper's next quarterly report on banks' conditions at the close of business on June 11, 1902, showed a noticeable drop in deposits of $1,202,611.63. Not to worry—as one newspaper commented on the troubling news, "There is always a falling off in deposits in Oklahoma at this time of the year."[2] Besides, the average reserve was 43½ percent, far more than the legal minimum of 15 percent. Eight territorial banks had opted for national charters, and twenty-three new banks had opened for business since Cooper's previous report. His report now included 156 territorial and private banks, and he ranked them according to their capital stock: 92 banks, $5,000; 2 banks, $6,000; 2 banks, $7,000; 3 banks, $8,000; 39 banks, $10,000; 1 bank, $12,500; 6 banks, $15,000; 1 bank, $20,000; 9 banks, $25,000; and 1 bank, $30,000.[3] Not included in Cooper's report were about sixty national banks whose reporting went not to his office in Guthrie, but rather to the comptroller of the currency in Washington, D.C.

By September 1, 1902, the Oklahoma Territory's 180 territorial banks had combined deposits of $7,738,747.21. Deposits in the territory's national banks were $11,028,635.23, making for a grand total of $18,767,382.44. For those concerned about the preponderance of national bank deposits, there was a simple explanation: "The excessive amount of deposits held by the national banks over the amount held by the territorial banks may be accounted for to a large extent from the fact that many national banks of the territory are used as reserve agents by the territorial banks."[4] Reports from Washington, D.C., were equally upbeat. For the year ending on November 25, 1902, the Oklahoma Territory's national banks were among the strongest in the West. Failures of the Capitol National Bank of Guthrie and the National Bank of Holdenville were still in the future when the comptroller of the currency praised the territory's unblemished record: "Since the organization of the Guthrie National Bank at Guthrie, which obtained a charter June 24, 1890, not a national bank receiver has been appointed in the territory."[5] Growth was attributed largely to immigration. When the Kiowa and

Comanche country opened in early 1902, new banks were spawned and old banks swelled with deposits.

Compared with eastern states, the territory had more banks than New Hampshire, Vermont, Rhode Island, Delaware, and West Virginia. In terms of deposits, loans, and discounts, the territory compared favorably with eastern banks. Impending statehood invited comparisons with other territories. Here again, the Oklahoma Territory was in the catbird seat, with sixty-eight national banks compared to New Mexico Territory's fifteen and Arizona Territory's eight. National bank deposits in excess of $10,000,000 in the Oklahoma Territory dwarfed deposits in New Mexico ($5,200,000) and Arizona Territories ($3,025,000).[6]

In his consolidated report on 232 territorial banks at the close of business on June 10, 1903, bank commissioner Cooper cited an increase of 76 banks over the past year, an increase of $2,774,809.80 in total footings, $1,775,751.76 in loans and discounts, and $1,333,507.38 in individual deposits as signs that "the condition this year is better than last year." The average reserve was 52 percent compared to 43½ percent in June 1902. Territorial and national banks reported combined resources of $28,482,504.69 and included deposits of $20,738,763.37.[7]

At the close of business on December 31, 1903, the number of territorial banks stood at 244. Combined deposits in territorial and national banks were $22,456,510.26, "the largest in the history of Oklahoma." On December 31, the reserve fund in territorial banks was 47 percent, almost twice the 25 percent now required by law. The territory's eighty-seven national banks had a reserve fund of 30 percent on December 10, even though federal laws required only 15 percent in reserves. Overdrafts were large because the year-end report was issued "when banks were furnishing large sums for the movement of cotton."[8] Since June 1903, twelve new territorial banks with capital stock of $173,370 had gone into business, and individual deposits were up $180,319.54.

The good news continued in bank commissioner Cooper's report on the condition of the territory's 262 territorial banks as of November 17, 1905. Resources, loans, and discounts were $6,765,244.66; banking house furniture and fixtures were $598,938.07; and individual deposits were $8,908,543.25. Good news in the banking sector meant good news for the territorial government in Guthrie. The newspaper reported, "With a larger appropriation than in any other year, the expenses of the commissioner's office were less. In the year 271 examinations of banks were made and fees to the amount of $4,185 turned into the territorial treasury."[9]

Reports on the condition of banks were not the only source of good financial news. On October 1, 1902, Oklahoma Territory treasurer C. W. Rambo made a historic announcement: for the first time, general revenue fund receipts were in excess of expenditures. The fiscal year ending June 30 began with $17,000 in the treasury and ended with $184,000, an increase by September 1 of $167,000. Measured against expenses of $145,000, the territory reached the end of the fiscal year with a balance of almost $40,000—more than enough to pay the principal and interest on the government's bonded indebtedness of $48,000.[10]

In his annual report for the fiscal year ending June 30, 1902, to the U.S. secretary of the interior, territorial governor Thompson B. Ferguson, a native of Iowa who had arrived in the territory at the time of the Cheyenne and Arapaho lands opening in 1892, was rhapsodic in his summary of the territory's prosperity.[11] The population had increased by 143,149 since 1901 to 541,480. Taxable property was valued at $72,677,423, an increase of more than $12 million over 1901. Revenue for the year was $566,950, an increase of more than $113,000 since 1901. A total of 2,968,000 acres were settled, leaving 3,769,000 acres—mainly grazing lands in the western counties—that were yet to be settled. Beaver County alone (then comprising the entire Panhandle) comprised 3 million acres. Governor Ferguson described advances in education at length and was particularly proud of the fact that "a pupil may advance step by step without interruption from the usual school to the university." Advances in transportation and communication were bringing territorial towns closer together. "Fully 500 miles of new railway was built in the year," crowed the governor, "and more railway is now building than ever before in the history of Oklahoma. Charters to twenty-three railway companies were issued in the year. Freight traffic increased largely. Every county except Day, has telegraphic communication."[12]

Down on the farm, wheat, cotton, and livestock topped the list of agricultural production. As homesteaders filed and fenced their claims, stockmen were pushed further west, and small ranches and farms were dotting the open range. "If there is an idle man in Oklahoma it is from choice rather than necessity," wrote Governor Ferguson. "The enormous amount of railroad building during the past year has given steady employment to hundreds of men, many of whom had to be imported from the North and East."[13] Manufacturing and building were gaining ground to the extent that they were draining the labor supply in spite of the ever-increasing flow of immigration. The governor touted territorial wages as equal, if not greater than, any in the nation.

But there was still room for improvement, particularly in banking and finance. In 1901, the legislature passed safeguards pertaining to building and loan associations, only to have them vetoed by the governor. Yet Governor Ferguson predicted a day when safeguards would be crucial. "Properly safeguarded by law and with ample security, they [building and loan associations] bring the blessings of homes to people who could not otherwise obtain them. Especially is that true in a new country like this." Because of the scramble in banking since the passage of laws in 1897 and their revision in 1899, Governor Ferguson's report could not begin to provide a thorough review of banking. But his report did note that the "prosperity of Oklahoma bankers has long been phenomenal."[14]

Figures coming out of the Indian Territory were equally sanguine, particularly with regard to agriculture. Estimates in January 1905 showed that the Indian Territory's 708,823 hogs were valued at $4.73 a head—$1 million more than their fellow swine in the Oklahoma Territory. Inexplicably, Arkansas's 1,031,245 hogs were valued at only $3.63 each. Nationwide, the Indian Territory ranked tenth in the production of cotton, eleventh in corn, seventeenth in oats, and twenty-first in hogs. Although less than a fourth of the Indian Territory's agricultural land was under cultivation and not even a tenth of its coal and oil was under development, its union with the Oklahoma Territory would create a state ranking seventh in the production of wheat, eighth in corn, ninth in cotton and potatoes, tenth in oats, eleventh in horses and mules, and twelfth in hogs.[15]

In early 1906, the Census Bureau published a bulletin reporting that the Twin Territories' advances in manufacturing during the previous five years surpassed all other states as well as the Arizona and New Mexico Territories. As reported in the press, the bulletin noted that runaway population growth was not enough to keep up with the growth in manufacturing: "Great as has been the increase in population in these territories during this period it has not kept pace with the increase in manufactures."[16] Citing close parallels between the Indian and Oklahoma Territories, the report focused on progress in key economic sectors: an increase in manufacturing establishments of 160 percent in the

Indian Territory and 107 percent in the Oklahoma Territory; an increase in capital investment of 215 percent in the Indian Territory and a whopping 351 percent in the Oklahoma Territory; and an increase in the value of products of 200 percent in both territories. Flour and grist ranked first, followed by cotton seed oil and coke. On a list of five western states, the Twin Territories led Nevada, Idaho, and Utah in the number of their industries and the value of their products.[17]

In November 1906, territorial treasurer Rambo assured Governor Frank Franz that the territory's financial condition had never been so good: "At the present time there is more money on hand to the credit of the territory than ever before, the total being $919,012.15." Territorial secretary Fred L. Wenner agreed and added, "Altogether I have now on hand a sum exceeding $200,000, all deposited in the banks designated as school land depositories, and fully secured." Territorial funds were deposited in thirty-one banks. In his semiannual bank statement, territorial bank commissioner Herbert H. Smock (1906–1909) showed an increase of $2,500,000 in deposits in territorial banks at the close of business on November 20, 1906. There were 299 territorial banks on November 20, 1906, up from 283 banks on May 24.[18]

Almost four decades would pass before Rodgers and Hammerstein put it all to music. *Oklahoma!* was set in the vicinity of Claremore, Indian Territory, in 1906—as good a place and time as any to imagine the excitement that heralded the coming of statehood. Long after the number crunchers in Guthrie and Washington, D.C., had quantified the galloping pace of commerce in the Twin Territories, actors dressed as cowboys and farmers cut to the chase in a refrain that has rung across the generations: "You're doin' fine, Oklahoma!"

Another way to measure economic development is through the lens of capital formation. In the spring of 1903, Oklahoma City was buzzing with news that a trust company capitalized at $1 million was being organized. There was speculation that former territorial delegate D. T. Flynn would be the largest stockholder in the territory. Controlling interest, however, would be "held by one of the big insurance companies."[19] Two years later, Caleb R. Brooks of Guthrie and W. E. Hodges of Stillwater struck a deal with businessmen in Cincinnati to organize a trust and surety bond company with capital stock of $200,000. Hodges retired as cashier and sold his interest in the First National Bank of Stillwater to engage in the new enterprise. Stockholders would decide whether to locate the new concern in Oklahoma City or Guthrie.[20] Henceforth, increasing numbers of Oklahomans would have the ability to hold their assets in trust in their home state for the benefit of their descendants.

Then there were those who took Horatio Alger's advice, went west, and struck it rich. By 1906, many people already had private fortunes in the $40,000–$50,000 range. Some had amassed modest fortunes of $250,000, "and in at least one instance a million dollars has been accumulated by a single individual." Not surprisingly, real estate was a preferred route to riches. A newspaper account of fortune building on the prairies has a familiar ring: "It has been possible for a man to begin with nothing, only a few feet of bare ground, and by holding it find himself in possession of a fortune that would permit him to retire from active business with a competency for old age."[21]

A 1906 newspaper account told the tale of James Weaver who made his way from Cincinnati to the Oklahoma Territory, staked two lots where he expected Oklahoma City's business district to grow, and hung onto them through the hard times until he had an extraordinary competency for old age. "This is going to be a big town some day," he said, "and I am going to hold these two lots for an old age investment. They cost me nothing, and if I am mistaken my loss will not be great." Weaver eventually secured a position as a clerk in a Cincinnati shoe store and traveled periodically to Oklahoma City to check on his lots. Sure enough, their value grew. Railroads came to town and the retail district spread to encompass his lots, but still he refused to sell. In 1906, he turned down an offer from owners of a wholesale establishment to buy his two lots for $40,000. But Cincinnati was his home and shoes were his business. "He is unmarried," concluded a profile of the reluctant tycoon. "Some day he may sell his lots, but not now. He believes they will be worth more money."[22]

James Weaver had plenty of company. Thanks largely to press reports on the statehood question, the Twin Territories were attracting capitalists like swallows to Capistrano. In the fall of 1906, one of the biggest construction projects was a million-dollar dam and power plant near Muskogee and Fort Gibson. The city of Muskogee was raising $200,000; businessmen from Chicago were prepared to furnish the rest. Other projects luring outside capital in late 1906 were a cement plant in Ada that was expected to employ 300 people; a pottery plant in El Reno

Ada National Bank, Ada, Indian Territory. Courtesy Oklahoma Historical Society.

expected to employ as many as 350; and the Great Western Glass Plant in Bartlesville that would eventually put 150 men on its payroll. Bartlesville was also bracing for a four-block smelter that would require 80 men to keep the furnaces in operation. The Midland Valley Railroad was building its general shops in Muskogee. To take advantage of an abundance of sand, boosters in Cleveland were working hard to attract a glass factory. Coal, lead, and zinc mines were being opened practically every day. In the Choctaw and Chickasaw Nations, asphalt and lumber were becoming the drivers of local economies. Almost without exception, these and other concerns were drawing outside capital to create "a flourishing industrial atmosphere in the new state."[23]

Even as they greeted industries and the prospect of new loans and deposits, bankers were surely heartened to find that lawmen were taking a bite out of crime. In January 1904, Leo E. Bennett, marshal for the western district of the Indian Territory whose service dated back to 1897, prepared a comprehensive report on crime in his jurisdiction. Between 1897 and January 1904, a total of 6,042 prisoners were received.

Marshal Bennett listed charges according to their frequency: larceny, 2,326; liquor (attendant crimes unspecified), 1,146; assault to kill, 403; murder, 386; attacks on women, 147; robbery, 138; burglary, 159; adultery, 137; arson, 33; counterfeiting, 12; perjury, 45; disposing of mortgaged property, 69; forgery, 40; kidnapping, 38; and all other crimes, 963. All four districts in the Indian Territory were building new jails so that prisoners could finally be confined safely. "The old shed used now is made of wood and is so unsafe that ten guards are kept constantly on duty day and night," said the veteran lawman, adding, "The walls are so flimsy that a determined rush on the part of the prisoners would force it to yield. The prisoners know this, but they know also that on the outside of the walls there are ten men with Winchesters and revolvers, and the chances are that once outside the prison they would be shot."[24] Marshal Bennett did not need to single out bank robberies to remind bankers that theft remained a problem. At least they could take comfort in knowing that statistics were being kept and prisons were being built in an effort to mitigate the Twin Territories' reputation for lawlessness.

Efforts were also under way to stamp out illegal gambling. In early April 1903, Oklahoma City prosecuting attorney Remer stated publicly that gambling houses would be closed and slot machines confiscated.[25] (One wonders how well that went over among frequenters of Oklahoma City's most notorious gambling den, the Blue Front.) In October 1904, thirty-seven white men were arrested and jailed by United States officers in Ardmore. Gambling houses were raided and paraphernalia was piled in the street and burned. Authorities in the southern district of the Indian Territory vowed to continue their crusade against gamblers. Territorial newspapers made light of their vow "inasmuch as gambling had continued wide open here since the beginning of the town."[26] In April 1905, it was Altus's turn to turn up the heat when warrants were served on thirty-six people for gambling. A news brief on the roundup read simply, "Every year brings a stronger enforcement of law against gambling in Oklahoma."[27]

Territorial and federal lawmen were aided in their war on crime by a voluntary organization whose exploits provided fodder for western legend and, as a practical corollary, made bankers' collateral on agricultural loans a lot safer: the Anti–Horse Thief Association, known far and wide by its acronym, the AHTA. "The Anti-Horsethief association has done more to suppress lawlessness and capture criminals in Oklahoma and the

Indian Territory than any other organization," boasted James Kirkwood, two-term president of the association in the Oklahoma Territory, in an October 1902 newspaper interview. He bragged, "The association is thoroughly organized, and never abandons pursuit when once on the trail of a fugitive." In three years, the de facto army grew from 2,500 to 12,000 members who were spread among 318 lodges in the Twin Territories and Texas. Kirkwood relied on statistics to back up his bravado: "Members of lodges in Oklahoma alone lost seventy-eight head of horses last year, of which seventy were recovered and returned to their owners, a record of which we are proud. Altogether we got 101 head of stock. Thirty-six thieves were rounded up and sixteen sent to the penitentiary."[28]

Bankers who lived in fear of robbers were surely encouraged by the AHTA president's opinion that carrying concealed weapons should be discouraged. In Kirkwood's estimation, the hallowed western tradition of packing heat was going out of vogue. "The indiscriminate carrying of pistols has given Oklahoma a bad name," he said with a flair for understatement, "and caused many killings that would not have taken place had the principals been unarmed. I believe that the number of 'pistol-toters' is decreasing."[29]

By October 1904, the AHTA's membership in the Twin Territories was the largest in the country, and Guthrie was bracing for 3,000 delegates to arrive in town for their annual convention. Membership had grown to 20,000 people scattered among nearly 1,000 lodges. A hot topic of conversation was the use of technology in putting thieves out of business. The telegraph, "a device which has done more to eradicate the horse thief and his methods than any other agent," was becoming indispensable to the AHTA and other crime-fighting organizations. Technological innovations in law enforcement were clearly having an impact on the bottom line. During the previous year, rapid communication helped the AHTA to capture 137 horse thieves and recover $12,000 worth of stolen horses. One hundred and twenty-four horses were stolen and 136 were recovered, some from previous years.[30]

Modern technology had little to do with the discovery of a moonshine distillery in the Choctaw Nation. In June 1905, officers stumbled across a "wild cat" still in the Jack Fork Mountains near Antlers, an area that was populated by asphalt miners who were willing to risk a trip to the penitentiary for the chance to indulge in strong spirits. Aware that a still was in production but unable to find it, lawmen enlisted the aid of "several cowpunchers who had ridden all over the country hundreds of times to assist them." Their efforts came to naught, and it was only by accident that railroad engineers discovered the illegal enterprise. According to a newspaper account, "One of them started to drive a stake under some bushes and logs and his stake struck the still. There was no one about the place and no evidence of habitation, but there was 180 gallons of whisky there. It was confiscated."[31]

That was good news for lawmen, but bad news for entrepreneurs in the Choctaw Nation who had their own ideas about economic development.

While bankers, politicians, and capitalists were taking stock of the territories and lawmen were making the land safer for commerce, homeseekers were showing their enthusiasm for landownership with their feet. In December 1902, six thousand to eight thousand people bound for the territories passed through the Union Depot in Kansas City in a single day. Seeking relief from a pounding rain, many lingered in the depot for hours, some in seats and many on the floor, and resigned to "the utter inadequacy of the ramshackle old place."[32]

This particular day of December 1902 was the last opportunity for homeseekers to take advantage of excursions offered by the railway. Most were from northern and central states, and they included sturdy Swedes from Minnesota wrapped in fur overcoats, heavy mittens, and winter caps. Whatever their provenance, the travelers shared the same hopes and dreams as they scrambled aboard the Frisco for the trip to Eagle City, a new town in western Blaine County some 450 miles to the southwest. A newspaper reporter on the scene, more than likely Frederick Barde, knew what lay in store for the traveling host: "While Eagle City is spoken of as a municipality, yet in reality there is little or nothing there yet but the town site. It is a town that is to be settled in a day, but everything has been prepared for this hasty settlement. To-day there will be a drawing of townsite lots."[33]

The conductor's familiar refrain "All aboard!" was the signal for some 600 people to pile into 12 coaches. Two brass bands consisting of 20 musical instruments each gave a short concert before clambering aboard. Everyone was anxious to participate in the drawing for 2,800 townsite lots that was expected to last for 2 days. Out in Eagle City, town boosters were preparing for their guests by issuing last-minute instructions to speakers and vaudeville entertainers. Fifteen buildings had already been erected, including 2 banks. The village had "a guaranteed population" (whatever that meant) of 500. Newshound Barde ended on a typically optimistic note: "Oil and gas have already been located on the property."[34]

The speed of commercial development can also be gauged by the flurry of activity in commercial clubs across the territories. The Chickasha Commercial Club reorganized in mid-January 1903 and elected C. L. Greer as president, D. D. Sayer as vice president, H. L. Jarboe as secretary, H. F. Owsley as assistant secretary, and B. P. Smith as treasurer. Committees were appointed to solicit funds to secure two railways in search of southwestern outlets: the Missouri, Kansas and Texas Railway; and the Ozark and Cherokee Central Railway.[35] Later that month, the Chickasha Commercial Club accepted the invitation of Oklahoma City mayor Charles "Gristmill" Jones, who was also president of the Oklahoma and Southwestern Railroad, to join him on an excursion to Greer County on the Frisco extension. Wives and families were welcomed to join them.[36] Over in the Indian Territory, the ninety-one members of the Tulsa Commercial Club reorganized on January 28, 1903. G. L. Williams was elected president, and S. F. Aby was elected secretary.[37]

News briefs on commercial club activities were a staple of newspaper reporting at the turn of the twentieth century, and they provide insight into communities' grassroots campaigns to lure businesses to their areas and develop infrastructure to keep them. When their gambits worked, town boosters were not shy about sharing their good news. Interviewed at the Union Depot in Kansas City in the fall of 1902, Guthrie businessman Paul Newman seized the opportunity to extol the tide of immigrants and eastern capital that were fulfilling the promise of the Promised Land. With characteristic pride in his community, Newman could not help but feed the rivalry between the territory's principal cities. "Guthrie and Oklahoma City are rivals," he explained, "just as they were on the day they were founded thirteen years ago. I believe my town is growing faster than Oklahoma City and is destined to be the metropolis of the territory." As evidence, Newman cited four railroads that were building toward Guthrie, the completion of an elegant city hall, and $65,000 in improvements to the sewer system. Then he went hyperbolic: "It is the most prosperous and most hustling little city of 15,000 people on the continent."[38]

Not to be outdone by his northern rival, Oklahoma City insurance man C. S. Avery rallied to the cause of his town: "Oklahoma City is growing faster, without suffering the disadvantages and dangers of a real estate boom, than almost any city of its size in the country. The street car line is almost completed, and we are now paving our principal business streets, many substantial business houses and a large number of new residences are being erected, and people are coming into the city by the score."[39]

Charles B. Adams, an attorney for the venerable firm of Hoffman, Charles and Conklin of Chandler, reserved his accolades for all of Oklahoma, a moniker that was gradually replacing the territorial designations in the common vernacular, if not on the map. He and E. L. Conklin were in Kansas City when he was asked about the goings-on down south. "Oklahoma is prospering in fine shape," said Adams. "Everybody is making money, and the banks are full of deposits. The crop prospects are excellent. The unparalleled period of railroad activity which set in last year is still on."[40]

While Guthrie and Oklahoma City vied for supremacy in the Oklahoma Territory, towns in the Indian Territory were clustering wherever the land could be tapped for natural resources. The initial boom in the oil business cooled somewhat in 1905 "pending the completion of increased carrying facilities." But that did not mean that commercial activity was stalling. Bartlesville's glory days as an oil center were still on the horizon in 1902, when the village consisted of little more than a few one-story pine sheds along the Caney River bottom. The proliferation of oil derricks forced developers to move to higher ground, and it was not until 1903 that the first modern building was constructed. By the summer of 1905, brick and stone structures sprawled across four city blocks, and there was not a vacant house or shack to be found. The city had a waterworks, a gas plant, and an electric light plant, and sewer lines were under construction. In mid-August 1905, there was speculation that the city council would authorize street paving, "and it will undoubtedly go through because everybody here appears to be for everything that is deemed essential anywhere else."[41] A new hotel was completed in March 1905, and one story of its white cut stone structure on the corner was occupied by the First National Bank. The hotel lobby had a tiled floor and was lit by electricity.

Fifty miles south of Bartlesville, Tulsa was shaping up as the de facto capital of the Indian Territory. Settlement dated back to 1836, when Creek Indians from Lochapoka (Place of Turtles) in present-day Alabama completed their cross-country trek by kindling their council fire beneath a mighty oak tree that towered above the Arkansas River. The Council Oak Tree at 1730 South Cheyenne testifies to Tulsa's roots—not terribly deep in the eastern scheme of things, but practically ancient compared to cities in the Oklahoma Territory that sprouted overnight from the prairies. The sleepy trading center and ceremonial grounds was widely known as Lochapoka until March 25, 1879, when Josiah C. Perryman, a town founder of Creek descent, was assigned as U.S. postmaster and his office was designated as "Tulsa" (originally "Tulsey" or "Tulsee," a shortened version of "Tallasi," and almost certainly derived from "Tallahassee" or "Tullahassee," meaning "Old Town").[42] Another milestone came in 1881 when officials with the Saint Louis and San Francisco Railroad decided to extend a line from Vinita in the Cherokee Nation through the Creek Nation to intercept cattle herds on their way north.[43]

MAIN STREET, LOOKING SOUTH.

Looking south on Main Street in Tulsa, Indian Territory, ca. 1900. Courtesy Western History Collections, University of Oklahoma Libraries (Howard Studio No. 3. SE9-4).

Much as the kindling of a sacred fire signaled Tulsa's birth, the arrival of the railroad marked the origin of modern Tulsa.

Laws aimed at discouraging non-Indians from settling in the Creek Nation were hard enough to maintain before the arrival of the railroads; in the ensuing years, Creek sovereignty seemed destined for oblivion. The first passenger train reached Tulsa on August 21, 1882.[44] To accommodate the quickening tempo of business, Josiah Perryman opened a store in May 1882 near the Third Street viaduct, where the surveyor's stakes crossed the old "river road" to Sand Springs. Assisted in his enterprise by his brothers, George and Legus, Josiah's firm became known as Perryman Brothers. When the brothers took on a white partner from Coffeyville, Kansas, the store was designated as Perryman and Reed. Two white clerks were employed, and advertisements enticed shoppers to the store's "complete full line of groceries, dry goods, and farm implements." For the grand sum of a dollar, they could purchase twenty yards of calico, ten yards of bleached muslin, or eight yards of "fine dress goods, all colors."[45] When the post office was moved from George Perryman's ranch house to Perryman and Reed, Tulsans boasted of having the nicest post office in the Creek Nation. It also became one of the busiest as mail came in daily on the Frisco. But there were still no banks—except, of course, for the cattlemen, who were the real bankers. The cash that they procured from cattle sales was about all there was to keep Tulsa stores afloat.[46]

Keeping their distance from Creek tribal politics, Tulsans in the 1880s and 1890s coped with the dearth of law by creating a business district where Creeks mingled freely with visitors from the Sac and Fox Reservation to the west and the Osage Reservation to the north to produce a vibrant commercial culture. Laden with buckskins and slabs of venison and other samples of the land's bounty, Indians traded for farm implements, cooking utensils, calico, sugar, coffee, and whatever else the land could not provide. Storekeepers made it easy for them by employing educated Creeks to serve as bilingual clerks. Commerce was augmented as white cattlemen, already profiting from the region's hardy grasses, capitalized on the expanding network of railroads to position Tulsa as one of the West's premier cow towns. Historian Angie Debo captured the zeitgeist of those freewheeling days in her classic history of early-day Tulsa: "The cowboys were sober, hard-working young men on the range, but they celebrated at Tulsa. On paydays they rode into town, filled up on forbidden whiskey, and dashed up and down the streets shooting at the lighted windows. Prudent citizens closed their stores, put out their lights, and lay flat on the floors of their houses until the frolic was over. The boys often fired pistols over the heads of a congregation as it left the church, not from any irreligious motive, but because the screams of the women added to the gaiety of living."[47]

Wherever commerce thrived, outlaws were soon to follow. Throughout the 1880s and 1890s, bandits emerged from their hideouts near Tulsa to steal horses, rob trains, and stir up whatever trouble their profession demanded. As Tulsa's first bank was not opened until 1895, merchants' safes made for easy pickings. Although members of the West's most notorious gangs were a familiar sight in Tulsa and committed sporadic crimes against people and property, there was never an organized raid. "There was a sort of gentleman's agreement with the outlaws," wrote Debo, "by which the town furnished them asylum in exchange for immunity."[48] As late as the 1940s, Tulsans remembered with affection the kind and courteous Daltons who behaved themselves in town, even as their lurid escapades elsewhere filled the newspapers and confirmed the Indian Territory's reputation for lawlessness.

Prescient observers knew that the Wild West's days were numbered. The first federal court in the Indian Territory was established in Muskogee in 1889; from then on, courts were established and jurisdictions were extended at a rapid clip. In 1893, the Dawes Commission began its work of shutting down tribal affairs and converting Indians to whites' insistence on individual ownership of land. When a federal judge ruled in 1895 that towns in the Indian Territory had the right to incorporate under existing statutes, yet another scramble was unleashed, this time to organize towns under U.S. laws and thereby circumvent the complexity of tribal land tenure. By then, Tulsa had thirty-eight businesses operating under traders' licenses. Competition came from Indian businesses, which were not saddled with licensing fees. Meanwhile, legions of non-Indian intruders increased their profit margins by evading Creek and U.S. laws as best they could.

Among these commercial enterprises was the Tulsa Banking Company. Opened on July 29, 1895, when Tulsa was still a cow town with a population of 650, the bank was capitalized with $10,000 and led by three men: John Forsythe, a Texan who, along with the legendary cowman "Shanghai" Pierce, had leased southwestern parts of the Perry-mans' vast holdings; Forsythe's brother-in-law, B. F. Colley; and his son-in-law, C. W. Brown, who actually had experience in banking.[49] With the nearest banks in Vinita and Muskogee, the principals were confident that there was enough farming and ranching in the vicinity of Tulsa to support an upstart bank. Operating from a small two-story build-ing on Main Street, they received deposits and loaned money on notes with maximum terms of ten years and whose annual interest rates were between 8 and 10 percent. The bank and numerous other businesses were consumed by a fire in December 1897. The safe, however, was found intact, and Forsythe and the others reopened in a nearby stone building the same day. On January 3, 1899, the Tulsa Banking Company was reorganized with $50,000 in capital and received a national bank charter as the First National Bank of Tulsa. Under the presidency of William H. Halsell, a cattleman from Vinita who had participated in the reorganization, the bank relocated in 1905 to a five-story building, a veritable skyscraper described as "the finest in the Southwest," to take its place among the strongest banks in mid-America.[50]

Tulsa's opportunity to build a more stable foundation for commerce than Indian land tenure came on January 18, 1898, when the town was incorporated. With the stroke of a pen, Tulsans had the right to establish a system of taxation other than paying licensing fees to the Creek trea-sury. Like any city in America, Tulsa could establish public schools, build water systems, pave streets—in short, develop an infrastructure commen-surate with the needs of a modern metropolis. Yet Tulsa was not about to shed its frontier persona without a show of western bluster. When a mass meeting was called to settle issues of landownership, reasoned debate quickly degenerated into a free-for-all of pistol shots and fist fights.[51]

Literally and figuratively, the Wild West was closing with a bang.

If Tulsa's history as a cow town ended with a bang, its emergence as an oil capital began with a roar. In the summer of 1901, Pennsylvania oil-men John S. Wick and Jesse A. Heydrick were prospecting in the vicinity of Red Fork, a tiny village some four miles from Tulsa on the opposite side of the Arkansas River. When the Frisco agent at Red Fork refused to accept a draft on their Pennsylvania backers to release their drill-ing equipment, they turned to two local doctors, John C. W. Bland and

Fred S. Clinton, for a loan. In return, they agreed to drill a well on the allotment of Sue A. Bland, Dr. Bland's wife, at Red Fork.[52]

With financing secured, Wick and Heydrick spudded their well on May 10, 1901. Shortly before midnight on June 24, their drill bit hit a gas pocket at a depth of 537 feet. With a roar that surely sent workers scrambling for cover and cattle stampeding across the prairies, a greenish-yellow plume cascaded from the derrick and rained down on dazed onlookers. Within days, newspapers nationwide were announcing the dawning of a new age. "Great Oil Strike," "Greatest Oil Well West of the Mississippi," "A Geyser of Oil Spouts at Red Fork"—these and similar headlines lured thousands of fortune seekers to Red Fork in a frantic scramble for land leases.[53] Not even the realization that the well was producing only ten barrels or so a day was enough to discourage the faithful from getting in on the oil boom.

Determined to benefit from the bonanza in nearby Red Fork, Tulsans organized the Tulsa Commercial Club in 1902 and elected G. W.

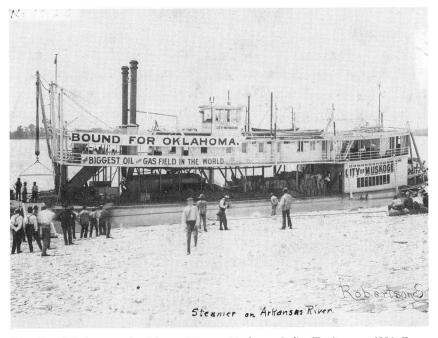

The *City of Muskogee* on the Arkansas River at Muskogee, Indian Territory, ca. 1906. Courtesy Oklahoma Historical Society.

Mowbray as their first president. The Tulsa Commercial Club's first order of business was to attract railroads as they expanded their lines across the Twin Territories. Another concern was the lack of a pedestrian bridge across the Arkansas River. Except for the railroad bridge, the only way to cross the river was by ferry or the more dangerous ford. Efforts to build a wagon bridge by floating bonds had already come to naught when skeptical Tulsans voted against a bond issue. Tulsa's conundrum was solved when Tulsa business leaders M. L. Baird, George T. Williamson, and J. D. Hagler used their own capital to build a toll bridge. When the bridge was completed on January 2, 1904, its owners put up a sign at the entrance that came to symbolize Tulsa's can-do spirit: "You said we couldn't do it, but we did."[54]

With easy access to the *rive gauche* of the Arkansas River, Tulsans were ready for the event that clinched their city's claim as the oil capital of the world. In the fall of 1905, Robert Galbreath, who had been involved in the Red Fork boom, and Frank Chesley spudded a wildcat well on the allotment of Ida E. Glenn about twelve miles south of Tulsa. On November 22, their drill bit reached 1,481 feet and tapped into a sandbar on the shores of an ancient sea.[55] A familiar rumble was followed by a gusher that dwarfed the Red Fork strike. By the middle of 1907, 516 wells were producing 117,440 barrels a day.[56] The drillers did their best to avoid the kind of pandemonium that accompanied the Red Fork strike, but to no avail. Derricks above the Glenn Pool soon cluttered the countryside, and Tulsa was open for business as the undisputed center of global oil production.

The Glenn Pool strike sent Tulsa into a frenzy of construction. It seems fitting that Tulsa's first skyscraper, towering to an astonishing five stories and equipped with an elevator, was built to house the First National Bank. Construction began in 1904 and was completed a few months after the pool was opened. The symbiotic relationship between bankers and oilmen did not begin with the Glenn Pool strike, but it certainly received a powerful boost on that fateful day of November 1905, and it remained a cornerstone of Oklahoma's commercial culture. As Angie Debo wrote more than six decades ago in *Tulsa: From Creek Town to Oil Capital,* "When oil started spouting over the top of a derrick, the man who got there first was the one who profited; thus the independent Oklahoma producers backed by Tulsa bankers had an advantage even over the great corporations, which had to await the impersonal action of Eastern financial centers. The story of the development of any major field, of the meteoric rise of any individual in this area, almost invariably begins with the courage and insight of Tulsa bankers willing to stake an audacious venture."[57]

"This is a boom town," recorded one chronicler in August 1905. "Everyone in Tulsa is a boomer, but not for revenue only. All the inhabitants believe that destiny has marked it for its own." There was a consensus that Tulsa's destiny hinged on four attributes: a favorable location at the "center of a great section of the Southwest"; railroads, of which there were already five; oil, "the best along the line Tulsa believes"; and a clinching argument that it was "the best town anywhere for manufactories." Banks were doing their best to keep pace with development. Aggregate deposits in Tulsa banks exploded from $100,000 in 1904 to $1,100,000 in the summer of 1905. During the same period, the population grew from 3,000 to 7,000, and many expected that number to grow to 25,000 within five years.[58]

The strikes at Red Fork and Ida Glenn's farm clinched Tulsa's position at the center of global oil production. But other Indian Territory fields were coming online, and output of five hundred barrels a day was becoming the new norm. In late 1904, the tiny village of Ochelata boasted three wells that started at one thousand barrels a day. After two months, the first well drilled in those environs was still pumping seven hundred barrels every twenty-four hours.[59] Meanwhile, entrepreneurs and engineers were figuring out what else lay beneath the surface and how to bring it to market. Creek Nation oil was complemented by natural gas and coal. The Cherokee Nation sat above vast deposits of oil, natural gas, and zinc. Sleepy Choctaw communities were being transformed by oil, coal, asphalt, and pine timber.

Nowhere were underground riches more apparent than in the Chickasaw Nation, "the mineral bargain counter of Indian territory," where wealth hidden for eons included oil, coal, copper, manganese, iron, asphalt, Gilsonite, red and yellow ochre, granite, and even quicksilver. Asphalt, known to grow harder and firmer over time, was the mineral of choice for sidewalk construction. By the fall of 1903, a foreign syndicate already controlled Chickasaw asphalt leases. One of the most productive asphalt plants was at Loco, about fifteen miles from Comanche. It was owned and operated by the Tar Springs Asphalt Company and received financing from capitalists in the Oklahoma Territory and back east. A catastrophic fire that gutted the plant was only a bump in the road; it was quickly rebuilt until five carloads of asphalt a week were being shipped to market. "Asphalt beds are everywhere in the Chickasaw nation," concluded a feature story on the Indian Territory's mineral wealth. "All mineral on an allotment will belong to the allottee, and when patents issue to allottees, the mineral resources will be developed rapidly by syndicates."[60]

Not all the riches, of course, were underground. In spite of three years of bad crops, fertile cropland was bringing farmers to the Indian Territory and causing towns to double in population. Statehood was expected to open the floodgates even further. "The farmer who has made his crop will have money," said one observer. "The newcomers will bring money and spend it. More money will be in circulation in I.T. in the fall of 1905 than any other year in its history."[61] Following tours of Kansas, the Twin Territories, Texas, and most of Mexico, George H. Findley of Topeka chimed in with his own assessment: "Indian territory will be the richest country that has ever come into statehood from an unorganized territory. Right now that country is filling up with farmers from Missouri, Iowa, Illinois, Kansas and Texas. They have sold farms for $50 and $75 an acre, and, when they go to Indian territory, they buy land and pay cash for it. They have enough money to improve their land and still have some money in the bank. They do not mortgage their property for all it is worth. The Indians from whom they buy are improving the land they do not sell and spending the money right at home."[62]

Clearly a true believer in free enterprise, Findley marveled to witness patterns of settlement and homesteading in which money was not siphoned into the U.S. Treasury. In his home state of Kansas, subsistence farmers began tilling the soil with little more than an ox team and a mortgage. Findley reflected, "It was a tough time we had in Kansas in early days to wring from the stubborn sod a living." Conditions could not have been more different in the Indian Territory, where settlers arrived with money and were blessed with natural resources. "Under statehood," concluded Findley, "it will be a wonderful country."[63]

Statehood was in the future, but signs of modernity were already ubiquitous, and they provide yet another gauge of commercial development. In February 1903, the Metropolitan Railway Company in Oklahoma

City rolled one of its new electric railway cars from the barn to make its initial run.[64] Principals in the development of Oklahoma City's urban transportation system were John W. Shartel and Anton H. Classen. Under the aegis of the Metropolitan Railway Company and its successor, the Oklahoma Railway Company, these and other business leaders launched their city into a stellar role as one of America's fastest-growing cities by promoting an electric streetcar and interurban rail system. Long before automobiles muscled their way onto the urban landscape, the Oklahoma Railway Company "accelerated the construction of graded and paved streets, the laying of gas and sewer lines, the platting of housing additions, and the creation of hundreds of jobs. It was an economic dynamo."[65]

Improvements in transportation continued on May 25, 1905, when the Colonial Construction Company of Oklahoma was chartered with a capital stock of $100,000 to build an interurban electric railroad from Oklahoma City through Lexington and on to Sulphur Springs, Indian Territory.[66] Further north, citizens of Guthrie were "enjoying the novelty of riding in electric street cars, and boast that now they have one of the necessary conveniences of a genuine state capital."[67] Oklahoma City, Guthrie, and Shawnee had electric streetcar systems by the spring of 1905. Shartel promoted the systems in Guthrie and Oklahoma City. Although many interurban lines had been proposed, Shartel said that the line between Oklahoma City and Guthrie was the first priority. Among the heaviest investors in urban transportation was Anton Classen. He and Shartel encouraged the citizens of Guthrie to complement their streetcar system with a beautiful park and summer resort. Features of the proposed park included an artificial lake with a sandy beach and a ballpark. In December, Shartel announced that financing was in place for the interurban line between Oklahoma City and Guthrie. By June 1, 1906, cars would be running as far as Edmond.[68]

Telephone and electric lines, too, were bringing the Twin Territories in ever-closer proximity. In December 1905, the Shawnee City Council granted a twenty-one-year franchise to the Pioneer Telephone Company to install a $100,000 system. At the same time, the Shawnee Light Company, headed by former territorial delegate to Congress Dennis Flynn, announced plans to build electric lights in Tecumseh. An electric line would later be built to Oklahoma City.[69]

But not all signs of modernity were electrical. Citizens of Hulbert claimed distinction as the only town in the Indian Territory with a female mail carrier. Not to be outdone, nearby Melvin countered that it had the only female bank manager in the territory. Known as a shrewd businesswoman with large land holdings, Jennie Taylor was so dissatisfied with the way things were going at the Bank of Melvin that she bought a majority share of the bank stock and took over its management.[70]

Businesspeople and bankers, including the thoroughly modern Taylor, thus had much to celebrate on the eve of Oklahoma statehood in 1907. What they did not read in the newspaper and glean from officialdom, they saw with their eyes and felt in their hearts. Frontier scarcity and lawlessness were giving up the ghost. Improvements in communication and transportation were erasing the line between the Twin Territories and hastening their inclusion in the national polity. Entrepreneurs were sniffing out opportunities and exploiting them for all they were worth, and farmers were turning a prairie wilderness into a horn of plenty. Through it all, bankers were greasing the wheels of commerce by employing their considerable skills in the management of currency and credit. One of humankind's oldest challenges—the equitable production, acquisition, and distribution of goods—was in very good hands indeed. Those uneasy bedfellows, capitalism and democracy, seemed to be getting along reasonably as the Twin Territories prepared to affix a single star to Old Glory.

But if that is true, then why were people so vexed by the Indians' management of their newfound wealth? A newspaper article filed the day after Christmas in 1902 cited the Osage agent's annual report to announce that the Osage Indians, of which there were 1,800, had $8,584,498 to their credit in the U.S. Treasury. What is more, they owned 400,000 acres, and their per capita income made them some of the wealthiest people on earth. Osage receipts for 1902 alone amounted to $579,866.[71] So how did these warriors-turned-tycoons manage their piles of money? Apparently, not very well, by many accounts—unless you happened to operate a retail establishment. As one press report claimed, "The improvidence of the American Indian is one of his remarkable characteristics."[72]

Rolling in wealth, the Osages were perceived as people who squandered their government annuities on extravagances. Annuity funds "pass through their fingers like water." Half-bloods who made it onto the tribal rolls were apparently the worst offenders. Mired in poverty long before the oil money flowed, many were prone to reckless spending. It was not unusual for an Osage family to purchase sugar by the barrel, fruit by the case, and everything else in proportion. A passerby recalled with disgust the heaps of food and luxury items that lay discarded in a yard for children and dogs to frolic on. One man who needed only one wagon had three. "Every child on the place was provided with a pony and saddle and they had guns galore. They had one built by special order at a fancy price by an Eastern firm."[73]

Farther west, members of the Cheyenne and Arapaho tribes were purportedly behaving no better. Characterizing them in his annual report to the Indian Bureau as frivolous, extravagant, and confirmed loafers, Indian superintendent John H. Seger was clearly miffed that his charges were so slow to catch on to the ways of capitalism. His report read in part, "These Indians spend their money so extravagantly that they soon use it up and then have to run into debt, which causes them to pay high prices for what they buy. . . . The Indians have not shown a disposition to settle down and improve their places as they should. Their greatest drawbacks are drinking, gambling, eating mescal and dancing. They have too much money, which they get without working."[74] Superintendant Seger singled out one Indian who lamented that he did not have a dead sister's land to sell and therefore had no choice but to raise corn.

It is not that Rodgers and Hammerstein got it wrong. On the contrary: Oklahoma *was* doing fine. Commerce was on a roll. Farms were prospering. Mines and wells were producing. Towns were growing, and buildings were reaching for the sky. Both cause and effect of the commercial frenzy were banks—full of money, and ready to extend credit to the next promising venture. But not everybody was on the free-market bandwagon. Clearly unwilling or unable to shed their ancient traditions and blend into the dominant commercial culture, Native Americans could neither stem the capitalist juggernaut nor participate fully in its bounty. Democracy, it seems, was not for everyone. As the Twin Territories careened toward statehood, there were plenty of folks who were happy to help Native Americans assimilate, but not in ways that augured well for democracy in the embrace of capitalism.

CHAPTER THIRTEEN

Other People's Money

Anybody likes to be acquainted with a man who has charge of a bank; they are mighty good people to be well acquainted with; they come in handy; there comes a time in every man's life when they come in handy to make a little borrow from. They are mighty good people and we are proud to have them with us.

J. S. Messenbaugh, Oklahoma City mayor

The tenth annual convention of the Oklahoma Territory Bankers Association, and the second annual meeting of the Oklahoma–Indian Territory Bankers Association, convened in Oklahoma City on May 21, 1906. When Oklahoma City mayor J. S. Messenbaugh rose to give his welcoming address, he knew that he could count on an attentive crowd. He was, after all, one of them—a onetime banker whose banking experience from 1893 to early 1896 coincided with the Panic of 1893, a debacle that everyone in his audience would have just as soon forgotten. "We hope and trust that we will never have a repetition of that particular time," said the banker-turned-politician as heads surely bobbed around the room. "Everything was long in the banking business, practically. The loans were long, the overdrafts were long, and the bills payable were long. In fact everything was long except their deposits and profits. They were short and gradually grew shorter."[1]

The bottom line for Mayor Messenbaugh was that banking was far from the cushy profession that outsiders assumed it was. "I quit the

Oklahoma National Bank, Oklahoma City, Oklahoma Territory. Courtesy Oklahoma Historical Society.

banking business," he said, "and I never go into a bank now unless I have business with it. I hurry by, I never stop. It always has a kind of horror for me."[2] But that did not mean that the mayor had lost respect for either bankers or their profession. On the contrary, he depicted bankers with the flattering description that begins this chapter.

Mayor Messenbaugh took great pride in Oklahoma City's development. "While our city is not yet finished," he once quipped in an interview for the *Daily Oklahoman,* "we have covered up about all the rough spots."[3] Like everyone else in the audience, he also looked forward to the day when the Twin Territories would unite as a single state. Other than positive vibes from Washington, D.C., exact evidence of impending statehood was hard to come by. The mayor likened the situation to a little old lady who believed that heaven was reserved for members of her congregation. When asked why, she replied that her belief was a matter of faith—nothing more, and nothing less. Messenbaugh explained, "That is the way we are on the statehood question, we are going to get it, but our main reason for thinking so is a matter of faith."[4]

Faith turned to hyperbole when Mayor Messenbaugh lauded citizens of the Twin Territories for their pioneer grit: "We have here some of the best people on earth, and I ought to say that Oklahoma and Indian Territory has the best people in the United States, and when I say it, I do not say it with any fear of contradiction, but I cannot furnish the evidence to prove it."[5] The mayor had more conviction than evidence to suggest "that the people down here are all expansionists"—not necessarily all Democrats, which he deemed unfortunate, but certainly united in their zeal for economic development. "They are making good cities all over these two territories," he concluded with a flourish, "making these territories so if we get into the union you will be proud of us."[6]

Next at the podium was Frank Craig of South McAlester, Indian Territory. Even though he came from a small town, he, too, took great pride in Oklahoma City. He reflected, "It is a marvel to people who come here from other states to see it, and so I say for us who live in the smaller towns, it is a matter of pride to us to say that we are a part of this country that has helped to make Oklahoma City this great town."[7] After praising the host city, Craig made the point that Oklahoma City's banks, whose gross deposits were then approaching $5 million, were owned and operated by men who were friends: "You will not hear, unless I am very much mistaken, a single knock on a banker from another banker while you are here." Craig fervently hoped that the spirit of cooperation and friendship exhibited by bankers would thrive throughout the territories and hasten the day when Oklahoma would join "the sisterhood of states."[8] United under a single flag, Oklahoma would surely become the envy of the nation.

Craig took his seat, and the president of the Oklahoma–Indian Territory Bankers Association, N. T. Gilbert of Madill, Indian Territory, stepped to the podium to deliver the president's annual address. He began with yet another compliment for the assembled bankers, this time by referring to the previous year's convention in Muskogee. No doubt scouting for business, several bankers from back east had been in attendance. One of them had attended bankers' conventions in nearly every state in the Union, and he was moved to comment that the Oklahoma–Indian Territory Bankers Association convention in 1905 "was composed of the brightest, best dressed and best looking lot of men he had ever seen together."[9]

Amidst much grinning and chuckling and straightening of collars, the dashing moneymen listened as their president did the numbers. In the Oklahoma Territory, there were 112 national banks with total resources of $27 million and 290 state (i.e., territorial) banks with total resources of $14 million, making for total resources of $41 million. Across the line in the Indian Territory, there were 142 national banks with total resources of nearly $27 million. In the absence of territorial banking laws in the Indian Territory, there was no way to offer precise figures on private banks. Gilbert postulated, "But judging from the closeness of the resources of the national banks in the two territories, we assume their resources are about the same as the state banks in Oklahoma which would make a grand total of 80 millions, making us number 21 among the states of the union."[10] Not bad, considering the fact that ten years earlier banks in the territories had numbered a mere fifty.

After citing favorable comparisons with other states, Gilbert cut to the heart of his message: "As nearly 90 per cent of the business of the country is done on confidence, it is certainly gratifying that bankers stand at the head of all professions for honesty."[11] He went on to suggest a motto to be inscribed above the door of every banking house in the land—"Other People's Money." Thus inspired, bankers would surely steer clear of speculation, reckless investments, and other pitfalls of their profession that had brought so many of their brethren to ruin. Their responsibility as trustees, intoned Gilbert, was to "stand there with the first duty impressed upon you to preserve for those that have trusted you the funds they have put in your charge, and all considerations of profit to the stockholder, of advantage to the corporation, shall be secondary and subordinate to the performance faithfully, at all times and against all temptations, of that first and highest trust that is entailed upon those who deal with Other People's Money."[12]

Gilbert concluded his remarks with a dual message of optimism: that single statehood was coming, and *soon;* and that bankers would do their part to make it happen: "As it seems morally certain we will soon be admitted to statehood, and the laws to be enacted will be of vital importance to the bankers, we should, each and every one, give our legislative committee every aid and encouragement in assisting to frame these laws."[13]

As the convention adjourned and bankers looked forward to mustering one year hence under the same state flag (actually, it would not be until 1908 that they would convene as citizens of the same state), the Twin Territories remained mired in a swamp of bad publicity. Under the despairing headline "Oklahoma Tired of It," the press in the spring of 1905 told the story of an Oklahoman who had been trying to convince Congress that the territories were not the wild and woolly wilderness they were reputed to be—"the frolic ground of grizzly bears," where settlers lived in constant terror of Indian uprisings, and where "the shaggy and unlettered sons of the wilderness" drank moonshine by the barrel before breakfast and staggered home at night "filled with enough lead to sink a steamboat." Such perceptions were ruinous to the territories' bid to join the Union and promote business. "I want to whisper to you that this thing has reached the jumping off place," declared the fed-up publicist. "By all our household gods we hope to get statehood next winter, but we are going to run against the same old bristles of Eastern distrust unless we start an advertising factory."[14]

Clearly bent on starting the factory himself, the unnamed defender of territorial ways vented his spleen on Oklahomans who got a kick out of playing jokes on greenhorns back east. He declared, "It's time a good many Oklahomans were learning that every time they lie about the country in 'stringing' a tenderfoot they are gouging up splinters in the statehood plank, and that sooner or later they will have to slide on this plank." Our publicist concluded his rant with a paean to Oklahoma exceptionalism that has lost none of its resonance among folks who relish the opportunity to sing at the top of their lungs, "You're doin' fine, Oklahoma!": "The main difference between the people of Oklahoma and the people in other states is that the Oklahomans are accustomed to doing more work in a day than the others do in a week, that they know a 'bunc' the minute they see it and that with them the wild, wild West is ancient history, while to the man beyond the Mississippi this Occidental realm still drips with gore."[15] This was not the first time, and it certainly would not be the last, that state pride revealed its inverse relationship to public relations.

Oklahoma exceptionalism notwithstanding, history offered reasons to be wary about the future. Just as there were ways to measure the ascending arc of economic development, so, too, were there ways to gauge the impediments to progress. Of particular concern to conservative bankers were the liberal laws that allowed banks to organize with a minimum capital stock of $5,000 and to begin business with only half of this amount paid in. In the fall of 1902, there were nearly one hundred such banks in operation, and many of them were little more than offices for lending money at high interest rates. All it would take was a single season of bad crops to push these institutions to the wall and threaten the stability of well-capitalized banks. Bank Commissioner Paul F. Cooper was blunt in his criticism of liberal banking laws dating back to January 1899, when the Oklahoma Territory's banking laws of 1897 were revised: "Under the present state of the law $2,500 in actual money is all that is required to open a bank and receive an unlimited amount of money on deposit, and a one-third portion of that grossly inadequate sum may immediately after opening be invested in real estate or fixtures." Convinced that that there should be a reasonable ratio between capital and deposits, the bank commissioner added his voice to a chorus of conservative bankers in urging the legislature to raise the minimum capitalization to $10,000 and insist that it be fully paid in. "The best bankers in the Territory and in fact the large majority of experienced bankers everywhere share this opinion."[16]

Another problem was the revolving door at the heart of officialdom in Guthrie. Cooper was the fourth person to hold the office of bank commissioner in less than two years (1901–1902). "Changes occurring so frequently necessarily disorganize the work of the department, and detract greatly from its efficiency," said the bank commissioner. The causes for the high turnover were not hard to find: the rapid increase in bank charters (there were four times as many banks in late 1902 as there were in 1899, when the banking laws were revised); the bank commissioner's paltry salary; and an annual appropriation of only five hundred dollars from the legislature to cover rent, office supplies, and travel. As if this were not enough, there was only one territorial bank examiner charged with the herculean task of examining every bank in the territory. As Cooper explained, "One examination is worth half a dozen reports prepared by the officers of the bank and forwarded by mail to the examiner."[17] National bank examiner Myron Sturtevant, whose travails ranged from ridiculous to dangerous, would have agreed wholeheartedly.

To create a functional banking system, Cooper recommended a host of amendments to the laws: vesting more regulatory powers in the office of bank commissioner; changing methods of accounting; consolidating corporations; bonding bank officers; raising the number of people required to subscribe to a bank's articles of incorporation as stockholders from three to five; scheduling banks' annual meetings to facilitate record keeping and reporting; and making stockholders personally liable for losses occasioned by excessive loans and overdrafts.

Defective laws and inadequate supervision were compounded by threats from within. Like the proverbial serpent in the garden, Charles E.

Billingsley, president of the failed Capitol National Bank of Guthrie and the National Bank of Holdenville, served as a reminder for bankers to guard against perils lurking at the heart of their profession. The Capitol National Bank of Guthrie closed in April 1904 in an aura of secrecy. The silence was shattered on September 9, 1904, when attorneys for the receiver filed suit against the Fidelity and Deposit Company of Maryland to collect a surety bond of $10,000 in favor of Billingsley. The petition alleged that Billingsley had abstracted from the bank a demand note for $5,000 given by his mother, Lizzie, and another demand note for the same amount given by his wife, Iva Zoe. Other banks caught in the web of Billingsley's malfeasance included the Citizens Bank of McLoud and the First National Bank of Perry. Total losses to the Capitol National Bank of Guthrie "caused by Billingsley's alleged dishonesty" amounted to $58,670.[18] When demand was made on July 1, 1904, for payment of its $10,000 surety bond, the Maryland company declined to pay.

Things went from bad to worse when R. M. McFarland, vice president of the defunct National Bank of Holdenville, was arrested on October 10 and placed under $50,000 bond, which he was unable to furnish. Charges included embezzlement, willful misappropriation of funds, abstraction of funds, and disposing of mortgaged property. Billingsley, not yet indicted but surely feeling the heat, was in France at the time of his former colleague's arrest. Evidence before the grand jury was that McFarland had used $60,000 of misappropriated (i.e., other people's) money "to finance schemes for his personal benefit." It was alleged that "he made loans to relatives and employees whom he knew were not good security and that he would have persons come in and execute mortgages to him on property which they did not own."[19] National Bank examiners Myron Sturtevant and W. A. Pollack assisted in bringing in the indictments. The day after McFarland's arrest, three other directors and stockholders of the National Bank of Holdenville were arrested: C. B. Schaff (relation to the Hughes County contractor J. W. Schaff unknown), E. A. Utrey, and J. D. Bosley. They were accused of obtaining money under false pretenses and disposing of mortgaged property. By then, McFarland was able to scrounge up enough money to post his $50,000 bond. As indictments rained down on Holdenville, several stockholders mysteriously disappeared.[20]

A federal grand jury was impaneled in Logan County in November 1904 to consider evidence that banking laws were broken in the Capitol

National Bank's failure.[21] Few were surprised when Billingsley, presumably sated with wine and cheese after his sojourn in France, was indicted on seven counts. But suddenly, the trail went cold. In spite of evidence of bad loans and cooked books, the grand jury could not produce a smoking gun. The grand jury report read simply, "There is evidence showing strongly that other violations of the law have taken place in the bank and probably other persons are guilty, but we could not get some evidence which is either destroyed or left in wrong boxes or other places in the bank which we failed to discover. We think this matter should be submitted to the next grand jury for further investigation."[22]

Over the ensuing months and even years, Billingsley's nefarious doings garnered their share of the spotlight. In February 1905, the territorial legislature appointed a committee to inquire into the condition of territorial funds, amounting to more than $200,000, which were deposited in the defunct Capitol National Bank. The committee had a letter from the comptroller of the currency instructing the bank's receiver to issue a complete disclosure.[23] On July 15, Capitol National Bank receiver J. A. Willoughby retired after fifteen stressful months and was succeeded by Charles T. Cherry of Oswego, Illinois. Among Willoughby's headaches was his inability to get his hands on certain assets tied up in the defunct National Bank of Holdenville. A press report on July 15, 1905, claimed that this bank owed the Capitol National Bank of Guthrie about $170,000.[24]

Willoughby's problems extended far beyond the territories. Prior to the Capitol National Bank's failure, the Fourth National Bank of Saint Louis sued the incredible Billingsley for money he had loaned to the Holdenville bank. The suit was apparently unsuccessful.[25] Before the year was out, McFarland was back in the hot seat, this time as a defendant in a Wewoka courtroom for his complicity in the National Bank of Holdenville's demise, the first such calamity in the history of the Indian Territory. By then, the bank was in the hands of a receiver. Few of the banking cognoscenti expected depositors to "realize anything out of their claims."[26]

Billingsley and company were by no means the only ones on the road to perdition. A perusal of press reports in late 1904 and 1905 indicates that they had plenty of company. In late October 1904, R. F. Baird, assistant cashier of the Bank of Wagoner, was arrested for embezzling $2,300 and delivered to Muskogee for trial. Baird had been dismissed from the bank a month earlier because he was short by three hundred dollars. Further investigation revealed a much larger debt, and the case quickly became a morality tale. A press account of the banker's fall from grace asserted that Baird "moved in the best society, but is said to have lived above his income. He is also said to have lost considerable money gambling."[27]

On December 1, a grand jury indicted H. H. Watkins of the defunct Citizens Bank of Enid on twelve counts: eight for receiving deposits when he knew that his bank was insolvent; two for embezzlement; one for forgery; and one for making a false statement to bank commissioners. His bond was fixed at $9,800. Bank president William Kennedy was not indicted.[28] The day after Watkins was indicted, U.S. marshals in Sapulpa received word that W. T. Hart, wanted on a charge of defrauding the First National Bank of Tulsa of $1,500, had been arrested in Galveston, Texas. A deputy marshal was dispatched to Texas to fetch him.[29] Two days later, personnel at the First National Bank of Madill reported a shortage of $22,600 to $25,000. Assistant cashier Roy E. Smith had been gone since November 23, supposedly on a vacation trip to Dallas occasioned by poor health. His colleagues put two and two together and alerted the authorities. The twenty-seven-year-old banker hailed from Iowa and had been with the bank for four years. Perhaps of primary importance, Smith was not bonded.[30]

Playing fast and loose with other people's money continued in 1905. In late March, the law caught up with J. S. McDuffie, cashier of a defunct bank in Lawton and, not incidentally, the city treasurer. He was caught in El Paso, Texas, while under a grand jury indictment for receiving deposits when he knew that his bank was failing. What is more, McDuffie's sworn statement that the bank had $10,000 in paid-in capital did not quite square with the $7,000 on the bank's books.[31] In June, S. A. Hays, cashier of the First National Bank of Lexington, was arrested on a federal warrant charging him with making false entries to deceive the national bank examiner and making a false report to the comptroller of the currency. "The bank had a capital stock of $25,000," ran a press report on the drama in Lexington. "It was found to have so much worthless paper that a 50 per cent assessment was made upon its stockholders and paid. Then another assessment was ordered, but the stockholders declined to pay, and the bank was closed."[32]

In late August, stockholders in the Union Exchange Bank of South McAlester filed a petition in federal court asking for a receiver. After examining the bank's books, a plaintiff alleged that the cashier, Julian Lockard, had loaned $10,000 to his brother-in-law, W. F. Hailey. At the same time, large sums had been loaned to the Central Trust Company and the Eastern Construction Company, both of which were partially owned by the bank's president, J. A. Hill. Hill and Lockard resigned from the bank. Capitalized at the impressive sum of $100,000, the bank had only $212.25 in cash. The trustees paid depositors as they called for money.[33]

C. J. Hill's route to fast money took him to the Indian reservations of southwestern Oklahoma Territory. After a three-day investigation, U.S. Attorney Horace Speed and Assistant U.S. Attorney L. S. McNight of Anadarko prosecuted Hill, a resident of Hobart, for trespassing on the Indian reservation to collect on loans when government payments were being distributed. "It has been a bitter fight," ran an account in the press. "The jury was out only fifteen minutes. It brought in a verdict for the government and assessed a fine of $1,000 and costs." Described as "one of the most noted cases ever in the courts of Southwestern Oklahoma" because of its proximity to the Anadarko Indian Agency, the case against Hill was strikingly similar to two cases pending against Frank Meyers, president of the First National Bank and the Citizens National Bank— both of Anadarko, and both connected with banks in Kansas. According to U.S. Attorney Speed, the seventy-year-old Meyers "was caught on the reservation in an Indian teepee, disguised in Indian garb, collecting Indian loans in violation of law."[34] The duplicitous Meyers was scheduled to appear in Anadarko district court in November.

In October 1905, it was Weleetka's turn to garner unwanted attention when a federal grand jury charged banker and politician Lake Moore, who was also a prominent member of the Creek Nation, with larceny. Irregularities in Moore's real estate dealings surfaced after he paid $6,000 for land belonging to Malinda Fife, an Indian woman who had cleared restrictions on her allotment adjoining the Weleetka townsite before agreeing to sell it. Upon receiving a certified check for her land, Fife turned it over to Moore with the understanding that he would cash it. Moore refused to turn the money over to her because (according to the banker) she owed him money, and he was holding the check as payment of her debt. The second charge stemmed from Moore's purchase of Yarner Hill's allotment under similar conditions. Again, an unsuspecting Indian received a certified check; again, the check was turned over to Moore; and again, the check was kept as payment for a debt. When Fife and Hill complained to the Dawes Commission, the matter was referred to the U.S. commissioner. Moore was promptly arrested. Even though the debts were likely legitimate, it was up to the court, and not the banker, to decide upon the legality of his collection method.[35]

T. G. Cutlipp, a Tecumseh attorney and former president of the defunct Exchange Bank of Wewoka, was next to reap the whirlwind. During the night of October 23, he was arrested and placed on $5,000 bond. The witch's brew of charges against him included embezzlement, larceny, and making false entries in the books. Those charges were made shortly after the bank suspended business but were not made public because Cutlipp "had disappeared immediately after the bank's failure and the officers had not been able to locate him."[36]

A. B. Davis's sleight of hand reverberated far beyond the Twin Territories. Formerly connected with the bank in Wapanucka, Davis was accused of embezzlement in connection with a savings bank in Denver. The defiant banker expressed a willingness to travel to Denver to face charges.[37] Other territorial bankers who might have been eligible for an all-expenses-paid trip to Colorado included (presumably, the aforementioned) J. A. Hill and R. Rappe, president and vice president, respectively, of the Farmers National Bank of Kingfisher. Organized in 1903 with capital stock of $25,000, loans of $10,000, and deposits of $30,000, the bank was closed by order of the comptroller of the currency. Nearly all of the bank's stock was held as collateral security or owned by the Denver Savings Bank, which had failed recently and was in the hands of a receiver.[38] In early November, Oklahoma Territory governor Thompson Ferguson issued a warrant for the arrest of E. E. Hull, formerly connected with Farmers National Bank of Kingfisher, for complicity in the failure of the Denver Savings Bank. Hull's attorneys were doing their best to prevent his extradition to Colorado.[39]

A detailed account of one bank's slide to ignominy comes to us from the Chickasaw Nation. The Bank of the Chickasaw Nation in Tishomingo was housed in one of the most beautiful, ornate buildings in the Twin Territories. It was built by former governor of the Chickasaw

Nation Robert Maxwell Harris who, among other things, was proprietor of the Harris General Store, located across the street, west of the building that became home to the bank. Intended to embellish his tribe's capital, the building's granite color and texture became the envy of bankers throughout the Southwest.[40] No less impressive were the up-to-date fixtures inside—all expensive, and all aimed at assuring tribal members that their money was in good hands. Such was the expense of its construction and furnishings that the building, used early on for offices, was never profitable as an office building, and it eventually became home to the bank.

Nearly all of the bank's officers were members of the Chickasaw tribe: Benjamin H. Colbert, U.S. marshal in the Indian Territory's southern district and onetime cashier and later vice president; T. A. Ward, who doubled as tribal treasurer; and others who, by the summer of 1905, found themselves under indictment for conspiracy to defraud the U.S. government as well as banks in Kansas and Missouri. A feature story published under the headline "How a Bank Graft Grew," told a tale that has unfolded countless times across the ages and that was now playing out in the Indian Territory: "It was in this granite walled edifice that the alleged conspiracies were hatched, and the thousands of dollars' worth of school and general fund warrants of the Chickasaw nation alleged to have been sold a second and a third time after they had been paid, but not canceled by the treasurer of the nation, who was in collusion with the bank's officials."[41]

As recently as 1902, the bank was in good shape. Scouting for a bookkeeper, bank officials settled on Kirby Purdom, a onetime grocery clerk in Denison, Texas. His rise was meteoric, and he was eventually promoted to the bank's presidency. Purdom was known as an affable fellow, but nobody thought of him as wealthy. An acquaintance once boasted that, on the morning of Purdom's arrival in Tishomingo, he loaned Purdom thirty-five cents for breakfast.[42]

It was thus with considerable surprise that folks awoke one crisp morning of October 1903 to discover that the Bank of the Chickasaw Nation had closed its doors and that the genial Purdom had skipped town. The bank had capital stock of $50,000, of which $38,000 was paid up, and deposits of about $54,000. When the vaults were opened, only $66.00 in cash was found. In winding up its affairs, officials were able to recover only $5,000 from the bank's assets; of this amount, $2,500 came from the sale of furniture and fixtures. The Chickasaw Nation lost about $5,000, but the tribal treasurer was not required to pay it because the bank had been designated as the official depository of the Chickasaw Nation.[43] The federal government eventually recovered its deposit of $1,700 by declaring that it belonged to a trust fund. Depositors, alas, recovered nary a cent. Stockholders, too, were left out in the cold. Purdom remained in hiding. Some people claimed to know where he was, but nobody was talking. The rumor mill placed him on the Isthmus of Panama. No one from his home town of Joplin laid eyes on him after the robbery. There is no evidence that he bothered to visit his mother in Oklahoma City.

Further investigation by special examiner T. E. Jenkins revealed fraud in school warrants that had been paid but never canceled. The tribal treasurer at the time the frauds were perpetrated, William T. Ward, was also a director of the defunct bank. Irregularities apparently dated back to 1899. In early June 1905, Judge Hosea Townsend was about to adjourn a federal grand jury in Ardmore, Indian Territory, when Jenkins showed up and made an urgent plea for the judge to retain the jury. The jury was reconvened on June 19, 1905. Indictments were returned against the bank's officers and directors: the mysterious Purdom, president in absentia; Benjamin H. Colbert, vice president; and directors William T. Ward, S. M. White, E. B. Hinshaw, and T. A. Teel. The article covering the story revealed, "The alleged peculations of these bank officers were made possible only by the connivance of Ward, treasurer of the Chickasaw Nation, in whose possession the warrants were kept."[44]

Problems of a less egregious nature greeted national bank examiner Charles F. Filson as he was passing through Tahlequah aboard the Frisco on a mission to examine a bank. No stranger to the peculiarities of territorial banking, Filson knew that a charter was not always the clearest indication that a bank existed, any more than boosters' testimonials guaranteed the existence of a town. On this particular day in July 1905, all Filson found when he stepped off the train was a whistling station and a section house. Perhaps his spirits lifted when he spotted "a half breed on an Arkansas mule."

"Can you tell me where the First National bank is?" queried Filson.

"The what?" answered the man.

"The First National bank."

"Well, stranger," responded the man, "I have been here nigh onto thirty year and I haint seen nothing like that yit. Is it sand or clay youns are looking fer?"

Filson apparently knew better than to press the matter. He caught the last coach as the train pulled away from the station. A black porter picked up his grip and grinned.[45]

Some men rob with a pen, others with a gun. Either way, robbery is not good for business, and it was most definitely an impediment to Oklahoma's economic development. In spite of law enforcement's best efforts to keep outlaws' hands off other people's money, the last few years before statehood saw plenty of mayhem. Lots of it played out in southeastern Pottawatomie County. Remote and rugged, this region was one of the last holdouts for bootleggers and pistol toters. Citizens were understandably afraid to confront them for fear of reprisal.

Territorial attorney general P. C. Simon aimed to do something about it. His goal was to create an environment that would "secure convictions and maintain the pressure of law so firmly that the bullies, thugs and night riders will find it dangerous to remain." His biggest challenge was Younger's Crossing on the South Canadian River at the border of the Chickasaw and Seminole Nations. Notorious as a center of the illegal whisky trade, the saloon that was apparently the center of Younger's Crossing's social life was described by one old-timer as "the lowest pit of hell he ever saw. Indians, halfbreed negroes and white men even more vicious and dangerous, came there regularly to carouse. All were armed and their debaucheries resulted usually in bloody encounters." The only rule in that bullet-scarred tavern was never to fire in the direction of the barkeeper, "whose duties made it impossible for him to serve his patrons promptly if he were compelled to keep a lookout for bullets."[46]

Far to the west, the up-and-coming town of Leger was undergoing its own trials at the hands of outlaws. Better known as Altus, the town changed its name to Leger in July 1901 in deference to a railroad official by that name who agreed to run tracks through the town on the condition that residents name the town after him. The name "Leger" did not stick, however, and by the spring of 1904, Altus was back in business.[47]

On the night of April 3, 1903, robbers less concerned about the bank's name than its contents staged a robbery. They arrived in town aboard a Frisco freight train and promptly surveyed the Bank of Leger. Finding that the bank had an unusual amount of money, they sprang into action. One guarded the front of the bank, another guarded the back, and a third with a yen for chemistry swabbed the safe with nitroglycerine. When residents realized what was happening, armed men rushed the bank and encountered a fusillade of bullets. J. W. Roberts fell, mortally wounded. The robbers eventually made their way to the Frisco yard and escaped on a handcar toward Quanah, Texas. As a sheriff's posse took to the trail, bank officials determined that about $8,000, including a large Indian payment, had been stolen.[48] Within two days, Sheriff Morrison of Kiowa County, Sheriff Thompson of Caddo County, Sheriff Porter of Garfield County, and Sheriff Bottom of Washita County surrounded a ranch near Cordell and captured six members of the Bert Casey gang who were supposed to have robbed the Bank of Leger. A newspaper reported, "The bandits were surprised and taken without trouble."[49]

But there were plenty of other bandits to take their place. A sample of heists in 1904 and 1905 reveals that robbers were getting increasingly bold and sophisticated. On December 8, 1904, two robbers drilled holes in the safe at Farmers State Bank of Lambert in Woods County and blew it to pieces with nitroglycerine. Rallying with a third gang member who had been holding their horses, the robbers escaped with $3,000 and rode toward the Glass Mountains with a sheriff and posse in hot pursuit. Fortunately, the bank carried burglar insurance and lost nothing.[50] In the early morning hours of March 1, 1905, the First State Bank of Clarksville was victimized by robbers who used a crowbar to enter the rear of the building and demolished the safe with nitro. They escaped with $500. At about the same time, the safe in the Frisco depot in Boynton, some fifteen miles from Clarksville, was blown by the same method. About $300 was taken. Law officers suspected the same thieves and no doubt braced for more of the same.[51] Robbers got away with more than $3,000 when they "wrecked the safe" of the Citizens National Bank of Owl near Shawnee in late November.[52] On Christmas Eve of 1905, authorities discovered that the Grinch had arrived in Muskogee with counterfeit bills and silver dollars in his stocking. Because of the rush of last-minute shoppers, many no doubt scouting for deals at the Patterson Mercantile Company, merchants were slow to catch on. No arrests were made.[53] Three days later, early-morning robbers blew up the safe at the Bank of Moore and removed a whopping $10,000. Authorities believed that four to six men were involved in the heist.[54]

And so it went. Operating inside and outside of the territories' banks, ne'er-do-wells helped themselves to other people's money, often with impunity. With pens, guns, and nitro, bank robbers created a giant stumbling block to economic development. With a few notable exceptions, law enforcement was stymied in its attempts to curtail rampant thievery. Not even hard-riding members of the Anti–Horse Thief Association and well-groomed members of the Oklahoma–Indian Territory Bankers Association were able to guarantee the safety and security of banks.

A final impediment to Oklahoma's economic development takes us straight to the troubled intersection of democracy and capitalism: the workings of the Dawes Commission. To be sure, American history offers plenty of evidence that capitalism has not always squared with ideals enshrined in the national narrative. Slavery surely ranks first on the list; discrimination against certain immigrant groups and the conditions that spawned prairie populism belong somewhere near the top. But it is hard to find more blatant perfidy than land fraud in the Indian Territory. If ever there was an instance of inequitable production, acquisition, and distribution of resources—in this case, the most fundamental resource of all—this is it. Like a polluted tributary feeding into a river, the theft of Indian land contributed a toxic element to Oklahoma's culture. The most common form of theft was the practice of locating non-Indians on Indian allotments, known in the common vernacular as grafting. One territorial resident went so far as to claim that this grafting of Indian land was "the chief and most thriving industry in the whole community."[55]

More than any other state, Oklahoma was founded on what territorial governor Thompson B. Ferguson (1901–1906) called "energetic individuality"—that is, the ability and effort of the individual dreamer.[56] Settlers came to build cities and businesses, grow crops, and extract resources—all with the unambiguous purpose of making money, and all at warp speed. In the rush to carve out a slice of the American Dream, the ends justified the means, and the means ran the gamut from legitimate transactions to outright theft. Bankers, caught between an imperative to grow their institutions and a responsibility to regulate the flow of currency and credit, were not always receptive to the voice of their better angels. And Indians, unless they were blessed with extraordinary business acumen or were just plain lucky, were the ultimate victims of runaway economic development.

As unavoidable as it is shameful, Indian land fraud was written into the final chapter of Oklahoma's territorial history, and it is inextricably tied to the Dawes Commission's well-intentioned mission to turn tribal members into American citizens. Determined to end tribal landownership and convert Indians into independent yeoman farmers, the Dawes Commission set up shop in Muskogee in 1893 to begin the extraordinary task of honing America's original inhabitants to the contours of capitalism. A decade into its mission, the secretary of the interior took on a project that demonstrated the government's good intentions when he appointed Levi Chubbuck of Saint Louis to teach Indians how to farm. In his capacity as a special inspector for the Indian Service, Chubbuck was assigned to provide lessons in farming and animal husbandry on Indian reservations. Ideally, Indians would be self-sufficient farmers by the time the Dawes Commission wound up its work.[57] In reality, Indians remained in a precarious position—socialized in the tradition of tribal landownership, and hopelessly inept at protecting their rights when white men in suits came calling.

A glimpse into the gathering storm comes in the form of an investigation headed by Charles J. Bonaparte of Baltimore, Maryland, a friend of President Theodore Roosevelt who was appointed to investigate land fraud in the Indian Territory. His lineage represented a fascinating blend of old and new worlds. The Baltimore attorney was a grandson of Jerome Bonaparte, who was made ruler of Westphalia by his brother, Napoleon I. Since the death of his brother, Jerome Napoleon Bonaparte, in 1894, Charles had been the head of the Bonaparte family in America. And as a sixty-something bachelor, he was the end of the line for America's connection to a man whose battle cry—"*de l'audace, encore de l'audace, et toujours de l'audace!*"—once echoed across Europe and struck fear into the hearts of kings.[58]

But it was Indians, and not kings, who commanded Bonaparte's attention as he prepared to establish his headquarters in Muskogee, Indian Territory, as a special commissioner in the Office of Indian Affairs. Known as one of the most successful lawyers of the Baltimore bar, Bonaparte not only was conversant with Indian issues, but he was also a member of the Board of Indian Commissioners, an honorary board charged with advising the commissioner of Indian Affairs on issues pertaining to contracts for Indian supplies. Before leaving for his summer home in New Hampshire in mid–September 1903, Secretary of the Interior Ethan Allen Hitchcock (1899–1907) expressed his confidence in Bonaparte's ability to get to the bottom of the matter: "Everyone who knows Mr. Bonaparte will feel sure that he will investigate the charges against Indian territory officials fearlessly and that he will disclose all the facts in regard to the connection of members of the Dawes commission with land companies and irregularities charged against them and against other officials engaged in the work of allotting lands."[59]

Expectations were thus running high as Bonaparte prepared to leave for Muskogee. Some hoped that he would expose even more sensational scandals than those already uncovered in the ongoing investigation by the U.S. Postal Inspection Service (USPIS), one of the nation's oldest law enforcement agencies whose lineage points straight back to Benjamin Franklin. Others were concerned that Bonaparte did not quite grasp the magnitude of his undertaking, particularly when he hinted that he would do much of his work in Washington, D.C., and that his trips to Muskogee would be infrequent and brief.[60] Meanwhile, reporting in popular magazines was drawing attention to the goings-on in the Indian Territory. A feature story in *Collier's Weekly magazine* in September 1903 captured the essence of the corruption. Much to the chagrin of boosters in the Twin Territories, the story exacerbated the region's public relations problem: "If anything is meaner than the behavior of members of the Dawes commission, we do not know what it is. They accept the duty of protecting a few last rights of the helpless Indian, and then begin promptly to 'graft' at his expense. Pretending to see that he receives full value for what little land he has to sell, they work in collusion with the very persons from whom they are supposed to protect him. . . . The members of the Dawes commission ought to be punished for their peculiarly mean dishonor."[61]

Tensions ramped up a notch when S. M. Brosius, special agent for the Indian Rights Association who had filed charges at the Department of the Interior against suspected grafters, returned to Washington, D.C., from a trip to the Indian Territory with incriminating evidence. He expected to turn his evidence over to Bonaparte to help in his probe. Before reporting to officials at the headquarters of the Indian Rights Association in Philadelphia, Brosius expressed cautious optimism about Bonaparte's investigation. "Everybody in the Indian territory except the grafters is anxious that the investigation be started," he said. "The people have confidence in Mr. Bonaparte, but they think he should begin his work without further delay."[62]

The months passed. As the investigation wound toward its conclusion, Charles Bonaparte—now assisted by another presidential appointee, Clinton Rogers Woodruff—sent signals that they were satisfied with their findings. Even Dawes Commission chairman Tams Bixby seemed satisfied with the spotlight that investigators had shined on the allotment system. "I believe that Mr. Bonaparte and Mr. Woodruff are now competent to pass upon the matter," he said in a newspaper interview in December 1903. "If they say that we are incompetent or are guilty of wrongdoing in connection with outside business interests, I am willing to accept their decision without dispute."[63]

Bonaparte, too, was satisfied with the investigation that he and his colleague had accepted from President Roosevelt. Announcing in late 1903 that they were putting the finishing touches on their report before sending it to the secretary of the interior, Bonaparte was ready to let the chips fall where they may. He stated, "Mr. Woodruff and I have, I think, made a thorough investigation of all matters referred to us; indeed, we have interpreted our instructions rather broadly, although they were broad in their scope as given to us. Every person who has had a complaint which was brought to our notice, unless it was trivial indeed, or was entirely out of our jurisdiction, was given a hearing, under oath, and every person against whom complaint was made was, so far as possible, given an opportunity for explanation or denial."[64]

An account of Bonaparte and Woodruff's findings lies beyond the scope of this book. Suffice it to say that some abuses were brought to light, and others were not; that some wrongs were righted, and others were left to fester for generations. It is surely a testament to American ideals that get-rich-quick schemes undertaken at the expense of a vulnerable population were found so repugnant in the land's highest office that an investigation was undertaken to root out the rascals and see that justice prevailed. Chalk up a win for democracy in its tug-of-war with capitalism.

It is also a testament to sound business principles that not everybody participated in the orgy. History does not record how many bankers heeded the advice of N. T. Gilbert, who suggested at the Oklahoma-

Indian Territory Bankers Association's annual convention in May 1906 that every banking house in the land be festooned with the simple motto "Other People's Money."[65] More than likely, some did, and quite a few others at least thought about it.

And then, bankers went back to work. The Bank of Beaver City's failure in early 1905 drew attention to the fact that some banks had not been examined for two years, even though banking law required annual examinations. Veteran Panhandle banker Fred C. Tracy complained that some banks in Beaver County, then comprising the entire Panhandle, had gone unexamined for three years. Upon his arrival in Beaver County to make up for lost time, an assistant bank examiner quickly discovered that an "old gentleman" had borrowed the bank's stock and $9,600 of the depositors' money. "In other words," wrote an incredulous Fred Tracy in his memoir, "until he paid that note the bank was short $19,600." With two other wrecked banks to his credit and no money to repay his loan at the Bank of Beaver City, the old gentleman joined the ranks of territorial businessmen whose gambles fell short of winning the jackpot.[66]

Oklahoma Territory governor Ferguson blamed neither the bank commissioner nor the harried examiner. After all, who could be expected to examine 250 banks in one year? But he did have to wonder about a legislature that would not allocate more resources to something as crucial to banking in Oklahoma as bank examinations. Ever the optimist, the governor expected more from the legislature of 1905.[67]

Bankers and their customers were depending on it.

Oklahoma Exceptionalism and the Legacy of Pioneer Banking

Clearly, then, we agree that government itself is a business proposition, requiring the application of business experience, of business sense, of business judgment, as absolutely free as possible, from petty politics and political intrigue, no more the proper subject of favoritism than is the business of the bank itself.

"New State of Oklahoma Is Born," *Daily Ardmoreite,* November 17, 1907

The Twin Territories' journey from frontier to statehood ended with a bang in Guthrie on November 16, 1907, when territorial secretary Charles Filson read President Roosevelt's proclamation admitting Oklahoma to the Union as a single state. To signal his affinity for the West, the president had signed the proclamation with a quill plucked from the wing of an American eagle. The quill was later entrusted to the Oklahoma Historical Society for the edification of future generations. Joining Secretary Filson and other dignitaries on the ceremonial platform was a beaming Charles N. Haskell, governor-elect of the new state, who was itching to put his populist-inspired policies into action. The festivities on that dazzling, sun-drenched day were punctuated by pistol shots and whoops and hollers that one might expect from America's last generation of pioneers.

Taking center stage in the celebration was a wedding ceremony symbolizing the union of east and west. The groom, dubbed "Mr. Oklahoma," was Charles G. "Gristmill" Jones, an Oklahoma City businessman whose activities ran the gamut of politics and commercial enterprise. Tall and fair-haired, Jones sported striped trousers and a black coat in keeping with so solemn an occasion. The role of his bride, "Miss Indian Territory," was played by Mrs. Leo Bennett, a young Native American from Muskogee. She was clad not as an Indian princess, as members of the eastern press on hand for the occasion might have expected, but wore a floor-length lavender satin dress with long sleeves and a high collar, a large picture hat, and gloves—as then was fashionable for Anglo-American brides. Clutching one large, mauve-colored chrysanthemum, Mrs. Bennett waited backstage as her husband-to-be summoned his oratorical skills to put his stamp on history and the stamp of legitimacy on the new state. History is silent as to whether Mr. Jones or Mrs. Bennett suffered from premarital jitters as William A. Durant, a young Choctaw from Bryan County who had served as sergeant at arms during the Oklahoma Constitutional Convention (1906–1907) and would later serve as speaker in the Oklahoma House of Representatives, prepared to give the bride away in marriage.[1]

The Reverend W. H. Dodson of the First Baptist Church in Guthrie performed the ceremony in front of the Carnegie Library. Introductions given and crowd more or less subdued, the groom stepped to the front of the platform, bowed to the right and left, and asked for silence. Without further ado, he delivered his wedding vows. Spoken before a congregation of thousands, his carefully chosen words conveyed a sense of the challenges that the Oklahoma and Indian Territories had overcome to be deemed worthy of statehood, even as they anticipated a glorious future:

> I have been asked to perform the agreeable duty of proposing marriage to Miss Indian Territory. Permit me to say that nothing gives me more pleasure, as the President advises us of his Proclamation and that the marriage will be strictly legal, without regard to age, condition, or previous servitude. The bridegroom is only 18 years old, but is capable of assuming all the matrimonial responsibilities of a stalwart youth. Though he was born in tribulation, in the city of Washington in 1889, his life of 18 years on the plains has been one of tremendous activity and he has grown to the size of a giant. . . . On account of his youth and

inexperience, he is possessed of an unconquerable modesty and has asked me to propose marriage to the Indian Territory.[2]

Wedding vows delivered, Jones ceded the stage to Durant, who then accepted Mr. Oklahoma's proposal on behalf of Miss Indian Territory. By alluding to "the unhappy circumstances of her youth, which have cast a shadow of sorrow over a face by nature only intended to give back only warm smiles of God's pure sunshine," Durant acknowledged the troubled history of Anglo-Indian relations that had cast a pall for the better part of a century across what was to become eastern Oklahoma. Durant's lament was mercifully brief, and it was quickly forgotten as he wound toward his upbeat conclusion: "Mr. Oklahoma into whose identity Indian Territory is about to be merged forever, must be entrusted to care for this princely estate. We resign it to you in confident hope that it will be cared for, developed and conserved to the unending glory of our new state and the untold benefit of her people."[3]

Cheering erupted when Miss Indian Territory, heretofore hidden from view and her identity kept secret, strode onto the platform. The wedding march blared as she took her place at Mr. Oklahoma's side. Cradling her chrysanthemum and bowing to the multitudes, she shielded her eyes from the glare of the midday sun as Reverend Dodson joined her in matrimony to her gallant groom. A group of Cherokee girls added a patriotic flourish to the ensuing speeches, oaths of office, and paper signing with a rendition of "The Star Spangled Banner."[4]

Parade marshals then sprang into action, and the crowd went wild. The *Beaver Herald* brought the festivities to life for its readers in western Oklahoma: "The inaugural parade formed at the Carnegie library and was the longest procession ever witnessed in the new state, being fully two miles in length and including 1,500 militiamen and cadets, ten bands, thirty carriages carrying state officials and committees, which were followed by hundreds of surreys and buggies carrying visitors, besides the different city delegations, civic organizations, etc."[5] Among the biggest crowd pleasers was a delegation from the Anti–Horse Thief Association. According to the *Oklahoma State Capital,* "The members walked their horses four abreast and many were the rounds of applause to which they responded with good humored smiles."[6]

Tulsans celebrated statehood with a daylong party, followed by an evening of congratulatory speeches at the opera house. As the *Oklahoma*

State Capital reported, "Everybody here is glad that the new state is at last an actuality and that [the] territorial regime is at an end."[7] Down in the old Chickasaw Nation, the *Daily Ardmorite* reminded revelers (as though anyone needed reminding!) that Oklahoma was a businessman's state, pure and simple—a message meant for politicians as well as businessmen: "The farmer is a business man. The laborer is a business man. Those engaged in finance, commerce, manufacturing, mining, or transportation, are business men, each and all; and in the aggregate they must, for stability and prosperity, depend upon their government. Clearly, then, we agree that government itself is a business proposition, requiring the application of business experience, of business sense, of business judgment, as absolutely free as possible, from petty politics and political intrigue, no more the proper subject of favoritism than is the business of the bank itself."[8] The *Muskogee Cimeter* championed the strides that the Twin Territories had made in banking and commerce in spite of the money powers' nefarious doings back east: "The financial condition is gradually growing better. All of our banks are in good shape and if the people will only have confidence and be patient all will be well. Present conditions are not due to mismanagement of the banks, but by speculators and gamblers on Wall Street."[9]

Clearly, a new day was dawning in the brand-new state. The journey to statehood had taken eighteen long years, and its completion on November 16, 1907, deserved the kind of celebration that pioneers were uniquely qualified to put on. But none doubted that statehood was a foregone conclusion whose postponement since 1890 had more to do with politics than the Twin Territories' qualifications for admission to the Union. Economically and politically, the Oklahoma and Indian Territories had long since eclipsed older and more settled states to become a powerhouse of free enterprise. Always more interested in forging ahead than looking over their shoulders, newly branded Oklahomans anticipated even better days ahead.

As catalysts of free enterprise, bankers shared in that optimism, and they were likewise drawn more to the future than the past. Yet the legacy of pioneer banking survived the celebratory hoopla of 1907 to form a deep stratum of Oklahoma's commercial culture. That legacy revealed itself in a conviction that Oklahomans were a breed apart—confident in their ability to coax both crops and cities from virgin soil, willing to gamble all they had for a shot at a new beginning, and wary of outsiders who did not see things their way. Not surprisingly in a region that beckoned non-Indian settlers with the promise of free land, Oklahomans prized economic development above everything else in measuring quality of life.

Values forged in the crucible of frontier and territorial commerce crystallized in banking. As noted in the preface to this book, Oklahoma City civic leader Henry Overholser characterized his adopted city as "a businessman's town" whose "people are for anything that will help business."[10] George Patterson (also known as Kemoha) was equally prescient when he described Oklahoma as "home to the bullshitter and the wildcatter. You've always had the gambling spirit in Oklahoma."[11] Although they drew on different cultural traditions, Overholser and Patterson were on the same page when it came to expressing values that shaped Oklahoma banking and commerce. To add a dash of sociological seasoning to the mix, those values can be distilled into five themes that pervade the state's pioneer banking narrative: (1) tolerance for risk; (2) self-reliance and its corollary in wariness toward outsiders; (3) a willingness to experiment; (4) egalitarianism, with due deference to social norms that excluded huge swaths of the population; and (5) regional pride bordering on jingoism. Those themes were apparent to some of the frontier's most prescient observers, including Tocqueville, Turner, and Bryce in the nineteenth century and Weber at the dawn of the twentieth. Nowhere were they expressed more clearly than in the Twin Territories, where frontier values survived the union of east and west to form the deepest stratum of Oklahoma's commercial culture.

The through-line, of course, is the dynamic tension between capitalism and democracy. Rarely has history offered a more robust laboratory for the problematic and shifting relationship between these pillars of the great American experiment than bartering and banking on the Oklahoma frontier. Just as the generation of 1789 spawned theories about American exceptionalism in the community of nations, so, too, did frontier values forged at the contested intersection of capitalism and democracy render Oklahoma a unique place to do business.

As promised, I have relied heavily on social history derived from journalism and oral histories to weave this narrative. Through the experiences and observations of non-Indian settlers, bankers, and businessmen, it is possible to discern the genesis of a commercial culture based on risk taking, self-reliance, egalitarianism, and a penchant for experimentation.

Those values hardened into something akin to ideology against a deluge of bad publicity that branded the Twin Territories as a risky venue for commerce. As anyone who has spent more than a few minutes in Oklahoma knows, deep-rooted values came to express themselves in an extraordinary pride of place. Well into the twenty-first century, "sooner pride" remained central to Oklahomans' sense of who they are, where they come from, and what they stand for.

Relying on precedent when possible or expedient and frontier ingenuity when all else failed, Oklahoma's pioneer bankers created and participated in a distinctive brand of resource allocation. It was left to later generations to figure out what to do with it. And the tug-of-war between capitalism and democracy? It seems safe to say that the tension never let up, and it continued to shape Oklahoma's commercial culture long after the wedding bells of 1907 fell silent. It certainly gave the newlyweds something to think about as they began their new lives together.

Notes

PREFACE

Epigraph: Angie Debo, *Prairie City: The Story of an American Community* (Tulsa: Council Oak Books, 1985), 3.

1. Joyce Appleby, *The Relentless Revolution: A History of Capitalism* (New York: W. W. Norton, 2010), 14, 20–26.

2. Tocqueville quoted in Leo Damrosch, *Tocqueville's Discovery of America* (New York: Farrar, Straus and Giroux, 2010), 143.

3. Coolidge quoted in Appleby, *Relentless Revolution,* 197.

4. Overholser quoted in Albert McRill, *And Satan Came Also: An Inside Story of a City's Social and Political History* (Oklahoma City: Britton Publishing, 1955), 58.

5. Patterson quoted in Phillip L. Zweig, *Belly Up: The Collapse of the Penn Square Bank* (New York: Crown, 1985), 87.

6. Alexis de Tocqueville, *Democracy in America,* ed. Phillips Bradley (New York: Knopf, 1945), 1:3.

7. Robert B. Reich, *Supercapitalism: The Transformation of Business, Democracy, and Everyday Life* (New York: Vintage Books, 2008), 4. Robert B. Reich served as secretary of labor during the Clinton administration. He was later named as Chancellor's Professor of Public Policy at the Goldman School of Public Policy at the University of California, Berkeley.

8. H. W. Brands, *American Colossus: The Triumph of Capitalism, 1865–1900* (New York: Anchor Books, 2010), 5.

9. Hayes quoted in Jack Beatty, *Age of Betrayal: The Triumph of Money in America, 1865–1900* (New York: Vintage Books, 2008), xv.

10. Lease quoted in ibid., 318.

11. Stiglitz quoted in Robert Borosage and Katrina vanden Heuvel, "The American Dream: Can a Movement Save It?" *Nation,* October 10, 2011, 11.

12. John Marshall, interview by author and Rodger Harris, May 1, 2009, Oklahoma City, Oklahoma.

CHAPTER 1

Epigraph: Jefferson quoted in Robert F. Bruner and Sean D. Carr, *The Panic of 1907: Lessons Learned from the Market's Perfect Storm* (Hoboken, N.J.: Wiley, 2007), 146, 236n18.

1. General Charles Cornwallis to Sir Henry Clinton, October 20, 1781, Yorktown, Virginia, in Henry B. Dawson, "Siege and Surrender of Yorktown (A.D. 1781)," in *The Great Events by Famous Historians,* ed. Rossiter Johnson (New York: National Alumni, 1905), 14:114.

2. Ibid., 111.

3. Ibid., 114–15.

4. Robert E. Wright, *The First Wall Street: Chestnut Street, Philadelphia, and the Birth of American Finance* (Chicago: University of Chicago Press, 2005), 47.

5. John Steele Gordon, *An Empire of Wealth: The Epic History of American Economic Power* (New York: Harper Perennial, 2005), 45.

6. Quoted in Davis Rich Dewey, *Financial History of the United States* (New York: Longmans, Green, 1931), 19.

7. Gordon, *Empire of Wealth,* 42; Shirley Donald Southworth and John M. Chapman, *Banking Facilities for Bankless Towns* (New York: American Economists Council for the Study of Branch Banking, 1941), 8–9.

8. Gordon, *Empire of Wealth,* 44; Murray N. Rothbard, *A History of Money and Banking in the United States: The Colonial Era to World War II* (Auburn, Ala.: Ludwig von Mises Institute, 2002), 49.

9. Dewey, *Financial History,* 20.

10. Robert E. Wright, *Origins of Commercial Banking in America, 1750–1800* (Lanham, Md.: Rowman and Littlefield, 2001), 20.

11. Gordon, *Empire of Wealth,* 44.

12. Dewey, *Financial History,* 20–21.

13. Ibid., 8.

14. Wright, *First Wall Street,* 33.

15. Robert E. Wright and David J. Cowen, *Financial Founding Fathers: The Men who Made America Rich* (Chicago: University of Chicago Press, 2006), 188.

16. Rothbard, *History of Money and Banking,* 51.

17. Dewey, *Financial History,* 22–24.

18. Gordon, *Empire of Wealth,* 46–47.

19. Rothbard, *History of Money and Banking,* 53.

20. Ibid., 59.

21. Gordon, *Empire of Wealth,* 60; Bray Hammond, *Banks and Politics in America from the Revolution to the Civil War* (Princeton: Princeton University Press, 1957), 29.

22. Paul Johnson, *A History of the American People* (New York: HarperCollins, 1997), 187–88.

23. Hammond, *Banks and Politics,* 50.

24. Lawrence Lewis Jr., "Establishment of the United States Bank, A.D. 1791," in Johnson, *Great Events,* 14:230.

25. Wright and Cowen, *Financial Founding Fathers,* 16.

26. Paine quoted in Hammond, *Banks and Politics,* 60.

27. Gordon, *Empire of Wealth,* 53.

28. Wright, *First Wall Street,* 36.

29. H. W. Brands, *The Money Men: Capitalism, Democracy, and the Hundred Years' War over the American Dollar* (New York: W. W. Norton, 2006), 22.

30. Ibid., 30–31.

31. Hamilton quoted in Hammond, *Banks and Politics,* 36.

32. Gordon, *Empire of Wealth,* 68–71.

33. Hammond, *Banks and Politics,* 101.

34. Ibid., 66–67.

35. Ibid., 72.

36. Wright and Cowen, *Financial Founding Fathers,* 16.

37. Dewey, *Financial History,* 99; Hammond, *Banks and Politics,* 114–15; Rothbard, *History of Money and Banking,* 68.

38. Hamilton quoted in Paul B. Trescott, *Financing American Enterprise: The Story of Commercial Banking* (New York: Harper & Row, 1963), 2.

39. Dewey, *Financial History,* 99.

40. Wright, *Origins of Commercial Banking,* 27.

41. Adams quoted in Hammond, *Banks and Politics,* 196; John Steele Gordon, *Hamilton's Blessing: The Extraordinary Life and Times of Our National Debt* (New York: Walker, 2010), 26.

42. Adams quoted in Gordon, *Hamilton's Blessing,* 17.

43. Hammond, *Banks and Politics,* 103.

44. Wright and Cowen, *Financial Founding Fathers,* 11.

45. Hammond, *Banks and Politics,* 114–18.

46. Hamilton quoted in Wright and Cowen, *Financial Founding Fathers,* 13.

47. Dewey, *Financial History,* 98–101; Gordon, *Empire of Wealth,* 77.

48. The South Sea Company was a British joint-stock company that traded in South America during the eighteenth century. Founded in 1711, the company was granted a monopoly to trade in Spain's South American colonies as part of a treaty during the War of Spanish Succession. In return, the company assumed the national debt England had incurred during the war. Speculation in the company's stock led in 1720 to a great economic bubble known as the South Sea Bubble, which led many down the path of financial ruin.

49. Wright and Cowen, *Financial Founding Fathers,* 27–30.

50. Washington quoted in James MacGregor Burns, *The Vineyard of Liberty* (New York: Knopf, 1982), 134.

51. Joseph J. Ellis, *American Creation: Triumphs and Tragedies at the Founding of the Republic* (New York: Random House, 2007), 170.

52. Jefferson quoted in Bruner and Carr, *Panic of 1907,* 146, 236n18.

53. Dewey, *Financial History,* 73.

54. Ibid., 100; Gordon, *Empire of Wealth,* 116; Hammond, *Banks and Politics,* 127.

55. Hammond, *Banks and Politics,* 144–45.

56. Ibid., 168–70.

57. Wright, *First Wall Street,* 67.

58. Rothbard, *History of Money and Banking,* 67.

59. Hamilton quoted in Wright and Cowen, *Financial Founding Fathers,* 30.

60. Wright, *First Wall Street,* 70.

61. Alston quoted in Hammond, *Banks and Politics,* 218.

62. Ibid., 172; Dewey, *Financial History,* 127.

63. Gordon, *Empire of Wealth,* 120–21; Hammond, *Banks and Politics,* 172–78.

64. Desha quoted in Hammond, *Banks and Politics,* 176.

65. Ibid., 210.

66. Dewey, *Financial History,* 144–45.

67. Rothbard, *History of Money and Banking,* 83.

68. Dewey, *Financial History,* 150–51; Arthur M. Schlesinger Jr., *The Almanac of American History* (New York: Putnam, 1983), 203–204.

69. Wright and Cowen, *Financial Founding Fathers,* 165.

70. Hammond, *Banks and Politics,* 264–68; Rothbard, *History of Money and Banking,* 70n37.

71. Wright and Cowen, *Financial Founding Fathers,* 176; Dewey, *Financial History,* 150–53; Hammond, *Banks and Politics,* 262–68.

72. Hammond, *Banks and Politics,* 340–41.

73. Benton quoted in ibid., 37.

74. David Dary, *The Santa Fe Trail: Its History, Legends, and Lore* (New York: Knopf, 2000), 152.

75. Gordon, *Empire of Wealth,* 122; Rothbard, *History of Money and Banking,* 78.

76. Howard Bodenhorn, *A History of Banking in Antebellum America: Financial Markets and Economic Development in an Era of Nation-Building* (New York: Cambridge University Press, 2000), 215.

77. Joseph J. Ellis, *After the Revolution: Profiles of Early American Culture* (New York: W. W. Norton, 2002), 29.

78. Brands, *Money Men,* 15–17.

CHAPTER 2

Epigraph: Anonymous source quoted in Wright, *First Wall Street,* 77.

1. Hamilton quoted in Joseph J. Ellis, *Founding Brothers: The Revolutionary Generation* (New York: Random House, 2000), 20–25.

2. Bartlett Naylor, "Bankers Spilled Blood in Nation's Early Years," in *Banking's Past, Financial Services' Future,* ed. William Zimmerman (New York: American Banker, 1986), 18; Hammond, *Banks and Politics,* 385.

3. Gallatin quoted in Dewey, *Financial History,* 153–54.

4. Hammond, *Banks and Politics,* 289.

5. Wright and Cowen, *Financial Founding Fathers,* 176–77.

6. Hammond, *Banks and Politics,* 291–92.

7. Ibid., 412.

8. Wright and Cowen, *Financial Founding Fathers,* 178.

9. Rush quoted in Dewey, *Financial History,* 157.

10. Smith quoted in Robert V. Remini, *The Life of Andrew Jackson* (New York: Harper-Collins, 2009), 178–81. The complete text of Margaret Bayard Smith's letter to Mrs. Kirkpatrick, dated March 11, 1829, can be found on the website of the White House Historical Association, s.v. "A Letter of Margaret Bayard Smith to Mrs. Kirkpatrick," http://www .whitehousehistory.org/whha_classroom/classroom_documents-1828_g.html. Much of what we know about polite society in the age of Jackson comes from Margaret Bayard Smith's astute and often hilarious commentary. See Jon Meacham, *American Lion: Andrew Jackson in the White House* (New York: Random House, 2008).

11. Story quoted in James Parton, "Jackson Elected President of the United States, A.D. 1828," in Johnson, *Great Events,* 16:149.

12. Jackson quoted in Hammond, *Banks and Politics,* 381.

13. Dewey, *Financial History,* 198–201.

14. Meacham, *American Lion,* 272.

15. Jackson quoted in ibid., 201. Emphasis Meacham's.

16. Benton quoted in Hammond, *Banks and Politics,* 259.

17. Kendall quoted in ibid., 334.

18. Taney quoted in ibid., 338.

19. Jackson quoted in Dewey, *Financial History,* 203; see also Hammond, *Banks and Politics,* 405–10.

20. Rothbard, *History of Money and Banking,* 93.

21. Biddle quoted in Hammond, *Banks and Politics,* 438.

22. Biddle quoted in Remini, *Life of Andrew Jackson,* 229.

23. Ibid., 274.

24. Jackson quoted in ibid., 274–75; and in Meacham, *American Lion,* 278.

25. Hammond, *Banks and Politics,* 439.

26. Paul Studenski and Herman E. Krooss, *Financial History of the United States* (New York: McGraw-Hill, 1963), 107.

27. Hammond, *Banks and Politics,* ix.

28. Anonymous source quoted in Naylor, "Bankers Spilled Blood," 20; and in Trescott, *Financing American Enterprise,* 17.

29. Naylor, "Bankers Spilled Blood," 23.

30. Gordon, *Empire of Wealth,* 130.

31. Schlesinger, *Almanac,* 235.

32. Charles W. Calomiris, *U.S. Bank Deregulation in Historical Perspective* (Cambridge: Cambridge University Press, 2000), 96.

33. Henry Dunning Macleod, *The Theory of Credit* (London: Longmans, Green, 1894), vol. 2, pt. 1, 630.

34. Naylor, "Bankers Spilled Blood," 18.

35. Studenski and Krooss, *Financial History,* 122; Hammond, *Banks and Politics,* 705–707.

36. Macleod, *Theory of Credit,* vol. 2, pt. 1, 629–30.

37. Calomiris, *U.S. Bank Deregulation,* 105–106.

38. Naylor, "Bankers Spilled Blood," 20; Southworth and Chapman, *Banking Facilities,* 10–11.

39. Locofocos quoted in Hammond, *Banks and Politics,* 493.

40. Locofocos quoted in ibid., 495.

41. Naylor, "Bankers Spilled Blood," 23. Contemporary scholarship indicates that branch banking lessens the effects of economic shocks in countries that allow it. Studies of Canada indicate that, "in the presence of a stable branch-banking system, financial shocks were not magnified by their effects on bank risk and, therefore, had more limited effects on economic activity." See Calomiris, *U.S. Bank Deregulation,* 101–102.

42. Editor quoted in Dary, *Santa Fe Trail,* 152. Emphasis in original.

43. Ibid., 152–53.

44. Ibid., 155.

45. Naylor, "Bankers Spilled Blood," 22–23.

46. McCulloch quoted in Hammond, *Banks and Politics,* 619.

47. Ibid., 338, 572–73.

48. Anonymous source quoted in Wright, *First Wall Street,* 77.

49. Dewey, *Financial History,* 155. Martin Van Buren, then senator from New York, was elected as governor at the same time as Andrew Jackson's election to the presidency. He served for only a few weeks before resigning and taking his place at the head of Jackson's Kitchen Cabinet. See Hammond, *Banks and Politics,* 351–52.

50. A. Piatt Andrew, "The Crux of the Currency Question," *Yale Review,* n.s., vol. 2 (July 1913): 600.

51. Thomas Bruce Robb, *The Guaranty of Bank Deposits* (Boston: Houghton Mifflin, 1921), 12.

52. Wright and Cowen, *Financial Founding Fathers,* 184–85.

53. Bodenhorn, *History of Banking,* 218–19.

54. Walker quoted in Dewey, *Financial History,* 257.

55. Corwin quoted in Hammond, *Banks and Politics,* 605.

56. Ibid., 617.

57. Studenski and Krooss, *Financial History,* 121.

58. Gouge quoted in Hammond, *Banks and Politics,* 607–608. Emphasis in original.

59. Dewey, *Financial History,* 262.

60. Naylor, "Bankers Spilled Blood," 24.

61. Trescott, *Financing American Enterprise,* 30.

62. Ibid., 38.

63. Quoted in ibid., 22.

64. Hammond, *Banks and Politics,* 698.

65. Gouge quoted in ibid., 679–80.

66. Naylor, "Bankers Spilled Blood," 24.

67. Chase quoted in ibid.

68. Calomiris, *U.S. Bank Deregulation,* 353; Hammond, *Banks and Politics,* 727.

69. *New York Tribune* quoted in Hammond, *Banks and Politics,* 727.

70. U.S. Office of the Comptroller of the Currency, *The National Bank Act, and other Laws Relating to National Banks, from the Revised Statutes of the United States; with Amendments and Additional Acts,* comp. Edward Wolcott (Washington: Government Printing Office, 1882), chapter 1, page 5, section 324.

71. Trescott, *Financing American Enterprise,* 48.

72. *National Banking Act,* chapter 1, page 5, section 324.

73. Ibid., chapter 1, page 7, section 333.

74. Trescott, *Financing American Enterprise,* 51.

75. Ibid., 21.

76. Sherman quoted in ibid., 53; see also Hammond, *Banks and Politics,* 733.

77. *Chicago Tribune* quoted in Hammond, *Banks and Politics,* 733.

78. Trescott, *Financing American Enterprise,* 53.

79. Rothbard, *History of Money and Banking,* 144–47.

80. Trescott, *Financing American Enterprise,* 55.

81. Ibid., 54–59.

82. U.S. Office of the Comptroller of the Currency, *Instructions and Suggestions of the Comptroller of the Currency in Regard to the Organization, Extension, and Management of National Banks* (Washington: Government Printing Office, 1884), revised statutes, page 26, section 5138.

83. Ibid., pages 29–30, section 5200.

84. Trescott, *Financing American Enterprise,* 10–11.

85. Wright, *Origins of Commercial Banking,* 111–13.

86. Bodenhorn, *History of Banking,* 45–53.

87. Ibid., 225–26.

88. Studenski and Krooss, *Financial History,* 108.

89. Tocqueville quoted in Damrosch, *Tocqueville's Discovery of America,* 136.

90. Tocqueville quoted in ibid., 138.

CHAPTER 3

Epigraph: Joseph B. Thoburn, "Steamboating on the Upper Arkansas," *Sturm's Oklahoma Magazine,* n.d., folder 7, box 33, Thoburn Collection, Research Division, Oklahoma Historical Society, Oklahoma City (hereafter cited as Thoburn Collection).

1. "Told of the Pioneer Days," unsourced newspaper article, dated by hand "December 21, 1915," folder 7, box 33, Thoburn Collection.

2. Ibid.

3. "Chouteaus Were Pioneer Trappers," unsourced and undated newspaper article, folder 19, box 6, Frederick Samuel Barde Collection, 1890–1916, Research Division, Oklahoma Historical Society, Oklahoma City (hereafter cited as Barde Collection).

4. Muriel H. Wright, "Early Navigation and Commerce along the Arkansas and Red Rivers in Oklahoma," *Chronicles of Oklahoma* 8, no. 1 (March 1930): 65.

5. Ibid., 66; "Chouteaus Were Pioneer Trappers"; Joseph B. Thoburn, "Trappers, Traders and the Epoch of Oklahoma Fur Trade," folder 13, box 10, 1–2, Barde Collection.

6. Wright, "Early Navigation and Commerce," 65–66; Thoburn, "Steamboating."

7. Thoburn, "Trappers, Traders," 2–3.

8. Douglas A. Hurt, "Brothers of Influence: Auguste and Pierre Chouteau and the Osages before 1804," *Chronicles of Oklahoma* 78, no. 3 (Fall 2000): 264–65.

9. Ibid., 266.

10. Wright, "Early Navigation and Commerce," 66–67.

11. Ibid., 66n2.

12. Hurt, "Brothers of Influence," 270.

13. Jno. B. Treat to the Honorable Henry Dearborn, secretary of war, July 13, 1806, folder 16, box 7, Carolyn Foreman Collection, Research Division, Oklahoma Historical Society, Oklahoma City (hereafter cited as Carolyn Foreman Collection).

14. Ibid.

15. Ibid.

16. Ibid.

17. Edwin C. McReynolds, *Oklahoma: A History of the Sooner State* (Norman: University of Oklahoma Press, 1954), 63; *Encyclopedia of Oklahoma History and Culture,* s.v. "Chouteau, Auguste Pierre (1786–1838)," by Douglas A. Hurt, http://digital.library.okstate.edu/encyclopedia/entries/C/CH057.html.

18. Hurt, "Brothers of Influence," 272–73; McReynolds, *Oklahoma: A History,* 62–65.

19. McReynolds, *Oklahoma: A History,* 63–64.

20. Washington Irving, *A Tour on the Prairies,* ed. John Francis McDermott (Norman: University of Oklahoma Press, 1956), 22–23.

21. Houston quoted in Grant Foreman, "Nathaniel Pryor," *Chronicles of Oklahoma* 7, no. 2 (June 1929): 162–63.

22. Houston quoted in ibid., 163.

23. Thoburn, "Steamboating."

24. McReynolds, *Oklahoma: A History,* 72–73.

25. Thoburn, "Steamboating."

26. Ibid.

27. Wright, "Early Navigation and Commerce," 70. Wright reports that four steamboats preceded the *Facility* to Fort Gibson in 1827. See also Thoburn, "Steamboating."

28. "Chouteaus Were Pioneer Trappers."

29. Thoburn, "Steamboating."

30. Dary, *Santa Fe Trail,* 162–63.

31. Howard F. Van Zandt, "The History of Camp Holmes and Chouteau's Trading Post," *Chronicles of Oklahoma* 13, no. 3 (September 1935): 317.

32. Ibid., 316–19.

33. Thoburn, "Trappers, Traders," 5.

34. Van Zandt, "History," 322; *Encyclopedia of Oklahoma History and Culture,* s.v. "Chouteau, Auguste Pierre."

35. Wright, "Early Navigation and Commerce," 77–81.

36. Shreve quoted in ibid., 81.

37. Thoburn, "Steamboating."

38. Wright, "Early Navigation and Commerce," 75.

39. Thoburn, "Steamboating."

40. Ibid.

41. Ibid.

42. "Webbers Falls . . . Rich in History," *Five Star News,* September 16, 1992, History File, in Jim Lucas Checotah Public Library, Checotah, Oklahoma.

43. The story of the sinking of the *Lucy Walker* was told by Oklahoma historian Clyde (or perhaps Claude) E. Hensely on the ninetieth anniversary of the disaster that was celebrated in Webbers Falls, Oklahoma, during the week of October 22, 1934. See "State Once Had Major Steanboat [*sic*] Tragedy," *Guymon Daily News,* October 21, 1934, folder 7, box 33, Thoburn Collection.

44. Ibid.

45. Thoburn, "Steamboating."

46. Alex Sykes, interview by L. W. Wilson, January 25, 1937, vol. 88, 578, in Indian-Pioneer Papers, Western History Collections, University of Oklahoma, Norman (http://digital.libraries.ou.edu/whc/pioneer/, hereafter cited as IPP online). The Indian-Pioneer Papers are also available on microfilm in the research library at the Oklahoma Historical Society, Oklahoma City (hereafter cited as IPP microfilm).

47. Bill Swimm, interview by L. W. Wilson, April 13, 1937, vol. 88, 550, IPP online.

48. B. M. Palmer, interview by L. W. Wilson, February 15, 1937, vol. 69, 60, IPP online.

49. Ibid., 61.

50. Ibid., 60.

51. Louis R. Jobe, interview by L. W. Wilson, n.d., vol. 48, 139, IPP online.

52. Lem W. Oakes, interview by Hazel B. Greene, April 12, 1937, vol. 68, 28, IPP online.

53. Ibid., 31.

54. "The Osage Chouteaus," newspaper submission, January 20, 1904, folder 19, box 6; Scrapbook, January 10–July 30, 1904, box 42, vol. 12, 5, Barde Collection.

55. Ibid.

56. Ibid.

57. Ibid.

CHAPTER 4

Epigraph: W. B. Napton, "The Santa Fe Trail, 1857, Part 1," *Kansas City Star,* January 12, 1902, folder 8, box 32, Thoburn Collection.

1. John Thompson, *Closing the Frontier: Radical Response in Oklahoma, 1889–1923* (Nor-

man: University of Oklahoma Press, 1986), 6. A succinct account of the Treaties of 1866 can be found in McReynolds, *Oklahoma: A History,* 229–34.

2. Long quoted in Henry Pickering Walker, *The Wagonmasters: High Plains Freighting from the Earliest Days of the Santa Fe Trail to 1880* (Norman: University of Oklahoma Press, 1966), 3–6.

3. Quoted in ibid., 116.

4. Dary, *Santa Fe Trail,* 92.

5. Ibid., 89–92.

6. Harris quoted in Donald Kaye, "Specie on the Santa Fe Trail," *Wagon Tracks* 14 (August 2000): 10.

7. Craig Crease, "Boom Times for Freighters on the Santa Fe Trail, 1848–1866," *Wagon Tracks* 23 (February 2009): 16.

8. *La jornado del muerto* translates as "the journey of death."

9. Josiah Gregg, *Commerce of the Prairies,* ed. Milo Milton Quaife (Lincoln: University of Nebraska Press, 1967), 8. Gregg was among the earliest and most frequent travelers on the Santa Fe Trail. His firsthand account of the Santa Fe trade, *Commerce of the Prairies,* was first published in two volumes simultaneously in New York and London in 1844. See Quaife's "Historical Introduction" to the book, specifically page xii.

10. David K. Clapsaddle, "'Cimarron Cutoff,' a 20th-Century Misnomer," *Wagon Tracks* 23 (May 2009): 26.

11. James E. Hudson, "Camp Nichols: Oklahoma's Outpost on the Santa Fe Trail," *Wagon Tracks* 14 (November 1999): 12.

12. Dary, *Santa Fe Trail,* endpapers.

13. Harry C. Myers, "As the Wheel Turns: The Evolution of Freighting on the Santa Fe Trail, An Introduction," *Wagon Tracks* 23 (November 2008), 8.

14. Crease, "Boom Times for Freighters," 20.

15. Ibid.

16. David K. Clapsaddle, "Old Dan and his Traveling Companions: Oxen on the Santa Fe Trail," *Wagon Tracks* 22 (February 2008): 10. For a firsthand description of these "exceedingly whimsical creatures," see Gregg, *Commerce of the Prairies,* 41, 95.

17. John T. Faws (?), "Freighting on the Plains," unsourced and undated article, folder 8, box 32, Thoburn Collection.

18. Crease, "Boom Times for Freighters," 21.

19. Phyllis Morgan, "Buffalo on the Santa Fe Trail," *Wagon Tracks* 18 (May 2004): 6.

20. Napton, "Santa Fe Trail, 1857, Part 1."

21. Morgan, "Buffalo on the Santa Fe Trail," 6.

22. Napton, "Santa Fe Trail, 1857, Part 1."

23. "Stories of Freighters: Life on the Santa Fe Trail in Early Days," unsourced and undated newspaper article, Scrapbook, May 6–November 10, 1897, box 36, vol. 1, 21, Barde Collection.

24. Walker, *Wagonmasters,* 3.

25. Ibid., 91.

26. "Stories of Freighters."

27. Napton, "Santa Fe Trail, 1857, Part 1."

28. Quoted in Walker, *Wagonmasters,* 129.

29. Gregg, *Commerce of the Prairies,* 72.

30. Napton, "Santa Fe Trail, 1857, Part 1."

31. Ibid.

32. McReynolds, *Oklahoma: A History,* 71; "Stories of Freighters."

33. Walker, *Wagonmasters,* 148.

34. "Stories of Freighters."

35. Walker, *Wagonmasters,* 48.

36. Napton, "Santa Fe Trail, 1857, Part 1."

37. Ibid., "The Santa Fe Trail, 1857, Part 2," *Kansas City Star,* January 12, 1902, Thoburn Collection.

38. Ibid., "Santa Fe Trail, 1857, Part 1."

39. Quoted in Walker, *Wagonmasters,* 73–74.

40. Gregg, *Commerce of the Prairies,* 102.

41. Emily E. Kieta, "The New Mexican Fandango," *Wagon Tracks* 19 (May 2005): 11–15.

42. Quoted in Walker, *Wagonmasters,* 154.

43. Napton, "Santa Fe Trail, 1857, Part 2."

44. Ibid.

45. Ibid., "Santa Fe Trail, 1857, Part 1."

46. Ibid.

47. M. C. Gottschalk, "Pioneer Merchants of the Las Vegas Plaza: The Booming Trail Days," *Wagon Tracks* 16 (February 2002): 8–19.

48. Ellis J. Smith, "When Rails Replaced the Santa Fe Trail," *Wagon Tracks* 12 (February 1998): 24.

49. Dary, *Santa Fe Trail,* 292.

50. *Junction City Union* quoted in Ralph P. Bieber, "Some Aspects of the Santa Fe Trail, 1848–1880," *Chronicles of Oklahoma* 2, no. 1 (March 1924): 5.

51. Napton, "Santa Fe Trail, 1857, Part 2."

52. Ibid., "Santa Fe Trail, 1857, Part 1."

53. *Encyclopedia of Oklahoma History and Culture,* s.v. "Warren's Post," by Larry O'Dell, http://digital.library.okstate.edu/encyclopedia/entries/W/WA027.html.

54. W. H. Clift, "Warren's Trading Post," *Chronicles of Oklahoma* 2, no. 2 (June 1924): 129.

55. Ibid., 132–33.

56. Ibid., 133–34.

57. Ibid., 135–40. Even though kidnappings occurred with some frequency on the Texas plains, none reverberated farther and wider than Cynthia Ann Parker's two abductions. Her first abduction occurred in May 1836 near present-day Mexia, Texas, northeast of Waco, when a band of Comanches snatched the nine-year-old girl from her Anglo family and raised her as one of their own. The blonde-haired, blue-eyed child eventually became the wife of a prominent war chief, Peta Nocona, and bore him three children, one of whom was the famed Quanah Parker. Cynthia Ann, known to her adopted Comanche kin as Naudah, was abducted a second time in the fall of 1860 by a party of Texas Rangers along the Pease River near present-day Crowell, Texas. Torn once again from the ones she loved, Cynthia Ann, now a mature woman of thirty-four, gained lasting celebrity for resisting assimilation into what was for her, by then, an alien culture. See Larry C. Floyd, "Quanah Parker's Star House: A Comanche Home along the White Man's Road," *Chronicles of Oklahoma* 90, no. 2 (Summer 2012): 134.

58. Ibid., 135.

59. Stan Hoig, "Jesse Chisholm: Peace-Maker, Trader, Forgotten Frontiersman," *Chronicles of Oklahoma* 66, no. 4 (Winter 1988): 352–57.

60. *Encyclopedia of Oklahoma History and Culture,* s.v. "Chisholm, Jesse (ca. 1805–1868)," by Stan Hoig, http://digital.library.okstate.edu/encyclopedia/entries/C/CH067.html.

61. Hoig, "Jesse Chisholm: Peace-Maker," 361.

62. Ibid., 362.

63. Whipple quoted in ibid., 364.

64. Waco chief quoted in ibid., 366.

65. Ibid., 351.

66. Mead quoted in ibid., 351, 370.

67. Michael Tower, "Traders along the Washita: A Short History of the Shirley Trading Company," *Chronicles of Oklahoma* 65, no. 1 (Spring 1987): 6.

68. Ibid., 8–9.

69. *Encyclopedia of Oklahoma History and Culture,* s.v. "Shirley Trading Company," by Michael Tower, http://digital.library.okstate.edu/encyclopedia/entries/S/SH026.html.

70. Ibid.; Tower, "Traders along the Washita," 13.

71. "Kiowa, Comanche and Apache Payment," *Fort Smith Weekly Elevator,* February 17, 1893, folder 15, box 7, Carolyn Foreman Collection.

72. R. A. Sneed, "The Reminiscences of an Indian Trader," *Chronicles of Oklahoma* 14, no. 2 (June 1936): 135.

73. Ibid., 136.

74. Ibid., 140.

75. Ibid.

76. Ibid., 142.

77. Ibid.

78. Ibid., 142–43.

79. Ibid., 154.

CHAPTER 5

Epigraph: W. A. West, interview by Robert W. Small, October 28, 1937, vol. 96, 481, IPP online.

1. *Encyclopedia of Oklahoma History and Culture,* s.v. "Kiowa-Comanche-Apache Opening," by Benjamin R. Kracht, http://digital.library.okstate.edu/encyclopedia/entries/K/KI020.html.

2. Kate Goodman, interview by Ruby Wolfenbarger, November 23, 1937, vol. 34, 446–47, IPP online.

3. Ibid., 447.

4. Ibid., 448.

5. Charles E. Boyer, interview by Ophelia D. Vestal, October 27, 1937, vol. 10, 144, IPP online.

6. Ibid., 147.

7. Ibid., 148.

8. Morris Brown, interview by James Russell Gray, December 10, 1937, vol. 12, 153, IPP online.

9. Ibid., 155.

10. Ibid., 154–55.

11. Ibid., 155.

12. Bell Haney Airington, interview by Lula Austin, October 25, 1937, vol. 1, 342, IPP online.

13. Hoyette North White, interview by Amelia F. Harris, July 16, 1937, vol. 97, 167, IPP online.

14. Ibid., 167–68.

15. Michael J. Hightower, "The Businessman's Frontier: C. C. Hightower, Commerce, and Old Greer County, 1891–1903," *Chronicles of Oklahoma* 86, no. 1 (Spring 2008): 20.

16. Lucy Sweet Wilson, interview by Ruth Kerbo, April 13, 1937, vol. 50, 218, IPP microfilm.

17. Ibid., 222.

18. Clara Tuton, interview by Ruth Kerbo, July 27, 1937, vol. 92, 426, IPP online.

19. Ibid., 428.

20. R. Beaumont, interview by Ruth Kerbo, April 9, 1937, vol. 6, 254, IPP online.

21. Ibid., 251.

22. J. B. McReynolds, interview by Ruth Kerbo, August 20, 1937, vol. 59, 346–47, IPP online.

23. Gordon, *Empire of Wealth,* 45; Dewey, *Financial History,* 19.

24. Dr. G. P. Cherry, interview by Eunice M. Mayer, May 10, 1937, vol. 17, 364, IPP online.

25. Ibid., 365.

26. *Encyclopedia of Oklahoma History and Culture,* s.v. "Cherokee Outlet Opening," by Alvin O. Turner, http://digital.library.okstate.edu/encyclopedia/entries/C/CH021.html.

27. Neely Mason, interview by Linnaeus B. Ranck, February 1, 1938, vol. 61, 67, IPP online.

28. In June 1952, Oklahoma State Bank of Buffalo vice president and cashier Walter Litz sent bank examiner E. H. Kelley a facsimile of a Lee and Reynolds trade check. His rummaging in the bank's archives also produced coins and a 101 Ranch check, drawn on the Winfield National Bank in Winfield, Kansas, and used as legal tender in the Cherokee Outlet, which he enclosed with the facsimile. As an amateur historian, Kelley planned to use currency and coins, along with other territorial trade relics, for a banking exhibit at the Oklahoma Historical Society. See Walter Litz to E. H. Kelley, June 21, 1952; and miscellaneous correspondence pertaining to banking exhibit, folder 11, box 8, all in E. H. Kelley Collection, Research Division, Oklahoma Historical Society, Oklahoma City (hereafter cited as Kelley Collection).

29. W. A. West, interview by Robert W. Small, October 28, 1937, vol. 96, 480–81, IPP online.

30. Ibid., 481.

31. Alexis de Tocqueville, *Democracy in America,* ed. Phillips Bradley (New York: Knopf, 1945), 1:3.

32. Nix quoted in Danney Goble, *Progressive Oklahoma* (Norman: University of Oklahoma Press, 1980), 36.

33. Andrew Oiler Crist, interview by Elizabeth L. Duncan, July 14, 1937, vol. 21, 493, IPP online.

34. Ibid., 495. Perhaps it is only coincidence that Mr. Crist was interviewed on July 14, 1937, the 148th anniversary of the fall of the Bastille in 1789, when the *sans-culottes* of Paris signaled their displeasure with the ancient regime by tearing down France's most reviled institution to leave posterity with a potent symbol of revolution. One wonders if any of those desperate homesteaders in the Cherokee Outlet stopped to think about rebellions in other times and places, when violence seemed to be the only way out of a tight spot.

35. Ibid., 496.

36. *Encyclopedia of Oklahoma History and Culture,* s.v. "Chickasaw," by James P. Pate, http://digital.library.okstate.edu/encyclopedia/entries/C/CH033.html.

37. Zack Redford, interview by Grace Kelley, December 21, 1937, vol. 74, 467, IPP online.

38. Ibid., 470.

39. Ibid., 471.

40. C. B. Queid, interview by Johnson H. Hampton, November 24, 1937, vol. 41, 68, IPP microfilm.

41. J. M. Lane, interview by John F. Dougherty, February 10, 1938, vol. 52, 261, IPP online.

42. Ibid., 262.

43. Ibid., 264.

44. Ibid., 265–66.

45. *Encyclopedia of Oklahoma History and Culture,* s.v. "Choctaw," by Clara Sue Kidwell, http://digital.library.okstate.edu/encyclopedia/entries/C/CH047.html.

46. W. C. Riggs, "Bits of Interesting History," *Chronicles of Oklahoma* 7, no. 2 (June 1929): 149.

47. Goble, *Progressive Oklahoma,* 45; Angie Debo, *The Rise and Fall of the Choctaw Republic* (Norman: University of Oklahoma Press, 1934), 114–15.

48. Jesse Green Robb, interview by Gomer Gower, May 13, 1937, vol. 76, 404, IPP online.

49. Hiram Quigley, interview by Thad Smith Jr., April 7, 1937, vol. 8, 299, IPP microfilm.

50. E. K. Hargrave, interview by Augusta H. Custer, August 17, 1937, vol. 38, 353, IPP online.

51. William Allred, interview by Jimmie Birdwell, June 21, 1937, vol. 2, 223, IPP online.

52. *Encyclopedia of Oklahoma History and Culture,* s.v. "Creek (Mvskoke)," by Theodore Isham and Blue Clark, http://digital.library.okstate.edu/encyclopedia/entries/C/CR006 .html.

53. Goble, *Progressive Oklahoma,* 52.

54. Helga H. Harriman, "Economic Conditions in the Creek Nation, 1865–1871," *Chronicles of Oklahoma* 51, no. 3 (Fall 1973): 325–26.

55. Dunn quoted in ibid., 332.

56. Mrs. A. Faltinson, interview by Effie S. Jackson, March 23, 1937, vol. 29, 30, IPP online.

57. Ibid., 34.

58. Eliza Palmer, interview by Grace Kelley, September 20, 1937, vol. 69, 73, IPP online.

59. Duncan M. Aldrich, "General Stores, Retail Merchants, and Assimilation: Retail Trade in the Cherokee Nation, 1838–1890," *Chronicles of Oklahoma* 57, no. 2 (Summer 1979): 120.

60. Ibid., 121–22.

61. *Encyclopedia of Oklahoma History and Culture,* s.v. "Cherokee," by Rennard Strickland, http://digital.library.okstate.edu/encyclopedia/entries/C/CH014.html.

62. Ellalee Pore, interview by Alene D. McDowell, December 14, 1937, vol. 72, 164, IPP online.

63. Ibid., 163.

64. Ibid., 166.

65. Ibid., 168.

66. Glove Morris, interview by W. J. B. Bigby, August 12, 1937, vol. 65, 31, IPP online.

67. Ibid., 34–35.

68. Ibid., 35.

69. J. Justin Castro, "From the Tennessee River to Tahlequah: A Brief History of Cherokee Fiddling," *Chronicles of Oklahoma* 87, no. 4 (Winter 2009–2010): 388–407.

70. Aldrich, "General Stores," 124–26.

CHAPTER 6

Epigraph: Jake Simmons, interview by L. W. Wilson, n.d., vol. 83, 234, IPP online.

1. John Mack Faragher, "The Frontier Trail: Rethinking Turner and Reimagining the American West," *American Historical Review* 98, no. 1 (February 1993): 106–17.

2. Frederick Jackson Turner, *The Frontier in American History* (Franklin Center, Pa.: Franklin Library, 1977), 3.

3. Ibid.

4. Turner certainly acknowledged Old World influence in shaping the American character, but he insisted that it be examined in the context of America's unique development. In essence, he was calling into question the so-called germ theory that conferred primary importance on the European origins of New World societies and posited that American institutions evolved in the forests of Europe among Teutonic tribes. See George Wilson Pierson, "The Frontier and American Institutions: A Criticism of the Turner Theory," in *Turner and the Sociology of the Frontier,* ed. Richard Hofstadter and Seymour Martin Lipset (New York: Basic Books, 1968), 16–17; and Wilbur R. Jacobs, *On Turner's Trail: 100 Years of Writing Western History* (Lawrence: University Press of Kansas, 1994), 6.

5. Ray Allen Billington, *America's Frontier Heritage* (New York: Holt, Rinehart and Winston, 1966), 3.

6. Frontier historian John Mack Faragher described Turner's characterization of the frontier as a determining factor in American character development as "the single most influential piece of writing in the history of American history." See John Mack Faragher, introduction to *Rereading Frederick Jackson Turner: "The Significance of the Frontier in American History" and Other Essays,* by Frederick Jackson Turner (New York: Henry Holt, 1994), 1. Walter Prescott Webb, who certainly ranks at the forefront of America's cadre of frontier historians, referred to Turner's paper as "the most influential single piece of historical writing ever done in the United States." See Walter Prescott Webb, *The Great Frontier* (Austin: University of Texas Press, 1964), 6. The resilience of the frontier thesis was perhaps best described by Ray Allen Billington when he wrote that, whatever their field of study, subsequent scholars "worshiped at Turner's shrine and glorified the frontier as a molding force that had shaped the course of civilization." See Billington, *America's Frontier Heritage,* 14–15.

7. For a fascinating exploration of Americans' antipathy to intellectuals, see Richard Hofstadter, *Anti-Intellectualism in American Life* (New York: Vintage Books, 1963).

8. Arrell M. Gibson, "The Homesteaders' Last Frontier," *American Scene* 4 (1962): 28.

9. Daniel J. Boorstin, *The Americans: The Democratic Experience* (New York: Random House, 1974), 14–17.

10. Michael J. Hightower, "Cattle, Coal, and Indian Land: A Tradition of Mining in Southeastern Oklahoma," *Chronicles of Oklahoma* 62, no. 1 (Spring 1984): 7.

11. Boorstin, *The Americans,* 119. Homesteaders were required to be twenty-one years old and head of the household. They had to live on the land, build a twelve-by-fourteen-foot

home, grow crops, and make improvements for five years before the land was titled to them. Citizens included single women who were head of household and freed slaves. Immigrants who had never borne arms against the United States or given aid to enemies of the United States could also claim land in the act ("Facts about the Homestead Act of 1862," eHow, http://www.ehow.com/facts_6751710_homestead-act-1862.html#ixzz2DiSCogEZ).

12. Edward E. Dale, "The Cow Country in Transition," *Mississippi Valley Historical Review* 24, no. 1 (June 1937): 3–20.

13. Carolyn Thomas Foreman, "Ferries in the Indian Territory," folder 10, box 3, Carolyn Foreman Collection.

14. Ibid.

15. Ibid.

16. Carolyn Thomas Foreman, "Red River," folder 20, box 3, Carolyn Foreman Collection.

17. Ibid.

18. Ibid.; Foreman, "Ferries in the Indian Territory."

19. B. M. Palmer, interview by L. W. Wilson, February 15, 1937, vol. 69, 57–59, IPP online.

20. W. R. Mulkey, interview by L. W. Wilson, n.d., vol. 65, 368, IPP online.

21. Ibid., 369–70.

22. Louis R. Jobe, interview by L. W. Wilson, n.d., vol. 48, 137–38, IPP online.

23. Berry quoted in Foreman, "Ferries in the Indian Territory."

24. Foreman, "Toll Gates and Roads in the Indian Territory," folder 21, box 3, Carolyn Foreman Collection.

25. Ibid.

26. Ibid.

27. Clinton quoted in "Toll Bridge Arkansas," folder 20, box 3, Carolyn Foreman Collection.

28. James M. Smallwood, *An Oklahoma Adventure of Banks and Bankers* (Norman: University of Oklahoma Press, 1979), 3–14.

29. Ibid., 91; Gum quoted in "Finance Has Had Big Part in Building Great State," *Daily Oklahoman,* April 23, 1939.

30. Mrs. Tom B. Ferguson, "Romance in Pioneer Banking," *Oklahoma Banker,* November 1932, 20.

31. Patricia Loosen and Joyce Treece, interview by author, August 30, 2010, Okarche, Oklahoma.

32. J. W. McNeal, "Pioneer Banking," in *Proceedings of the Sixth Annual Convention of the Oklahoma Bankers Association, November 7 and 8, 1902* (Oklahoma City: Oklahoma Bankers Association), 35.

33. A. T. Lowman, interview by Augusta H. Custer, December 10, 1937, vol. 33, 439, IPP microfilm.

34. Arthur Bynum, interview by Effie S. Jackson, March 22, 1937, vol. 14, 307, IPP online.

35. Ibid., 308.

36. Niall Ferguson, *The Ascent of Money: A Financial History of the World* (New York: Penguin, 2008), 30.

37. Smallwood, *Oklahoma Adventure of Banks,* 6.

38. For one merchant's perilous road to success in the dry goods business, see Hightower, "The Businessman's Frontier," 4–31.

39. Michael J. Hightower, "The Road to Russian Hill: A Story of Immigration and Coal Mining," *Chronicles of Oklahoma* 63, no. 3 (Fall 1985): 236.

40. Jake Simmons, interview by L. W. Wilson, n.d., vol. 83, 234, IPP online.

41. Ibid., 235.

42. Ibid., 235–36. For an excellent account of the Simmons oil dynasty, see Jonathan D. Greenberg, *Staking a Claim: Jake Simmons and the Making of an African American Oil Dynasty* (New York: Atheneum, 1990).

43. Henry Vogel, interview by L. W. Wilson, February 19, 1937, vol. 11, 91–92, IPP microfilm.

44. Alex Sykes, interview by L. W. Wilson, January 25, 1937, vol. 10, 270, IPP microfilm.

45. A. E. Dixon, interview by Jerome M. Emmons, June 8, 1937, vol. 24, 486–87, IPP online.

46. Ibid., 486.

47. Bill Swimm, interview by L. W. Wilson, April 13, 1937, vol. 88, 551, IPP online.

48. Ibid., 551–52.

49. Ibid., 558.

50. Smallwood, *Oklahoma Adventure of Banks,* 12.

51. M. W. Maupin, interview by Lula Austin, August 27, 1937, vol. 34, 243, IPP microfilm.

52. Thomas Lee Ballenger, *Story of the Banking Business in Tahlequah, Oklahoma* (Tahlequah, Okla.: Tahlequah Publishing, 1968), 7, 9.

53. Ibid., 9–10. John W. Stapler's other son was John B.

54. Ibid., 8.

55. Frederick Drummond, interview by author, March 17, 2011, Pawhuska, Oklahoma; John R. Drummond, *The Drummond Family History: A Story of Fred and Addie, their Ancestors and Children* (San Angelo, Tex.: Newsfoto Publishing, 1981), 15.

56. *Encyclopedia of Oklahoma History and Culture,* s.v. "Drummond Ranch," by Les Warehime, http://digital.library.okstate.edu/encyclopedia/entries/D/DR007.html.

57. Drummond, *Drummond Family History,* 15.

58. *Encyclopedia of Oklahoma History and Culture,* s.v. "Drummond Ranch."

59. Drummond, follow-up phone correspondence with author, August 29, 2011.

60. 2009 Historical Calendar, City National Bank and Trust Company of Guymon, Guymon, Oklahoma, City National Bank and Trust Company of Guymon Corporate Files (hereafter cited as City National Bank and Trust Company of Guymon Corporate Files).

61. Drummond, *Drummond Family History,* 15.

62. Drummond follow-up correspondence.

63. Beverly Whitcomb, interview by author, August 31, 2011, Hominy, Oklahoma; "Drummond Home, Hominy, Oklahoma," promotional brochure, Drummond Home Collection.

64. Drummond, *Drummond Family History,* 16.

65. E. H. Kelley, "Early Banking in Oklahoma," *Oklahoma Banker,* October 1954, 8.

66. "History of Patterson Mercantile Company: Experiences of Miss Ella Robinson, Employee, 4-5-37," submitted by Grant Foreman, Muskogee, Okla., folder 1, box 8, Carolyn Foreman Collection. See also Ella Robinson, "History of the Patterson Mercantile Company," *Chronicles of Oklahoma* 36, no. 1 (Spring 1958): 53–64.

67. "History of Patterson Mercantile Company: Experiences of Miss Ella Robinson," 3–4.

68. Ibid., 4.

69. Ibid., 5.

70. Ibid., 6.

71. Ibid.

CHAPTER 7

Epigraph: Ferguson, "Romance in Pioneer Banking," 20.

1. A. P. Jackson and E. C. Cole, *Oklahoma! Politically and Geographically Described—History and Guide to the Indian Territory* (Kansas City, Mo.: Ramsey, Millett & Hudson, 1885), 48–49. For information on E. C. Cole, see Stan Hoig, *The Oklahoma Land Rush of 1889* (Oklahoma City: Oklahoma Historical Society, 1984), 22, 23, 56, 79, 167.

2. Jackson and Cole, *Oklahoma!,* 54.

3. Carl Coke Rister, *Land Hunger: David L. Payne and the Oklahoma Boomers* (New York: Arno Press, 1975), 40.

4. Ibid., 41; McReynolds, *Oklahoma: A History,* 282.

5. Rister, *Land Hunger,* 41; Joseph B. Thoburn, *History of Oklahoma,* illus. L. P. Thompson (Oklahoma City: First National Bank and Trust Company of Oklahoma City, Oklahoma Publishing Company, 1957).

6. Quoted in Goble, *Progressive Oklahoma,* 69.

7. Berlin B. Chapman, "Oklahoma City, from Public Land to Private Property," *Chronicles of Oklahoma* 37, no. 2 (Summer 1959): 212.

8. Rister, *Land Hunger,* 41–49; Hoig, *Oklahoma Land Rush,* 5.

9. Rister, *Land Hunger,* 5.

10. Dan W. Peery, "Captain David L. Payne," *Chronicles of Oklahoma* 13, no. 4 (December 1935): 441.

11. Ibid., 446.

12. "Early Oklahoma History: The Hardships of D. L. Payne, the 'Original Boomer,'" unsourced newspaper article, December 3, 1903, Scrapbook, September 20, 1903–January 9, 1904, box 40, vol. 11, 50, Barde Collection. See also Charles W. Nuckolls, "The Cultural History of an Oklahoma Identity," in *The Culture of Oklahoma,* ed. Howard F. Stein and Robert F. Hill (Norman: University of Oklahoma Press, 1993), 127.

13. E. H. Kelley, "Early Banking in Oklahoma," *Oklahoma Banker,* August 1954, 14; Smallwood, *Oklahoma Adventure of Banks,* 13.

14. Brower quoted in "Early Oklahoma History: The Hardships of D. L. Payne," 50.

15. Quoted in Peery, "Captain David L. Payne," 446.

16. Rister, *Land Hunger,* 189–93.

17. Quoted in Howard R. Lamar, "The Most American Frontier: The Oklahoma Land Rushes, 1889–1893," *Humanities Interview* 7 (1989): 5.

18. McReynolds, *Oklahoma: A History,* 287.

19. Goble, *Progressive Oklahoma,* 8.

20. Chapman, "Oklahoma City," 216.

21. Bennington quoted in "And There Oklahoma City Stands," unsourced newspaper article, December 26, 1900, Scrapbook, September 1, 1900–March 22, 1901, box 38, vol. 6, 108, Barde Collection.

22. A. W. Durham [*sic,* Dunham], "Oklahoma City before the Run of 1889," *Chronicles of Oklahoma* 36, no. 1 (Spring 1958): 72. The station master is referenced as both "Durham" and "Dunham." See A. W. Dunham, "A Pioneer Railroad Agent," *Chronicles of Oklahoma* 2, no. 1 (March 1924): 48–62.

23. Durham [*sic,* Dunham], "Oklahoma City before the Run," 73.

24. Chapman, "Oklahoma City," 216–17.

25. The name of the post office, "Oklahoma Station," was shortened by the Post Office Department to "Oklahoma" on December 18, 1888. Samuel H. Radebaugh was the first postmaster. The name of this post office remained "Oklahoma" until July 1, 1923, when it was changed to "Oklahoma City." See George H. Shirk, "First Post Offices within the Boundaries of Oklahoma," *Chronicles of Oklahoma* 30, no. 1 (Spring 1952): 83.

26. Durham [*sic,* Durham], "Oklahoma City before the Run," 76.

27. Ibid.

28. Springer quoted in Hoig, *Oklahoma Land Rush,* 11–12.

29. McReynolds, *Oklahoma: A History,* 288.

30. Hamilton S. Wicks, "The Opening of Oklahoma," *Cosmopolitan Magazine* 7 (September 1889): 460.

31. Ibid., 460–61.

32. LeRoy H. Fischer, "Oklahoma Territory, 1890–1907," *Chronicles of Oklahoma* 53, no. 1 (Spring 1975): 4–5.

33. Dunham, "A Pioneer Railroad Agent," 56. Dunham read from notes at the annual meeting of the Oklahoma Historical Society on February 5, 1924. His notes were published in the *Chronicles of Oklahoma* in March 1924.

34. Fischer, "Oklahoma Territory," 3.

35. Hoig, *Oklahoma Land Rush,* 100.

36. "A Brighter View," *Los Angeles Times,* April 23, 1889.

37. T. M. Richardson Jr., interview by Harry M. Dreyer, April 6, 1937, vol. 8, 381, IPP microfilm.

38. Hoig, *Oklahoma Land Rush,* 159.

39. T. M. Richardson Jr. interview, 383.

40. Lerona Rosamond Morris, ed., *Oklahoma Yesterday-Today-Tomorrow* (Guthrie, Okla.: Co-Operative Publishing, 1930), 1:878.

41. Max Nichols and David R. Martin, *Continuing an Oklahoma Banking Tradition* (Oklahoma City: First Interstate Bank of Oklahoma, N.A., 1989), 4. The Oklahoma Bank's original location later became home to the Biltmore Hotel and, most recently, the Myriad Gardens and its centerpiece, the Crystal Bridge.

42. McRill, *And Satan Came Also,* 35.

43. Nichols and Martin, *Continuing an Oklahoma Banking Tradition,* 4; John Cecil Brown, "Early Days of the First National: A Bank as Old as the City It Serves," *Fifty Years Forward: The First National Bank and Trust Company of Oklahoma City, 1889–1939* (Oklahoma City: First National Bank and Trust Company of Oklahoma City, 1939), 47–48.

44. Nichols and Martin, *Continuing an Oklahoma Banking Tradition,* 4. See also Mary Marsh, ed., "Our First Seventy-Five Years," *Bank Life: 1889/1964—Our First 75* (Oklahoma City: First National Bank and Trust Company, April 1964), 2–3.

45. Elterman quoted in Brown, "Early Days of the First National," 48.

46. Ferguson, *Ascent of Money,* 34.

47. Dunham, "Pioneer Railroad Agent," 59.

48. Goble, *Progressive Oklahoma,* 15.

49. Myron R. Sturtevant, untitled manuscript beginning, "In March, 1901, I was appointed National Bank Examiner by Comptroller of the Currency, Charles E. Dawes," folder 11, box 8, Kelley Collection. See also "Cash Really Flew Back in Old Days," unsourced newspaper article, attributed in the text to 1956, folder 16, box 8, Kelley Collection.

50. "Oklahoma City Has Had 48 Banks Since 1889," *Daily Oklahoman,* April 23, 1939.

51. "Banks," unsourced newspaper article, n.d., folder 28, box 2, Barde Collection; Kelley, "Early Banking in Oklahoma," *Oklahoma Banker,* April 1954, 24.

52. "50th Anniversary of the First National Bank of Guthrie, 1889–1939," folder 5, box 7, Kelley Collection.

53. Brown, "Early Days of the First National," 48–49.

54. Advertisement quoted in ibid., 50. Similar advertisements were published throughout 1889 and 1890. See Oklahoma Bank advertisement, *Oklahoma City Evening Gazette,* June 3, 1890.

55. "Banks," unsourced newspaper article.

56. Ibid.

57. Debo, *Prairie City,* 63.

58. Ben Haller Jr., *A History of Banking in Nebraska, 1854–1990* (Lincoln: Nebraska Bankers Association, 1990), 27. Haller's chapter, "Banking in Nebraska," is reprinted in full from an essay written by one of Nebraska's most prominent early-day bankers. See Henry W. Yates, "Banking in Nebraska," in *Illustrated History of Nebraska* (Lincoln: Jacob North, 1906).

59. Tom J. Hartman, interview by Lawrence D. Hibbs, May 13, 1937, vol. 4, 453, IPP microfilm.

60. Ibid., 450–51.

61. William M. Jenkins to Bank of Hoffman Charles & Conklin, January 1, 1898, folder 62, box 2, Kelley Collection.

62. Hartman interview, 451–52. Mr. Hartman stated in his interview for the WPA that the First National Bank of Muskogee was chartered on August 1, 1890. He must have meant 1889.

63. Ibid.; "State's First Banks Trailed Act 26 Years," *Sunday Oklahoman,* February 24, 1963, Banks and Banking Vertical Files, in Research Division, Oklahoma Historical Society, Oklahoma City (hereafter cited as OHS Vertical Files).

64. "State's First Banks Trailed Act 26 Years," *The Sunday Oklahoman,* February 24, 1963, OHS Vertical Files.

65. W. A. Willibrand, "German in Okarche, 1892–1902," *Chronicles of Oklahoma* 28, no. 3 (Autumn 1950): 284.

66. "Okarche Has Million Dollar Bank," *Okarche (OK) Chieftain,* July 13, 1944; *Fifty Years 1892–1942* (Okarche, Oklahoma: First Bank of Okarche, 1942); certificate of citizenship issued to Julius Peter Loosen in Polk County, Nebraska, October 22, 1885, all in Loosen family archives, Okarche, Oklahoma.

67. *Fifty Years 1892–1942.*

68. E. H. Kelley, "The History of Banking in Oklahoma: Wagon Yard Banking," *Oklahoma Banker,* October 1956, 29.

69. Roma Lee Porter, William Paul Ellwanger, and Teresa Heater, interview by author, August 23, 2010, Lawton, Oklahoma.

70. 2010 Historical Calendar, City National Bank and Trust Company of Guymon, Guymon, Oklahoma, City National Bank and Trust Company of Guymon Corporate Files.

71. Bert Willis, "And Your Old Men Shall Dream Dreams," unpublished memoir, 1953, folder 6, box 7, 24, Kelley Collection.

72. Ibid., 26–27.

73. E. H. Kelley, "Early Day Banking in Oklahoma: An Interesting Early Charter," *Oklahoma Banker,* March 1954, 9.

74. B. L. Phipps, "Banking in Indian Territory during the 80's," *Chronicles of Oklahoma* 7, no. 2 (June 1929): 186–87.

75. Hoig, *Oklahoma Land Rush,* 197.

76. McReynolds, *Oklahoma: A History,* 292n28; William Cronon, George Miles, and Jay Gitlin, "Becoming West: Toward a New Meaning for Western History," in *Under an Open Sky: Rethinking America's Western Past,* ed. William Cronon, George Miles, and Jay Gitlin (New York: W. W. Norton, 1992), 17.

77. Fischer, "Oklahoma Territory," 3.

78. *Encyclopedia of Oklahoma History and Culture,* s.v. "Organic Act, 1890," by Dianna Everett, http://digital.library.okstate.edu/encyclopedia/entries/O/OR004.html. The boundary dispute was settled on March 16, 1896, when the U.S. Supreme Court directed that Old Greer County be made a part of Oklahoma Territory. See chapter five of this work, "Territorial Trading," and Hightower, "The Businessman's Frontier," 20.

79. Fischer, "Oklahoma Territory," 4; McReynolds, *Oklahoma: A History,* 292.

80. McReynolds, *Oklahoma: A History,* 298–99.

81. Harry E. Henslick, "The Life of Abraham Jefferson Seay" (master's thesis, Oklahoma State University, 1973), 109.

82. Roy P. Stewart, *Born Grown: An Oklahoma City History* (Oklahoma City: Fidelity Bank National Association, 1974), 66.

83. Goble, *Progressive Oklahoma,* 26–27.

84. Fischer, "Oklahoma Territory," 4.

85. Ibid.

86. Smallwood, *Oklahoma Adventure of Banks,* 20.

87. Norbert R. Mahnken, "No Oklahoman Lost a Penny: Oklahoma's State Bank Guarantee Law, 1907–1923," *Chronicles of Oklahoma* 71, no. 1 (Spring 1993): 43–44.

88. "History of Oklahoma Banking and the Oklahoma State Banking Department," unpublished history, n.d., Oklahoma State Banking Department Collection, Oklahoma City (hereafter cited as Oklahoma State Banking Department Collection).

89. Mrs. Nora Catlett, interview by Amelia Harris, n.d., vol. 19, 295–98, IPP microfilm.

90. Willard Johnston, interview by Carrie L. Boggs, April 12, 1932, manuscript in possession of George J. and Nancy J. Records, Oklahoma City (hereafter cited as Records Collection). Willard Johnston was Nancy J. Records's grandfather. See also Hightower, "Willard Johnston: Homesteader and Frontier Banker, 1881–1904," *Chronicles of Oklahoma* 87, no. 4 (Winter 2009–10): 408–31.

91. Will Turner, "A Brief Biography of Willard Johnston, 1863–1939," Records Collection.

92. George Gorton, *A "Big-Ass Boy" in the Oil Fields: My Adventures, 1918–28* (New Berlin, Wis.: Napco Graphic Arts, 1975), 30–31.

93. Ibid.

94. Ferguson, "Romance in Pioneer Banking," 20.

95. "Indians Massing," *Oklahoma City Evening Gazette,* November 28, 1890.

96. "The Southern Indians," *Oklahoma City Evening Gazette,* November 29, 1890.

97. C. A. McNabb, "Oklahoma City's Indian Scare," *Chronicles of Oklahoma* 2, no. 4 (December 1924): 395.

98. Mrs. Myrtle Hill Allen, interviewer unknown, n.d., vol. 77, 25, IPP microfilm. Judge J. P. Allen arrived in Oklahoma City from Kosciusko, Mississippi, several years after the Indian scare and moved into the brick house that had provided refuge to Mrs. Allen and her neighbors. He was elected mayor of Oklahoma City on April 12, 1897, to become the fifth person

to fill that office after Oklahoma City's incorporation. Following his term in the mayor's office, Judge Allen became a probate judge and served with distinction in the administration of Governor J. B. A. Robertson. J. P. Allen was the author's paternal great-great grandfather.

99. T. M. Richardson Jr., interview by Harry M. Dreyer, April 6, 1937, vol. 8, 384–85, IPP microfilm.

100. McNabb, "Oklahoma City's Indian Scare," 396.

101. Ibid.

102. Ibid., 397.

CHAPTER 8

Epigraph: News brief, *Daily Oklahoma State Capital,* August 5, 1893.

1. Brown, "Early Days of the First National," 51.

2. "Gone to the Wall," unsourced newspaper article, November 21, 1890, folder 26, box 2, Barde Collection.

3. Ibid.

4. Smallwood, *Oklahoma Adventure of Banks,* 16–17.

5. Ibid., 20; Debo, *Prairie City,* 63. The maximum interest rate was repealed in 1895, and a usury law fixing a maximum rate of 10 percent was placed in the Oklahoma Constitution. It was not removed until 1969.

6. Brown, "Early Days of the First National, 51; Marsh, "Our First Seventy-Five Years," 2; Nichols and Martin, *Continuing an Oklahoma Banking Tradition,* 7–8; First National Bank of Oklahoma City advertisements, *Oklahoma City Evening Gazette,* June 3, October 25, and December 30, 1890.

7. Lynne Pierson Doti and Larry Schweikart, *Banking the in the American West: From the Gold Rush to Deregulation* (Norman: University of Oklahoma Press, 1991), 19.

8. News brief, *Altus News,* March 15, 1900. C. C. Hightower was referenced by the *Altus News.* His role in settling Old Greer County is described in Hightower, "The Businessman's Frontier," 4–31. C. C. Hightower was the author's paternal great-grandfather.

9. Doti and Schweikart, *Banking the in the American West,* 44.

10. Boyle quoted in Brown, "Early Days of the First National," 54.

11. Richardson quoted in ibid.

12. Jeffrey Marshall, "Twixt Booms and Panics: Banking in the Gilded Age," in Zimmerman, *Banking's Past,* 25; Hugh Rockoff, "Banking and Finance, 1789–1914," in *The Cambridge Economic History of the United States,* ed. Stanley L. Engerman and Robert E. Gallman, vol. 2, *The Long Nineteenth Century* (Cambridge: Cambridge University Press, 2000), 657.

13. Rockoff, "Banking and Finance," 663.

14. Schlesinger, *Almanac,* 372. Journalist and business historian Jack Beatty claims that Ms. Lease never adjured farmers to raise less corn and more hell. Rather, she accepted it as good advice from reporters. See Beatty, *Age of Betrayal,* 320.

15. Editor quoted in Trescott, *Financing American Enterprise,* 102.

16. Schlesinger, *Almanac,* 376; Dewey, *Financial History,* 444–47; Studenski and Krooss, *Financial History,* 219.

17. Douglas quoted in Brown, "Early Days of the First National," 54–55.

18. "The Bank Suspensions," *Oklahoma Daily Times-Journal,* July 20, 1893.

19. Ibid.

20. Richardson quoted in Brown, "Early Days of the First National," 55–57; see also "'93 Bank Run Was Stopped by Audacity," *Daily Oklahoman,* April 23, 1939.

21. "Bank Suspensions."

22. "'93 Bank Run."

23. McRill, *And Satan Came Also*, 57.

24. Henry Overholser was married for the second time to Anna Murphy, Samuel Murphy's daughter, in 1890. One account has it that Overholser took the loot to Oklahoma City, displayed bills to customers before the closed doors of the bank, and asked them to be patient until tellers could count the money and deposit it properly. A rumor was planted that $25,000 was available for those who wanted it. See Stewart, *Born Grown*, 52.

25. "'93 Bank Run"; Nichols and Martin, *Continuing an Oklahoma Banking Tradition*, 10–12.

26. "Bank Suspensions."

27. "First Money Deposited in Canvas Tent," *Daily Oklahoman*, April 23, 1939.

28. Nichols and Martin, *Continuing an Oklahoma Banking Tradition*, 13.

29. "The Oklahoma of To-Day," *Oklahoma Daily Press-Gazette*, October 30, 1893.

30. News brief, *Daily Oklahoma State Capital*, August 5, 1893.

31. News brief, *Daily Oklahoma State Capital*, June 26, 1893.

32. Quoted in "Poker Game Was 'Bill's' Court of Final 'Justice,'" unsourced newspaper article, August 14, 1910, folder 14, box 10, Barde Collection.

33. A. T. Lowman, interview by Augusta H. Custer, December 10, 1937, vol. 33, 444, IPP microfilm.

34. Edward Everett Dale, *The West Wind Blows: The Autobiography of Edward Everett Dale*, ed. Arrell Morgan Gibson (Oklahoma City: Oklahoma Historical Society, 1984), 23.

35. "Making of a New Town," unsourced, newspaper article, n.d., folder 8, box 26, Barde Collection.

36. Ibid.

37. *Encyclopedia of Oklahoma History and Culture*, s.v. "Renfrow, William Cary (1845–1922)," by Dianna Everett, http://digital.library.okstate.edu/encyclopedia/entries/R/RE026.html.

38. Turner quoted in "What the Execs Will Do," unsourced newspaper article, May 5, 1897, Scrapbook, January 12–May 5, 1897, box 36, vol. 0, 169, Barde Collection.

39. Smallwood, *Oklahoma Adventure of Banks*, 33.

40. News brief, *Edmond Sun-Democrat*, February 22, 1895.

41. Advertisements for the Bank of Shawnee, *Shawnee Weekly News*, April 6, April 20, and September 28, 1895. For an account of pioneer banker Willard Johnston, see Hightower, "Willard Johnston," 408–31.

42. Advertisements for the T. M. Richardson Lumber Co., *Shawnee Weekly News*, April 6 and 20, 1895.

43. "Bank Failure at Shawnee," *Daily Oklahoman*, September 1, 1896.

44. Trescott, *Financing American Enterprise*, 115.

45. Quoted in "New Oklahoma Industry," unsourced newspaper article, May 25, 1897, Scrapbook, May 6–November 10, 1897, box 36, vol. 1, 36, Barde Collection.

46. Leonard quoted in "The Poultry Industry," unsourced newspaper article, June 2, 1897, Scrapbook, May 6–November 10, 1897, 56.

47. Ibid.

48. "Big Fruit Shipments," unsourced newspaper article, August 18, 1897, Scrapbook, May 6–November 10, 1897, 200.

49. "The First Bales Coming In," unsourced newspaper article, August 30, 1897, Scrapbook, May 6–November 10, 1897, 213.

50. Ibid.

51. Ibid., 213–14.

52. "An Additional Telegraph Wire," unsourced newspaper article, August 20, 1897, Scrapbook, May 6–November 10, 1897, 206.

53. "It Is Oklahoma's Big Year," unsourced newspaper article, September 16, 1897, Scrapbook, May 6–November 10, 1897, 237.

54. Ibid., 238.

55. Ibid.

56. James Bryce, *The American Commonwealth* (New York: MacMillan, 1914), 2:295.

57. Ibid., 2:895.

58. Ibid., 2:315–16.

59. Tocqueville quoted in Leo Damrosch, *Tocqueville's Discovery of America,* 215.

60. Bryce, *American Commonwealth,* 2:900–901.

61. First National Bank of Oklahoma City advertisement, *Oklahoma Champion,* May 7, 1897.

62. Smallwood, *Oklahoma Adventure of Banks,* 26–27.

63. Debo, *Prairie City,* 85. Dun & Bradstreet traces its history back to 1841 with the formation of The Mercantile Agency in New York City. It was later renamed R. G. Dun & Company. The company was formed to create a network of correspondents to provide reliable and objective credit information. In 1933, Dun merged with competitor John M. Bradstreet to form today's Dun & Bradstreet.

64. "The Wealth of Oklahoma," unsourced newspaper article, June 28, 1897, Scrapbook, May 6–November 10, 1897, box 36, vol. 1, 131, Barde Collection.

65. Ibid.

66. Ibid.

67. Let the good times roll!

CHAPTER 9

Epigraph: "Oklahoma Bankers Meet," unsourced newspaper article, November 26, 1900, Scrapbook, September 1, 1900–March 22, 1901, box 38, vol. 6, 77, Barde Collection.

1. Untitled newspaper submission, n.d., beginning, "When Oklahoma was opened to settlement," folder 14, box 10, Barde Collection.

2. Ibid.

3. Untitled newspaper submission, n.d., beginning, "There is scarcely an old-time gambler in the United States," Barde Collection.

4. Ibid.

5. Untitled newspaper submission, n.d., beginning, "At No. 7½ Grand Avenue house wreckers lately tore down a two-story frame building," Barde Collection.

6. Ibid.

7. Ibid.

8. Ibid.

9. Dell B. Kell, "When Oklahoma City Was Wide Open," *Oklahoma City Times,* n.d., Barde Collection.

10. Ibid.

11. "Busy Liars in Oklahoma," unsourced newspaper article, May 4, 1897, Scrapbook, January 12–May 5, 1897, box 36, vol. 0, 169, Barde Collection.

12. Ibid.

13. Ibid.

14. "Their Idea of the Wild West," unsourced newspaper article, March 5, 1898, Scrapbook, November 11, 1897–July 29, 1898, box 37, vol. 2, 101, Barde Collection.

15. Jenkins quoted in "Decline of the 'Bad Man,'" *McMaster's Weekly,* April 4, 1896.

16. Nagle quoted in "Oklahoma Rid of Bad Men," unsourced newspaper article, March 20, 1897, Scrapbook, January 12–May 5, 1897, box 36, vol. 0, 111, Barde Collection.

17. "A Pawnee Bank Robbed," *Edmond Sun-Democrat,* January 26, 1894.

18. "A Preacher a Bad Banker," *Daily Oklahoman,* October 29, 1897.

19. "Hold-Up at Earlsboro," *Oklahoma Champion,* December 16, 1898.

20. "May Be a Political Game," unsourced newspaper article, May 6, 1897, Scrapbook, May 6–November 10, 1897, box 36, vol. 1, 1, Barde Collection.

21. "A Bank's Receivership Ended: Affairs of the Defunct Guthrie Commercial Concern Wound Up," unsourced newspaper article, November 2, 1897, Scrapbook, May 6–November 10, 1897, 285.

22. E. H. Kelley, "A History of the Early Banks of Guthrie," compiled for the Historical Society of Oklahoma, August 18, 1948, 15, unpublished compilation, folder 7, box 7, Kelley Collection.

23. "Oklahoma Bankers in Jail," unsourced newspaper article, December 28, 1897, Scrapbook, November 11, 1897–July 29, 1898, box 37, vol. 2, 42, Barde Collection.

24. "'Wild Cat' Banking To Be Attacked—An Irate Populist—Notes," unsourced newspaper article, January 16, 1897, Scrapbook, January 12–May 5, 1897, box 36, vol. 0, n.p., Barde Collection.

25. May quoted in "To Boycott Bank Notes," unsourced newspaper article, February 23, 1897, Scrapbook, January 12–May 5, 1897, n.p.

26. "That Anti-Bank Wrecking Law," unsourced newspaper article, February 26, 1897, Scrapbook, January 12–May 5, 1897, 16. "Boodling" was the rather colorful term for bribery.

27. "Against 'Wild Cat' Banks," unsourced newspaper article, March 10, 1897, Scrapbook, January 12–May 5, 1897, 100–101.

28. "Representative D. S. Rose of the Second District," unsourced newspaper article, March 8, 1897, Scrapbook, January 12–May 5, 1897, 97.

29. Mahnken, "No Oklahoman Lost a Penny," 46; "History of Oklahoma Banking and the Oklahoma State Banking Department," Oklahoma State Banking Department Collection; "Against 'Wild Cat' Banks"; Smallwood, *Oklahoma Adventure of Banks,* 37; Robb, *Guaranty of Bank Deposits,* 39.

30. "Bill Thieves Outwitted," unsourced newspaper article, March 12, 1897, Scrapbook, January 12–May 5, 1897, box 36, vol. 0, 104, Barde Collection.

31. Ibid.

32. Doyle and Rose quoted in "Bribery Stories Believed," unsourced newspaper article, March 13, 1897, Scrapbook, January 12–May 5, 1897, 106.

33. "Oklahoma's New Laws," unsourced newspaper article, March 18, 1897, Scrapbook, January 12–May 5, 1897, 110.

34. "The New Banking Board," unsourced newspaper article, April 22, 1897, Scrapbook, January 12–May 5, 1897, 153.

35. "The New Bank Examiner," unsourced newspaper article, April 23, 1897, Scrapbook, January 12–May 5, 1897, 155.

36. Ibid.

37. "Bank Examiner Richardson's Bond Filed," unsourced newspaper article, April 24, 1897, Scrapbook, January 12–May 5, 1897, 159.

38. "Renfrow Becomes a Cyclist," unsourced newspaper article, May 18, 1897, Scrapbook, May 6–November 10, 1897, box 36, vol. 1, 26, Barde Collection.

39. "Barnes' Inauguration," unsourced newspaper article, May 26, 1897, Scrapbook, May 6–November 10, 1897, 40.

40. "The Banking Law Endorsed," unsourced newspaper article, June 19, 1897, Scrapbook, May 6–November 10, 1897, 122.

41. Tom J. Hartman, interview by Lawrence D. Hibbs, May 13, 1937, vol. 40, 66, IPP online.

42. Doti and Schweikart, *Banking the in the American West,* 82.

43. "Richardson's Game Stopped," unsourced newspaper article, June 19, 1897, Scrapbook, May 6–November 10, 1897, box 36, vol. 1, 122, Barde Collection.

44. T. M. Richardson Jr. to the Hon. C. M. Barnes, June 21, 1897, folder 5, box 1, Kelley Collection.

45. "To Govern the Bank Examiner," unsourced newspaper article, August 7, 1897, Scrapbook, May 6–November 10, 1897, box 36, vol. 1, 188, Barde Collection.

46. McNeal quoted in "Money Comes out of Hiding," unsourced newspaper article, August 7, 1897, Scrapbook, May 6–November 10, 1897, 188.

47. Barnes quoted in "Prosperity in Oklahoma," unsourced newspaper article, August 21, 1897, Scrapbook, May 6–November 10, 1897, 206.

48. "The Condition of Oklahoma National Banks," unsourced newspaper article, August 23, 1897, Scrapbook, May 6–November 10, 1897, 207.

49. "Oklahoma's Banks Thrive," unsourced newspaper article, September 11, 1897, Scrapbook, May 6–November 10, 1897, 232.

50. "The Banks Full of Money," unsourced newspaper article, October 14, 1897, Scrapbook, May 6–November 10, 1897, 267.

51. "Growth without a Boom," unsourced newspaper article, October 18, 1897, Scrapbook, May 6–November 10, 1897, 271.

52. Ibid.

53. Lenders quoted in "It Is a Debt-Paying Year," unsourced newspaper article, October 23, 1897, Scrapbook, May 6–November 10, 1897, 277–78.

54. Pugh quoted in "Failure Was Its Only End," unsourced newspaper article, December 15, 1897, Scrapbook, November 11, 1897–July 29, 1898, box 37, vol. 2, 31, Barde Collection.

55. Pugh quoted in ibid.

56. "Pugh Wants to Explain," unsourced newspaper article, December 31, 1897, Scrapbook, November 11, 1897–July 29, 1898, 45.

57. "Oklahoma Bankers Meet," 77.

58. Ibid.

59. "Early-Day Check Written on Wood," *Daily Oklahoman,* April 23, 1939.

CHAPTER 10

Epigraph: T. J. Ballew to William Jenkins, Esq., April 2, 1901, folder 54, box 2, Kelley Collection.

1. Untitled newspaper submission, May 25, attributed in the text to 1911–15, beginning, "A Golfer lately made the estimate," folder 26, box 10, Barde Collection.

2. Ibid.

3. "Oklahoma Banks Prosperous," unsourced newspaper article, January 8, 1898, Scrapbook, November 11, 1897–July 29, 1898, box 37, vol. 2, 53, Barde Collection.

4. Pugh quoted in "Good Advice to Bankers," unsourced newspaper article, January 22, 1898, Scrapbook, November 11, 1897–July 29, 1898, 64.

5. "Deposits of 21–2 Millions," unsourced newspaper article, July 26, 1898, Scrapbook, November 11, 1897–July 29, 1898, 197.

6. Ibid.

7. Ibid.

8. "Mr. Rose Defends his Bill," unsourced newspaper article, January 8, 1898, Scrapbook, November 11, 1897–July 29, 1898, 53.

9. Lofland quoted in "To Talk with Kansas City," unsourced newspaper article, January 29, 1898, Scrapbook, November 11, 1897–July 29, 1898, 73.

10. "Good Times in Oklahoma," unsourced newspaper article, April 30, 1898, Scrapbook, November 11, 1897–July 29, 1898, 139.

11. Ibid.

12. Ibid.

13. Ibid.

14. Hagan quoted in "Oklahoma Taking its Place," unsourced newspaper article, January 27, 1898, Scrapbook, November 11, 1897–July 29, 1898, 71.

15. Hagan quoted in ibid.

16. Allen quoted in "Bankers in Oklahoma City," unsourced newspaper article, December 7, 1898, Scrapbook, August 1, 1898–February 24, 1899, box 37, vol. 3, 95, Barde Collection. Mayor J. P. Allen was the father-in-law of Frank P. Johnson, president of the American National Bank and, later, the First National Bank and Trust Company of Oklahoma City from its inception in the late 1920s until his death in October 1935. Allen was also the author's paternal great-great grandfather. See Michael J. Hightower, "Brother Bankers: Frank P. and Hugh M. Johnson, Founders of the First National Bank and Trust Company of Oklahoma City," *Chronicles of Oklahoma* 88, no. 4 (Winter 2010–2011): 388–415.

17. Search quoted in "Bankers in Oklahoma City," 95.

18. Search quoted in ibid.

19. "Points for the Bankers," unsourced newspaper article, December 8, 1898, Scrapbook, August 1, 1898–February 24, 1899, box 37, vol. 3, 117, Barde Collection.

20. Pugh quoted in ibid.

21. Pugh quoted in ibid.

22. Fleming's paper, as read by Wheeler, quoted in ibid., 117–18.

23. "Most Vital Issue," *Oklahoma Champion,* December 9, 1898.

24. "Powerless as It Is," *Oklahoma Champion,* December 2, 1898.

25. "Absorbed by Interest," *Oklahoma Champion,* December 23, 1898.

26. "Reign of the Trusts," editorial cartoon, *Oklahoma Champion,* May 26, 1899.

27. "Points for the Bankers," 118.

28. Hogan quoted in ibid.

29. Guss quoted in ibid.

30. Guss quoted in ibid.

31. Ibid.

32. Smallwood, *Oklahoma Adventure of Banks,* 37–38; "History of Oklahoma Banking and the Oklahoma State Banking Department," Oklahoma State Banking Department Collection.

33. "A Watonga Bank Increases its Stock," unsourced newspaper article, April 12, 1900, Scrapbook, April 9–August 31, 1900, box 38, vol. 5, 5, Barde Collection.

34. "A New Bank for Manchester," unsourced newspaper article, April 21, 1900, Scrapbook, April 9–August 31, 1900, 13.

35. "A Charter to the Bank of Glencoe" and "Grimes and Thompson in a Bank," unsourced newspaper articles, April 23, 1900, both in Scrapbook, April 9–August 31, 1900, 14.

36. "Another Bank for Glencoe," unsourced newspaper article, April 24, 1900, Scrapbook, April 9–August 31, 1900, 16; "A Stillwater Savings and Loan Company," unsourced newspaper article, April 27, 1900, Scrapbook, April 9–August 31, 1900, 19.

37. "The First Bank on the Osage Reservation," unsourced newspaper article, May 7, 1900, Scrapbook, April 9–August 31, 1900, 27. The Bank of Pawhuska's charter is reported in "Flynn in a Pawhuska Bank," unsourced newspaper article, April 13, 1900, Scrapbook, April 9–August 31, 1900, 5. See chapter seven of this work, "Twilight of the Frontier," for an account of these gentlemen's participation in the Sac and Fox Indian Agency and the Union National Bank of Chandler.

38. "A New Bank for Cordell," unsourced newspaper article, May 19, 1900, Scrapbook, April 9–August 31, 1900, 42.

39. "Kremlin to Have a Bank" and "A Charter for a Bank for Granite," unsourced newspaper articles, May 21, 1900, both in Scrapbook, April 9–August 31, 1900, 46.

40. "A Lexington Bank Increases its Capital," unsourced newspaper article, June 1, 1900, Scrapbook, April 9–August 31, 1900, 56.

41. "A Bank for Lamont," unsourced newspaper article, June 6, 1900, Scrapbook, April 9–August 31, 1900, 61.

42. "A Charter for a Custer County Bank" and "A New Bank for Kildare," unsourced newspaper articles, June 13, 1900, both in Scrapbook, April 9–August 31, 1900, 74.

43. "A New Bank for Cleo," unsourced newspaper article, June 14, 1900, Scrapbook, April 9–August 31, 1900, 76.

44. "A New Bank for Tonkawa," unsourced newspaper article, July 21, 1900, Scrapbook, April 9–August 31, 1900, 113.

45. "Banks in Indian Territory," unsourced newspaper article, June 7, 1900, Scrapbook, April 9–August 31, 1900, 61–62.

46. O. B. Kee to Secretary Jenkins, Esq., May 18, 1900, folder 39, box 2, Kelley Collection.

47. M. Whitacre to the Hon. Wm. Grimes, May 5, 1902, folder 6, box 1, Kelley Collection.

48. J. A. Henry to Hon. Wm. M. Jenkins, May 31, 1900, folder 12, box 3, Kelley Collection. See Hightower, "The Businessman's Frontier," 4–31.

49. Geo. E. McKinnis to the Hon. W. M. Grimes, November 8, 1901, folder 6, box 1, Kelley Collection.

50. H. K. Bickford to Secy Jenkins or the Bank Commissioner, February 4, 1901, folder 20, box 3, Kelley Collection.

51. A. N. Leffingwell to the Secretary of Oklahoma Ter., April 13, 1901, folder 6, box 1, Kelley Collection.

52. A. N. Leffingwell to the Secretary of Okla. Ter., April 20, 1901, folder 6, box 1, Kelley Collection.

53. J. A. Mays to Secretary of State, July 22, 1902, folder 40, box 2, Kelley Collection.

54. J. J. Hughes to Hon. Wm. Grimes, March 24, 1903, folder 47, box 2, Kelley Collection.

55. [Name illegible] to Hon. J. J. [illegible], Secty, O.T., July 2, 1901, folder 6, box 1, Kelley Collection.

56. C. H. Brand to Wm. Grimes, Secy, March 19, 1903, folder 22, box 3, Kelley Collection.

57. W. T. Clark to Wm. Grimes, Esq., Sect., March 25, 1903, folder 6, box 2, Kelley Collection.

58. J. P. Whatley to Hon. Wm. Grimes Secretary, April 4, 1903, folder 26, box 2, Kelley Collection.

59. I. C. Thurmond to W.M. Grimes, Sec., October 10, 1901, folder 50, box 2, Kelley Collection.

60. H. M. Johnson to the Hon. Wm. Grimes, Sect., January 31, 1903, folder 48, box 2, Kelley Collection. H. M. Johnson was the author's paternal great-grand uncle.

61. H. Shelby Mason to the Secretary Oklahoma Teritory [sic], December 16, 1901, folder 11, box 1, Kelley Collection.

62. H. Shelby Mason to the Hon. Wm. Grimes, December 24, 1901, folder 11, box 1, Kelley Collection.

63. J. F. Cox to the Secretary of Okla. Ter., May 23, 1902, folder 11, box 1, Kelley Collection.

64. J. W. McLoud to Wm. M. Jenkins, Esq., April 2, 1901, folder 6, box 1, Kelley Collection.

65. Thomas A. Davis to the Secretary of State, April 21, 1904, folder 11, box 1, Kelley Collection.

66. Thomas A. Davis to the Secretary of State, April 27, 1904, folder 11, box 1, Kelley Collection.

67. J. L. Blanchard to the Secretary of State, January 4, 1901, folder 11, box 1, Kelley Collection.

68. N. C. Kohl to the Secretary of the Territory of Oklahoma, October 25, 1900, folder 11, box 1, Kelley Collection.

69. C. H. Holmes to the Secretary of the Territory of Oklahoma, December 4, 1900, folder 11, box 1, Kelley Collection.

70. F. C. Kriz to the Secretary of State, September 27, 1902; E. P. Blake to the Sec'y of Territory, October 16, 1902; C. W. Wiedemann to Secy of State, October 22, 1902; and Theo. A. Clarke to Secy of Territory, March 13, 1903, all in folder 11, box 1, Kelley Collection.

71. Harry Beam to the Hon. Secretary Grimes, June 14, 1902, folder 10, box 1; J. O. McCollister to William Grimes, February 6, 1903, folder 7, box 1; J. O. McCollister to William Grimes, February 21, 1903, folder 7, box 1; Bulow and Lambert to Wm. M. Grimes, Esq., February 18, 1902, folder 11, box 1; B. B. Blakeney to the Hon. Wm. Grimes, April 10, 1903, folder 7, box 1; H. E. Shaffer to the Secretary of the Territory, August 14, 1903, folder 7, box 1; Crossan & Crane to William Grimes, Esq., April 23, 1904, folder 7, box 1; and H. A. Noah to the Honorable William Grimes, November 28, 1903, folder 7, box 1, all in Kelley Collection.

72. J. D. Ford, Esq., to Wm. M. Jenkins, n.d., folder 8, box 1; W. J. Alder to Wm. M. Jenkins, October 15, 1900, and November 19, 1901, folder 8, box 1; E. M. Ellsworth to Territorial Secretary of Oklahoma, February 14 and March 22, 1901, folder 8, box 1; B. F. Griffith to the Territorial Secretary, January 31, 1900, folder 10, box 1; Homer J. Kendall to the Secretary of State, February 23, 1900, folder 11, box 1; George H. Hunker to Wm. Grimes, Esq., December 2, 1902, folder 11, box 1; Charles B. Rogers to the Secretary of Oklahoma Territory, September 24, 1903, folder 11, box 1; Will E. Lower to the Banking Board of Oklahoma Ty.,

June 6, 1903, folder 11, box 1; and George Lord to the Hon. W. S. Search [*sic*], November 27, 1901, folder 10, box 1, all in Kelley Collection.

73. Secretary William Grimes to A. L. McPherson, September 22, 1902, folder 4, box 1, Kelley Collection.

74. J. W. McCloud to the Honorable Wm. M. Jenkins, April 18, 1898, folder 54, box 2, Kelley Collection.

75. J. W. McLoud to the Honorable W. M. Jenkins, April 26, 1898, folder 54, box 2, Kelley Collection.

76. "Two New Banks Chartered," unsourced newspaper article, May 14, 1898, Scrapbook, November 11, 1897–July 29, 1898, box 37, vol. 2, 148, Barde collection.

77. J. H. Maxey to the Honorable Wm. M. Jenkins, May 20, 1898, folder 54, box 2, Kelley Collection.

78. John H. Dillon to the Honorable Wm. M. Jenkins, March 1, 1899, folder 54, box 2, Kelley Collection. The date on the letter appears to be March 1, 1899, but a handwritten scrawl renders the year not quite decipherable.

79. John H. Dillon to the Honorable Wm. M. Jenkins, February 1, 1900, folder 54, box 2, Kelley Collection.

80. T. J. Ballew to William Jenkins, Esq., April 2, 1901, folder 54, box 2, Kelley Collection.

81. T. J. Ballew to William Grimes, Esq., August 17, 1901, folder 54, box 2, Kelley Collection. William Grimes had recently assumed the position of territorial secretary.

82. For what amounts to a sociological study of the frontier businessman, see Norman L. Crockett, "The Opening of Oklahoma: A Businessman's Frontier," *Chronicles of Oklahoma* 56, no. 1 (Spring 1978): 85–95.

83. "Bank Examiner Pugh Resigns," unsourced newspaper article, July 9, 1900, Scrapbook, April 9–August 31, 1900, box 38, vol. 5, 101, Barde Collection.

84. "The New Bank Examiner," unsourced newspaper article, July 10, 1900, Scrapbook, April 9–August 31, 1900, 101.

85. "Oklahoma Banks Did Well," unsourced newspaper article, October 24, 1900, Scrapbook, September 1, 1900–March 22, 1901, box 38, vol. 6, 47, Barde Collection.

86. "An Oklahoma Bank Failed," unsourced newspaper article, August 13, 1900, Scrapbook, April 9–August 31, 1900, box 38, vol. 5, 131, Barde Collection.

87. "No Receivers at Kingfisher Yet," unsourced newspaper article, August 14, 1900, Scrapbook, April 9–August 31, 1900, 134.

88. "A Defective Banking Law," unsourced newspaper article, August 15, 1900, Scrapbook, April 9–August 31, 1900, 135.

89. "Guthrie Bank Closed Doors," *Daily Oklahoman,* April 5, 1904.

90. "Bad Management Is Blamed for Failure," *Daily Oklahoman,* April 6, 1904.

91. "Fifth Failure in Past Month," *Daily Oklahoman,* April 13, 1904.

92. Myron R. Sturtevant, untitled manuscript beginning, "In March, 1901, I was appointed National Bank Examiner by Comptroller of the Currency, Charles E. Dawes," folder 11, box 8, Kelley Collection.

93. "Tried to Kill a Banker," unsourced newspaper article, November 7, 1900, Scrapbook, September 1, 1900–March 22, 1901, box 38, vol. 6, 60, Barde Collection.

94. "Arrested for Embezzlement," unsourced newspaper article, November 19, 1900, Scrapbook, September 1, 1900–March 22, 1901, 70.

95. "Bank Robbers in Oklahoma," unsourced newspaper article, November 22, 1900, Scrapbook, September 1, 1900–March 22, 1901, 74.

96. "The Bank of Cashion Robbed," unsourced newspaper article, December 17, 1900, Scrapbook, September 1, 1900–March 22, 1901, 99.

97. "Perhaps Cashion Men Did It," unsourced newspaper article, December 31, 1900, Scrapbook, September 1, 1900–March 22, 1901, 112.

98. "The Safe Robbers Got $65," unsourced newspaper article, February 18, 1901, Scrapbook, September 1, 1900–March 22, 1901, 170.

99. Company's response in "No Safe Burglar Proof," unsourced newspaper article, December 18, 1900, Scrapbook, September 1, 1900–March 22, 1901, 101.

100. "The Oklahoma Cowboy," unsourced newspaper article, October 23, 1900, Scrapbook, September 1, 1900–March 22, 1901, 45.

101. Ibid., 46.

102. Ibid.

CHAPTER 11

Epigraph: "Indian Territory: The New Land of Promise," *Kansas City Star,* March 15, 1903, Scrapbook, October 1, 1902–March 16, 1903, box 39, vol. 9, Barde Collection.

1. "Oklahoma Bankers Meet," unsourced newspaper article, November 26, 1900, Scrapbook, September 1, 1900–March 22, 1901, box 38, vol. 6, 76, Barde Collection.

2. Search quoted in ibid., 77.

3. The masthead of the *Kosciusko Star* carried this moniker in the early 1890s, when Frank P. Johnson served as editor and Hugh M. Johnson served as business manager.

4. Frank Johnson's abrupt departure from the *Kosciusko Star* was published under the terse headline "Withdrawal" and reads as follows: "With this issue of The Star I withdraw from the ownership and editorial management of the paper having sold my entire interest to my brother, Mr. H. M. Johnson. On account of the late hour at which the contract was closed, I can not say more now; but next week will perhaps have a few words of farewell for my friends and associates." In the same issue of the *Kosciusko Star,* his successor, C. M. Brooke, was more specific about the causes of the shake-up. Under the equally terse headline "Notice," he wrote, "With the next week's issue of The Star the undersigned will take entire charge of the editorial department. The financial policy of the paper, in accordance with my convictions, will be changed and will vigorously advocate the free and unlimited coinage of silver at a ratio of 16 to 1. My connection with the paper was made too late for me to give more than this statement this week." See *Kosciusko Star,* August 2, 1895.

5. "Kosciusko Bar Meeting," *Kosciusko Star,* February 1, 1895.

6. F. T. Raiford to Mrs. Frank P. (Aida Allen) Johnson, October 10, 1935, Johnson-Hightower Family Archives, private collection, Oklahoma City. Senatobia, Mississippi, is approximately forty miles south of Memphis, Tennessee. The infant daughter was the author's paternal grandmother, Ethlyn.

7. Ibid.

8. "A People's Savings Bank at Oklahoma City," unsourced newspaper article, November 24, 1900, Scrapbook, September 1, 1900–March 22, 1901, box 38, vol. 6, 76, Barde Collection.

9. "A Good Day for Banks," unsourced newspaper article, January 9, 1901, Scrapbook, September 1, 1900–March 22, 1901, 122. See also "Johnson President American National," *Daily Oklahoman,* September 18, 1906.

10. "A New Bank in Roger Mills County," unsourced newspaper article, February 7, 1901, Scrapbook, September 1, 1900–March 22, 1901, box 38, vol. 6, 161, Barde Collection.

11. "Oklahoma City Gets Big Banking Institution," *Oklahoma Banker,* February 1927, 16.

12. "Something about the Oklahoma City Savings Bank," *Daily Oklahoman,* April 10, 1903.

13. Ibid.

14. Ibid.

15. "Big Deal Closed," *Daily Oklahoman,* July 25, 1903.

16. Stewart, *Born Grown,* 333.

17. "Big Deal Closed."

18. Ibid. Frank Johnson had actually been in Oklahoma City for almost eight years since the fall of 1895.

19. Ibid.

20. "Jas. H. Wheeler, Head of Financial Institution Formed by Merging Two Leading Banks," *Daily Oklahoman,* June 22, 1905.

21. Ibid; Nichols and Martin, *Continuing an Oklahoma Banking Tradition,* 21–22.

22. "Johnson President American National," *Daily Oklahoman,* September 18, 1906.

23. For a thorough account of Frank P. and Hugh M. Johnson from their newspaper careers in Mississippi to the historic merger of their banks in Oklahoma, see Hightower, "Brother Bankers."

24. Smallwood, *Oklahoma Adventure of Banks,* 38–39.

25. Quoted in Robb, *Guaranty of Bank Deposits,* 39.

26. Ibid; "Finance Has Had Big Part in Building Great State," *Daily Oklahoman,* April 23, 1939.

27. "Why Do Banks Fail?" *Beaver Herald,* February 16, 1905.

28. "W. S. Search Has Resigned," unsourced newspaper article, January 5, 1901, Scrapbook, September 1, 1900–March 22, 1901, box 38, vol. 6, 118, Barde Collection.

29. "The New Search Bank," unsourced newspaper article, January 8, 1901, Scrapbook, September 1, 1900–March 22, 1901, 121.

30. Sturtevant, quoted by Gum in "Finance Has Had Big Part in Building Great State."

31. Myron R. Sturtevant, untitled manuscript beginning, "In March, 1901, I was appointed National Bank Examiner by Comptroller of the Currency, Charles E. Dawes," folder 11, box 8, Kelley Collection. See also "Cash Really Flew Back in Old Days," unsourced newspaper article, attributed in the text to 1956, folder 16, box 8, Kelley Collection.

32. Sturtevant, untitled manuscript. See chapter seven of this work, "Twilight of the Frontier," for Sturtevant's recollections of Oklahoma's earliest banks, and chapter ten, "The Scramble," for his closure of the Capitol National Bank of Guthrie.

33. McReynolds, *Oklahoma: A History,* 310–13.

34. Bixby quoted in "Indian Territory: The New Land of Promise."

35. Bixby quoted in ibid.

36. Ibid.

37. Ibid.

38. Ibid.

39. "Oklahoma's Trade in Furs," unsourced newspaper article, January 8, 1901, Scrapbook, September 1, 1900–March 22, 1901, box 38, vol. 6, 121, Barde Collection.

40. Mahnken, "No Oklahoman Lost a Penny," 43; "History of Oklahoma Banking and the Oklahoma State Banking Department," Oklahoma State Banking Department Collection.

41. Smallwood, *Oklahoma Adventure of Banks,* 47.

42. "A New Bank in Muskogee, I.T.," unsourced newspaper article, April 22, 1902, Scrapbook, February 25–September 30, 1902, box 39, vol. 8, 48, Barde Collection.

43. "There'll Be No Muskogee State Bank," unsourced newspaper article, July 16, 1902, Scrapbook, February 25–September 30, 1902, 134.

44. "Buying Stock in Territory Banks," unsourced newspaper article, July 24, 1902, Scrapbook, February 25–September 30, 1902, 144.

45. "A New $10,000 Bank in Grove, I.T.," unsourced newspaper article, April 25, 1902, Scrapbook, February 25–September 30, 1902, 52.

46. "Muskogee's Mayor Will Be a Banker," unsourced newspaper article, July 31, 1902, Scrapbook, February 25–September 30, 1902, 151.

47. "A New Indian Territory Bank," unsourced newspaper article, September 25, 1902, Scrapbook, February 25–September 30, 1902, 198.

48. "Another Indian Territory Bank," unsourced newspaper article, March 26, 1903, Scrapbook, March 17–September 19, 1903, box 40, vol. 10, 10, Barde Collection.

49. "A New Bank for Muskogee, I.T.," unsourced newspaper article, April 8, 1903, Scrapbook, March 17–September 19, 1903, 24.

50. "More Banks for Indian Territory," unsourced newspaper articles, April 21 and April 22, 1903, Scrapbook, March 17–September 19, 1903, 37–38; "Another Bank for Indianola, I.T.," unsourced newspaper article, April 30, 1903, Scrapbook, March 17–September 19, 1903, 46.

51. "A Muskogee, I.T., Bank Sold," unsourced newspaper article, May 1, 1903, Scrapbook, March 17–September 19, 1903, 47.

52. "A Bank Incorporated for Stigler, I.T.," unsourced newspaper article, May 13, 1903, Scrapbook, March 17–September 19, 1903, 58.

53. John Nance, interview by L. W. Wilson, April 13, 1938, vol. 66, 92–93, IPP online.

54. "The Indian Territory Bankers," unsourced newspaper article, May 14, 1903, Scrapbook, March 17–September 19, 1903, box 40, vol. 10, 58, Barde Collection.

55. *Wikipedia,* s.v. "Louisiana Purchase Exposition," last modified November 2, 3012, http://en.wikipedia.org/wiki/Louisiana_Purchase_Exposition.

56. "Indian Territory at St. Louis," unsourced newspaper article, May 15, 1903, Scrapbook, March 17–September 19, 1903, box 40, vol. 10, 60, Barde Collection.

57. "A New Indian Territory Telephone Line," unsourced newspaper article, June 16, 1902, Scrapbook, February 25–September 30, 1902, box 39, vol. 8, 108, Barde Collection.

58. "The First Telephone in the Osage Country," unsourced newspaper article, May 28, 1902, Scrapbook, February 25–September 30, 1902, 89.

59. "Bankers for Joint Statehood," unsourced newspaper article, November 18, 1904, Scrapbook, August 1, 1904–February 1, 1905, box 40, vol. 13, 67, Barde Collection.

60. "Inter-Territorial Bankers to Meet," unsourced newspaper article, December 30, 1904, Scrapbook, August 1, 1904–February 1, 1905, 102.

61. "To Advertise Oklahoma," unsourced newspaper article, October 19, 1904, Scrapbook, August 1, 1904–February 1, 1905, 42. The twenty-two towns represented on the trip included Enid, Pawnee, Arapaho, Clinton, Thomas, Hobart, Anadarko, Alva, Cherokee, Carmen, Cleo, Helena, Drummond, Carrier, Garber, Kremlin, Hunter, Perry, Wakita, Lamont, Blackwell, and Waukomis.

62. *Proceedings of the Ninth Annual Convention of the Oklahoma–Indian Territory Bankers Association, Held at Muskogee, I. T., May 25–26, 1905* (Guthrie: State Capital Company, 1905), 18.

63. Ibid.

64. Ibid., 19.

65. Ibid., 19–20.

66. Ibid., 20.

67. Ibid.

68. Ibid., 21.

69. Ibid., 22.

70. Marianne Weber, *Max Weber: A Biography,* trans. and ed. Harry Zohn (New York: Wiley, 1975), 285.

71. Ibid., 286.

72. Ibid., 287.

73. Eugene Halton, *The Great Brain Suck and other American Epiphanies* (Chicago: University of Chicago Press, 2008), 70–85.

74. Weber, *Max Weber,* 291.

75. Ibid.

76. Ibid., 292.

77. Ibid.

78. Ibid.

79. Ibid., 293.

80. Ibid.

81. Ibid., 294.

CHAPTER 12

Epigraph: Refrain from the theme song of the Broadway musical *Oklahoma!,* music by Richard Rodgers, lyrics by Oscar Hammerstein II, opened on Broadway in New York on March 31, 1943.

1. "The Banks in Oklahoma," unsourced newspaper article, April 11, 1902, Scrapbook, February 25–September 30, 1902, box 39, vol. 8, 38, Barde Collection.

2. "The 156 Banks in Oklahoma," unsourced newspaper article, July 10, 1902, Scrapbook, February 25–September 30, 1902, unsourced newspaper article, September 16, 1902, Scrapbook, February 25–September 30, 1902, 128.

3. Ibid., 128–29.

4. "The Banks in Oklahoma," unsourced newspaper article, September 16, 1902, Scrapbook, February 25–September 30, 1902, 191.

5. "Oklahoma Finances Good," unsourced newspaper article, December 18, 1902, Scrapbook, October 1, 1902–March 16, 1903, box 39, vol. 9, 70, Barde Collection.

6. Ibid.

7. "More Oklahoma Banks," unsourced newspaper article, July 14, 1903, Scrapbook, March 17–September 19, 1903, box 40, vol. 10, 97, Barde Collection.

8. "Bank Deposits Increased," unsourced newspaper article, January 6, 1904, Scrapbook, September 20, 1903–January 9, 1904, box 40, vol. 11, 82, Barde Collection.

9. "An Oklahoma Bank Report," unsourced newspaper article, December 20, 1905, Scrapbook, December 1, 1905–March 24, 1906, box 42, vol. 16, 22, Barde Collection.

10. "Oklahoma Is Making Money," unsourced newspaper article, October 1, 1902, Scrapbook, October 1, 1902–March 16, 1903, box 39, vol. 9, 2, Barde Collection.

11. McReynolds, *Oklahoma: A History,* 305.

12. Ferguson quoted in "How Oklahoma Prospers," unsourced newspaper article, November 28, 1902, Scrapbook, October 1, 1902–March 16, 1903, box 39, vol. 9, 51, Barde Collection.

13. Ferguson quoted in ibid., 52.

14. Ferguson quoted in ibid.

15. "Prosperous Indian Territory," unsourced newspaper article, July 22, 1905, Scrapbook, July 11–November 29, 1905, box 41, vol. 15, 12, Barde Collection.

16. "The Territories' Growth," unsourced newspaper article, February 18, 1906, Scrapbook, December 1, 1905–March 24, 1906, box 42, vol. 16, 93, Barde Collection.

17. "Territories Lead the List," unsourced newspaper article, February 22, 1906, Scrapbook, December 1, 1905–March 24, 1906, 98.

18. Rambo, Wenner, and Smock quoted in "Oklahoma Treasury Full," unsourced newspaper article, December 15, 1906, Scrapbook, November 23, 1906–July 8, 1907, box 43, vol. 18, 21, Barde Collection. H. H. Smock was appointed as the state's first bank commissioner on November 16, 1907, and served in that capacity until his resignation on January 1, 1909. See *Fifth Biennial Report of the Bank Commissioner of the State of Oklahoma* (Oklahoma City: Harlow, December 31, 1916), Oklahoma State Banking Department Collection.

19. "A Trust Company for Oklahoma City," unsourced newspaper article, May 1, 1903, Scrapbook, March 17–September 19, 1903, box 40, vol. 10, 47, Barde Collection.

20. "An Oklahoma Trust Company," unsourced newspaper article, June 6, 1905, Scrapbook, February 1–July 10, 1905, box 41, vol. 14, 105, Barde Collection.

21. "Rich Men in Oklahoma," unsourced newspaper article, June 14, 1906, Scrapbook, March 25–November 22, 1906, box 42, vol. 17, 80, Barde Collection.

22. Ibid.

23. "New State Draws Capital," unsourced newspaper article, October 12, 1906, Scrapbook, March 25–November 22, 1906, 174.

24. Bennett quoted in "Crime Still Increasing," unsourced newspaper article, January 5, 1904, Scrapbook, September 20, 1903–January 9, 1904, box 40, vol. 11, 84, Barde Collection.

25. "No More OKC Gambling," unsourced newspaper article, April 9, 1903, Scrapbook, March 17–September 19, 1903, box 40, vol. 10, 25, Barde Collection.

26. "A Crusade in Ardmore, I.T.," unsourced newspaper article, October 11, 1904, Scrapbook, August 1, 1904–February 1, 1905, box 40, vol. 13, 35, Barde Collection.

27. "Notes of Two Territories," unsourced newspaper article, n.d., Scrapbook, February 1–July 10, 1905, box 41, vol. 14, 59, Barde Collection.

28. Kirkwood quoted in "To Stop Horse Stealing," unsourced newspaper article, October 2, 1902, Scrapbook, October 1, 1902–March 16, 1903, box 39, vol. 9, 2, Barde Collection.

29. Kirkwood quoted in ibid.

30. "Heads an Army," unsourced newspaper article, October 18, 1904, folder 3, box 2, Barde Collection.

31. "Moonshine in the Territory," unsourced newspaper article, June 8, 1905, Scrapbook, February 1–July 10, 1905, box 41, vol. 14, 107, Barde Collection.

32. "Homeseekers by Thousands," unsourced newspaper article, n.d., Scrapbook, October 1, 1902–March 16, 1903, box 39, vol. 9, 56, Barde Collection.

33. Ibid.

34. Ibid.

35. "The Chickasha Commercial Club," unsourced newspaper article, January 15, 1903, Scrapbook, October 1, 1902–March 16, 1903, 100.

36. "A Commercial Club Going Visiting," unsourced newspaper article, January 20, 1903, Scrapbook, October 1, 1902–March 16, 1903, 105. For an in-depth study of the ubiquitous "Gristmill" Jones, see Aaron Bachhofer, "Forgotten Founder: Charles G. 'Gristmill' Jones and

the Growth of Oklahoma City, 1889–1911," *Chronicles of Oklahoma* 80, no. 1 (Spring 2002): 44–61.

37. "Tulsa Commercial Club Reorganized," unsourced newspaper article, January 28, 1903, Scrapbook, October 1, 1902–March 16, 1903, box 39, vol. 9, 116, Barde Collection.

38. Newman quoted in "Guthrie Is Having a Boom," unsourced newspaper article, n.d., Scrapbook, October 1, 1902–March 16, 1903, 4.

39. Avery quoted in "Oklahoma City Going Ahead," unsourced newspaper article, n.d., Scrapbook, October 1, 1902–March 16, 1903, 12.

40. Adams quoted in "Oklahoma Is Still Booming," unsourced newspaper article, n.d., Scrapbook, March 17–September 19, 1903, box 40, vol. 10, 30, Barde Collection.

41. "Territory Town's Boom," unsourced newspaper article, August 19, 1905, Scrapbook, July 11–November 29, 1905, box 41, vol. 15, 37, Barde Collection.

42. Angie Debo, *Tulsa: From Creek Town to Oil Capital* (Norman: University of Oklahoma Press, 1943), 3–4, 37.

43. Ibid., 51.

44. Ibid., 54.

45. Ibid., 55.

46. Susan Dornblaser, *Liberty and Tulsa: Making History Together for 100 Years, 1895–1995* (Tulsa: Liberty Bank and Trust Company, N.A., 1995), 1.

47. Debo, *Tulsa,* 71.

48. Ibid., 74.

49. Ibid., 69, 78; Smallwood, *Oklahoma Adventure of Banks,* 26–27; Dornblaser, *Liberty and Tulsa,* 1–2.

50. Dornblaser, *Liberty and Tulsa,* 9.

51. Debo, *Tulsa,* 59, 78.

52. *Encyclopedia of Oklahoma History and Culture,* s.v. "Red Fork Field," by Bobby D. Weaver, http://digital.library.okstate.edu/encyclopedia/entries/R/RE004.html.

53. Debo, *Tulsa,* 80.

54. Ibid., 87–88.

55. *Encyclopedia of Oklahoma History and Culture,* s.v. "Glenn Pool Field," by Bobby D. Weaver, http://digital.library.okstate.edu/encyclopedia/entries/G/GL005.html.

56. Debo, *Tulsa,* 88.

57. Ibid., 98.

58. "Tulsa a Boom Town," unsourced newspaper article, August 26, 1905, Scrapbook, July 11–November 29, 1905, box 41, vol. 15, 44, Barde Collection.

59. "Big Territory Oil Wells," unsourced newspaper article, December 1, 1904, Scrapbook, August 1, 1904–February 1, 1905, box 40, vol. 13, 75, Barde Collection.

60. "Indian Territory Riches," unsourced newspaper article, September 24, 1903, Scrapbook, September 20, 1903–January 9, 1904, box 40, vol. 11, 2, Barde Collection.

61. Quoted in "To Be Its Money Year," unsourced newspaper article, July 27, 1905, Scrapbook, July 11–November 29, 1905, box 41, vol. 15, 16, Barde Collection.

62. Findley quoted in "Indian Territory Is Rich," unsourced newspaper article, December 8, 1905, Scrapbook, December 1, 1905–March 24, 1906, box 42, vol. 16, 9, Barde Collection.

63. Ibid.

64. Kim K. Bender, "Oklahoma City's First Mass Transit System: Who Brought the Streetcars for People to Ride?" *Chronicles of Oklahoma* 72, no. 2 (Summer 1994): 138.

65. Ibid., 141.

66. "For a Territory Interurban," unsourced newspaper article, May 25, 1905, Scrapbook, February 1–July 10, 1905, box 41, vol. 14, 97, Barde Collection.

67. "A Guthrie–Oklahoma City Line," unsourced newspaper article, May 29, 1905, Scrapbook, February 1–July 10, 1905, 99.

68. "An Interurban Line Financed," unsourced newspaper article, December 17, 1905, Scrapbook, December 1, 1905–March 24, 1906, box 42, vol. 16, 19, Barde Collection.

69. "A $100,000 Telephone System for Shawnee" and "Will Connect Shawnee and Tecumseh," unsourced newspaper articles, December 20, 1905, both in Scrapbook, December 1, 1905–March 24, 1906, 22.

70. "Only Woman Bank Manager," unsourced newspaper article, December 30, 1905, Scrapbook, December 1, 1905–March 24, 1906, 32.

71. "Per Capita of the Osage Indians Greater than that of any Nation," unsourced newspaper article, December 26, 1902, Scrapbook, October 1, 1902–March 16, 1903, box 39, vol. 9, 79, Bard Collection.

72. "Where Indian Money Goes," unsourced newspaper article, May 31, 1905, Scrapbook, February 1–July 10, 1905, box 41, vol. 14, 100, Barde Collection.

73. Quoted in ibid.

74. Seger quoted in "These Indians Extravagant," unsourced newspaper article, September 2, 1904, Scrapbook, August 1, 1904–February 1, 1905, box 40, vol. 13, 9, Barde Collection.

CHAPTER 13

Epigraph: Proceedings of the Tenth Annual Convention of the Oklahoma–Indian Territory Bankers Association, Held at Oklahoma City, Okla., May 21–22, 1906 (Guthrie: State Capital Company, 1906), 11.

1. Messenbaugh quoted in ibid., 12.

2. Messenbaugh quoted in ibid., 13.

3. Messenbaugh quoted in "Mayors Trace Development of this Great and Growing City," *Daily Oklahoman,* March 10, 1907.

4. Messenbaugh quoted in *Proceedings (1906),* 10–11.

5. Messenbaugh quoted in ibid., 13.

6. Messenbaugh quoted in ibid., 14–15.

7. Craig quoted in ibid.

8. Craig quoted in ibid., 20–21.

9. Gilbert quoted in ibid., 21.

10. Gilbert quoted in ibid., 21–22.

11. Gilbert quoted in ibid., 22.

12. Gilbert quoted in ibid., 22–23.

13. Gilbert quoted in ibid., 27.

14. Quoted in "Oklahoma Tired of It," unsourced newspaper article, April 17, 1905, Scrapbook, February 1–July 10, 1905, box 41, vol. 14, 59, Barde Collection.

15. Quoted in ibid.

16. Cooper quoted in "The Banks of Oklahoma," unsourced newspaper article, September 16, 1902, Scrapbook, February 25–September 30, 1902, box 39, vol. 8, 191, Barde Collection.

17. Cooper quoted in ibid.

18. "Accuse a Banker of Theft," unsourced newspaper article, September 9, 1904, Scrapbook, August 1, 1904–February 1, 1905, box 40, vol. 13, 13, Barde Collection.

19. "The Arrest of a Banker," unsourced newspaper article, October 10, 1904, Scrapbook, August 1, 1904–February 1, 1905, 35.

20. "More Bankers Arrested," unsourced newspaper article, October 11, 1904, Scrapbook, August 1, 1904–February 1, 1905, 35.

21. "May Indict Guthrie Bankers," unsourced newspaper article, November 16, 1904, Scrapbook, August 1, 1904–February 1, 1905, 65.

22. "Indicted C. E. Billingsley," unsourced newspaper article, December 31, 1904, Scrapbook, August 1, 1904–February 1, 1905, 105.

23. "To Examine the Bank's Books," unsourced newspaper article, February 24, 1905, Scrapbook, February 1–July 10, 1905, box 41, vol. 14, 32, Barde Collection.

24. "New Guthrie Bank Receiver," unsourced newspaper article, July 15, 1905, Scrapbook, July 11–November 29, 1905, box 41, vol. 15, 7, Barde Collection.

25. Ibid.

26. "Trying a Territorial Banker," unsourced newspaper article, October 25, 1905, Scrapbook, July 11–November 29, 1905, 103.

27. "Say He Lived Too High," unsourced newspaper article, October 28, 1904, Scrapbook, August 1, 1904–February 1, 1905, box 40, vol. 13, 49, Barde Collection.

28. "An Enid, OK, Banker Indicted," unsourced newspaper article, December 1, 1904, Scrapbook, August 1, 1904–February 1, 1905, 75.

29. "W. T. Hart Arrested in Texas," unsourced newspaper article, December 2, 1904, Scrapbook, August 1, 1904–February 1, 1905, 75.

30. "A Madill I.T. Bank Shortage," unsourced newspaper article, December 4, 1904, Scrapbook, August 1, 1904–February 1, 1905, 79.

31. "The Lawton Cashier Caught," unsourced newspaper article, April 1, 1905, Scrapbook, February 1–July 10, 1905, box 41, vol. 14, 51, Barde Collection.

32. "Oklahoma Banker Arrested," unsourced newspaper article, June 12, 1905, Scrapbook, February 1–July 10, 1905, 113.

33. "Ask Receiver for a Bank," unsourced newspaper article, August 28, 1905, Scrapbook, July 11–November 29, 1905, box 41, vol. 15, 45, Barde Collection.

34. "For Collecting Indian Loans," unsourced newspaper article, September 25, 1905, Scrapbook, July 11–November 29, 1905, 75.

35. "Territory Banker Indicted," unsourced newspaper article, October 5, 1905, Scrapbook, July 11–November 29, 1905, 85.

36. "A Territory Ex-Banker Arrested," unsourced newspaper article, October 23, 1905, and "A Territory Banker Arrested," unsourced newspaper article, October 24, 1905, both in Scrapbook, July 11–November 29, 1905, 103.

37. "Territory Banker to Denver," unsourced newspaper article, October 31, 1905, Scrapbook, July 11–November 29, 1905, 106.

38. "An Oklahoma Bank Fails," unsourced newspaper article, November 1, 1905, Scrapbook, July 11–November 29, 1905, 107.

39. "A Warrant for Banker Hull in Oklahoma," unsourced newspaper article, November 7, 1905, Scrapbook, July 11–November 29, 1905, 112.

40. Lynn Rogers, Norman, Oklahoma, email correspondence with the author, July 17, 2010. Chickasaw Governor Robert Maxwell Harris was Lynn Rogers's great-great grandfather. According to Lynn Rogers, Governor Harris furnished the granite for both the capitol and the bank building.

41. "How a Bank Graft Grew," unsourced newspaper article, July 9, 1905, Scrapbook, February 1–July 10, 1905, box 41, vol. 14, 135, Barde Collection.

42. Ibid.

43. Ibid., 135–36.

44. Ibid., 136.

45. Filson quoted in "One Bank that Couldn't Fail," unsourced newspaper article, July 31, 1905, Scrapbook, July 11–November 29, 1905, box 41, vol. 15, 20, Barde Collection.

46. "A Paradise for Thugs," unsourced newspaper article, May 24, 1905, Scrapbook, February 1–July 10, 1905, box 41, vol. 14, 96, Barde Collection.

47. Hightower, "The Businessman's Frontier," 23.

48. "Bank Robbers in Oklahoma," unsourced newspaper article, April 4, 1903, Scrapbook, March 17–September 19, 1903, box 40, vol. 10, 20, Barde Collection.

49. "Six Oklahoma Bandits Taken," unsourced newspaper article, April 6, 1903, Scrapbook, March 17–September 19, 1903, 21.

50. "Robbed an Oklahoma Bank," unsourced newspaper article, December 8, 1904, Scrapbook, August 1, 1904–February 1, 1905, box 40, vol. 13, 83, Barde Collection.

51. "Robbed Territory Banks," unsourced newspaper article, March 1, 1905, Scrapbook, February 1–July 10, 1905, box 41, vol. 14, 34, Barde Collection.

52. "Owl, I.T. Bank Robbers Got $3,000," unsourced newspaper article, November 30, 1905, Scrapbook, December 1, 1905–March 24, 1906, box 42, vol. 16, 1, Barde Collection.

53. "Bad Money in Muskogee," unsourced newspaper article, December 24, 1905, Scrapbook, December 1, 1905–March 24, 1906, 27.

54. "An Oklahoma Bank Robbed," unsourced newspaper article, December 27, 1905, Scrapbook, December 1, 1905–March 24, 1906, 27.

55. Goble, *Progressive Oklahoma*, 78.

56. Ibid., 39.

57. "To Teach Indians to Farm," unsourced newspaper article, May 29, 1902, Scrapbook, February 25–September 30, 1902, box 39, vol. 8, 89, Barde Collection.

58. "The American Bonaparte," unsourced newspaper article, September 17, 1903, Scrapbook, March 17–September 19, 1903, box 40, vol. 10, 151, Barde Collection. Napoleon Bonaparte's battle cry translates from the French as "audacity, more audacity, and ever more audacity!"

59. Hitchcock quoted in "Bonaparte to Investigate," unsourced newspaper article, September 14, 1903, Scrapbook, March 17–September 19, 1903, 145.

60. "Does Bonaparte Grasp It?" unsourced newspaper article, September 19, 1903, Scrapbook, March 17–September 19, 1903, 153.

61. *Collier's Weekly* quoted in "Investigation Next Week," unsourced newspaper article, September 15, 1903, Scrapbook, March 17–September 19, 1903, 146.

62. Brosius quoted in "It Will Help Bonaparte," unsourced newspaper article, September 29, 1903, Scrapbook, September 20, 1903–January 9, 1904, box 40, vol. 11, 7, Barde Collection.

63. Bixby quoted in "Territory System Probed," unsourced newspaper article, December 19, 1903, Scrapbook, September 20, 1903–January 9, 1904, 66.

64. Bonaparte quoted in ibid.

65. *Proceedings (1906)*, 22–23.

66. Fred Carter Tracy, *Recollections of No Man's Land from the Memoirs of Fred Carter Tracy*, ed. V. Pauline Hodges (Goodwell, Okla.: No Man's Land Historical Society, 1998), 178.

67. "Not Examined in Two Years," unsourced newspaper article, January 21, 1905, Scrapbook, August 1, 1904–February 1, 1905, box 40, vol. 13, 128, Barde Collection.

EPILOGUE

1. Muriel H. Wright, "The Wedding of Oklahoma and Miss Indian Territory," *Chronicles of Oklahoma* 35, no. 3 (Fall 1957): 255–58. See also "Inaugural Day Plans Maturing," *Guthrie Daily Leader,* November 11, 1907; and "Oklahoma a State," *Beaver Herald,* November 21, 1907. (Founded in 1886, the *Beaver Herald* branded itself as the Oklahoma Territory's oldest newspaper.)

2. Wright, "Wedding," 259. For an in-depth study of the ubiquitous "Gristmill" Jones, see Bachhofer, "Forgotten Founder."

3. Wright, "Wedding," 259.

4. Ibid., 260.

5. "Oklahoma a State."

6. "Celebration in New State," *Oklahoma State Capital,* November 17, 1907.

7. Ibid.

8. "New State of Oklahoma Is Born," *Daily Ardmoreite,* November 17, 1907.

9. News brief, *Muskogee Cimeter,* November 22, 1907. The *Guthrie Daily Leader* (1893–1908), the *Beaver Herald* (1895–1922), the *Daily Ardmoreite* (1893–current), the *Muskogee Cimeter* (1901–19??), and other select Oklahoma newspapers can be found online at the Library of Congress, in partnership with the National Endowment for the Humanities, at Chronicling America: Historic American Newspapers, 1836–1922, http://chroniclingamerica.loc.gov/.

10. Overholser quoted in McRill, *And Satan Came Also,* 58.

11. Patterson quoted in Zweig, *Belly Up,* 87.

Bibliography

ARCHIVAL, CORPORATE, PERSONAL, AND VERTICAL FILE COLLECTIONS

Banks and Banking Vertical Files. Research Division, Oklahoma Historical Society, Oklahoma City.

Frederick. S. Barde Collection, 1890–1916. Research Division, Oklahoma Historical Society, Oklahoma City.

City National Bank and Trust Company of Guymon Corporate Files. Guymon, Oklahoma.

Drummond Home Collection. Hominy, Oklahoma.

Carolyn Foreman Collection. Research Division, Oklahoma Historical Society, Oklahoma City.

Indian-Pioneer Papers. Research Division, Oklahoma Historical Society, Oklahoma City.

Indian-Pioneer Papers. Western History Collections, University of Oklahoma, Norman, Oklahoma.

Johnson-Hightower Family Archives. Private Collection. Oklahoma City, Oklahoma.

E. H. Kelley Collection. Research Division, Oklahoma Historical Society, Oklahoma City.

Loosen Family Archives. Private collection. Okarche, Oklahoma.

Jim Lucas Checotah Public Library History File. Checotah, Oklahoma.

Oklahoma State Banking Department Collection. Oklahoma City, Oklahoma.

George J. and Nancy J. Records Collection. Private collection. Oklahoma City, Oklahoma.

Joseph B. Thoburn Collection. Research Division, Oklahoma Historical Society, Oklahoma City.

NEWSPAPERS AND MAGAZINES

Altus News
Beaver Herald
Daily Ardmoreite

Daily Oklahoman
Edmond Sun-Democrat
Guthrie Daily Leader
Kansas City Star
Kosciusko (MS) Star
Los Angeles Times
McMaster's Weekly
Muskogee Cimeter
Oklahoma Banker
Oklahoma Champion
Oklahoma City Evening Gazette
Oklahoma City Times
Oklahoma Daily Press-Gazette
Oklahoma Daily Times-Journal
[Daily] Oklahoma State Capital
Shawnee Weekly News

BOOKS AND THESES

Appleby, Joyce. *The Relentless Revolution: A History of Capitalism.* New York: W. W. Norton, 2010.

Ballenger, Thomas Lee. *Story of the Banking Business in Tahlequah, Oklahoma.* Tahlequah, Okla.: Tahlequah Publishing, 1968.

Beatty, Jack. *Age of Betrayal: The Triumph of Money in America, 1865–1900.* New York: Vintage Books, 2008.

Billington, Ray Allen. *America's Frontier Heritage.* New York: Holt, Rinehart and Winston, 1966.

Bodenhorn, Howard. *A History of Banking in Antebellum America: Financial Markets and Economic Development in an Era of Nation-Building.* New York: Cambridge University Press, 2000.

Boorstin, Daniel J. *The Americans: The Democratic Experience.* New York: Random House, 1974.

Brands, H. W. *American Colossus: The Triumph of Capitalism, 1865–1900.* New York: Anchor Books, 2010.

———. *The Money Men: Capitalism, Democracy, and the Hundred Years' War over the American Dollar.* New York: W. W. Norton, 2006.

Brown, John Cecil. "Early Days of the First National: A Bank as Old as the City It Serves." In *Fifty Years Forward: The First National Bank and Trust Company of Oklahoma City, 1889–1939.* Oklahoma City: First National Bank and Trust Company of Oklahoma City, 1939.

Bruner, Robert F., and Sean D. Carr. *The Panic of 1907: Lessons Learned from the Market's Perfect Storm.* Hoboken, N.J.: Wiley, 2007.

Bryce, James. *The American Commonwealth.* 2 vols. New York: MacMillan, 1914.

Burns, James MacGregor. *The Vineyard of Liberty.* New York: Knopf, 1982.

Calomiris, Charles W. *U.S. Bank Deregulation in Historical Perspective.* Cambridge: Cambridge University Press, 2000.

Dale, Edward Everett. *The West Wind Blows: The Autobiography of Edward Everett Dale.* Edited by Arrell Morgan Gibson. Oklahoma City: Oklahoma Historical Society, 1984.

Damrosch, Leo. *Tocqueville's Discovery of America*. New York: Farrar, Straus and Giroux, 2010.

Dary, David. *The Santa Fe Trail: Its History, Legends, and Lore*. New York: Knopf, 2000.

Debo, Angie. *Prairie City: The Story of an American Community*. Tulsa: Council Oak Books, 1985.

———. *The Rise and Fall of the Choctaw Republic*. Norman: University of Oklahoma Press, 1934.

———. *Tulsa: From Creek Town to Oil Capital*. Norman: University of Oklahoma Press, 1943.

Dewey, Davis Rich. *Financial History of the United States*. New York: Longmans, Green, 1931.

Dornblaser, Susan. *Liberty and Tulsa: Making History Together for 100 Years, 1895–1995*. Tulsa: Liberty Bank and Trust Company, N.A., 1995.

Doti, Lynne Pierson, and Larry Schweikart. *Banking the in the American West: From the Gold Rush to Deregulation*. Norman: University of Oklahoma Press, 1991.

Drummond, John R. *The Drummond Family History: A Story of Fred and Addie, Their Ancestors and Children*. San Angelo, Texas: Newsfoto, 1981.

Ellis, Joseph J. *After the Revolution: Profiles of Early American Culture*. New York: W. W. Norton, 2002.

———. *American Creation: Triumphs and Tragedies at the Founding of the Republic*. New York: Random House, 2007.

———. *Founding Brothers: The Revolutionary Generation*. New York: Random House, 2000.

Ferguson, Niall. *The Ascent of Money: A Financial History of the World*. New York: Penguin, 2008.

Fifth Biennial Report of the Bank Commissioner of the State of Oklahoma. Oklahoma City: Harlow, December 31, 1916.

Goble, Danney. *Progressive Oklahoma*. Norman: University of Oklahoma Press, 1980.

Gordon, John Steele. *An Empire of Wealth: The Epic History of American Economic Power*. New York: Harper Perennial, 2005.

———. *Hamilton's Blessing: The Extraordinary Life and Times of Our National Debt*. New York: Walker, 2010.

Gorton, George. *A "Big-Ass Boy" in the Oil Fields: My Adventures, 1918–28*. New Berlin, Wis.: Napco Graphic Arts, 1975.

Greenberg, Jonathan D. *Staking a Claim: Jake Simmons and the Making of an African American Oil Dynasty*. New York: Atheneum, 1990.

Gregg, Josiah. *Commerce of the Prairies*. Edited by Milo Milton Quaife. Lincoln: University of Nebraska Press, 1967.

Haller, Ben, Jr. *A History of Banking in Nebraska, 1854–1990*. Lincoln: Nebraska Bankers Association, 1990.

Halton, Eugene. *The Great Brain Suck and other American Epiphanies*. Chicago: University of Chicago Press, 2008.

Hammond, Bray. *Banks and Politics in America from the Revolution to the Civil War*. Princeton: Princeton University Press, 1957.

Henslick, Harry E. "The Life of Abraham Jefferson Seay." Master's thesis, Oklahoma State University, 1973.

Hofstadter, Richard. *Anti-intellectualism in American Life*. New York: Vintage Books, 1963.

Hoig, Stan. *The Oklahoma Land Rush of 1889*. Oklahoma City: Oklahoma Historical Society, 1984.

Irving, Washington. *A Tour on the Prairies.* Edited by John Francis McDermott. Norman: University of Oklahoma Press, 1956.

Jackson, A. P., and E. C. Cole. *Oklahoma! Politically and Geographically Described—History and Guide to the Indian Territory.* Kansas City, Mo.: Ramsey, Millett & Hudson, 1885.

Jacobs, Wilbur R. *On Turner's Trail: 100 Years of Writing Western History.* Lawrence: University Press of Kansas, 1994.

Johnson, Rossiter, ed. *The Great Events by Famous Historians.* 20 vols. New York: National Alumni, 1905.

Macleod, Henry Dunning. *The Theory of Credit.* 2 vols. London: Longmans, Green., 1894.

McReynolds, Edwin C. *Oklahoma: A History of the Sooner State.* Norman: University of Oklahoma Press, 1954.

McRill, Albert. *And Satan Came Also: An Inside Story of a City's Social and Political History.* Oklahoma City: Britton Publishing, 1955.

Meacham, Jon. *American Lion: Andrew Jackson in the White House.* New York: Random House, 2008.

Morris, Lerona Rosamond, ed. *Oklahoma Yesterday-Today-Tomorrow.* 2 vols. Guthrie, Okla.: Co-operative Publishing, 1930.

Nichols, Max, and David R. Martin. *Continuing an Oklahoma Banking Tradition.* Oklahoma City: First Interstate Bank of Oklahoma, N.A., 1989.

Proceedings of the Ninth Annual Convention of the Oklahoma–Indian Territory Bankers Association, Held at Muskogee, I. T., May 25–26, 1905. Guthrie: State Capital Company, 1905.

Proceedings of the Tenth Annual Convention of the Oklahoma–Indian Territory Bankers Association, Held at Oklahoma City, Okla., May 21–22, 1906. Guthrie: State Capital Company, 1906.

Reich, Robert B. *Supercapitalism: The Transformation of Business, Democracy, and Everyday Life.* New York: Vintage Books, 2008.

Remini, Robert V. *The Life of Andrew Jackson.* New York: HarperCollins, 2009.

Rister, Carl Coke. *Land Hunger: David L. Payne and the Oklahoma Boomers.* New York: Arno Press, 1975.

Robb, Thomas Bruce. *The Guaranty of Bank Deposits.* Boston: Houghton Mifflin, 1921.

Rothbard, Murray N. *A History of Money and Banking in the United States: The Colonial Era to World War II.* Auburn, Ala.: Ludwig von Mises Institute, 2002.

Schlesinger, Arthur M., Jr., ed. *The Almanac of American History.* New York: Putnam, 1983.

Smallwood, James M. *An Oklahoma Adventure of Banks and Bankers.* Norman: University of Oklahoma Press, 1979.

Southworth, Shirley Donald, and John M. Chapman. *Banking Facilities for Bankless Towns.* New York: American Economists Council for the Study of Branch Banking, 1941.

Stewart, Roy P. *Born Grown: An Oklahoma City History.* Oklahoma City: Fidelity Bank, N.A., 1974.

Studenski, Paul, and Herman E. Krooss. *Financial History of the United States.* New York: McGraw-Hill, 1963.

Thoburn, Joseph B. *History of Oklahoma.* Illustrated by L. P. Thompson. *History of Oklahoma.* Oklahoma City: First National Bank and Trust Company of Oklahoma City, Oklahoma Publishing Company, 1957.

Thompson, John. *Closing the Frontier: Radical Response in Oklahoma, 1889–1923.* Norman: University of Oklahoma Press, 1986.

Tocqueville, Alexis de. *Democracy in America.* Edited by Phillips Bradley. 2 vols. New York: Knopf, 1945.

Tracy, Fred Carter. *Recollections of No Man's Land from the Memoirs of Fred Carter Tracy*. Edited by V. Pauline Hodges. Goodwell, Okla.: No Man's Land Historical Society, 1998.

Trescott, Paul B. *Financing American Enterprise: The Story of Commercial Banking*. New York: Harper & Row, 1963.

Turner, Frederick Jackson. *The Frontier in American History*. Franklin Center, Pa.: Franklin Library, 1977.

———. *Rereading Frederick Jackson Turner: "The Significance of the Frontier in American History" and Other Essays*. With commentary by John Mack Faragher. New York: Henry Holt, 1994.

U.S. Office of the Comptroller of the Currency. *Instructions and Suggestions of the Comptroller of the Currency in Regard to the Organization, Extension, and Management of National Banks*. Washington: Government Printing Office, 1884.

———. *The National Bank Act, and other Laws Relating to National Banks, from the Revised Statutes of the United States; with Amendments and Additional Acts*. Compiled by Edward Wolcott. Washington: Government Printing Office, 1882.

Walker, Henry Pickering. *The Wagonmasters: High Plains Freighting from the Earliest Days of the Santa Fe Trail to 1880*. Norman: University of Oklahoma Press, 1966.

Webb, Walter Prescott. *The Great Frontier*. Austin: University of Texas Press, 1964.

Weber, Marianne. *Max Weber: A Biography*. Translated and edited by Harry Zohn. New York: Wiley, 1975.

Wright, Robert E. *The First Wall Street: Chestnut Street, Philadelphia, & the Birth of Modern Finance*. Chicago: University of Chicago Press, 2005.

———. *Origins of Commercial Banking in America, 1750–1800*. Lanham, Md.: Rowman and Littlefield, 2001.

Wright, Robert E., and David J. Cowen. *Financial Founding Fathers: The Men Who Made America Rich*. Chicago: University of Chicago Press, 2006.

Zimmerman, William, ed. *Banking's Past, Financial Services' Future*. New York: American Banker, 1986.

Zweig, Phillip L. *Belly Up: The Collapse of the Penn Square Bank*. New York: Crown, 1985.

ARTICLES AND BOOK CHAPTERS

Aldrich, Duncan M. "General Stores, Retail Merchants, and Assimilation: Retail Trade in the Cherokee Nation, 1838–1890." *Chronicles of Oklahoma* 57, no. 2 (Summer 1979): 119–36.

Andrew, A. Piatt. "The Crux of the Currency Question." *Yale Review,* n.s., 2 (July 1913): 595–620.

Bachhofer, Aaron. "Forgotten Founder: Charles G. 'Gristmill' Jones and the Growth of Oklahoma City, 1889–1911." *Chronicles of Oklahoma* 80, no. 1 (Spring 2002): 44–61.

Bender, Kim K. "Oklahoma City's First Mass Transit System: Who Brought the Streetcars for People to Ride?" *Chronicles of Oklahoma* 72, no. 2 (Summer 1994): 138–59.

Bieber, Ralph P. "Some Aspects of the Santa Fe Trail, 1848–1880." *Chronicles of Oklahoma* 2, no. 1 (March 1924): 1–8.

Borosage, Robert, and Katrina vanden Heuvel. "The American Dream: Can a Movement Save It?" *Nation,* October 16, 2011, 1–2.

Castro, J. Justin. "From the Tennessee River to Tahlequah: A Brief History of Cherokee Fiddling." *Chronicles of Oklahoma* 87, no. 4 (Winter 2009–2010): 388–407.

Chapman, Berlin B. "Oklahoma City, from Public Land to Private Property." *Chronicles of Oklahoma* 37, no. 2 (Summer 1959): 211–37.

Clapsaddle, David K. "'Cimarron Cutoff,' a 20th-Century Misnomer." *Wagon Tracks* 23 (May 2009): 25–26.

———. "Old Dan and his Traveling Companions: Oxen on the Santa Fe Trail." *Wagon Tracks* 22 (February 2008): 6–11.

Clift, W. H. "Warren's Trading Post." *Chronicles of Oklahoma* 2, no. 2 (June 1924): 129–40.

Crease, Craig. "Boom Times for Freighters on the Santa Fe Trail, 1848–1866." *Wagon Tracks* 23 (February 2009): 16–21.

Crockett, Norman L. "The Opening of Oklahoma: A Businessman's Frontier." *Chronicles of Oklahoma* 56, no. 1 (Spring 1978): 85–95.

Cronon, William, George Miles, and Jay Gitlin. "Becoming West: Toward a New Meaning for Western History." In *Under an Open Sky: Rethinking America's Western Past,* edited by William Cronon, George Miles, and Jay Gitlin, 3–27. New York: W. W. Norton, 1992.

Dale, Edward E. "The Cow Country in Transition." *Mississippi Valley Historical Review* 24, no. 1 (June 1937): 3–20.

Dawson, Henry B. "Siege and Surrender of Yorktown (A.D. 1781)." In vol. 14 of *The Great Events by Famous Historians,* edited by Rossiter Johnson, 97–115. New York: National Alumni, 1905.

Du[n]ham, A. W. "Oklahoma City before the Run of 1889." *Chronicles of Oklahoma* 36, no. 1 (Spring 1958): 72–78.

Dunham, A. W. "A Pioneer Railroad Agent." *Chronicles of Oklahoma* 2, no. 1 (March 1924): 48–62.

Faragher, John Mack. "The Frontier Trail: Rethinking Turner and Reimagining the American West." *American Historical Review* 98, no. 1 (February 1993): 106–17.

Fischer, LeRoy H. "Oklahoma Territory, 1890–1907." *Chronicles of Oklahoma* 53, no. 1 (Spring 1975): 3–8.

Floyd, Larry C. "Quanah Parker's Star House: A Comanche Home along the White Man's Road." *Chronicles of Oklahoma* 90, no. 2 (Summer 2012): 132–59.

Foreman, Grant. "Nathaniel Pryor." *Chronicles of Oklahoma* 7, no. 2 (June 1929): 152–63.

Gottschalk, M. C. "Pioneer Merchants of the Las Vegas Plaza: The Booming Trail Days." *Wagon Tracks* 16 (February 2002): 8–19.

Gibson, Arrell M. "The Homesteaders' Last Frontier." *American Scene* 4 (1962): 27–69.

Harriman, Helga H. "Economic Conditions in the Creek Nation, 1865–1871." *Chronicles of Oklahoma* 51, no. 3 (Fall 1973): 325–34.

Hightower, Michael J. "Brother Bankers: Frank P. and Hugh M. Johnson, Founders of the First National Bank and Trust Company of Oklahoma City." *Chronicles of Oklahoma* 88, no. 4 (Winter 2010–2011): 388–415.

———. "The Businessman's Frontier: C. C. Hightower, Commerce, and Old Greer County, 1891–1903." *Chronicles of Oklahoma* 86, no. 1 (Spring 2008): 4–31.

———. "Cattle, Coal and Indian Land: A Tradition of Mining in Southeastern Oklahoma." *Chronicles of Oklahoma* 62, no. 1 (Spring 1984): 4–25.

———. "The Road to Russian Hill: A Story of Immigration and Coal Mining." *Chronicles of Oklahoma* 63, no. 3 (Fall 1985): 228–49.

———. "Willard Johnston: Homesteader and Frontier Banker, 1881–1904." *Chronicles of Oklahoma* 87, no. 4 (Winter 2009–2010): 408–31.

Hoig, Stan. "Jesse Chisholm: Peace-Maker, Trader, Forgotten Frontiersman." *Chronicles of Oklahoma* 66, no. 4 (Winter 1988): 350–73.

Hudson, James E. "Camp Nichols: Oklahoma's Outpost on the Santa Fe Trail." *Wagon Tracks* 14 (November 1999): 12–17.

Hurt, Douglas A. "Brothers of Influence: Auguste and Pierre Chouteau and the Osages before 1804." *Chronicles of Oklahoma* 78, no. 3 (Fall 2000): 260–77.

Kaye, Donald. "Specie on the Santa Fe Trail." *Wagon Tracks* 14 (August 2000): 10–13.

Kieta, Emily E. "The New Mexican Fandango." *Wagon Tracks* 19 (May 2005): 11–15.

Lamar, Howard R. "The Most American Frontier: The Oklahoma Land Rushes, 1889–1893." *Humanities Interview* 7 (1989): 4–9.

Lewis, Lawrence, Jr. "Establishment of the United States Bank, A.D. 1791." In vol. 14 of *The Great Events by Famous Historians,* edited by Rossiter Johnson, 230–35. New York: National Alumni, 1905.

Mahnken, Norbert R. "No Oklahoman Lost a Penny: Oklahoma's State Bank Guarantee Law, 1907–1923." *Chronicles of Oklahoma* 71, no. 1 (Spring 1993): 42–63.

Marsh, Mary, ed. "Our First Seventy-Five Years." In *Bank Life: 1889/1964—Our First 75.* Oklahoma City: First National Bank and Trust Company, 1964.

Marshall, Jeffrey. "Twixt Booms and Panics: Banking in the Gilded Age." In *Banking's Past, Financial Services' Future,* edited by William Zimmerman, 25–32. New York: American Banker, 1986.

McNabb, C. A. "Oklahoma City's Indian Scare." *Chronicles of Oklahoma* 2, no. 4 (December 1924): 396.

McNeal, J. W. "Pioneer Banking." In *Proceedings of the Sixth Annual Convention of the Oklahoma Bankers Association, November 7 and 8, 1902.* Oklahoma City: Oklahoma Bankers Association.

Morgan, Phyllis. "Buffalo on the Santa Fe Trail." *Wagon Tracks* 18 (May 2004): 5–9.

Myers, Harry C. "As the Wheel Turns: The Evolution of Freighting on the Santa Fe Trail, An Introduction." *Wagon Tracks* 23 (November 2008): 7–9.

Naylor, Bartlett. "Bankers Spilled Blood in Nation's Early Years." In *Banking's Past, Financial Services' Future,* edited by William Zimmerman, 19–23. New York: American Banker, 1986.

Parton, James. "Jackson Elected President of the United States, A.D. 1828." In vol. 16 of *The Great Events by Famous Historians,* edited by Rossiter Johnson, 143–56. New York: National Alumni, 1905.

Peery, Dan W. "Captain David L. Payne." *Chronicles of Oklahoma* 13, no. 4 (December 1935): 438–56.

Phipps, B. L. "Banking in Indian Territory during the 80's." *Chronicles of Oklahoma* 7, no. 2 (June 1929): 186–87.

Pierson, George Wilson. "The Frontier and American Institutions: A Criticism of the Turner Theory." In *Turner and the Sociology of the Frontier,* ed. Richard Hofstadter and Seymour Martin Lipset, 15–42. New York: Basic Books, 1968.

Riggs, W. C. "Bits of Interesting History." *Chronicles of Oklahoma* 7, no. 2 (June 1929): 148–51.

Robinson, Ella. "History of the Patterson Mercantile Company. *Chronicles of Oklahoma* 36, no. 1 (Spring 1958): 53–64.

Rockoff, Hugh. "Banking and Finance, 1789–1914." In *The Long Nineteenth Century.* Vol. 2 of *The Cambridge Economic History of the United States,* edited by Stanley L. Engerman and Robert E. Gallman, 643–84. Cambridge: Cambridge University Press, 2000.

Shirk, George H. "First Post Offices within the Boundaries of Oklahoma." *Chronicles of Oklahoma* 30, no. 1 (Spring 1952): 38–104.

Smith, Ellis J. "When Rails Replaced the Santa Fe Trail." *Wagon Tracks* 12 (February 1998): 23–24.

Sneed, R. A. "The Reminiscences of an Indian Trader." *Chronicles of Oklahoma* 14, no. 2 (June 1936): 135–55.

Tower, Michael. "Traders along the Washita: A Short History of the Shirley Trading Company." *Chronicles of Oklahoma* 65, no. 1 (Spring 1987): 4–15.

Van Zandt, Howard F. "The History of Camp Holmes and Chouteau's Trading Post." *Chronicles of Oklahoma* 13, no. 3 (September 1935): 316–37.

Wicks, Hamilton S. "The Opening of Oklahoma." *Cosmopolitan Magazine* 7 (September 1889): 460–70.

Willibrand, W. A. "German in Okarche, 1892–1902." *Chronicles of Oklahoma* 28, no. 3 (Autumn 1950): 284–91.

Wright, Muriel H. "Early Navigation and Commerce along the Arkansas and Red Rivers in Oklahoma." *Chronicles of Oklahoma* 8, no. 1 (March 1930): 65–88.

———. "The Wedding of Oklahoma and Indian Territory." *Chronicles of Oklahoma* 35, no. 3 (Fall 1957): 255–63.

Yates, Henry W. "Banking in Nebraska." In *Illustrated History of Nebraska*. Lincoln: Jacob North, 1906.

INTERVIEWS

Frederick Drummond, March 17, 2011. Pawhuska, Oklahoma; follow-up correspondence by phone, August 29, 2011.

Patricia Loosen and Joyce Treece, August 30, 2010. Okarche, Oklahoma.

John Marshall, with Rodger Harris, May 1, 2009. Oklahoma City, Oklahoma; follow-up correspondence by email, summer 2009.

Roma Lee Porter, William Paul Ellwanger, and Teresa Heater, August 23, 2010. Lawton, Oklahoma.

Beverly Whitcomb, August 31, 2011. Hominy, Oklahoma.

Index